# THE CAMBRIDGE HISTORY OF
# CLASSICAL LITERATURE

GENERAL EDITORS

Mrs P. E. Easterling *Fellow of Newnham College, Cambridge*

E. J. Kenney *Fellow of Peterhouse, Cambridge*

ADVISORY EDITORS

B. M. W. Knox *The Center for Hellenic Studies, Washington*

W. V. Clausen *Department of the Classics, Harvard University*

# VOLUME II PART 4
# THE EARLY PRINCIPATE

# THE CAMBRIDGE HISTORY OF
# CLASSICAL LITERATURE

# VOLUME II: LATIN LITERATURE

# THE CAMBRIDGE HISTORY OF CLASSICAL LITERATURE

## VOLUME II

### PART 4

# The Early Principate

EDITED BY

## E. J. KENNEY

*Fellow of Peterhouse, Cambridge*

ADVISORY EDITOR

## W. V. CLAUSEN

*Professor of Greek and Latin*
*Harvard University*

# CAMBRIDGE UNIVERSITY PRESS

CAMBRIDGE

LONDON   NEW YORK   NEW ROCHELLE

MELBOURNE   SYDNEY

Published by the Press Syndicate of the University of Cambridge
The Pitt Building, Trumpington Street, Cambridge CB2 1RP
32 East 57th Street, NewYork, NY 10022, USA
296 Beaconsfield Parade, Middle Park, Melbourne 3206, Australia

© Cambridge University Press 1982

First published 1982 as chapters 24–34 of *The Cambridge History of Classical Literature*, Volume II
First paperback edition 1983

Printed in Great Britain by the University Press, Cambridge

Library of Congress catalogue card number: 82-19782

*British Library Cataloguing in Publication Data*
The Cambridge history of classical literature.
Vol. 2: Latin literature
The Early principate
1. Classical literature – History and criticism
I. Kenney, E. J. II. Clausen, W. V.
880′.09   PA3001
ISBN 0 521 27372 2

# CONTENTS

# CONTENTS

# CONTENTS

# 1

# CHALLENGE AND RESPONSE

The first century of the Christian era has often been termed the 'age of rhetoric'. Such a designation, which has been used polemically, can be misleading. Nearly all human communication involves 'rhetoric' to some degree: for it is nothing other than the art of effective speaking and writing. It is only in relatively recent times that the hypothesis that such a skill can be schematized and taught has passed out of fashion. Among the Greeks and Romans it was the pivot of a whole educational system; they would have found it hard to understand a critical terminology that equates the rhetorical with the artificial and insincere. Just as they recognized medicine or astronomy as sciences (*artes*) with their own rules and expertise, so the ancients believed that a man could acquire specific techniques to aid him in public speaking and in literary composition. The techniques alone might not suffice, but they were nonetheless indispensable as prerequisites. A young Roman received the rudiments of his education from a *litterator*; thereafter he studied literature under a *grammaticus*; a *rhetor* finally instructed him in the practice of oratory itself. *Disertus, eloquens, facundus*: the epithets express the aim and object of the whole process. An educated Roman was expected to possess the power of speaking impressively and convincingly in the senate, in the courts and elsewhere. The technicalities of the law could be left to the jurisconsults: but eloquence was universally desirable. There was nothing new in such an outlook. Nor was it any more revolutionary for the precepts and principles of the schools to be adapted to creative writing. Poetry and prose in the Republic and during the Augustan principate were deeply affected by rhetoric. Yet there is a real and obvious disparity between the style of Virgil and Lucan, Cicero and Seneca, Livy and Tacitus. To attribute the change – frequently in tones of regret – solely or largely to the rise of a malign 'rhetoric' is fallacious. Other considerations too have to be given due weight.

The establishment of Augustus' restored Republic, however much a sham it has appeared to later historians, gave birth to a truly classical or 'golden' age of Roman letters. With hopes of the emergence of a peaceful and stable society after long years of civil turmoil arose also a miraculous flowering of literature. The pre-eminence of the early Augustan writers was quickly acknowledged.

Their immediate successors – of whom Ovid, harbinger of the 'silver' age, may be reckoned the first – sought for new ways to validate their own work within the tradition of which they were part. Classical periods are normally followed by a reaction: artists, while implicitly or explicitly conceding and profiting from the achievements of their forerunners, try to avoid sterile imitation. They explore fresh dimensions in style, thought and content, in quest of a justifiable claim to originality and to circumvent odious comparisons.

Tacitus' *Dialogus* is a valuable witness to the attitudes and aspirations of the first century. The arguments of Vipstanus Messalla (25–6, 28–32, 33–6) have been cited to prove the corrupting effects of rhetorical education. Messalla is an advocate of older values in oratory, a stern antagonist of contemporary developments. For him the late Republic was the zenith of oratorical splendour, with Cicero as indisputable master. But the discourse of his impetuous opponent, the modernist Marcus Aper, is equally revealing, for it typifies what must have been a not uncommon viewpoint. Aper sensibly prefaces his exposition with the opinion that the style and types of oratory change with the times (*mutari cum temporibus formas quoque et genera dicendi*, 18). In 19, he remarks that, whereas once a knowledge of rhetorical doctrines (*praecepta rhetorum*) and of philosophical aphorisms (*philosophorum placita*) was something of a rarity, the situation had now radically altered:

at hercule peruulgatis iam omnibus, cum uix in cortina quisquam adsistat quin elementis studiorum, etsi non instructus, at certe imbutus sit, nouis et exquisitis eloquentiae itineribus opus est, per quae orator fastidium aurium effugiat.

> *But now everything is common knowledge. There is scarcely anyone in the body of the court who, even if he has not been fully instructed, has not at least acquired some acquaintance with the basic tenets of the schools. There is, therefore, a need for new and subtle paths of eloquence, by which an orator may avoid boring his audience.*

Changed conditions demanded novelty. Rhetoric and philosophy, at least at a superficial level, were more widely disseminated. Orators had to respond to the situation. Audiences were more critical, more prone to boredom (*fastidium*) if their attention was not firmly held. A little later, Aper comments further on the predilections of the day:

iam uero iuuenes et in ipsa studiorum incude positi, qui profectus sui causa oratores sectantur, non solum audire, sed etiam referre domum aliquid inlustre et dignum memoria uolunt; traduntque in uicem ac saepe in colonias ac prouincias suas scribunt, siue sensus aliquis arguta et breui sententia effulsit, siue locus exquisito et poetico cultu enituit. (20)

> *What is more, the young men, still at the formative stage of their training, who are seeking to make progress by attaching themselves to established orators, desire not merely to hear but to carry away with them some brilliant and memorable passage. They pass such things on to each other and often cite them in letters to their*

*home towns among the colonies and provinces: perhaps some idea that glitters with a*
*pointed and brief epigram or a paragraph that is illuminated by a subtle and poetic*
*beauty.*

His words present a vivid picture of Rome as an educational centre for the whole empire. (It is indeed notable that, in the early Imperial period, men from the provinces, and especially from Spain, played a leading role in oratory and literature.) Aper stresses the love of verbal brilliance, the eagerness to invent epigrams (*sententiae*) and the borrowing of poetic devices by orators. All three of these traits have been repeatedly traced as characteristic qualities of the post-Augustan style. These were the days when, according to H. E. Butler, we find above all 'a straining after effect, a love of startling colour, produced now by over-gorgeous or over-minute imagery, now by a surfeit of brilliant epigram'.[1] To him, the 'silver' writers lacked restraint and propriety.

Butler's tone is pejorative. Such trends have always been objectionable to critics directly or indirectly oriented towards Romanticism. They were equally repugnant to Quintilian, whose *Institutio oratoria* was aimed at revivifying classical ideals – in part an ethical programme, for Quintilian held that morality and stylistics were closely interrelated. Perverse, degenerate rhetoric was, for him, symptomatic of a malaise infecting society and individuals.

Leaving aside modern critical and ancient moral presuppositions, we may still plausibly link the rise of the 'new style' with one feature of rhetorical education: *declamatio*. *Declamationes* were set speeches on given themes, either deliberative (*suasoriae*) or forensic (*controversiae*). They were not merely scholastic exercises. Professors of rhetoric found in them a vehicle to display their own talents, to attract a clientele. The declamations became, therefore, a form of public entertainment. Seneca the Elder, who compiled a large collection of *declamationes* delivered by rhetors and others in his lifetime (with introductions and commentary), states that declamation first became a widespread activity in the reign of Augustus. Teachers, it appears, entered into what amounted to a contest with each other as purveyors of words and conceits. That these performances were conducive to the growth of exotic and extreme styles is not surprising. They doubtless imbued their audiences with a sophisticated appreciation of that dazzling 'brilliance' which, as we have seen, was much esteemed by Marcus Aper. Seneca's compilation reveals that the results were often hollow and strained, sometimes *outré*. Yet the fault did not lie in rhetoric itself; rather it was in the ends to which rhetoric was prostituted. *Declamatio* was attacked at the time as one of the causes of the 'decline of eloquence'. Messalla in the *Dialogus* (35) voices a standard criticism: the themes chosen for declamation were bizarre and unrelated to the real-life situations pupils would

---

[1] Butler (1909) 1.

eventually have to face in the courts. Such attacks should not be taken too literally: it is certainly erroneous to regard the declamations as valueless in preparing youths for practical advocacy.[1] On the other hand, the subject matter of the *suasoriae* was more prone to be fantastic (and hence susceptible to stylistic floridity) than that of the *controversiae*: and it was the former which often had direct points of contact with the material treated by poets, historians and philosophers. The commonplaces and 'purple patches' beloved by the declaimers are often recognizable in first-century literature – as also the forms, structures and methods of deliberative orations. But it may be said that if rhetoric affected poetry the reverse process was also true. Ovid's style was much admired by the declaimers. Quintilian, hardly with approval, said that Lucan was 'fit rather to be imitated by orators than by poets' (*Inst.* 10.1.90). Sententiousness and *panni purpurei* were, after all, more obviously a legacy of poetry than prose: and the adoption of a poetic style by prose writers (which is as true of Livy as of the 'silver' historians) inevitably led to the inclusion of poetic/declamatory *topoi* and attitudes in their work. Historiography had, in any case, traditionally been viewed as a genre akin to poetry, and especially to tragedy and epic.

So far as poetry was concerned the rising popularity of public readings (*recitationes*) at this time – in many ways parallel to the burgeoning of *declamatio* in the schools – may have provided an impetus for the assumption of more overtly declamatory techniques. Marcus Aper in the *Dialogus* (9) speaks slightingly of poets who, after all their labours, are constrained to plead with people to attend their recitations – and to pay for hiring a hall and chairs and for producing programmes (*libelli*) into the bargain. Satirists like Persius, Petronius and Juvenal are no less scathing in their allusions to *recitatio*. Nonetheless, it had a real function. It was a form of cultural recreation as well as a means by which poets could establish a reputation. Audiences might well have to face effusions of bad verse (as Juvenal grumbles at the beginning of his first satire), but they also had the chance of hearing more skilful writers. Pliny saw in *recitatio* a way for authors to subject their work to independent assessment (*Epist.* 7.17.13). For a professional poet in need of patronage the recitation must have been of some assistance. Statius, for instance, at one point refers to the fact that senators were in the habit of attending his readings (*Silv.* 5.2.160–3) – and Juvenal, in sarcastic vein, confirms their success, though denying that they brought Statius any financial benefit (*Sat.* 7.82ff.).[2] For poets like Statius and Martial, the problem of finding patrons was urgent and pressing. The days of such coteries as those presided over by Maecenas and Messalla Corvinus

---

[1] Cf., esp., Parks (1945) 61ff.

[2] On Juvenal's allusion to Statius, cf. Tandoi (1969) 103–22. The satirist's remarks on Statius' financial status should not be taken at face value.

under Augustus had passed.[1] Commissions had now to be canvassed among the denizens of a new aristocracy of wealth. For many of the poets of the first century known to us this difficulty did not arise: they were rich men themselves. For them *recitationes* were more a self-indulgence than a necessity. One thinks of the millionaire consular Silius Italicus who, according to Pliny, frequently submitted his *Punica* to criticism by recitations (*Epist.* 3.7.5): it is improbable that he encountered much candour. The contrast between two figures like Silius and Statius is instructive: in this period, we see side by side the dilettante and the professional. The climate of the times did not endow poets with the status once enjoyed by Virgil and Horace. Martial bewailed the altered scene (1.107).

If the 'silver' writers have been lambasted for their addiction to 'rhetoric', their supposed pedantry has been no less thoroughly vilified. It is true that the tradition of *doctrina* in poetry, deriving from the innovations of the republican *novi poetae* and hence from the Alexandrians, could be taken too far, that allusiveness and obscurity can be fatiguing for a modern reader. One sometimes gains the impression that a poet such as Statius deliberately set out *épater les savants*. This 'learning' too has been viewed as a façade: the outgrowth of an overzealous culling of earlier authors and of handbooks. For the first century was a time of encyclopaedism. The gathering of information on diverse subjects into a convenient form was educationally helpful: for the rhetoricians liked to pose as polymaths, to have ready to hand those *exempla* and anecdotes which could easily be worked into their orations. To fill this need, digests and handbooks were produced, an extant example of which is Valerius Maximus' *Facta et dicta memorabilia*. This work, in nine books, was dedicated to the Emperor Tiberius some time after the disgrace of Sejanus in A.D. 31. It comprises a loosely-constructed collection of historical instances and quotable aphorisms. Valerius makes it clear in his preface that the purpose of his work is to save the reader from the arduous task of searching directly for such material in the many distinguished authors he claims to have consulted. For the sake of easy reference, each book is subdivided under various headings, with most sections presenting Roman and non-Roman instances. As well as anecdotal expositions on such topics as religion (Book 1), social, political and military institutions (Book 2) and well-known legal causes (Book 8), he cites illustrations of moral qualities both good (Books 3 to 6) and bad (Book 9), interlarded with disquisitions, at a generally superficial level, on well-worn philosophical themes. In such a work it would be wrong to expect deep insight or originality. Valerius' approach is declamatory, his style often pedantically sententious, his ideas

---

[1] C. Calpurnius Piso, forced to suicide by Nero in 65, may be seen, in his encouragement of a literary circle, as a pale reflection of his Augustan forerunners. On the background, cf. Cizek (1972) esp. 67–9.

threadbare and hackneyed. Yet, for orators and writers wishing to add a veneer of learning to their narratives, such a compendium would have been of considerable service. In later antiquity it was more than once abridged; in the Middle Ages and Renaissance it became a favourite educational text. Valerius has now lost both his usefulness and his appeal; but as a sidelight on first-century rhetoric he is worthy of examination.

In assessing other possible influences on changing stylistic fashions in this period, caution is always necessary. The autocratic rule of the emperors may have affected profoundly the outlook of such writers as Lucan and Tacitus: but it is dangerous to speak too glibly of forms of government engendering particular literary or oratorical styles. The creed of Stoicism – dominant at this time – impregnated a great deal of poetry and prose: but the Stoic theory of style, which emphasized the necessity of 'naturalness' and 'clarity' does not seem to have produced the results we might have predicted on such men as Seneca, Lucan, Persius or Statius. To see the literature of the first century in perspective, it seems best to bear in mind a number of disparate but possibly cumulative factors, educational, social, political and philosophical, all of which are, to a greater or lesser degree, relevant to the whole picture. The most satisfactory starting-point, however, is surely to be found in an analysis of literary developments in terms of a response to the challenge of the 'golden' age that had occurred so shortly before: for in coming to terms with himself, an artist has first to come to terms with his predecessors.

# 2

# PERSIUS

The satires of Persius are preceded by fourteen choliambic lines, which say in effect: 'I have not undergone any of the usual rituals of consecration; I only half belong to the bards' fraternity. But, as we know, the prospect of cash makes all kinds of untalented people poetic.' By this disclaimer Persius hopes to win indulgence. The clichés of inspiration are presented with unmistakable irony: Persius has not drunk from the *fons caballinus* 'the nag's spring' (a deflationary translation of the Greek Hippocrene); 'as far as he remembers' he has not had any dreams on Mt Parnassus (a satirical reference to the dreams of Callimachus and Ennius); and he leaves the *Heliconides* 'the daughters of Helicon' to established writers. Nevertheless, although he is only 'a half clansman' (*semipaganus*), Persius does regard himself as in some sense a *poeta* with a *carmen* to contribute; and since his pose as a starving hack is clearly a comic device (because he was quite well off), we assume he has other reasons for writing.

The lines have caused much dispute, but while the choice of metre is odd (cf. Petronius, *Satyricon* 5), there is no good reason to doubt that they form a single piece and were intended to serve as a prologue, not as an epilogue.

### Satire 1

In Ovid (*Met.* 11.180ff.) we read how King Midas' barber discovered that his master had asses' ears and whispered the secret into a hole in the ground. Persius' secret, however, is that everyone in Rome has asses' ears; and instead of trying to bury it he confides it to his book. In the myth Midas was given the ears as a punishment for his critical incompetence – he had judged Pan superior to Apollo in a musical contest. So in Persius the Romans' asininity is shown in their corrupt literary taste. Poets become fashionable without serving a proper apprenticeship, their recitals are occasions for affectation and self-advertisement, and their main purpose is to win applause. The works themselves are objectionable for various reasons. Some are grandiose (epic and tragedy), some are sentimental (pastoral and elegy), some are a mixture of both (epyllion and romantic epic), but all are artificial in the sense that they are not based on any profound experience and offer no serious interpretation of life. Poetry has become a social pastime.

Some of the best lines describe recitations:

> scilicet haec populo pexusque togaque recenti
> et natalicia tandem cum sardonyche albus
> sede leges celsa, liquido cum plasmate guttur
> mobile collueris, patranti fractus ocello.
> tunc neque more probo uideas nec uoce serena
> ingentis trepidare Titos, cum carmina lumbum
> intrant et tremulo scalpuntur ubi intima uersu.

> *On your birthday you will finally read this stuff*
> *from a public platform, carefully combed, in a new white toga,*
> *flashing a gem on your finger, rinsing your supple throat*
> *with a clear preparatory warble, your eyes swooning in ecstasy.*
> *Then, what a sight! The mighty sons of Rome in a dither,*
> *losing control of voice and movement as the quivering strains*
> *steal under the spine and scratch the secret passage.*

This and other examples show that although the satire is primarily about literature it also carries a wider condemnation; for a degenerate taste is the sign of a degenerate character. Romans have lost their virility. Later, after quoting lines from a wild Bacchic scene in which the vocabulary is markedly Greek and the musical effects overdone, Persius is warned about the dangers of writing satire – not unreasonably, for exotic subjects of that kind were employed by Nero and his acquaintances. But Persius evades the point by a clever manoeuvre: he won't tell anyone about Rome's stupidity, he will simply confide it to his book. That, he says, will be read only by the discerning few. The vulgar can find their entertainment elsewhere.

*Satire 2*

In describing wrong types of prayer Persius moves from hypocrisy to super-stition and then to sheer stupidity (e.g. the man who prays for a long and healthy life while gorging himself on rich food); offerings of livestock and gold are really an insult, for they imply that the gods are as greedy as the people who worship them.

Images of grossness recur: e.g. *pulmone et lactibus unctis* 'offal and greasy guts', *grandes patinae tuccetaque crassa* 'huge platefuls of thick goulash', *extis et opimo ferto* 'innards and rich cakes'. Even the qualities mentioned at the end are presented in culinary terms: human and divine law are to be 'blended in the mind' (*compositum animo*) and the heart is to be 'cooked in high-quality honour' (*incoctum generoso honesto*). Such spiritual food-offerings, however, *are* acceptable to heaven.

Several people are addressed, but as Persius' presence is not acknowledged in return, no dialogue develops. Instead the poet assumes the worshippers' voices, quotes their prayers (often in a ridiculous form), and then comments satirically *in propria persona*. The liveliness of the style comes partly from the varied use of statement, question, and prayer, partly from the comic device whereby things are treated as living agents and vice versa (a prayer is acquisitive – *emax*, a coin sighs in despair, a dead man is a *bidental* – i.e. a piece of ground which has been fenced off after being struck by lightning), and partly from the shifts of tone produced by different levels of diction. Thus some prayers run as follows: 'If only my uncle would pop off (*ebulliat*)' and 'O that I might rub out (*expungam*) that ward of mine.' At the other end of the scale we have a line worthy of a Hebrew prophet:

> o curuae in terris animae caelestium inanes!

> *O souls bent on earth, devoid of the things of heaven!*

And sometimes the two effects come together, when a sordid prayer is offered in the solemn language of supplication.

Although the second satire lacks the breadth and variety of Juvenal's tenth, it is more consistently noble in spirit. This quality gained esteem for Persius among the Church Fathers, the monks of the Middle Ages, and all who had been taught that 'to obey is better than sacrifice and to hearken than the fat of rams'.[1]

## Satire 3

Late in the morning a lazy student, who is a comic representation of Persius himself, is wakened by a companion. He tries in a rather hectic and dishevelled way to start work, but fails to make any progress. The companion lectures him on indolence and complacency, and finally launches into a sermon on remorse:

> magne pater diuum, saeuos punire tyrannos
> haut alia ratione uelis, cum dira libido
> mouerit ingenium feruenti tincta ueneno:
> uirtutem uideant intabescantque relicta.

> *O mighty father of the gods, when sadistic lust with its point*
> *dipped in fiery poison incites despots to savage*
> *cruelty, may it please thee to inflict just one punishment on them:*
> *let them behold Goodness and waste with remorse at having spurned her.*

These lines have a grandeur which impressed even Milton.[2] We tend to forget that they are addressed to an audience of one student with a hangover.

---

[1] Samuel 1.15.22. Cf. Plato, *Alcibiades* 2 149ff.     [2] Milton, *P.L.* 4.846ff.

9

Soon after, the student disappears and the friend's voice merges with that of the poet as he goes on to stress the supreme importance of philosophy – knowing why we're here and what really matters. Objections are supposed to come from a centurion – 'one of that smelly breed' – who ridicules philosophers and their dreary rubbish in language well beyond the range of a simple soldier. And then comes the best passage of all. A glutton disobeys his doctor:

> turgidus hic epulis atque albo uentre lauatur,
> gutture sulpureas lente exhalante mefites.
> sed tremor inter uina subit calidumque trientem
> excutit e manibus, dentes crepuere retecti,
> uncta cadunt laxis tunc pulmentaria labris.
> hinc tuba, candelae, tandemque beatulus alto
> compositus lecto crassisque lutatus amomis
> in portam rigidas calces extendit. at illum
> hesterni capite induto subiere Quirites.

> *Bloated with food and queasy in the stomach our friend goes off*
> *to his bath, with long sulphurous belches issuing from his throat.*
> *As he drinks his wine a fit of the shakes comes over him, knocking*
> *the warm tumbler from his fingers; his bared teeth chatter;*
> *suddenly greasy savouries come slithering from his loose lips.*
> *The sequel is funeral-march and candles. And then the late lamented*
> *plastered with heavy odours reclines on a high bed,*
> *pointing his stiff heels to the door. He is raised on the shoulders*
> *of pall bearers with freedmen's caps – citizens as of yesterday.*

Though loose dramatically, the satire is held together by its theme, which might be summed up as 'health requires training.' Physical and spiritual interact; thus pallor, swelling, fever, and shivering are related to moral defects, while gluttony, rage, lust, and fear produce bodily symptoms. Medical language came naturally to the Stoics, who laid much stress on the therapy of the emotions.

## Satire 4

In the opening section Socrates takes the young Alcibiades to task:[1] although clever at managing the mob, he doesn't know right from wrong and cares only for his own pleasures. No one tries to know himself; everyone criticizes the defects of others. A successful farmer is dismissed as a miser; one who lazes in the sun is accused of being a male prostitute. In this malicious world a man may try to hide his sores, even from himself. He gets used to depending on other people's admiration. But it's better to face the truth, however unflattering.

The poem begins well, and arresting phrases occur throughout. The two samples of abuse, directed at the farmer and the idler, have a Juvenalian force.

---

[1] The setting is taken from Plato, *Alcibiades 1*.

(In the second, one notes the figurative vulgarisms and the use of terminology from the *Georgics* to describe homosexual depilation.) The satire as a whole, however, is rather weak. The ridicule of the demagogue Alcibiades has little bearing on imperial Rome. The sequence of thought is sometimes confusing. For example, after comparing malicious talk to a battle (42f.), Persius mentions someone with a secret wound. We assume it has been inflicted by a fellow-citizen, but in fact it is a moral defect which the man is concealing from his neighbours. Finally, some apparent links between the Greek/political background of the first half and the Roman/social background of the second prove illusory – or rather they connect things which don't belong together. Thus the sunbather is abused by a stranger for showing his posterior to the public (36). Clearly we are meant to condemn this foul attack, yet the insulting words recall what Socrates has previously said to Alcibiades: 'Your highest aim is to pamper your skin with sunshine' (17f.) and 'stop wagging your tail at the admiring public' (15f.). These blemishes cannot be explained away.

*Satire 5*

After a discussion of style, in which tragedy (pompous, artificial, insincere) is contrasted with satire (plain, down-to-earth, genuine), Persius goes on to speak of his friendship with the Stoic Cornutus, who held that only the truly free man could live a virtuous life.[1] About sixty lines explore the distinction between legal and moral freedom, and then another sixty demonstrate that greed, sex, ambition, and superstition are all forms of slavery. In an ironical coda Pulfenius, a massive centurion, sweeps all this Greek nonsense away with a coarse guffaw.

In this, the longest and most elaborate of the satires, several forms are employed, including dialogue, autobiographical narrative, monologue, diatribe (with hypothetical protests), and a dramatic scene based on Menander's *Eunuch*. Of many excellent passages the following is perhaps the most lively:

> mane piger stertis. 'surge' inquit Auaritia, 'eia
> surge.' negas. instat. 'surge' inquit. 'non queo.' 'surge.'
> 'et quid agam?' 'rogat! en saperdas aduehe Ponto,
> castoreum, stuppas, hebenum, tus, lubrica Coa.
> tolle recens primus piper et sitiente camelo.
> uerte aliquid; iura.' 'sed Iuppiter audiet.' 'eheu,
> baro, regustatum digito terebrare salinum
> contentus perages, si uiuere cum Ioue tendis.'

*It's daylight and you're lying snoring. 'Get up' says Lady Greed,*
*'Hey, get up!' You won't. She persists, 'Up!'*

[1] For the idea that 'Only the wise man is free' see Cicero, *Paradoxa Stoicorum* 5 and Horace, *Sat.* 2.7.

'*I can't.*

'*Up!*'
  '*What for?*'
    '*What a question! Go and fetch kippers from Pontus,*
*plus beaver-musk oakum ebony frankincense slippery silk.*
*Grab that fresh pepper before the camel's had a drink.*
*Get there first. Do a deal; swear an oath.*'
                            '*But God will hear.*'
'*Ha! Listen, you numbskull, if you want God on your side,*
*you'll spend your days happily scraping the bottom of the barrel.*'

The fifth satire is particularly interesting for its ingenious transformations of Horace. The *Satires* and *Epistles* were always near the surface of Persius' mind, and he drew on them again and again in a spirit of admiring emulation. In 5.52ff. we hear of men's various pursuits:

> hic satur irriguo mauult turgescere somno.

> *Another lies replete and bloated in well soaked sleep.*

The source of *irriguo somno* is Horace, *Sat.* 2.1.8–9:

> transnanto Tiberim, somno quibus est opus alto,
> irriguumque mero sub noctem corpus habento.

> *For sound sleep: swim across the Tiber; before retiring*
> *ensure that the system is thoroughly soaked in strong wine.*

Persius has compressed 'sound sleep' and 'a body well soaked in wine' into 'well soaked sleep'. That is an example of a clever *iunctura*, i.e. a combination of ordinary words which produces a new and striking phrase.

## Satire 6

This is a letter in which Persius develops an idea found in Horace, *Epist.* 2.2. 190ff., namely that one should live to the limit of one's income and not worry unduly about the claims of an heir. Other Horatian features are the procedure whereby objections are stated and overcome, the epistolary framework which implies a friendly interest in someone else's doings, the pleasant description of Luna and its climate,[1] and above all the advocacy of enjoyment as a principle of behaviour. This relaxed manner is no doubt partly due to the addressee, for Caesius Bassus was a lyric poet who carried on Horace's tradition by his interest in metres and his lighthearted approach to love; he even had a Sabine farm.

Yet the poem is not quite so genial as the opening suggests. While gluttony and parsimony are attacked with typical vigour, the *via media* has few positive features. Perhaps that is why, unlike Horace, Persius 'fails to convince us that

---

[1] The modern Luni, now inland from the bay of Spezia.

12

enlightened self-indulgence is a true facet of his character'.[1] Nevertheless, the satire succeeds in a number of respects. There is a splendid scene where a despatch arrives from Caesar reporting that the pride of Germany has crashed to defeat; plans are being eagerly made for a public celebration. Then the whole edifice begins to crumble as we learn that the occasion in question is Caligula's farcical triumph in which men in yellow wigs were passed off as German prisoners. There follows an argument between Persius and his heir, in which we don't actually hear the latter speak and yet we know what he's saying. The technique is like that of an actor talking on the telephone. The literary texture is also very rich. Several expressions recall the language of Propertius, a repulsive slave-dealer is satirized through a parody of Virgil, and Ennius is directly quoted.[2] This is learned satire for a sophisticated audience; there can be no question of general reform.

The poems outlined above were written by a well-to-do young man in his mid twenties. Aules Persius Flaccus was an *eques* from the Etruscan town of Volaterrae. He went to school in Rome, where he came under the influence of the Stoic Cornutus, a freedman of the Seneca household. He also knew other Stoics, like the senator Thrasea Paetus. Such men had little use for Nero, and the Emperor regarded them with suspicion. After an unsuccessful plot in A.D. 65 (three years after Persius' death) a number of them perished; others were exiled. Had Persius been alive he could hardly have escaped. The satires themselves were politically harmless, except for the first, which attacked the writings of wealthy dilettanti and *ipso facto* the poetry of Nero and his friends. Nothing, however, was published in Persius' lifetime, nor did he finish the book. According to the *Vita* (42–5) some lines were removed from *Sat.* 6 to give the impression of completeness; then the poems were handed over to Caesius Bassus, who produced the first edition.

The poet's interest in Stoicism had some bearing on his choice of themes, and it helps to explain his earnest tone and his rather intolerant attitude to human failings. Unlike Lucilius and Horace, he does not really care about places or people; he is primarily interested in behaviour and in ethical (which includes literary) ideas. These ideas are worked out within a very restricted social framework. The *plebs* exists only as an anonymous mass (*plebecula, popellus*); the mercantile class is insensitive and greedy; politicians have no constructive role – their only function is to placate the mob; soldiers are boors; women are largely ignored. Happiness appears to consist in having a comfortable income from land, which makes it possible to spend one's time studying and discussing philosophy.

[1] Nisbet (1963) 67.

[2] With *turdarum saliuas* (24), *surda uota* (28), *cinere ulterior* (41) cf. Propertius 4.8.28, 5.58; 3.1.36; with *nec sit praestantior alter* (76) cf. Virgil, *Aen.* 6.164; l. 9 is from the *Satires* of Ennius – see Skutsch (1968) 25–7.

These limitations disqualify Persius from greatness, but he never claimed to be a major poet, and it is the critic's business to appreciate him for what he was. The ideals implied in his work are sensible and honourable (1, 4, 6) and at times noble (2, 3, 5). If he doesn't always affirm them with dignity – well, dignity is not a satirist's prime concern. And if there is some flexibility of viewpoint between, say, 2.64ff. and 6.68ff., that may tell in his favour. He is certainly consistent enough not to raise doubts about his sincerity – doubts of a kind which will always hamper any interpretation of Juvenal as a serious moralist. Persius *can* laugh at himself (see the Prologue and the beginning of 1 and 3), and for all his loyalty to Stoicism his picture of the school is not oppressively reverent (3.53–5). It is mainly his verbal artistry, however, which claims permanent attention. Some of his words are rarely encountered elsewhere (e.g. *canthus*, *obba*, and *tucceta*); others are given extended meanings (e.g. *aqualiculus*, *aristae*, *pulpa*); others he made up himself (e.g. *Pegaseius*, *semipaganus*, and *poetrides*); grammatical forms have odd functions (e.g. infinitives are used as nouns, and nouns are used as adjectives); there are strong tonal contrasts and abrupt transitions of thought. But Persius' most interesting feature is his gift for compressed and unusual metaphors. Sometimes these can be understood in the light of their origins; thus in 5.92 'tearing old granny-weeds out of someone's lungs' – i.e. 'getting rid of his long-standing misconceptions' – is a variation of 'pulling thorns (i.e. vicious desires) from the heart' (Horace, *Epist.* 1.14.4–5). Sometimes the metaphor unfolds itself, as in 3.20ff. where it gradually becomes plain that the student is a badly made pot. But sometimes the strands are so tightly twisted that they cannot easily be unravelled. Thus when the untalented are tempted by cash (Prologue 14), *cantare credas Pegaseium nectar* 'you'd swear they were carolling nectar worthy of Pegasus' spring';[1] and philosophers walk about staring at the ground, *murmura cum secum et rabiosa silentia rodunt* (3.81) – literally 'gnawing mutterings and mad silences with themselves'.

When all these features are taken together they add up to an idiosyncratic but nonetheless impressive achievement. In recommending the poet today we can do no better than quote his own appeal (1.125):

aspice et haec, si forte aliquid decoctius audis

*If you've an ear for a concentrated brew, then have a look at this –*

which reminds us that for reading Persius one sense is not enough.

---

[1] This seems to be derived from a line of Honestos: Πηγασίδος κρήνης νεκταρέων λιβάδων '[You had your fill of] the nectar-flow of Pegasus' spring.' See Gow and Page (1968) 1 270.

# 3

# THE YOUNGER SENECA

## I. INTRODUCTION: THE STYLISTIC REVOLUTIONARY

A generation after Seneca's suicide Quintilian composed his survey of Greek and Roman authors, classified by genres. Only in its very last paragraph (*Inst.* 10.1.125–31) does he mention Seneca:

In treating each genre of literature I have deliberately postponed discussion of Seneca. The reason is a belief which has falsely circulated concerning me: it has been supposed that I condemn him, and even that I detest him. This befell me in the course of my efforts to bring style back into conformity with stricter standards at a time when it was depraved, and paralysed by every kind of fault. Now at that period Seneca was practically the only author being read by the young. I protest that I was not trying to banish him entirely; but neither was I about to let him be preferred to his betters. These Seneca had attacked endlessly, realizing that his own style was utterly different from theirs... And the young did not so much imitate him as worship him; they dropped as far away below him as he himself had fallen from the heights of the ancient authors... Generally speaking, however, Seneca had many virtues as a writer. His mind was ready, and well stocked. He was capable of immense application. His factual knowledge was great (although in this he was sometimes misled by the people to whom he delegated some of his researches). He treated almost every subject of literary study: speeches of his, poems, letters, and dialogues are all before the public. In philosophy he was not thorough enough; and yet he was a superlative assailant of the vices. There are many brilliant *sententiae* [see below, p. 17] in him, as there is also much that is worth reading for moral improvement. In style, however, much of his writing is depraved; and its effect is all the deadlier because it is rich in attractive faults.

This passage has naturally exerted enormous influence on Seneca's literary reputation; but it has not always been read critically and in its historical context. On objective questions of style and ancient literary history, Quintilian's opinion may usually be accepted; and so here. He is to be believed when he represents Seneca's work as nothing less than a one-man revolution against the entire tradition of Rome, and indeed of Greece also. All the other authors in Quintilian's survey could be neatly slotted into a traditional genre; Seneca, alone, attempted almost all the genres. Other Romans might painfully acquire a style, like pupils in the eighteenth-century Royal Academy, by sedulous imitation of the Old Masters, and delicate variations on them; Seneca both neglected and despised the ancient models, substituting a manner of writing that was all his own. We may further believe Quintilian when he indicates that the Senecan revolution might well have succeeded, had not Quintilian himself laboured in the classrooms of Flavian Rome to recall Latin style to the norms of antiquity.

So much is literary history. The rest is a matter of sympathy and taste, and here Quintilian cannot be allowed the same absolute authority, any more than any other critic. Style is his primary interest. For all his openmindedness he cannot be expected to sympathize with the style which has dominated the preceding generation, which violates all his principles, and which he has spent a lifetime in eradicating. Still less can he be fairly expected to probe beneath that style's surface, and to attempt a balanced evaluation of Seneca's literary achievement in all its aspects. In fact, a very long time was to pass before anybody attempted such a thing. The life-work of Seneca resembles many other artistic and political phenomena of the later Julio-Claudian dynasty, in that it is innovative, contemptuous of earlier categories and conventions, hyperbolic – and shortlived, barely surviving the catastrophic collapse of the dynasty. In the reaction towards classicism which followed (and is nobly represented by Quintilian), it had little hope of sympathy. Almost the only later Roman authors who show a genuine admiration for Seneca as a writer are the Christians; and this is no accident, inasmuch as they themselves are anticlassicists and revolutionaries in their way.[1] The era of his greatest influence on European literature belongs, in fact, not to the classical period at all, but to the sixteenth and seventeenth centuries.[2] Thereafter it declined, approximately *pari passu* with the decline of Latin itself from the status of a major literary dialect to that of a scholastic pursuit. With the exception of T. S. Eliot,[3] no literary critic of the first rank has seriously occupied himself with any part of Seneca's work in the twentieth century. Professional classicists, on the other hand, have been paying ever-increasing attention to him; yet even among these there have been relatively few attempts at a general literary-critical estimate, and nothing approaching a *communis opinio* has yet emerged. There is, indeed, a general disposition to take Seneca more seriously than was customary at any time between the ideological upheavals of the seventeenth century and those of the twentieth; but he continues to resist conventional literary categorization as stoutly as he did in Quintilian's day. For these reasons the present survey,

---

[1] For the pagan and Christian *testimonia* to Seneca, see Trillitzsch (1971) 11.

[2] See, e.g., Eliot (1927), for his effect on dramatic poetry; Williamson (1951), for his importance in the story of English prose style; and Regenbogen (1927/8) for a general summary of his influence on continental European literature.

[3] Eliot (1927).

while it endeavours to respect both the ancient texts and the enormous variety of modern opinions, must necessarily be tentative, and in some degree personal.

## 2. LIFE AND WORKS

Seneca was no more free of extremes in his life than in his writings, and his biography is as dramatic in its vicissitudes as any in the story of Rome. Here, however, we are to consider only the aspects of it that seem directly related to his education as a writer. Broadly speaking, these are three: his family connexion with the declamation-schools, his early-acquired enthusiasm for philosophical studies, and his prolonged, intimate experience of despotic power.

His father Seneca (usually distinguished as 'the Elder' or – inaccurately – 'the Rhetor') has recorded his vivid memories of the Augustan declamation-schools in the *Suasoriae* and *Controversiae*. The latter work was composed in about A.D. 37, at the express request of his three sons Novatus, our Seneca, and Mela. They were passionately interested, the father informs us, in the declamatory skills of the generation that had just passed, and above all in the *sententiae* uttered by the declaimers: that is, the concisely formulated generalities *tamquam quae de fortuna, de crudelitate, de saeculo, de diuitiis dicuntur* 'such as those which are pronounced about Fortune, cruelty, the times we live in, and riches' (*Controversiae* 1 *praef.* 23). Among those who were present at such exhibitions the elder Seneca records many of his most able contemporaries in all fields: statesmen, from Augustus himself downwards; historians such as Livy and Cremutius Cordus; poets, most notably Ovid; and the philosophers Papirius Fabianus and Attalus. With some of them he formed close personal ties. For example, L. Junius Gallio, a senator and a friend of Ovid's, later adopted his eldest son, Novatus. This inherited familiarity with the declaimers seems to have been decisive in the formation of the younger Seneca's prose style; all the major characteristics of that style can already be discerned in the elder's verbatim accounts of the extemporary debates.

To the same cause, no doubt, the younger Seneca owed his special interest in Ovid and his poetry (below, section 4); and also his abiding enthusiasm for philosophy. Two out of the three philosophers whom he mentions as having inspired him in his youth were in fact also declaimers – Fabianus and the Stoic Attalus.[1] Fabianus in particular was admired for his *dulces sententiae*, his attacks on the wickedness of the age, his copious descriptions of rural and urban landscapes and of national customs (Seneca the Elder, *Controversiae* 2 *praef.* 1–3). In these men's oral discourses on philosophy, therefore, Seneca may already have noted that application of school-rhetoric to moral instruction

---

[1] Motto (1970) 187 collects Seneca's references to his philosophical teachers; the most extensive is *Epist.* 108.

which is such an important characteristic of his own literary achievement. The third teacher whom he mentions, Sotion the Pythagorean, is not known to have declaimed; but as a lecturer he was eloquent enough to convert the youthful Seneca, temporarily, to vegetarianism – an instance of that quasi-religious zealotry which recurred sporadically during Seneca's life, and in his hour of death.

Yet for long periods this gifted and inconsistent man was at least equally attracted to the charms of power. The elder Seneca, even as he was composing the *Controversiae* to satisfy his sons' passion for rhetoric, noticed that to the two elder ones *ambitiosa curae sunt; foroque se et honoribus parant, in quibus ipsa quae sperantur timenda sunt* 'they are concerned with a political career, preparing for the law and for public office – in which our very hopes are what we have to fear' (*Controversiae* 2 *praef.* 4). That double-edged prediction justified itself for the rest of the younger Seneca's life. Before Caligula's reign was over, he was prominent enough as an orator to excite the Emperor's hatred. From then on his fortunes, good and ill, were tied directly to the imperial house. Exiled to Corsica by Claudius in A.D. 41; recalled by Agrippina in 49, and appointed tutor to Nero; joint adviser to the latter on the administration of the empire from 54 to 62; retired (in effect) by Nero in 62, and instructed by him to commit suicide in the spring of 65 – Seneca was to experience, as few major writers in the history of the world have ever experienced, the nature and effects of unlimited political power. He was to observe how those effects radiated from the psychology of the rulers themselves to the entire commonwealth; how an emperor's passion might work havoc among populations. *Principum saeuitia bellum est* 'the savagery of princes is war', he says in the *De clementia* (1.5.2); and in the *De beneficiis* (7.20.4) the extreme of wickedness in a tyrant is *portenti loco habita, sicut hiatus terrae et e cauernis maris ignium eruptio* 'equated with a portent, like the opening of a chasm in the earth, like fire flaring out of ocean-caves'.

School-rhetoric, the lectures of the philosophers, and the long practical experience of power: although innumerable nuances of Seneca's biography no doubt elude us, these are securely documented as major elements in his formation. Out of them above all, it seems, he wrought a new kind of literature, both in prose and in verse.

### 3. SENECAN PROSE

'Tu me' inquis 'uitare turbam iubes, secedere et conscientia esse contentum? Ubi illa praecepta uestra quae imperant in actu mori?' Quid? Ego tibi uideor inertiam suadere? In hoc me recondidi et fores clusi, ut prodesse pluribus possem. Nullus mihi per otium dies exit; partem noctium studiis uindico; non uaco somno sed succumbo, et oculos uigilia fatigatos in opere detineo. Secessi non tantum ab hominibus sed a rebus, et in primis a meis rebus; posterorum negotium ago.

*You tell me (you say) to shun the crowd, to withdraw, to find my satisfaction in a good conscience? What happened to those famous [Stoic] doctrines of yours which tell us to die while doing? Really! Do you think that I am advising you just to be lazy? I have hidden myself away and barred the door for one reason only: to help more people. No day of mine expires in idleness; I claim possession of part of the nights for my studies. I leave no time for sleep; I only collapse under it. My eyes weary, they drop with sleeplessness, yet still I hold them to their work. I have withdrawn my presence not just from mankind but from business, my own business above all. My deals are done for our posterity.*

The reader fresh from Cicero on the one hand, or from Quintilian on the other, will at once be struck by the *staccato* effect of this typical sample of Seneca's prose (*Epist.* 8.1–2). The sentences are short and grammatical subordination is avoided. The insistence of most earlier classical prose writers that a sentence should seem to glide logically out of its predecessor, the transition being smoothed by a connective particle or relative pronoun, is no longer to be felt (as it happens, this passage contains not a single instance). Senecan prose, although no less contrived than its predecessors, depends for its effect on a series of discrete shocks: paradox, antithesis, graphic physical detail, personification (here the nights, sleep, and Seneca's own eyes all become transient aggressors or victims), and metaphor or simile (most often drawn from military life, medicine, law, or – as in the final sentence here – commerce).[1] There is great insistence on metrical clause-endings, all the more evident to the ear because the clauses are so short, and Seneca's range of clausulae[2] is rather limited (his favourite, $- \cup - - -$, occurs half a dozen times in this passage). But perhaps the most significant single characteristic of Senecan prose style is *the relative infrequency of the third person* in it. The grammatical persons natural to Seneca are the first and second. In the Letters, of course, this phenomenon is to be expected (although even here one is struck by the heavy emphasis: *Tu me! Ego tibi!*). But the fact is that it is universal in Seneca's prose works, whatever their nominal genre or subject. Each of these works is addressed to an individual, and the direct 'I–thou' relationship thus established is maintained throughout the book.

To sum up: Senecan prose stands to the prose of Cicero or Livy much as pointillism stands to the style of the Old Masters. Instead of a clear-lined, integrated design, Seneca relies on the abrupt juxtaposition of glaring colours. For the real or apparent objectivity of the periodic style, depicting in the third person a situation that is *out there*, he substitutes the subjectivity – or the egocentricity – of the first person imposing himself on the second. Well might Quintilian disapprove! This is an intellectual as well as a stylistic revolution.

[1] Summers (1910), Introduction, offers an excellent characterization of Seneca's prose style. The metaphors and similes of Senecan prose are catalogued by Steyns (1906).
[2] Norden (1898) I 310–12; Bourgery (1922) 145–9.

It is a denial of the finest achievements of Graeco-Roman classical culture – the seeming detachment, the creative use of traditional modes, the imposition of coherent and harmonious form on the chaos of the phenomena.

Seneca's approach to composition on the grand scale is similar. Again one misses the architectonic faculty possessed by the earlier classical masters. His procedure – no doubt based on the practice of the impromptu orators in the schools – seems to have been to block out the main headings to be treated in a given book, sometimes announcing them in a formal *divisio* immediately after his proem (e.g. *Constant.* 5.1, *Helv.* 4.1), sometimes not. Within those headings it is often difficult to observe much order in the argument.[1] The effect is again that of an impromptu speaker, developing various aspects of his topic as they occur to him, often at inordinate length and with much repetition. Here may be formulated the most important criticism to which Seneca is liable, in his prose and – to a lesser extent – in his verse: his deficiency in a sense of proportion, his inability to stop. Like so much of the best and worst in Seneca, this is essentially the attribute of a *speaker* rather than a writer – of a supreme virtuoso among conversationalists, whose *métier* is to captivate his hearer from moment to moment.

In the school-declamations and in the diatribes of the philosophers the art of the *exemplum* and the description had long been cultivated: the hearer was to be convinced by an appeal to some exemplary precedent in myth or history, his imagination to be conducted wholly into those scenes or situations which would best illustrate the speaker's point. Seneca consummated that art. His talent perhaps appears at its finest in the paragraphs of *exemplum* or description that are so frequent in his prose works; some of which are scarcely equalled for majesty in all Latin prose. Examples are *Q. Nat.* 1 *praef.* (the greatness of the universe, the littleness of man); *Q. Nat.* 3.27–end (the vision of the Deluge); *Consolatio ad Marciam* 17 (the voyage that is the life of man); *De brevitate vitae* 14–15 (the wise man's converse with the wise of all ages); *De providentia* 2.8–11 (Cato's gladiatorial duel with Fortune); *Ben.* 4.5–6 (the vision of God's *beneficia* to man); *Helv.* 8.4–6 (the heavens circling above the exile, reminding him of his true home). In such passages above all we glimpse the Stoic world-vision, which is in a sense the only subject of Seneca's extant prose works. He never described it systematically or as a whole, for only a *sapiens*, a perfect Stoic sage, was capable of so comprehending it (*Epist.* 89.2); and Seneca repeatedly disclaimed this status (e.g. *Helv.* 5.2, *Ben.* 7.17.1, *Epist.* 57.3, *Epist.* 87.4–5). All his treatises either describe a facet of that majestic vision (e.g. in the *De ira* and *Q. Nat.*), or apply the principles deducible from it to a given human situation (e.g. in *Clem.*, *Helv.*, and the majority of the Dialogues and Epistles).

[1] A more favourable view of Seneca's compositional art, as it is seen in the *Dialogi*, will be found in Abel (1967).

In either case, however – even in the *Naturales quaestiones* – his prime concern is to explore its practical consequences for daily moral conduct, *omnia ad mores et ad sedandam rabiem adfectuum referens* 'applying all to morals, and to calming the fury of the passions' (*Epist.* 89.23). Seneca was by no means a slavish follower of the Stoics. He would readily accept a moral hint from a Cynic, or from Epicurus himself;[1] and in one important doctrinal matter, the ethics of suicide, he seems to have made his own original contribution.[2] But on the whole his mind dwells in the Stoic universe as naturally and securely as the mind of a medieval thinker dwelt in the universe pictured by the Church. Its splendours and terrors, its vastness, its periodic destruction by fire or water, were ever present in his thoughts and his visual imagination;[3] but present above all was the inseparable bond between it and the soul of any individual man. The painter's saying, 'There are no lines in Nature', well applies to the Senecan universe. Its unity is perhaps most simply grasped by a consideration of the relations which exist in it between man and God. *Quid est deus? Mens uniuersi. Quid est deus? Quod uides totum et quod non uides totum* 'What is God? Mind of the whole. What is God? All that you see and, of what you don't see, all' (*Q. Nat.* I *praef.* 13). He is also Nature, Fate, and Reason (*ratio*) as we learn from other passages.[4] Below the stars, visible reminders of his majesty and peace, however, the universe is alive with apparent terrors: not merely the physical terrors of thunderbolt, earthquake, and deluge, but also those which surge out of the soul of man, the *rabies adfectuum* ('fury of the passions') which may have an equally disastrous impact on the visible world. Passion set free in the soul will distort features and gestures first, and then lay waste the individual and his surroundings. It may destroy a vast region, above all if it captures the soul of a prince (*De ira* 1, 2, *Clem.* 1.5.2). The individual who seeks peace or freedom inside or outside himself has one hope only: all men's souls contain a particle of the *ratio* which is God, and to perfect that *ratio*, to purge it of all contact with the passions, is to become God's equal in all respects save personal immortality (e.g. *Constant.* 8.2). And this way, Seneca insists, is open to all human beings, whatever their external condition. To this tenet we owe his famous and moving protests against the maltreatment of slaves and the inhumanity of the gladiatorial games.[5] The noble mind, he says, is a god that sojourns in a human body, *deum in corpore humano hospitantem*. That body may be a Roman knight's, a freedman's, or a slave's (*Epist.* 31.11).

---

[1] Motto (1970) 149 collects his admiring references to his friend Demetrius the Cynic; for Epicurus, see ibid. 150–1.

[2] Rist (1969) 246–50.　　　　　　　　　　　　　　[3] See below, p. 33 n. 1.

[4] Motto (1970) 92 item 2.

[5] On slaves, *Epist.* 47 is the *locus classicus*; the many further references are collected in Motto (1970) 195–6. For the games, see especially *Epist.* 7.3–5.

Such, in general terms, is the central doctrine which irradiates all his extant prose treatises. Seneca may, and does, discuss it from many angles and apply its consequences to many political and moral dilemmas; but in its essentials it is invariable. This invariability of theme is paralleled by a remarkable invariability of style. Although the prose works extend over a period of at least twenty-five years, it has so far proved impossible to establish objective criteria for dating any of them on purely stylistic grounds, where they lack allusion to any datable historical event. For example, the *De providentia* has been placed by modern scholars as early as A.D. 41/2 and as late as A.D. 64.[1] Seneca in fact seems to have formed his style while still relatively young, before the period of any of his extant works, and never to have substantially modified it. The most that may be said regarding his literary development – and that subjectively – is that in the works of his last phase (A.D. 62–5), the *Naturales quaestiones* and the *Epistulae morales*, one may perhaps sense a greater maturity, a greater urgency and conviction.

It remains to consider the nature of Seneca's achievement in prose, and the measure of his success. Technically, his major innovation consisted in taking over a personal, extempore, *speaking* style which had been developed by the declaimers and philosophical preachers, and implanting it in formal Latin literature. In that rhetorical technique he was a supreme master, far outranging his predecessors (if their quality is fairly to be judged by Seneca the Elder's reports of them). Yet it will not do to dismiss him as a mere rhetorician, as has been customary since the Romantic period. Obviously he was a rhetorician, as are all serious writers; the proper question is, what did he express through his rhetoric, and how effectively? He had indeed much to express: a profound imaginative grasp of this universe as the Stoics understood it, a keen and sensitive observation of the visible world, and a prolonged acquaintance with human nature and politics. If he is not consistently successful, the prime reasons are his diffuseness and his lack of a sense of proportion. From a compositional point of view, there is no masterpiece among the prose works of Seneca. Perhaps the least disconcerting in that respect are the *Consolatio ad Helviam*, which in many other respects also is the most carefully finished of his treatises, and the *Epistulae morales*. The *Epistulae* have always been the most popular of his works, and understandably so; for here Seneca finally discovered the literary medium that suited his genius. The formlessness, the spontaneity, the powerful exercise of the writer's personality upon the reader, are both natural to Seneca and natural to the letter.

The diffuseness is indeed a grave fault. It is quite possible that Seneca's reputation as thinker and stylist might today stand infinitely higher if his work, like that of Pascal, had never progressed beyond the stage of disconnected

[1] Münscher (1922) 75; Abel (1967) 158.

*Pensées* – a paragraph here, a sentence there, each projecting its separate shaft of light into the mystery of human existence. For in short, or momentary, effects he is at his finest. He is a world master in the art of crystallizing a notable thought in a few, lasting words; and the unexampled force of his great descriptive passages has already been noted. Nevertheless, there remains a half-forgotten way of appreciating the prose works even as they stand; which is to *hear* them. Possibly the best advice yet given in modern times on reading Seneca is to be found in the following paragraph:

It is interminable. As we go round and round like a horse in a mill, we perceive that we are thus clogged with sound because we are reading what we should be hearing. The amplifications and the repetitions, the emphasis like that of a fist pounding the edge of a pulpit, are for the benefit of the slow and sensual ear which loves to dally over sense and luxuriate in sound – the ear which brings in, along with the spoken word, the look of the speaker and his gestures, which gives a dramatic value to what he says and adds to the crest of an extravagance some modulation which makes the word wing its way to the precise spot aimed at in the hearer's heart. (Virginia Woolf, *The second common reader*, pp. 9–10; she is actually referring here to the Elizabethan stylist, Gabriel Harvey.)

## 4. SENECAN TRAGEDY

The Appendix on the tragedies will show that the external evidence concerning Senecan tragedy is minimal – far less than exists for any other dramatic (or supposedly dramatic) corpus of comparable importance in the history of European literature. Above all, there is no indication, either in the manuscripts or in the relatively few ancient allusions to the tragedies,[1] as to when or how they were performed; or even whether they were performed at all. Until about 150 years ago the general assumption was that they were regular stage dramas. Only after A. W. Schlegel's onslaught on them[2] did the opinion begin to prevail that they were intended merely for recitation, either in the recitation-auditorium or by the solitary reader. The question is far more doubtful than it is sometimes made to seem. Yet certain fundamental points may be agreed on. First: in the later first century B.C. tragedies were certainly being performed *both* in the live theatre *and* by simple recitation, but we have almost no knowledge of the conventions obtaining in either category of performance. The most concise of much evidence for the co-existence of both kinds of tragedy is found in Quintilian, *Inst.* 11.3.73: *itaque in iis quae ad scaenam componuntur fabulis artifices pronuntiandi a personis quoque adfectus mutuantur, ut sit Aerope in tragoedia tristis, atrox Medea...* 'Thus *in those plays that are composed for*

---

[1] Collected in Peiper and Richter (1902) xxiv–xxx.
[2] In his *Vorlesungen über dramatische Kunst und Litteratur* of 1809; the relevant extract is reprinted in Lefèvre (1972) 13–14.

*the stage* the actors likewise borrow the emotional tones of their pronunciation from the masks, so that in tragedy Aerope is mournful, and Medea savage...'[1] Second: to decide on the category to which the Senecan tragedies may have belonged we have one recourse only, and that is to analysis of their texts. Third: such analysis has so far produced no passage that is physically impossible to stage. Zwierlein, in his valuable discussion of the texts from this point of view,[2] has indeed shown that many passages defy the conventions of the fifth-century B.C. Attic stage; but has taken no account of the possibility, or probability, that the Neronian live theatre may have been as different from that of classical Greece as the Golden House was from the Parthenon. There remains nothing in the Senecan tragedies that could not have been staged with, for example, the resources of English Restoration drama. The atrocious *Oedipus* of Dryden and Lee (1679) is, by Zwierlein's standards, far less stageable than any scene in Seneca (the stage-direction for Oedipus' death, for example, reads: 'Thunder. He flings himself from the window. The Thebans gather around his body'). Yet it was composed for the stage; all that was necessary was some miming, and some machinery – neither of them by any means unknown to Neronian public entertainment. It may finally be noted that the only actable English poetic translation of any of Seneca's plays, Ted Hughes's *Oedipus* (1969) has responded well to the production-methods and theatrical expectations of the later twentieth century.

In view of the extreme deficiency of relevant data, the question of the manner of performance of the tragedies should probably, in method, be left open. The following discussion of their literary character will aim rather at those aspects which would be equally significant whether Seneca intended performance on the stage, or in the salon, or in the mind's eye. The works primarily referred to will be the seven tragedies which are both complete and generally acknowledged as authentic. Much of what is said will apply also to the *Phoenissae*, which is incomplete (it lacks choruses, and is apparently an ill-coordinated series of draft scenes for a play covering the events in the Theban saga that followed the deposition of Oedipus),[3] and to the remaining mythological play in the corpus, the probably spurious *Hercules Oetaeus*. A Senecan tragedy takes for its subject a Greek mythical episode, and in presenting that episode follows, *in outline*, a play by one of the great Attic tragedians. As it happens, almost all the Greek prototypes have survived for comparison[4] – perhaps an indication

---

[1] For live theatre in Seneca's time see *Epist.* 80.7–8 and *De ira* 2.17.1. The evidence for 'recitation drama' is assembled by Zwierlein (1966) 127–66.

[2] Zwierlein (1966).

[3] Such is the school of thought to which the present writer inclines; it presents far less difficulty than the alternative view, that the *Phoenissae* was originally completed by Seneca, but has been mutilated in the course of transmission. There is a recent survey of the piece by Opelt (1969).

[4] A general survey of the probable prototypes of the Senecan tragedies is found in Herrmann (1924) 247–327. The subject in detail still presents much uncertainty. There are many cases where

that the literate public of Seneca's time was already beginning to narrow its reading in Greek tragedy towards the limits of the 'Selection' of the tragedians preserved in the medieval Greek manuscripts. The major exception to this rule is the *Thyestes*; its theme was enormously popular among both Greek and Roman playwrights. Nauck[1] indexes eight Greek authors of a *Thyestes*, and one of an *Atreus*; Ribbeck[2] indexes seven Roman plays (besides Seneca's) named *Thyestes*, and four named *Atreus*. Of the Roman plays, no less than ten are datable in the Roman Imperial period. But none of these other versions survives, and it is impossible to be sure which of them Seneca may have followed. Yet the Senecan tragedies cannot properly be called *translations* from the Greek, any more than Virgil's Eclogues can be called translations from Theocritean pastoral. There is hardly a line in which Seneca reproduces the Greek word for word; there are very many scenes (including all the Prologues)[3] which have no parallel at all in the Greek; and even those scenes that do follow the general shape of a Greek prototype are given new colours and different proportions. The critic can make no more disastrous initial error than to assume that Seneca is merely aping the Greeks, or that Attic tragedy can serve as a point of reference for the assessment of Senecan tragedy.

Nor does it seem satisfactory to dismiss the tragedies out of hand, as so many critics have done under the influence of Schlegel and above all of Leo, as empty displays of rhetoric and nothing more. Leo[4] offers, indeed, a superb statement of the observable facts; but the literary-critical principles there applied require careful scrutiny. Leo's judgement on the subject is summed up in a sentence on his p. 158, which may be translated: 'These are no tragedies! They are declamations, composed according to the norm of tragedy and spun into acts. An elegant or penetrating saying, a flowery description with the requisite tropes, an eloquent narration – in these compositions that was enough: the audience would clap, and Art's claims would have been satisfied.' Before anyone adopts so easy an exit from his critical responsibilities, he should perhaps take the following considerations into account. First: while Senecan dramatic poetry is admittedly rhetorical, and indeed declamatory, it is hardly more or less so than the great bulk of Imperial Roman poetry in other genres, from Ovid to Juvenal. Ovid indeed, the founding father of this poetic manner, a star of the late-Augustan declamation-halls, and a family acquaintance (above, p. 17; cf. Seneca the Elder, *Controversiae* 2.2.8–12), was of enormous importance to Seneca, as numerous quotations in his prose works testify.[5] In the

contamination of a surviving Greek prototype with one or more lost plays is reasonably posited; for example the *Phaedra*, where elements of both the Euripidean Hippolytus-plays and of Sophocles' *Phaedra* have been detected by some scholars.

[1] *TGF* 964–5.        [2] *TRF* 364–5.        [3] See Anliker (1960).
[4] Leo (1878) I 147–59 (the chapter 'De tragoedia rhetorica').
[5] Haase (1852) Index.

tragedies his influence is even more pervasive, being apparent in the diction, in the phrasing, in the rhetoric, in characters, and in situations. All these points may be compendiously verified by a comparison of two admired passages in Seneca's *Phaedra*, 110–28 and 646–66, with Ovid's *Heroides* 4 (*Phaedra Hippolyto*) 37–62 and 63–78 respectively. Many more instances could be cited.[1] If Ovid's one essay in tragedy, the *Medea*, had survived, there can be little doubt that the debt of Senecan tragedy to him would be seen to be even greater, in many aspects.[2] But where Ovid fails to supply a parallel to Senecan dramatic poetry, one can generally be found without long search in the Latin poetry of the following two generations – most notably in the *De bello civili* of Seneca's nephew Lucan. In short, the rhetoric and the poetic manner of Senecan tragedy belong squarely in the tradition of what is commonly called Silver Latin poetry; and it is against the standards of that tradition – not against the standards of Euripides or even of Virgil – that his work deserves to be judged in the first instance. Almost all those features in it which have so displeased critics who insist on reading the tragedies with one eye misdirected towards Attic drama, are in fact shared with post-Ovidian Roman poetry: its pointed *sententiae*, its generalizations from one or a few instances, its habit of attaining its effects by caricature-like exaggeration of the literal facts, its powerful and often horrific realism, its tendency to enforce a point by piling up mythological or geographical instances in long catalogues, its abandonment of narrative architecture and a smooth story-line in favour of a series of discrete, brilliantly-worked episodes. If these features are to be condemned in themselves, then so is the bulk of later Roman poetry. Perhaps a more fruitful procedure will be to accept them as given for a poet of Seneca's time, and to enquire how he applies them to the creation of a poetic drama. Are they there for themselves alone, mere showpieces of technical virtuosity? Or are they media for the artistic expression of a coherent statement?

In recent decades, especially since Regenbogen's essay,[3] there has been an increasing tendency to suppose that the latter alternative is the correct one; or in other words, that Senecan tragedy is somehow to be taken seriously as literature. In the details of interpretation there remains a vast diversity. The most that may be undertaken here is a general theory of Seneca's dramatic aims and methods, illustrated by a brief consideration of a single play, the *Thyestes*.

Each of the Senecan tragedies, viewed as a whole, will make coherent sense as a concentrated study in one or more of the elemental terrors which ever threaten to disrupt human existence: omnipresent death, the passions, guilt voluntary and involuntary, and political tyranny. Each is pervaded from end to end by an appalling aura of *evil*, as are perhaps no other works of ancient

---

[1] Cf. Canter (1925) 42–54.  [2] Leo (1878) I 148–9.
[3] Regenbogen (1927/8).

literature (modern parallels might be found in the fiction of Edgar Allan Poe). It is above all to communicate that aura that Seneca consistently applies the contemporary stylistic techniques which were surveyed above – techniques which happen to be excellently adapted to his purpose. Since the emphasis of his drama is on the evil and its workings, rather than on the activities of individuals for their own sake, a logically developing plot at the human level is not his main concern. At the same time the evil in itself, and the dread effects of its operation, may be most graphically expressed (as they are also in Lucan and Juvenal) through images that in other contexts would appear monstrous, grotesque, or revolting.

The evils which thus dominate the tragedies, and in a sense are their main actors, are none other than those which preoccupy Seneca the prose-writer. The tragedies too, although Dante did not mean as much when he uttered the phrase, are clear manifestations of *Seneca morale*.[1] Yet there is an important difference: whereas the Senecan prose corpus endeavours to combat these moral terrors, primarily with the weapon of Stoic doctrine, the tragedies scarcely go beyond presenting them. It seems misleading to characterize Seneca's plays as 'Stoic tragedy'. Indeed, one may doubt whether such a thing can exist, strictly speaking; as Plato long ago saw (*Laws* 7.817a–d), the absolute acceptance of any coherent and exclusive metaphysical system, and the composition of tragedy, are mutually exclusive. In Senecan tragedy the remedies against evil, with which a practising Stoic was most profoundly concerned, are hardly touched on; and uniquely Stoic doctrine of any kind is rare. The most important exceptions to this rule will be observed in the *Thyestes*. Other major exceptions are the analyses of the onset and progress of passion, notably in those in the *Medea* and the *Phaedra*;[2] and the idea, which surfaces in almost all the plays but is most pervasive in the *Troades*, of death (often by suicide) as the ultimate guarantor of human liberty.[3] A number of other evident allusions to Stoic doctrine will of course be found, but they are brief, and not firmly woven into the tragic fabric; for example: *H.F.* 463–4 and *Phoen.* 188–95 (evidently on the qualities of the *sapiens*, the Stoic sage); *Phaedra* 959–89 and *Oed.* 980–94 (thoughts on Providence and Fate, respectively, which are closely paralleled in the prose writings). Here and there a Senecan character seems to show some of the attitudes of a *sapiens* or *proficiens* ('progressor', the technical term for one who is still seeking to attain the state of a *sapiens*): Thyestes; Hippolytus;

---

[1] *Inferno* 4.141; cf. Eliot (1927) vi.

[2] The *locus classicus* for the onset of passion is Act II of the *Phaedra* (85–273); its physiological and psychological impact on the individual is described, e.g. in *Phaedra* 360–83, and *Med.* 380–430; its ultimate triumph is best seen in the Atreus of the *Thyestes*, to be discussed below. The doctrines on passion implied in these plays are overtly stated in the prose treatise *De ira*, especially 1.1–8, 2.1–5.

[3] *Tro.* 142–63, 418–20, 574–7, 791; cf. *H.F.* 511–13, *Phaedra* 139, the great choral meditation on death in *Ag.* 589–611, and *Thy.* 442.

Polyxena and Astyanax in the *Troades*. On the whole, however, although the tragedies are no doubt related to Seneca's philosophical mission, their function here must be considered as almost entirely protreptic. They rest not so much on a philosophy as on the universal human experience of evil, typified in certain familiar myths and conveyed primarily by the resources of contemporary verse-rhetoric. They are addressed, in short, to unenlightened, non-Stoic, man – to the common reader, whether of Seneca's time or of our own.

Yet if the positive side of Stoic doctrine is rare in the tragedies, Seneca's Stoic habit of mind indirectly influences their composition at almost all points. His imaginative vision of the universe as a moral–physical unity, and his almost morbid sensitivity to evil, seem in fact largely responsible for that aspect of his theatre which has most vexed his critics since the early nineteenth century: the grotesque and often (to moderns) physically impossible exaggerations and horrors. In these tragedies, when evil once takes control of a human being it does not manifest itself merely in his features and walk,[1] or in bestial outrage against other human beings. The surrounding landscape may feel and reflect it (e.g. *Oed.* 569–81, *Med.* 785–6); and so, often, do the clouds, the sun, the stars, the very universe itself (e.g. *Phoen.* 6–8, *Med.* 739, *Ag.* 53–6). *Fecimus caelum nocens* 'we have put guilt into the sky!', is the cry of Oedipus at *Oed.* 36; *omnia nostrum sensere malum* 'all things have felt our evil', echoes the Chorus in line 159 of the same play, as it catalogues the ever-spreading horrors of the Theban plague. All these things are consequences of the Stoic sense of the vast power of evil, and of the Stoic vision of the universe as a whole interrelated in all its parts, which are expressed equally clearly in the prose treatises and also in Lucan. In the tragedies they seem to serve the same end as does Seneca's use of the contemporary techniques of verse-rhetoric: the realization, in almost palpable form, of evil.

Some consideration of a single tragedy in action (as it were) may help to clarify and complete the above general account of Seneca's dramaturgy. It may also suggest that a Senecan play, while obviously lacking in the Aristotelian virtues of consistently drawn character and satisfying story-line, may yet achieve a kind of unity peculiar to itself. The *Thyestes* has been chosen for this purpose, as being a play that has been particularly coolly treated by most critics later than the eighteenth century. The most recent full commentary on the *Thyestes* is still that originally published by Gronovius (1661 and 1682). Even Eliot[2] describes it as 'the most unpleasantly sanguinary' of Seneca's plays.[3] The coolness was justifiable only on their literal-minded assumption that the play's subjects were butchery and cannibalism photographically

---

[1] See above, p. 27 n. 2, for examples from the *Medea* and *Phaedra*.
[2] Eliot (1927) xxiii.
[3] Sympathetic critics are much rarer; Gigon (1938) is a valuable representative.

reproduced for their own gory sake. Thus read, it indeed makes little sense – either in itself or in the context of the rest of Seneca's *œuvre*. Yet all that we otherwise know of Seneca's mental and artistic habits would suggest a very different reading. Seneca has here adapted the hideous ancient fable to the combined expression of three themes which ever preoccupied him both as a prose-writer and as a politician: the temptations of political power, the passion of anger, and the dire effects of that passion once it has occupied the soul of a despot. On such a reading, the *Thyestes* might even be considered the most concise and powerful expression of Seneca's life-experience among all his extant works.

The *Thyestes*, like most of the Senecan tragedies, is divided into five acts (the Prologue being reckoned as Act I), with four choric songs in the intervals.[1] It opens before the palace at Mycenae, in darkness, and appropriately so. The traditional Thyestes story already contained a moment of unnatural night, when the Sun reversed his course in horror; but Seneca, to whom 'darkness' elsewhere signifies 'evil' (*Epist.* 110.6–7, 115.3–4, 122.4), effectively exploits this symbolism throughout the play, bringing it to a crashing climax in the fourth Ode. As usual, the Prologue involves little action, being dominated by one sombre figure, who carries with him the miasma of evil which will pervade the play.[2] This is the Ghost of Tantalus, the founder of the family and the initiator of its grim propensity to cannibalism in the furtherance of ambition. One of the simple, dreadful truths that are to be embodied in this play is that *ambition eats people*, including above all its own kindred. Another is that *ambition will never be sated* – a point which is now elaborated, by mythological means, in the first choral Ode.

Senecan choruses are in most respects quite unlike those of Attic tragedy. The precise identity of a chorus, or even its sex, can rarely be deduced from its utterances;[3] it is not always present during the actor-episodes;[4] and even when present it does not actually intervene in the dialogue if more than one speaking actor is on stage.[5] Scholars are now less inclined than they were to

---

[1] Possible exceptions to this rule among the genuine and complete plays are the *Phaedra* and *Oedipus*; cf. Anliker (1960) 93–7. The *Hercules Oetaeus* is also a five-act play. The *Octavia* can be so divided, as it is in Gronovius (1682) and Sluiter (1949); but the division is highly artificial, and obscures the real articulation of the play (see below, p. 35).

[2] The Prologue of the *Thyestes* is slightly more diversified than most; it contains, besides Tantalus, the subsidiary figure of a Fury, and some stage business (real, or to be imagined) is implied at lines 23–5, 67, 83–4, 100–5. The Prologue of the *Oedipus* also introduces two figures, Oedipus and Jocasta. The prologues of all the other complete plays contain one character alone.

[3] The exceptions in the genuine plays are the chorus of the *Troades*, and the second chorus of the *Agamemnon*; which both consist of captive Trojan women, and speak and act as such.

[4] The clearest, but not the only, evidence for this is found at *H.F.* 827–9 and *Ag.* 586–8. In each case the entrance of the singers of the ensuing choral ode is announced by an actor, in mid-play.

[5] This convention was observed by Leo (1897) 513. There is an apparent exception to it at *Phaedra* 404–5, which would be removed by Friedrich's convincing reassignment of the speakers, (1933) 24–38; and a probable exception at *Oed.* 1004–9.

attribute these technical peculiarities merely to Seneca's impudent contempt for the best Greek models; a certain amount of recent evidence suggests that Hellenistic conventions offered him some precedents, at least.[1] The metrical character of his choral odes, again, differs widely from that of Athenian dramatic lyric. The great majority consist simply of stretches of one or two verse-forms, repeated stichically. His favourite verse-form is the anapaestic dimeter, which occurs in all the complete plays, and which he handles, perhaps, as ably as any extant Latin poet. Next in his preference are a number of Horatian metres (notably lesser asclepiads, glyconics, and sapphic hendecasyllables). His solitary approach to a strophic arrangement is found in *Med.* 579–669 (sapphic hendecasyllables, punctuated as regular strophes by adonii). Only four of his odes exhibit anything near the metrical complexity and virtuosity of the Greek choral lyric.[2] The first Ode of the *Thyestes* is metrically of Seneca's simplest type – lesser asclepiads from one end to the other – and is in other respects also a fair specimen of his lyric manner. The thought-structure is not complex: a prayer to the gods of Peloponnese (catalogued) to end the series of crimes in the Tantalid house (catalogued); and in conclusion a description of Tantalus' torment in Hades by insatiable hunger and thirst. The style is influenced by Horace,[3] but at no point approaches Horace's mastery; if nothing else, Seneca's besetting sin of diffuseness, and the narrow range of his poetic vocabulary, would exclude him from that class. Yet it also often shows that peculiar vividness of description which has also been noted in Seneca's prose works; as here, in the final presentation (152–75) of the sinner's swivelling eyes, his desperately clenched teeth, the tempting apple-cluster looming ever nearer until he yields, and it tosses aloft into the sky; and, at the last, the deep, thirsty, swig from the swirling river of. . .dust.

Act I and Ode I have developed the moral atmosphere of the play – a prodigal expenditure of versification indeed, if (but only if) Senecan dramaturgy aimed primarily at the sadistic representation of physical horrors for their own sake. With Act II (176–335) the play's movement – it can hardly yet be termed *action* – begins. King Atreus enters, lashing himself into a rage against his exiled brother Thyestes. This rage is almost all we shall learn about Atreus in the course of the play. If it could, it would embroil the world in war, set fields and cities aglow with flames,[4] and annihilate Atreus himself, provided that in so doing it might destroy his brother.[5] Atreus is now encountered by a *satelles*,

[1] Herington (1966) 445, with note 57.
[2] These 'polymetric odes' are restricted to the *Oedipus* (403–508, 709–37) and the *Agamemnon* (589–637 and 808–66). Technically, they are unparalleled in extant Latin verse before the Renaissance. On their metrical character see, e.g., Leo (1878) 1 110–34, and Pighi (1963).
[3] Keseling (1941).  [4] *Thy.* 180–3, closely paralleled in *De ira* 1.2.1, *fin.*
[5] *Thy.* 190–1. The self-destructive effect of anger is likewise emphasized in *De ira* 1.1.1–2, and in the great allegorical portrait of Anger, ibid. 2.35.5 (which might serve almost equally effectively as a portrait of Seneca's Atreus, Medea, or Phaedra).

an Attendant; and the rest of the act is a debate between them on issues connected with Atreus' revenge-plot. The Attendant at first opposes the plot as contrary to the principles of right government, religion, and morality, but finally submits to becoming the passive instrument of Atreus' rage. Such scenes, often called 'dissuasion scenes', are a characteristic feature of Senecan tragedy; in most cases they are placed, as here, in Act II. Fine shades of characterization will be found neither in them nor elsewhere in the tragedies, with very few exceptions. There are perhaps only two extensive scenes in which the modern reader may feel something of that sympathetic interest in the characters as human individuals which he feels throughout a Shakespearean play: *Troades* 524–813 (the confrontation between Andromacha and Ulysses) and *Phaedra* 589–718 (Phaedra's revelation of her passion to Hippolytus). The reasons behind these two exceptions present a critical problem too great to be entered into here; it need hardly be said that the customary response is to assume that these superb scenes must be 'translations' from lost Greek 'originals'. But in general Seneca's speakers are accorded no personal background, very few modulations of tone, and no distinctive syntax or diction. They 'all seem to speak with the same voice, and at the top of it', as T. S. Eliot justly remarked.[1] Atreus here presents himself bluntly as *iratus Atreus* (180), while his Attendant is quite without fixed characteristics, being a conduit now for words of justice and piety, now for words of tame assent.

The second Ode is the most overtly Stoic of all Senecan tragic passages, setting up as it does the antithesis between the true kingship of the soul and the false kingship of political power; even as an adolescent, Seneca had thrilled to the discourse of Attalus the Stoic on this fundamental doctrine (*Epist.* 108.13, *Ben.* 7.2.5–3.3). It also coheres perfectly with the dramatic context, for that is precisely the choice which Thyestes is to make before our eyes in the ensuing act. The ode used to be one of the most admired poems of Seneca; [*chorus*] *ille divinus* 'that divine chorus', the scholar Daniel Heinsius called it.[2] The closing period (391–403) has become part of English poetry in translations by Wyatt, Heywood, and Cowley,[3] and by Marvell. Simply composed in lightly-running glyconics, the ode can be reproached only for the usual diffuseness, the tendency to catalogue. Even that fault is absent from the noble period at its close.

In Act III Thyestes arrives before the palace with his three sons. He has been invited by Atreus, in accordance with the plans laid in the preceding act, to share the throne of Mycenae. Yet exile and privation have taught Thyestes the nature of true kingship: *immane regnum est posse sine regno pati* 'it is a vast kingdom to be able to bear a kingdom's absence' (407). He would rather live

[1] Eliot (1927) ix.       [2] *Ap.* Scriverius (1621) II 297.
[3] Mason (1959) 181–5.

the natural life, in the woods, without fear; only under pressure from his son, significantly named Tantalus, does he sadly resign himself to advancing and greeting Atreus. The act closes with what may be one of the finest symbolic spectacles in ancient drama, next to Aeschylus' tapestry-scene in the *Agamemnon*. The exile, dirty, unkempt, and ragged (505–7, 524), stands grasping the sceptre (532–3) and crowned with the royal diadem (531, 544), pressed on him by his smiling brother. In full understanding of the true kingship, he has accepted the false. This rich act is, further, the only one in the play that requires as many as three speaking actors. Like the Attic tragedians, Seneca is economical with speaking parts, and follows the Attic precedent in limiting their number to three, with rare exceptions.[1]

The third Ode (546–622) consists almost entirely of a series of general reflections on fraternal piety, the terrors of imminent war, and the vicissitudes of Fortune. Odes of this character occur at some point in most of the plays. While their sentiments are blameless, and while they may often include impressive descriptions by way of example,[2] one feels that they would be almost equally appropriate anywhere – even outside a play altogether. Yet in this case some such pause for the hearer's emotions may be justified, for he is nearing the climax of horror. By a pattern that is discernible in most of Senecan tragedy, the climate of evil has been established in the first, static, movement of the play (here in Act I and Ode I); in the second, deliberative, movement (here Acts II–III), choices have been made through which the evil has taken root in the souls of the human actors; in the third and last, it will burst over the people and the landscape like a firestorm. In Act IV a messenger describes to the Chorus the things that Atreus has done within the palace – a palace which he first describes at length, from its pompous and glittering front to its inmost courtyard, where eternal darkness reigns and hellish beings walk. That description is no mere verbal ornament; for the scene is both a just emblem of false kingship, and an appropriately dark setting for Atreus' maniacal sacrifice of Thyestes' sons, which is next described. Then follows the butchery of the bodies, then the cookery, in atrocious detail. The Sun has meanwhile recoiled in his course, and darkness has covered all – or is to be so imagined – throughout the act (*Thy.* 637–8, cf. 776–8, 784–8. Whether or not the *Thyestes* was staged in antiquity, a modern director might brilliantly exploit the opportunities which the darkness presents – and the contrasting glare of torchlight in the banqueting-hall at 908). This darkness is taken up in the fourth Ode (789–884); and is enlarged to the scale of the universe. The singers wonder whether it is a mere

---

[1] The exceptions are *Oed.* 291–402 and *Ag.* 981–1012, each of which episodes will be found to require the presence of four speaking actors. A recent discussion of the Senecan 'three-actor rule' is that of Zwierlein (1966) 46–7.

[2] Noteworthy in the present ode are the contrasting tableaux of the Storm and the Calm (577–95), emblems respectively of the threat of war and of *détente*.

eclipse, or is the prelude to a cosmic destruction, perhaps (880–1) as the consequence of human wickedness. The major movement of the song is occupied by a surrealist vision of the collapse of the flaming constellations into chaos – its effects marred only by the fact that every sign of the Zodiac is catalogued in detail.[1]

In Act V Seneca returns from the impact of evil on the skies, to describe its effects on the two chief human actors. Atreus enters, transfigured by passion. He has reached the ultimate delirium, in which he feels himself beyond common mortality, the king of kings (*Thy.* 911–12, *regum atque regem*, cf. 885–9); this final and irremediable degree of anger is further described in *De ira* 1.20.2 and 2.5.5. The themes of anger and false kingship are here consummated. Only one pain afflicts Atreus through this act. *He has not had revenge enough* (890–5, 1052–68); nor will he ever, if the figure of Tantalus at the play's beginning had any significance. The palace door is now swung open, displaying Thyestes at his torchlit banquet. He is singing a drunken song – a song with no close parallel in ancient tragedy – in which joy battles with uncanny fears. There follows a swift crescendo of horrors. Atreus serves Thyestes a cup of wine mixed with his children's blood; then (1004–5) reveals their remains; and lastly (1034) discloses that Thyestes himself has feasted on their flesh. As the play closes Thyestes is lamenting, Atreus responding with triumphant sarcasms. The rancorous interchange, one feels, will go on into eternity.

All Seneca's writings, the verse as well as the prose, are imperfect in some degree. In the tragedies the familar faults recur: the tendency to run on and on to the ruin of all proportion, the lapses from taste and humour,[2] the occasional inconsistencies, the general air of work produced in too great haste and with too great facility. There persists also that egocentricity which was already observed in the prose works. Here also, whoever the nominal speakers may be, the dominating moral ideas are Seneca's ideas, and the many voices are, in the end, the lone voice of Seneca. It might be said of him, as it might be said of most of the great moralists, that all his work is in a sense a dialogue with *himself.* Writing of this kind, as Quintilian saw, resists classification within any particular genre, whether ancient or modern. Accordingly the Senecan tragedies can only be in part reconciled with the genre of tragedy, as the Greeks or Elizabethans practised it. Like the prose works, they are best approached in the

---

[1] The destruction of the universe by fire or water is a Stoic theme that particularly fascinated Seneca: *Cons. ad Marciam* 26.6, *Cons. ad Polybium* 1.2, *Ben.* 6.22, *Epist.* 71.12–13, *Q. Nat.* 3.27–30 and 6.2.9; cf. *Octavia* 377–437 (in the mouth of the stage-character Seneca), where again the catastrophe is ascribed to the sins of men.

[2] These are relatively not so frequent as might be supposed from a perusal of the nineteenth- and early twentieth-century critics; but they certainly occur. Two striking examples will suffice: *Helv.* 16.3–4, where our author gravely commends his own mother for not wearing maternity-gowns to conceal her pregnancies, not resorting to abortions, and not wearing makeup; and *Thy.* 999–1004, where the noisy symptoms of Thyestes' indigestion after his banquet are described.

first instance as the unique expressions of an extraordinary mind – a mind sensitive as few others have been to the spiritual and political problems of the human condition. Unlike the prose works, however, the tragedies are controlled by the external limitations of metre, of dramatic form, and of mythic subject; and to that extent are perhaps Seneca's greater works of art.

## 5. EXCURSUS: THE OCTAVIA

As is explained in the Appendix, the *E*-recension of the Senecan tragic corpus contains nine plays only, whereas the *A*-manuscripts preserve a tenth, the *Octavia*, unanimously ascribing this little historical drama to Seneca. The arguments against that attribution, however, seem very strong. They are best studied in Helm's exhaustive article (1934). His historical arguments against Senecan authorship (notably the accurate knowledge of the exact manner of Nero's death displayed in the prophecy of *Oct.* 629–31) are impressive, but not totally convincing; overwhelming are his arguments from style. Some further considerations will be found in Coffey (1957) 174–84, and in Herington (1961). The majority of editors, in fact, from Gronovius (1661)[1] to Giardina (1966), have treated the *Octavia* as non-Senecan. Attempts to identify its author by name have failed for want of evidence, but certain of his characteristics can reasonably be inferred from the contents and style of the play. He was an opponent of Nero and all that Nero stood for; an admirer, possibly an acquaintance, of Claudius' ill-fated children, Britannicus and Octavia; and an impassioned believer in Seneca's moral and political ideals. He was completely familiar with the Senecan tragedies and prose works; indeed, one strong indication of the non-authenticity of the *Octavia* is its persistent and rather clumsy borrowings from them (notably 381–90, borrowed from *Helv.* 8.4–6, and 440–532, borrowed from *Clem.* 1 *passim*; many examples will be found in Hosius (1922)). Finally, although a man of some learning and of deep feeling, he was a mere amateur in the craft of verse-drama (Herington (1961)). The date of his play's composition cannot be earlier than A.D. 64, since it contains apparent allusions to the great fire of Rome (831–3) and to Nero's construction of the Golden House (624–5). How much later it may be than that is hard to determine. The view of most investigators, however, that it belongs to the early Flavian period (after the death of the tyrant in 68, before the strong reaction against Senecanism visible in Quintilian's work), seems reasonable. Tentatively one might set it in the decade A.D. 70–80.

If the individual who wrote the *Octavia* has here been correctly reconstructed, he is clearly of some interest as a minor witness both to imperial Roman politics and to the career and influence of Seneca (cf. Trillitzsch (1971) I 44–8). Even more significant, perhaps, is the contribution of his play to our understanding of the potentialities of ancient classical drama. It is one of the only two ancient plays on historical themes that have survived complete (the other, of course, being Aeschylus' *Persians*). Moreover, it is the sole extant survivor of an entire Roman dramatic genre, the *fabula praetexta* (on the genre as a whole see Helm (1954)). The title of our play often found

---

[1] Gronovius follows the practice of his age in reproducing the vulgate text, complete with the attribution to Seneca; but his own opinion is made quite clear in the notes (esp. *ad* 185 and 516).

34

in modern discussions, *Octavia praetexta*, is not in fact justified by the manuscripts or earlier editions, which entitle it simply *Octavia*. Yet there are reasons to suppose that it is a fair representative of the genre *praetexta* in the second, Imperial, phase of its development (*c.* A.D. 40–80). Possibly to the conventions of the genre the *Octavia* owes a singular structural feature: the three major movements into which its action falls are each set in one of three successive days.[1] The second of these days, the wedding-day of Nero and Poppaea,[2] is represented only by a brief *kommos* (646–89). The first and third days (1–592 and 690–983, respectively) approximately balance each other both in theme and in structure; the notable difference in length between them may well be due to the author's progressively failing powers of invention. Another unique feature is the apparition (593–645) of Agrippina's ghost, on a stage temporarily cleared of all human actors. In character this interlude is extremely like a Senecan prologue (especially those of the *Agamemnon* and *Thyestes*), but there is no parallel in the genuine Seneca, nor indeed in ancient tragedy, for the intrusion of such a totally detached episode into the middle of a play. The tragic function of Agrippina's apparition, in drawing together the historical and moral causes of the catastrophe, is paralleled to some extent by that of Darius' ghost in Aeschylus' *Persians*. But the Darius episode is no 'postponed prologue'; the only structural parallels to such a feature (and remote parallels, at that) are to be found in ancient comedy, e.g. Menander, *Aspis* 97–148. The final major difference to be noted between the *Octavia* and other ancient dramas is that its non-iambic portions – the choral odes, the two monodies, and the three *kommoi* – are all restricted to a single metre, the anapaestic dimeter; another sign, perhaps, of the composer's inexperience at his craft. In most other purely stylistic respects the *Octavia* closely resembles the genuine Senecan plays. One misses only the inimitable essence of Seneca: the wit, the descriptive power, the gift of apt comparison, the occasional concise and ever-memorable phrase.

Yet the author also shows certain qualities that Seneca lacks. Although the *Octavia* is not a great play, it can yet be read with pleasure, and even with profound sympathy – once one has ploughed through the rambling and repetitive opening sections (1–272), in which the writer seems still to be trying his hand at an unfamiliar task. His chosen theme is moving in itself. It is a story of the early summer of A.D. 62, when a young and orphaned princess is repudiated by the husband whom she was forced to marry; sees the Roman *plebs* rise up in vain to protest against that husband's remarriage to the radiant Poppaea; and finally, on the pretext of her responsibility for the uprising, is dragged off the stage to her exile on a lonely island and inevitable death. The characters in this story are hardly less moving. Here one becomes aware of what may be the most profound difference between the *Octavia* and Senecan tragedy. Whereas in the genuine plays (as has been seen above) the human figures are almost colourless in comparison with the evil which informs and dominates the action, the *Octavia*'s principal characters, and even its Choruses,[3] live and act independently, in their own right.

---

[1] Sluiter (1949) 9–10, and Herington (1961), esp. 24–5, on the indications that the 'unity of time' may also have been flouted in some *praetextae* of the Republican period.

[2] This is established by *Oct.* 646–7 and 669–73. The evidence that the play's first movement is set on the preceding day is provided by *Oct.* 592; the evidence that the third movement takes place on the day after the wedding is found in lines 712–17.

[3] There are evidently two Choruses in the *Octavia*, as there are in the genuine *Agamemnon* and in the probably spurious *Hercules Oetaeus*. The first Chorus consists of Roman citizens who are fervent

Evils enough, indeed, are involved in the events here; but none of them is represented as the central, controlling force in the shaping of the plot. Thus it comes about – possibly through the author's very incompetence in the creation of a truly Senecan-type drama – that his Nero, Poppaea, Seneca, and (above all) Octavia, however imperfectly rendered, are the most vivid and credible human figures in the entire Senecan tragic corpus.

The student of Seneca's works will perhaps be most interested by the representation of Seneca himself in *Oct.* 377–592. Both in ancient and modern times Seneca's personal character has been vilified by some critics,[1] although it needs to be said that the peculiar practice of using his supposed morals as a criterion for the literary criticism of his writings is comparatively recent.[2] At least the author of the *Octavia*, who may well have known him, offers us a believable portrait of the man. This stage-Seneca is strangely like the Senecan Thyestes in that he has learned from exile the true delights of philosophy, but has adopted the fatal choice of returning to power when power was offered him (*Oct.* 377–90; cf. *Thy.* 404–90). Yet, having fallen once more to the temptations of ambition, he still applies his philosophical insight as best he may, under the foul circumstances, to the betterment of humanity. Seneca is seen desperately attempting to convince a rabid Nero that the true model for imperial behaviour is the mature, benevolent Augustus, that clemency and respect for the opinion of his subjects are the only right way to rule,[3] that morality and piety forbid the divorce of Octavia. All this is in vain; *liceat facere quae Seneca improbat* (*Oct.* 589: 'Be it my right to do what Seneca condemns!') cries Nero; and the tragedy marches on to its terrible close. This stage-character does not, after all, seem too remote from the Seneca whom one reconstructs from his writings and the scattered testimonies to his life. Here is a man tragic in his inconsistency: an eloquent moralist fascinated, even to his own destruction, by power.

partisans of Octavia, and appears in the first and second of the play's three movements. The Chorus of the final movement is of a very different fibre: it adores Poppaea's beauty (762–77) and condemns (785, 806) the folly of the uprising perpetrated by the First Chorus (683–9, cf. 786–803).

[1] The earliest recorded is Suillius, in Tacitus, *Ann.* 13.42 (year A.D. 58). Some of Dio Cassius' sources were equally critical or more so (60.8.5, 61.10.1–6, 61.12.1, 62.2.1). Yet they must be balanced against another source, according to which Seneca 'excelled the Romans of his time, and many others too, in wisdom' (59.19.7); Dio himself, unfortunately, did not trouble to do this.

[2] An example: 'Of [Seneca's] works the writer finds it hard to judge fairly, owing to the loathing which his personality excites' – H. J. Rose *ap.* Motto (1973) 45.

[3] Just so the prose-writer Seneca had argued in the *De clementia*.

# 4

# LUCAN

Petronius' classicistic reaction to Lucan's Stoic epic, the *Bellum civile*, fore-shadows the later response: why the neglect of convention, the disregard for precedent, the carelessness about poetry? He prefaces his *Civil war* (*Satyricon* 119–24), a Virgilian pastiche on Lucan's theme, its style a mixture of the old and the new, with a prescription for the correct approach:

> ecce belli ciuilis ingens opus quisquis attigerit nisi plenus litteris sub onere labetur. non enim res gestae uersibus comprehendendae sunt, quod longe melius historici faciunt, sed per ambages deorumque ministeria et fabulosum sententiarum torrentem praecipitandus est liber spiritus, ut potius furentis animi uaticinatio appareat quam religiosae orationis sub testibus fides.          (*Satyricon* 118.6)

> *Look at the immense theme of the civil wars. Whoever takes on that without being immersed in literature must falter beneath the load. Historical events are not the stuff of verses – that's much better dealt with by historians. Instead, the free spirit must be plunged in complexities of plot, divine machinery, and a torrent of mytho-logical material. The result should be the prophecies of an inspired soul, not the exact testimony of a man on oath.* (Tr. M. Winterbottom)

Quintilian had no doubts: Lucan is a model for orators, not poets. Martial shows that prose and verse had become polarized – that sense was now distinct from sensibility – when he records that Lucan, for many, had forfeited the name of poet: there were rules, and the rules were there to be followed.[1] Fronto's judgement we might question, but he too helped in the devaluation of Neronian baroque.[2] What strikes the reader of the ancient *testimonia* is their conservatism about the proper limits of poetry and prose, their lack of sym-pathy for experiment and innovation, and their distrust of wit and intelligence in verse: poetry was to be rich, ornamental and mellifluous, not sparse, eco-nomical and cerebral. Lucan, of course, is both rhetorician and poet: the two are

---

[1] Quint. *Inst.* 10.90 *Lucanus ardens et concitatus et sententiis clarissimus, et ut dicam quod sentio, magis oratoribus quam poetis imitandus*; Mart. 14.194 *sunt quidam qui me dicant non esse poetam: | sed qui me uendit bibliopola putat.*

[2] Front. 2.105f. '. . . in the first seven verses at the beginning of his poem he has done nothing but paraphrase the words *wars worse than civil*. Count up the phrases in which he rings the changes on this . . . wilt never be done, Annaeus!' (tr. Haines, Loeb). An unfavourable contrast with Apollonius follows.

quite compatible. Yet modern estimates usually see fit to follow the ancients and undervalue a way of writing which, albeit extreme in Lucan's case, is quite in agreement with the trends of Roman poetry, if not of Roman criticism: Ennius on occasions and Lucretius, as well as Propertius, Manilius and Ovid, had prepa ed the way for his intellectualized conceits, and their rhetorical, often prosaic formulations. And his infrequent admirers have been more concerned with aesthetic vindication of his verbal and intellectual extravaganzas than with discovering a rationale for his rejection of tradition.[1]

Anything but unoriginal in the *Bellum civile*, Lucan began with tired neoteric essays, stylistically akin to those of the *princeps*, quite mainstream, and accomplished. One might compare his clever *Thebais Alcmene, qua dum frueretur Olympi | rector, luciferum ter iusserat Hesperon esse* 'while the lord of Olympus enjoyed Alcmene of Thebes he ordered three nights in succession', fr. 8 M, from the *Catachthonion*, with Nero's *colla Cytheriacae splendent agitata columbae* 'the necks of Venus' doves are ruffled then shine', fr. 2 M: except for a certain Ovidian flavour, both fragments could have been written in the late Republic, during the heyday of the epyllion – supporting evidence for Persius' demonstration that neoteric poetry continued to thrive at Rome.[2] Perhaps there was agreement then, between the Emperor and Lucan, but soon we hear of discord – of enmity arising after the publication of part of the epic. But there is little point in clinging to the *Vita* in pursuit of three books composed before the supposed quarrel: anti-Caesarian comment is rife in the *Bellum civile*, and consistently so; nor is there any reason to assume that Nero would have identified with Julius.[3] Domitius Ahenobarbus, the ancestor of Nero that mattered, is awarded an unrepresentatively heroic end in Book 7; and Nero is praised at the opening of Book 1 in terms which may be overly fulsome, but are hardly ironic.[4] Poetic rivalry there might have been: but there is nothing in the poem

---

[1] For the ancient response see Ahl (1976) 74–5, and Sandford (1931) 233–57.

[2] It is tempting to speculate as to the identity of the *noui poetae* in Seneca's *Apocolocyntosis* (12.29), but *nouus* there probably means no more than 'modern'. Nero's second fragment is more reminiscent of Lucan's epic style: *quique pererratam subductus Persida Tigris | deserit et longo terrarum tractus hiatu | reddit quaesitas iam non quaerentibus undas* 'the Tigris, which meanders through Persia then disappears and leaves it, drawn underground in a passage through many lands, then finally surrenders its lost waters to a people which does not expect them' (I owe the interpretation to Dr R. Mayer). This could be from one of Lucan's many geographical excursuses: but it still has a preciosity which we associate with the term 'neoteric'.

[3] *Vita Vaccae*, p. 335 Hosius: *cum inter amicos enim Caesaris tam conspicuus fieret profectus eius in poetica, frequenter offendebat; quippe et certamine pentaeterico acto in Pompei theatro laudibus recitatis in Neronem fuerat coronatus et ex tempore Orphea scriptum in experimentum aduersum complures ediderat poetas et tres libros, quales uidemus, quare inimicum sibi fecit imperatorem.* It used to be assumed that the first three books were the *tres libri, quales uidemus*, but there is nothing to distinguish them from the rest in terms of antipathy to Caesar; nor do other proposals convince. For Lucan's politics, see Brisset (1964); for the quarrel, Gresseth (1957).

[4] Lucan imitates the proem of Virgil's first *Georgic* in the latter passage: for the issues, see P. Grimal (1960).

to warrant the hypothesis of a growing discontent with Caesarism – a dubious concept anyway – culminating in the conspiracy and suicide of A.D. 65.[1]

As the epic unfolds, we find a greater sympathy for the Republican party: but that is inevitable, as Pompey moves towards his death, and Cato emerges as Stoic saint. Rhetoric may demand an increasing amount of anti-Caesarian invective, but that has no necessary bearing on Lucan's relations with the *princeps*. It has been argued that the completed epic's structure was to be tetradic, the first four books concerned with Caesar, and culminating in the death of the Caesarian Curio, the second four with Pompey, whose death occupies the last half of Book 8, while the projected final tetrad – the epic breaks off part way through Book 10 – was to end with the death and apotheosis of Cato.[2] If Lucan's aim was a vindication of the Republican cause through Cato's suicide – and Book 9, an allegory of the testing of the Stoic sage, gives every indication that it was – then structural requirements are sufficient explanation of any increase in his antipathy towards Caesar, the tyrannical egotist, and Stoic villain.

But we should not press the tetradic structure too closely: in the first two sets of four books, focus alternates between the Pompeians and Caesarians without overdue regard for a principle of organization, and Book 10 is as dedicated to Caesar as 9 is to Cato. Moreover there is some indication, tenuous though it may be, that Lucan thought in terms of two hexads: lists of sympathetic omens are common to Books 1 and 7, and 6, with its closing inferno, reminds us of the *Aeneid* and its twelve books.[3] But Lucan's method of composition, by the self-contained episode, paratactically arranged, as well as the unfinished state of the poem, should warn us against imposing schemata and eliciting interior correspondences: for instance, we cannot make much of the fact that Books 5 and 9 both have storms in common, while geographical excursuses – scientific, not pseudo-scientific – occupy a great deal of Books 2, 6 and 10.[4] Unlike the *Aeneid*, the *Bellum civile* shows few traces of organic design. And, again unlike the *Aeneid*, it has no single hero: tetradic structure, or, more plausibly, the exigencies of his theme, occasion the choice of three main characters, Pompey, Caesar, and Cato, along with various ancillary figures, like Julia and Curio.[5] Pompey, the least impressive of the three, comes across most forcefully in the oak tree and lightning simile of Book 1, but is a rather shadowy figure after that.[6] His stoical death in Book 8 is a literary failure,

[1] See Tac. *Ann.* 15.70, with its story of Lucan's narcissistic death-bed recitation of his own poetry.
[2] For structure see the summaries in Due (1962), Rutz (1965) 262–6, and Marti (1968).
[3] In general, see Guillemin (1951), and for particular Virgilian debts, Thompson and Bruère (1968).
[4] See Eckhardt (1936).
[5] For the characters, see Ahl (1976) 116–274. Julia, who could be a figure from Ovid's *Heroides*, needs a closer study.
[6] 1.136–43, contrasting with the lightning simile used of Caesar, 151–7.

Lucan devoting too much space to moralization, and little, if any, to narrative; and his apotheosis at the beginning of Book 9 is too abstract to reflect on him as an individual. As one of the initiators of civil war he must die in order that the Republican cause be satisfied; but whether he has reached any personal moral goal at the moment of his death – as Marti puts it, whether he is a προκόπτων, a Stoic acolyte progressing to salvation – is a doubtful proposition.[1] Cato is more obviously a product of the philosophy textbook, a negatively characterized moral archaist in Book 2,[2] yielding to the impersonal saint of Book 9, who prepares himself, and his men, for a death which will be the ultimate vindication of the Liberty destroyed by Caesar. Cato had long since been an *exemplum* for poets and moralizing historians: in Book 9 he is more fully drawn than ever before, an imaginative, at times incomprehensible counterpart to the rigid hero of Seneca's *De constantia sapientis* – the tract which helps explain the more extreme of Lucan's metaphysical Stoic conceits.[3] Where, in the case of Cato, Stoic abstractions called for a rarefied, almost mathematical manner of writing, with Caesar we find an unphilosophically passionate conception, a nervous enthusiasm, learnt from the rhetoricians in their declamations on Alexander. Caesar, like the *felix praedo* of Macedon at the opening of Book 10, is a predecessor of Christopher Marlowe's heroes – an overreacher, an evil genius who pits himself against nature and mankind in an attempt to subjugate their order to his individual will. Sallust, who likewise went to the rhetorical portrait of Alexander for his depiction of young Catiline, would have applauded the idea: the evil self-will of one person is responsible for chaos in the state, and beyond that, chaos in the universe.[4] But it would be romantic, and false, to give pride of place to the anti-hero: Book 9, abstract and difficult though it is, begins to redress any imbalance caused by the flagging of our spirits during Pompey's last hours, and Book 12 would surely have set Cato over Caesar. If the two Republican heroes are less convincing to us, that is a result of a failure of execution on Lucan's part, or a failure of understanding on ours: there is clearly no intention that Caesar should steal the epic.

No single hero, then: but what of theme? Civil war, as the title states, not the loss of Liberty, or any other ancillary topic implied in that title.[5] Rome had seen a good deal of civil war, and a literature had been adapted to the theme. No single genre claimed it as its own, but a series of stock motifs and conventional sentiments became the vehicle for its presentation: epic, history,

[1] Marti (1945).
[2] See especially 2.354–64, on Cato's unconventional marriage, with its remarkable number of negatives.
[3] For the figure of Cato in Roman literature, see Pecchiura (1965).
[4] See Levin (1952), and for Alexander, Sen. *Suas.* 1.
[5] See, for example, the rather inconsequential discussion in Marti (1945), and Due's summary (1962).

declamation, epode – all strike a common note when lamenting civil strife.[1]
Fabianus' declamatory piece is typical, showing the contribution of Cynic–
Stoic diatribe:

See! Armies of fellow-citizens and relatives often face each other in battle-order,
determined to engage in close combat. The hills are filled with horses and soldiers,
and shortly afterwards the whole region is covered with mutilated corpses. Among
that mass of corpses and of enemies robbing them one might wonder, What
cause brings man to such a crime against his fellow man? There are no wars among
animals, and even if there were, they would not be becoming to man... What pesti-
lence is it, what fury that drove you to mutual bloodshed, though you are of one origin
and of one blood? Is it worth murdering your kinsmen that banquets may be served
by hordes of people and that your roofs may be flashing with gold? Truly it is a great
and splendid aim, for which men have preferred to gaze upon their dinner-tables and
their gilded ceilings as murderers, rather than see the light of the sun as guiltless people!
(Sen. *Contr.* 2.1.10–11)[2]

and so on, in a similar associative vein, for another two pages or so. Not a far
cry from the proems of Lucan and Petronius, this way of looking at human
corruption finds its way into Sallust's monographs, Virgil's *Georgics*, Horatian
lyric, and even the elegy of Propertius. Behind it lie the history of Thucydides,
and, more generally, the sermons of the Hellenistic philosophers, and the
moralistic iambography of writers like Cercidas and Phoenix of Colophon.
A basic assumption of writing of this kind is that the cosmos is an ordered,
balanced entity, and that the ideal society is one which obeys the laws of nature,
each living thing observing its station within the grand design.[3] Any individual who oversteps the limits of the natural order is preparing his fellows for
internecine strife. By laying claim to a portion which is not his own, he unlooses
the forces of greed and ambition: nature becomes man's victim, ransacked for
what she will yield, and conflicting appetites lead to civil war.[4] Natural confusion, as much as human confusion, is the result of the primal rebellion. Lucan's
assumptions are the same: man and nature suffer as human values are reversed,
*fas* being replaced by *nefas*, while at the level of cosmic interdependence, the
breakdown of earthly order leads to the distressed protestations of a nature
whose laws have been defied. He states the theme of the reversal of values in
the second line of his proem:

iusque datum sceleri canimus

*I sing of legality conferred on crime*

[1] See Jal's impressive study (1963).     [2] Leeman's translation (1963) II 470.
[3] See Manil. 5.734ff. (above, p. 483). Ulysses' speech in Shakespeare's *Troilus and Cressida* is derived
from the ancient view, and expresses it admirably: see Tillyard (1943).
[4] See also, e.g., 1.226, 666–7; 9.190–1; contrast 2.381–2, of Cato. At Virg. *Geo.* 1.510–11, the
infringement of law and order is a prelude to civil strife. The translations of Lucan which follow are
those of J. D. Duff (Loeb), sometimes adapted.

and redeploys it in various forms throughout his epic, as at 1.667–8:

scelerique nefando
nomen erit uirtus

*atrocious crime shall be called heroism*

or again, at 6.147–8, as a preface to the inverted ἀριστεία of Scaeva:

pronus ad omne nefas et qui nesciret in armis
quam magnum uirtus crimen ciuilibus esset.

*Ready for any wickedness, he knew not that valour in civil war is a heinous crime.*

In the fourth line of the proem – *rupto foedere regni* – the bond which previously contained the ambitions of self-seeking individuals is broken; and the laws of Rome are rescinded by the onslaught of war at 1.176–7:

hinc leges et plebis scita coactae
et cum consulibus turbantes iura tribuni.

*Hence came laws and decrees of the people passed by violence; and consuls and tribunes alike threw justice into confusion.*

This confusion and transgression of law and proportion has its counterpart in nature. Cicero sees civil war as involving a violent and universal upheaval (*uis et mutatio omnium rerum et temporum*, *Fam.* 4.13.2), while Sallust connects political discord with lawlessness in nature: *considerate quam conuorsa rerum natura sit* (*Hist.* 1.77.13 M). And Petronius, like Lucan, connects cosmic disturbance with the onset of civil strife:

aedificant auro sedesque ad sidera mittunt,
expelluntur aquae saxis, mare nascitur aruis;
et permutata rerum statione rebellant.    (*Bell. Civ.* 87–9)

*They build in gold and raise their homes to the stars, expelling water from the seabed and introducing sea to the fields, rebels from an order they have changed.*

Lucan's version is more general:

iamque irae patuere deum, manifestaque belli
signa dedit mundus, legesque et foedera rerum
praescia monstrifero uertit natura tumultu
indixitque nefas.    (2.1ff.)

*And now Heaven's wrath was revealed; the universe gave clear signs of battle; and Nature, conscious of the future, reversed the laws and ordinances of life, and, while the hurly-burly bred monsters, proclaimed civil war.*

Another sign of nature's confusion prefaces the climactic battle:

segnior Oceano, quam lex aeterna uocabat
luctificus Titan numquam magis aethera contra
egit equos.    (7.1ff.)

*Unpunctual to the summons of eternal law, the sorrowing sun rose from Ocean, driving his steeds harder than ever against the revolution of the sky.*

The imminent rupture of all *lex* and *ius*, of all Roman values, on the field of Pharsalus, is foreshadowed by a parallel unwillingness in nature to perform her proper functions. Lucan then develops the theme through the omens which, like those of the first book, image Nature's involvement in Roman *furor*.[1]

No single source supplied the basic concepts, nor indeed the method of treatment. Livy is pointlessly, but necessarily invoked:[2] Augustan epic had attempted the civil war, but again, fragments yield as little as epitomes. The early-first-century *Bellum Actiacum*, partially preserved on a Herculaneum papyrus, proves that the epic continued to show interest, and that the style remained prosaic.[3] Lucan's ideas are those of the mass of civil war literature, his style an extension from the sparse, realistic idiom of Augustan civil war epic,[4] while the elements of his theme could have been derived from moral tradition, declamation, or any Republican-biased digest of the events.[5] Only one thing was anathema, mainstream epic, with its poetic embellishments and superannuated gods: the *deorum ministeria* of previous epic are replaced by the sympathetic reactions of an outraged cosmos, additional colour being supplied by frequent recourse to witchcraft, omens and magic, while the concepts of *fatum* and *fortuna* – with occasional invocations of generalized *dei* – supply the theological basis.[6] In the realms of diction, convention and narrative technique Lucan consistently adapts the resources of tradition to an unpoetic subject whose demands went quite counter to those of other epic themes. Homer and Virgil could not provide a model for the topic of civil war: their methods would have elevated where Lucan wants despair.

Moralization, cynical and pessimistic, takes the place of organized narrative: the rhetorical moment, seen whole, and interpreted for its moral implications, becomes the unit of composition, replacing sequential action. Lucan's plan is too large, his mood too negative, to dwell on the details of any individual event. Homer, in describing the act of shooting an arrow, maintains a complete step-by-step objectivity, *Il.* 4.122ff.:

...and now, gripping the notched end of the bow and the ox-gut string, he drew them back together till the string was near his breast and the iron point was by the bow. When he had bent the great bow to a circle, it gave a twang, the string sang out, and the sharp arrow leapt into the air, eager to wing its way into the enemy ranks.[7]

---

[1] There has been no full study of this theme, nor of the related topics of disease in the body politic and the decay of agriculture; nor of Lucan's images of collapse and cataclysm: all of which help create a picture of a world on the edge of dissolution.

[2] See especially Pichon (1912), who has influenced most later discussion.

[3] Text in *Anth. Lat.* I 3–6 R; see Bardon (1956) II 73–4.

[4] See *The Age of Augustus*, pp. 190–2.

[5] For instance, Valerius Maximus' handbook of *exempla* could have supplied material.

[6] For divine machinery, see Petron. 118.6, above, p. 37. In Lucan, fate and fortune are indistinct: but they do *not* take the place of the mythological interventions of previous epic, despite the impression conveyed by the secondary literature.　　　　　　　　　[7] Rieu's translation (1950).

The poet is not present in his own person: the only concern is with the exact, literal presentation of every single stage in a succession of events. Lucan, on the other hand, refuses to narrate: Virgil, admittedly, had introduced emotional and moral language into his narratives of such actions, but narratives they remained. But now sequence is minimal, ousted by static moral comment: when Crastinus launches the first javelin of the climactic battle of Book 7, the action itself is relegated to a subordinate clause:

> di tibi non mortem, quae cunctis poena paratur,
> sed sensum post fata tuae dent, Crastine, morti,
> *cuius torta manu commisit lancea bellum*
> primaque Thessaliam Romano sanguine tinxit.
> o praeceps rabies! cum Caesar tela teneret,
> inuenta est prior ulla manus?                    (7.470–5)

*Heaven punish Crastinus! and not with death alone, for that is a punishment in store for all mankind alike; but may his body after death keep the power to feel, because a lance that his hand brandished began the battle and first stained Pharsalia with Roman blood. O reckless madness! When Caesar held a weapon, was any other hand found to precede his?*

And even within the subordinate clause emphasis on action as such is minimal: the participle, *torta*, is the only word concerned with the actual throwing of the spear. It is the moral aspect of the deed, not the deed itself, which occupies the poet. *Nefas* – the *nefas* of civil war – here occasions the substitution of an indignant, moralistic rhetoric for Homeric-style narrative. In the historical accounts, the javelin cast of Crastinus occurred after the signal for battle, being thereby absolved of its guilt by the priority of the trumpet-sound.[1] In Lucan's account, the javelin is launched before the signal, immediately joining those other deeds of civil war which violate accepted values. Hence the acrimonious apostrophe, in lieu of epic treatment: for that would have glorified, where Lucan wants to denigrate. He begins to write his poem at a point where narrative has ceased to matter: his audience, with its knowledge of Livy, and of the paradigmatic history conveyed by the rhetoricians, is expected to supply the background, and the links. Pompey's death is not mentioned at the end of Book 8, although four hundred lines are devoted to his final hours; nor does Lucan record the outcome of the lengthy sea battle in front of Massilia at the end of Book 3. His interest is in interpretation, in throwing light on aspects of a story which we would not have noticed for ourselves.[2]

---

[1] See Dilke (1960) 24, 28.

[2] For Homer's narrative technique, see Auerbach (1953) ch. 1; for Virgil's, Otis (1963) ch. III: some interesting comments are to be found in Brower (1959), chh. IV and V. I am indebted to Seitz (1965) for his analysis of this episode: also for his treatment of the flight from Rome, below, pp. 49–52.

Likewise, in the sphere of diction and metre Lucan avoids the precedent of mainstream epic. He abandons the versatility of the Virgilian hexameter, opting for a rhythm which is unmusical and prosaic. *Logopoeia* – 'poetry that is akin to nothing but language, which is a dance of intelligence among words and ideas, and modifications of ideas and words'[1] – is his chosen mode, a more suitable vehicle for the abstractions and difficulties of his theme than the musicality of Virgil.[2] In diction he is less concerned to embellish his material than present it in a dry sardonic light. For instance, *cadauer*, a real and uncompromising word used only twice in the *Aeneid* and once in the *Metamorphoses*, occurs thirty-six times in the *Bellum civile*,[3] while *mors*, the everyday term, is preferred to the poetic *letum*[4] – for in civil war, death is not romantic. By the same token he prefers the realistic *pilum* to *iaculum*, the heroic word.[5] His prosaic tendency is seen again in the precedence of *terra* over *tellus*, *caelum* over *polus*, *uentus* over *aura*, *aqua* over *lympha* or *latex*;[6] and, once more, the modernity and realism of his subject matter dictate a predilection for *gladius*, with its forty incidences, against five in Virgil, two in Valerius, and one in Statius. Unpoetic verbs are rife, many of them compounds. Constantly at odds with conventional epic, Lucan is not averse to coinages, or taking words from other areas of Latin literature: but most of the innovations have a cold, metallic ring. There is nothing especially ornamental about his coinage *quassabilis* or his four otherwise unattested verbs, *circumlabi*, *dimadescere*, *intermanere*, *supereuolare*, or again, his cumbersome three new compounds, *illatrare*, *iniectare*, *superenatare*; *peritus*, *formonsus*, and *deliciae* have no place in the higher genres;[7] nor should *lassus* have been so frequent, when *fessus* was available. Nouns like *auctus*, *ductus* and *mixtura* are more reminiscent of Lucretius and Manilius than the vocabulary of epic,[8] and *uxor*, like *alloquium*, *arca*, *armamentum*, *bucetum*, *columen*, *constantia*, *excrementum*, *opera* and *sexus* would not have pleased the critics. Of his verbal nouns in *-tor*, which are many, seven of them new, several are unnecessarily prosaic, or even bizarre. Technical terms are frequent, for instance *bardus*, *biblus*, *bracae*, *cataracta*, *coccus* and *couinnus*: sparingly used by most poets, Lucan likes them for their scientific edge, which is especially

[1] Pound (1918).
[2] For details on Lucan's metre, see Ollfors (1967).
[3] *corpus* is the more usual word in poetry: see Norden on Virg. *Aen.* 6.149. In what follows, I am indebted to Axelson (1945).
[4] *mors* 126 times; *letum* 36; note *interficere* at 4.547, absent from Virg., Ov. *Met.*, Val., Sil.; also *obire* at 9.190, allowed in Senecan tragedy, but with only two occurrences in the Augustans.
[5] *pilum* 19; *iaculum* 8.
[6] Respectively 183:99; 84:32; 61:0:3. Cf. *pater* 20 (5 times it means senator), against *genitor* 5; and *mater* 17, *genetrix* 8; yet *equus* 12, against *sonipes* 11, and *cornipes* 2.
[7] Before Lucan, *peritus* only occurs once each in Virgil (*Eclogues*) and Ovid, twice in Propertius, and three times in Horace (twice in the more prosaic hexameter works); *formonsus* is a lyric and elegiac word, like *deliciae*.
[8] For Manilius' influence on Lucan – which was considerable – see Hosius (1893).

apt for digressions.[1] He has also read his Virgil with an eye for such terms: from the *Georgics* he takes *ardea, defectus, dilectus, donarium* and *monstrator*; from the *Aeneid, asylum* and *caetra*. Virgil's 'poetic' vocabulary, on the other hand, is consistently avoided. Ovid too supplied him with several prosaic or technical words, and there is a relatively high frequency of Ovidian adjectives – usually more poetic.

We find the same suspicion of poeticism and ornament when it comes to groups of terms: for example, in those relating to fear, joy and colour, where other epicists deploy a large and varied range, Lucan limits himself to the more neutral and more obvious words. He uses the conventional *dirus* as frequently as the other epicists, but has a marked distaste for the Virgilian *horreo* and compounds, along with related adjectives such as *horridus*; nor is he as fond of *terreo* as his predecessors. Conversely, he likes the less colourful *metuo*, the prosaic *timeo* and *uereor*, and the un-Virgilian *paueo*, as well as its adjective, *pauidus*.[2] He also reacts against Virgil in his use of the vocabulary of joy: ignoring the stronger words – *alacer, laetitia, ouans* – as also the Homeric *subrideo*, he prefers the more ordinary *laetus, laetor, gaudeo* and *iuuat*.[3]

Similarly, his colour vocabulary[4] is less rich than that of mainstream epic; roughly half as many terms, used rather less then half as frequently. From a total of 34 terms, white, grey and black are the dominant tones, accounting for 15 terms with 64 occurrences. Black is preferred to white, but Lucan draws no distinction between the epic *ater*, Virgil's option, and the more ordinary *niger*:[5] likewise, he rejects the Virgilian *albus* and the evocative *niueus*, in favour of the neutral *pallidus* and *palleo*.[6] Red is Lucan's next favourite colour – we remember the frequency of deaths in his epic – but the conventional *purpureus* which accounts for 15 of Virgil's 38 reds, and the decorative *roseus* are entirely absent, replaced by *rubere* and cognates, which claim 14 out of the 25 incidences in the *Bellum civile*. Blues, yellows, and greens are sparse: *caeruleus* and *caerulus* only appear once each, ousted by the duller *liuens* and *liuor*; the epic *fuluus* has only three incidences, *flauus* five, and *croceus* one; while *uirens*, at 9.523, is the only green in this predominantly monochrome epic. A dark and negative theme, and the spirit of revolt: these explain the style. Traditional epic was too wordy, too august.

---

[1] Lucan's serpent catalogue at 9.700–33 is rich in technical terms: cf. the sole poetic incidence of *musculus* at 9.771, during the serpent-bite episode.

[2] See MacKay (1961) for full statistics.

[3] See Miniconi (1962).

[4] I rely on André (1949) for what follows.

[5] Lucan has 13 incidences of *ater*, 14 of *niger*. Val. and Stat. likewise do not discriminate; Sil. has a liking for *nigrans*.

[6] *albus* accounts for 22 of Virgil's 48 whites; Sil. and Stat. like *niueus*, 19 out of 44, and 19 out of 33. Lucan has only 5 conventional whites, *albus* 2.720, *candidus* 2.355, 5.144, 10.141, and *niveus* 10.144.

As with poetic diction, so with epic convention. The stock ingredients are either missing, or accommodated to the themes of the reversal of values and the breakdown of order. Where, for example, in Virgil's underworld scene we have the founder of Rome, a venerable Sibyl, and a parade of future heroes, in Lucan's νέκυια we find a coward, a witch, and the triumph of Rome's villains. The cycle is at an end: decay replaces birth, discord follows greatness.[1] Likewise, single combat – the ἀριστεία of Homeric and Virgilian epic – is not at home in its usual form in a poem on civil war. It occurs but once – the Scaeva episode of Book 6 – and even then Lucan takes pains to modify its meaning, 6.189–92:

> illum tota premit moles, illum omnia tela,
> nulla fuit non certa manus, non lancea felix
> parque nouum Fortuna uidet concurrere, bellum
> atque uirum.

*All the host and all the weapons made him their sole object; no hand missed its aim, no lance failed of its mark; and Fortune sees a new pair meet in combat – a man against an army.*

Because this is a time of civil strife, *uirtus* is now a crime:[2] hence the extravagance of the episode, the claim to novelty – *par nouum*, one man against an army – and the absence of the convention elsewhere in the epic. True, the Homeric colour crops up in the sea fight at the end of Book 3: but the ναυμαχία itself is devoid of epic precedent.[3] His only other concession to the ἀριστεία is to nod at the related motif of the dying hero's words, during the death of Ahenobarbus in Book 7, a book singularly lacking in Homeric or Virgilian narrative action: but there the heroic send-off is more ignobly motivated – by Nero's ancestry, not the nature of his theme.

Lucan is at his best when he has some pattern to follow, adapting, reversing, or negating it. Declamation alone does not stand him in good stead during his account of the battle of Pharsalus, despite his feeling that the event was too big to warrant mere narrative:[4] apart from the death of Domitius, his only conventional gesture is his variation on the motif of the signal for battle.[5] In Virgil, women and children tremble at Allecto's trumpet blast:

> et trepidae matres pressere ad pectora natos                    (*Aen.* 7.518)

*and trembling mothers pressed their children to their breasts.*

---

[1] As Lucan says at 6.780–1, *effera Romanos agitat discordia manes | impiaque infernam ruperunt arma quietem*; civil war affects the underworld as well.

[2] See 6.147–8, quoted above, p. 42.

[3] For details, see Miniconi (1951), and Opelt (1957).

[4] See 7.633–4 *illic per fata uirorum, | per populos hic Roma perit*. Lucan has just refused to write of *singula fata* – a rejection of the Homeric tradition – giving instead a précis which catalogues the elements of a battle, 7.617ff.

[5] In my analysis I follow Seitz (1965).

The legacy of Apollonius Rhodius 4.129ff., these women and children reappear in Virgil's imitators, Valerius and Statius: in Lucan, the stereotype is changed. Gone is the pathetic terror of the innocent: it is the belligerents themselves who fear their own actions:

> uocesque furoris
> expauere sui tota tellure relatas.         (*Bell. Civ.* 7.483–4)

*The armies were terrified of their own madness repeated from all the earth.*

One of the keynotes of the proem was the self-destruction of a powerful people:

> populumque potentem
> in sua uictrici conuersum uiscera dextra.      (*Bell. Civ.* 1.2–3)

*I tell how a powerful people turned their victorious hands against their own vitals.*

Like the hand which turns in on its own entrails, the signal for battle rebounds on the impious armies, their guilt increased by their shouts. A simple adjustment to convention continues the notion that in civil war, the normal laws no longer hold. Earlier in the book, another reversal had done the same work: Cicero, the traditional champion of liberty, martyred for peace by Antony, had been shown counselling war. Historical accuracy – Cicero was not in fact at Pharsalus – is subordinated to the theme of the triumph of *nefas*. But apart from these touches, and the general anti-Virgilian tenor of the book, there is insufficient connexion with epic, and insufficient action. Originality needs some basis: Lucan's private rhetoric cannot support the battle. We find a new direction in the last few pages, where Caesar gloats over the dead: but although the gory innovation caught on with Silius, it is no real substitute for the adaptation of tradition.[1]

When faced with tired or unsuitable conventions, Lucan has constant recourse to one particular mannerism: the negation antithesis, *non* followed by *sed*. Sometimes it merely indicates formal divergence, like *nouus* or *insolitus*; at others it enacts the themes of discord and disorder.[2] During the *descriptio luci* (3.399ff.), we find several examples of the negation antithesis, partly formal in intention, partly thematic: at one and the same time, Lucan claims literary originality, and mirrors his theme. Nature's laws cease to operate, and the grove becomes original, and forbidding, as Lucan denies Virgilian associations, replacing conventions with personal fancy:

> hunc *non* ruricolae Panes nemorumque potentes
> Siluani Nymphaeque tenent; *sed* barbara ritu
> sacra deum; structae diris altaribus arae,
> omnisque humanis lustrata cruoribus arbor.      (3.402–5)

---

[1] See Miniconi (1962) for details.

[2] Nowak's thesis (1955), part III, 'Negationsantithesen', discusses the interior mechanics of the device. For Lucan's grove, see Phillips (1968).

*No rural Pan dwelt there, no Silvanus, ruler of the woods, no Nymphs; but gods were worshipped there with savage rites, the altars were heaped with hideous offerings, and every tree was sprinkled with human gore.*

Virgil's pastoral ideal is deliberately revoked:

> est ingens gelidum lucus prope Caeritis amnem,
> religione patrum late sacer; undique colles
> inclusere caui et nigra nemus abiete cingunt.
> Siluano fama est ueteres sacrasse Pelasgos,
> aruorum pecorisque deo, lucumque diemque,
> qui primi finis aliquando habuere Latinos.     (*Aen.* 8.597ff.)

> *There's an extensive woodland near the cool stream of Caere*
> *Reverenced by all around in the faith of their fathers; encircled*
> *By hills, that wood of dark green fir-trees lay in a hollow.*
> *The legend is that the ancient Pelasgians, the first settlers*
> *Of Latium in the old days, had dedicated the wood*
> *And a festival day to Silvanus, the god of fields and cattle.*
>
> (Tr. C. Day Lewis)

Not only that: Lucan's variation strips Nature of her functions, suggesting an uncanny automatism:

> nec uentus in illas
> incubuit siluas excussaque nubibus atris
> fulgura; *non* ulli frondem praebentibus aurae
> arboribus suus horror inest.     (3.408–11)

*No wind ever bore down upon that wood, nor thunderbolt hurled from black clouds; the trees, even when they spread their leaves to no breeze, rustled of themselves.*

The reader's response to the norm, exploited by the negatives, provides the basis for the paradox: order and disorder, comprehended in sequence, present a vision of a world that is awry.

In the first book's account of the abandonment of Rome the same techniques recur: civil war transforms a rhetorical prescription accepted by history and epic alike. Reminded of what ought to happen, we deplore the breach of the code. Quintilian gives the ingredients:

sic et urbium captarum crescit miseratio...apparebunt effusae per domus ac templa flammae et ruentium tectorum fragor et ex diuersis clamoribus unus quidam sonus, aliorum fuga incerta, alii extremo complexu suorum cohaerentes et infantium feminarumque ploratus et male usque in illum diem seruati fato senes.     (8.3.67)

*So, too, we may move our hearers to tears by the picture of a captured town...we shall see the flames pouring from house and temple, and hear the crash of falling roofs and one confused clamour blended of many cries; we shall behold some in doubt whither to fly, others clinging to their nearest and dearest in one last embrace, while the wailing of women and children and the laments of old men that the cruelty of fate should have spared them to see that day will strike our ears.* (Tr. H. E. Butler)

Fire, crashing buildings, shouts, uncertain flight, final embraces, wailing women and children, old men: the possibilities are exploited by Petronius, Virgil and Silius, as well as Dio and Livy.[1]

Lucan begins his treatment with a version of the negation antithesis, reproving the flight of the Senate:

> *nec* solum uolgus inani
> percussum terrore pauet, *sed* curia et ipsi
> sedibus exiluere patres inuisaque belli
> consulibus fugiens mandat decreta senatus.　　　(1.486–8)

*Nor was the populace alone stricken with groundless fear. The Senate House was moved; the Fathers themselves sprang up from their seats and the Senate fled, deputing to the consuls the dreaded declaration of war.*

We might excuse the flight of the *uolgus*: but that of the Senate is not to be pardoned. Two similes follow, neatly adapted again to the irregular state of affairs. In the first, Lucan recalls the rhetorical formula, then implicitly denies its application:

> credas aut tecta nefandas
> corripuisse faces aut iam quatiente ruina
> nutantes pendere domos: sic turba per urbem
> praecipiti lymphata gradu, uelut unica rebus
> spes foret adflictis patrios excedere muros,
> inconsulta ruit.　　　(1.493–8)

*One might think that impious firebrands had seized hold of the houses, or that the buildings were swaying and tottering in an earthquake shock. For the frenzied crowd rushed headlong through the city with no fixed purpose, and as if the one chance of relief from ruin were to get outside their native walls.*

'One might have thought...but one would be wrong': that is the upshot. Lucan's *faces* and *ruina*, the equivalent of the *effusae per domus ac templa flammae* and *ruentium tectorum fragor* prescribed by Quintilian, would normally be just reason for deserting a city. But on this occasion, the absence of the usual causes is an indictment of Rome's unnatural susceptibility to rumour and panic. By abrogating the rule, Lucan highlights the guilt. His nautical simile has a like effect. Plutarch uses it straightforwardly: οἰκτρότατον δὲ τὸ θέαμα τῆς πόλεως ἦν, ἐπιφερομένου τοσούτου χειμῶνος ὥσπερ νεὼς ὑπὸ κυβερνητῶν ἀπαγορευόντων πρὸς τὸ συντυχὸν ἐμπεσεῖν κομιζομένης. 'But most pitiful was the sight of the city, now that so great a tempest was bearing down upon her, carried along like a ship abandoned of her helmsman to dash against whatever lay in her path' (*Vit. Caes.* 34.3). Lucan, on the other hand, shows that the

---

[1] See Nowak (1955) 8ff., and Seitz (1965); also Caplan on *Rhet. ad Her.* 4.39.51.

desertion is premature; worse than that, it is a flight into war. After an orthodox start and central section, a final accommodation to the motif of reversal:

> *nondum* sparsa compage carinae
> naufragium sibi quisque facit.         (1.502–3)

*and each man makes shipwreck for himself before the planks of the hull are broken asunder.*

If the timbers really had broken up, the ship might reasonably have been abandoned: as it is, the crew is too hasty. And as Lucan adds, desertion makes things worse:

>                 sic urbe relicta
> in bellum fugitur.         (1.503–4)

Thus Rome is abandoned, and flight is the preparation for war. Corresponding to *nondum...carinae* and *naufragium...facit*, the two parts of the epigram bring the perversity to a head. Panic in the face of civil war causes men to forsake the natural patterns of behaviour, breaking the natural bonds of family and home: the idea is developed at lines 504–9, where the individual points of the rhetorical scheme are prefixed by negatives:

> *nullum* iam languidus aeuo
> eualuit reuocare parens coniunxue maritum
> fletibus, aut patrii, dubiae dum uota salutis
> conciperent, tenuere lares; *nec* limine quisquam
> haesit, et extremo tunc forsitan urbis amatae
> plenus abit uisu; *ruit inreuocabile uolgus.*

*No aged father had the power to keep back his son, nor weeping wife her husband; none was detained by the ancestral gods of his household, till he could frame a prayer for preservation from danger; none lingered on his threshold ere he departed, to satiate his eye with the sight of the city he loved and might never see again. Nothing could keep back the wild rush of the people.*

That this was novel, and noticed, is borne out by Petronius, who sets the record straight by omitting the negatives:

> hos inter motus populus, miserabile uisu,
> quo mens icta iubet, deserta ducitur urbe.
> gaudet Roma fuga, debellatique Quirites
> rumoris sonitu maerentia tecta relinquunt.     225
> ille manu pauida natos tenet, ille penates
> occultat gremio deploratumque reliquit
> limen et absentem uotis interficit hostem.
> sunt qui coniugibus maerentia pectora iungunt
> grandaeuosque patres umeris uehit aegra iuuentus.
>                        (*Bell. Civ.* 221–30)

*In the turmoil the people themselves, a woeful sight, are led out of the deserted city,*
*whither their stricken heart drives them. Rome is glad to flee, her true sons are cowed*
*by war, and at a rumour's breath leave their houses to mourn. One holds his*
*children with a shaking hand, one hides his household gods in his bosom, and weeping,*
*leaves his door and calls down death on the unseen enemy. Some clasp their wives*
*to them in tears, weary youths carry their aged sires on their shoulders.*

(Tr. M. Heseltine)

Despite the occasional bow to the theme of civil war – note the impious behaviour of 224–5, and the unexpected *absentem* at 228 – the account is the antithesis of Lucan's, a classicistic refusal to violate convention. Behind this orthodoxy, and Lucan's nonconformism, is the sad but responsible exodus from Troy, treated correctly, and with dignity, at the end of *Aeneid* 2. Father, *penates*, son and wife: Aeneas' retinue summarizes the piety so signally lacking in Lucan.[1] But what Petronius forgets is the disparity of theme: the Rome of Aeneas is falling to Caesar. No reason, then, for the conventional antics of rhetorical prescription. Instead, unruly headlong flight.

Traditional patterns are likewise adapted at the end of Book 4, in the account of Curio's defeat. Epic had its formulae for treating the pitched battle: and, once again, the negation antithesis is prominent in Lucan's redeployment. Encouraged by Hercules' victory over Antaeus, Curio decides to give battle to King Juba, heedless of the fact that the mission must be pious for the *fortuna locorum* to work.[2] The struggle of Hercules and Antaeus – of good against evil – is developed along orthodox lines. For Curio, on the other hand, Lucan invents a battle which breaks the literary rules, but coheres with the over-all theme: when civil war claims its instigator, the ordinary cannot be excepted. Lucan sets the tone with:

> bellumque trahebat
> auctorem ciuile suum. (4.738–9)

*and civil war was claiming the man who made it.*

Curio is out of step with fortune. At line 747, the Romans are surrounded and a standstill ensues; at 750–64 the Roman cavalry attempts an ineffectual charge, answered by a counter-charge at 765–8. The focus now switches to the beleaguered infantry, and its inability to move, leading up to the climactic paradoxes of 781–7. Negatives are rife – 749 (*bis*), 750, 759, 760, 761, 762, 770, 775, 781, 784, 785: Curio's defeat is not like other battles. It is only in the treatment of the African attack that traditional motifs are employed without demur – the noise of the galloping horse, and the cloud of dust, complete with Homeric simile:

---

[1] See Virg. *Aen.* 2.657f., 710f., 717, 723f., 728f., and 3.10–12: Silius adopts the orthodox Virgilian scheme at 4.27ff.

[2] There is some discussion in Longi (1955), Grimal (1949), and now Ahl (1976) ch. III.

at uagus Afer equos ut primum emisit in agmen
tum campi tremuere sono, terraque soluta,
quantus Bistonio torquetur turbine puluis
aera nube sua texit traxitque tenebras.              (4.765–8)

*But as soon as the African skirmishers launched their steeds at the host, the plains
shook with their trampling, the earth was loosened, and a pillar of dust, vast as is
whirled by Thracian stormwinds, veiled the sky with its cloud and brought on
darkness.[1]*

Elsewhere, the battle is unheroic and abnormal: for the Romans, unlike the
Africans, are at war with one another.

At 749 the brave man and the coward are refused their usual actions, the
negatives creating an air of paralysis:

*non* timidi petiere fugam, *non* proelia fortes.

*the coward did not flee, nor the brave man fight.*

And then, in contrast to the ensuing African charge, follow the feeble, listless
movements of the Roman war horses, all epic associations denied, and replaced
by reminiscence of the plague of *Georgic* 3. Firstly, the negations:

quippe ubi *non* sonipes motus clangore tubarum
saxa quatit pulsu rigidos uexantia frenos
ora terens spargitque iubas et subrigit aures
incertoque pedum pugnat *non* stare tumultu.        (4.750–3)

*For there the war-horse was not roused by the trumpet's blare, nor did he scatter
the stones with stamping hoof, or champ the hard bit that chafes his mouth, with
flying mane and ears erect, or refuse to stand still, and shift his clattering feet.*

The Roman horse is not roused by the trumpet; nor does it strike the ground
with its hoof; nor champ at the bit; nor shake its mane; nor prick up its ears;
nor refuse to stand its ground – a far cry from Virgil's noble animal:

tum, si qua sonum procul arma dedere
stare loco nescit, micat auribus et tremit artus     (*Geo.* 3.83–4)

*If he hears armour clang in the distance,
He can't keep still, the ears prick up, the limbs quiver*

or the fiery creature of Statius:

qui dominis, idem ardor equis; face lumina surgunt,
ora sonant morsu, spumisque et sanguine ferrum
uritur, impulsi nequeunt obsistere postes

---

[1] The motif of the galloping horse begins with Hom. *Il.* 10.535, passes into Ennius, *Ann.* 439 V,
and thence to Lucr. 2.329–30, Virg. *Aen.* 8.596, 9.599–600, and 975, Stat. *Theb.* 12.651, and Sil.
4.95–6. The dust cloud was equipped with a wind simile at Hom. *Il.* 3.10ff: Virgil drops it at *Aen.*
11.876–7, 908–9, 12.407–8, and 444–5. See Miniconi (1951).

claustraque, compressae transfumat anhelitus irae.
stare adeo miserum est, pereunt uestigia mille
ante fugam, absentemque ferit grauis ungula campum.

(*Theb.* 6.396–401)

*The steeds are as ardent as their masters: their eyes dart flame, they loudly champ
the bits, and blood and foam corrode the iron; scarce do the confining posts resist
their pressure, they smoke and pant in stifled rage. Such misery it is to stand still,
a thousand steps are lost ere they start, and, on the absent plain, their hooves ring
loud.* (Tr. J. H. Mozley)

Bereft of heroic features, Lucan's horse looks sick and weary, 754ff.:

> fessa iacet ceruix, fumant sudoribus artus,
> oraque proiecta squalent arentia lingua,
> pectora rauca gemunt, quae creber anhelitus urguet,
> et defecta grauis longe trahit ilia pulsus,
> siccaque sanguineis durescit spuma lupatis.

*The weary neck sinks down; the limbs reek with sweat, the tongue protrudes and the
mouth is rough and dry; the lungs, driven by quick pants, give a hoarse murmur;
the labouring breath works the spent flanks hard; and the froth dries and cakes on the
blood-stained bit.*

Here we have an amalgam of Virgil's plague symptoms: *fessa iacet ceruix*
corresponds to *Geo.* 3.500 *demissae aures* and 524 *ad terramque fluit deuexo
pondere ceruix*; *fumant sudoribus artus* to 500–1 *incertus ibidem | sudor* and 515
*duro fumans sub uomere taurus*; *oraque proiecta squalent arentia lingua* to 501–2
*aret | pellis* and 508 *obsessas fauces premit aspera lingua*; *pectora rauca gemunt, quae
creber anhelitus urguet* to 497 *tussis anhela* and 505–6 *attractus ab alto | spiritus*;
*et defecta grauis longe trahit ilia pulsus* to 506–7 *interdum gemitu grauis, imaque
longo | ilia singultu tendunt*; and *siccaque sanguineis durescit spuma lupatis* to
507–8 *it naribus ater | sanguis* and 516 *mixtum spumis uomit ore cruorem*. Static
as ever in his narrative technique, Lucan remodels tradition to reflect his ignoble
theme. Even the purported narrative of 759–64 – the actual Roman charge –
is subordinate to a pair of antitheses which increase our awareness that the rules
no longer hold:

> iamque gradum, *neque* uerberibus stimulisque coacti
> *nec* quamuis crebris iussi calcaribus, addunt:
> *uolneribus coguntur equi; nec* profuit ulli
> cornipedis rupisse moras, *neque* enim impetus ille
> incursusque fuit; *tantum perfertur ad hostes
> et spatium iaculis oblato uolnere donat.*

*Neither blows nor goads, nor constant spurring can make the horses increase their
pace: they are stabbed to make them move; yet no man profited by overcoming the
resistance of his horse; for no charge and onset happened there: the rider was merely
carried close to the foe, and by offering a mark, saved the javelin a long flight.*

The horses are stabbed, not spurred; yet even when this is effective, the increased speed merely brings the rider nearer to the spears of the enemy. Lucan has begun to make the battle into a non-battle: there was no *impetus* or *incursus*, as would have been natural from a charging horse. For what follows at 769ff., the epigram *pugna perit* might have been a suitable motto.

Death takes the place of fighting, the paradox explained by two flanking negations:

> ut uero in pedites fatum miserabile belli
> incubuit, *nullo* dubii discrimine Martis
> ancipites steterunt casus, *sed tempora pugnae*
> *mors tenuit*; *neque* enim licuit procurrere contra
> et miscere manus.                       (4.769–73)

*And when the piteous doom of battle bore down upon the Roman infantry, the issue never hung uncertain through any chance of war's lottery, but all the time of fighting was filled by death: it was impossible to rush forward in attack and close with the enemy.*

There were none of the usual hazards of a two-sided battle; nor could anyone advance and join in the conflict. We find a similar one-sidedness in the seventh book's culminating battle:

> perdidit inde modum caedes, ac *nulla* secuta est
> pugna, *sed* hinc iugulis, hinc ferro bella geruntur.     (7.532–3)

*Unlimited slaughter followed: there was no battle, but only steel on one side and throats to pierce on the other*

where the abnormality once again displays the special nature of the war. Lucan continues to innovate with the motif of the cloud of weapons – found in Homer, Ennius and Virgil[1] – which not only transfixes its victims, but also crushes them under its weight:

> sic undique saepta iuuentus
> comminus obliquis et rectis eminus hastis
> obruitur, *non* uolneribus *nec* sanguine solum,
> telorum nimbo peritura et pondere ferri.          (4.773–6)

*So the soldiers, surrounded on all sides, were crushed by slanting thrusts from close quarters and spears hurled straight forward from a distance – doomed to destruction not merely by wounds and blood but by the hail of weapons and the sheer weight of steel.*

A new type of destruction joins the old, as yet another convention is altered.

---

[1] See Hom. *Il.* 17.243, Enn. *Ann.* 284 V, Virg. *Aen.* 10.801–9, 12.284: also Lucan 7.519–20 – an orthodox usage of the motif: cf. 2.501–2 – and *Il. Lat.* 359, 743–4. See Miniconi (1951).

Death from the swords of their companions awaits those who step out of line: so densely packed are the Romans:[1]

> uix impune suos inter conuertitur enses. (4.779)

*he could scarce move about unhurt amongst the swords of his comrades.*

Here we are back in the civil war ambience, where the harm and violence is done to oneself. Prefiguring his treatment of the trumpet signal in Book 7, Lucan lets self-destruction take over from the normal pattern of conflict:

> *non* arma mouendi
> iam locus est pressis, *stipataque membra teruntur,*
> *frangitur armatum conliso pectore pectus.* (4.781–3)

*The crowded soldiers have no longer space to ply their weapons; their bodies are squeezed and ground together; and the armoured breast is broken by pressure against another breast.*

After the prefatory negative – never before was there a battle in which one side could not move – a bold inversion: dispensing with one set of combatants, Lucan sets Roman against Roman with a verbal scheme more appropriate to two opposing forces. Homer, admittedly, had used it of one army; but Virgil, and Lucan himself, had established a more natural usage.[2] On reading *stipataque membra teruntur; | frangitur armatum conliso pectore pectus,* we think of Virgil's equivalent of *Iliad* 16.215:

> haud aliter Troianae acies aciesque Latinae
> concurrunt; haeret *pede pes* densusque *uiro uir* (*Aen.* 10.360–1)

*Just so did the ranks of Troy and Latium clash*
*Together, foot to foot, man to man locked in the mêlée,*

or again, of the pattern Virgil uses for two opposing chargers:

> perfractaque quadrupedantum
> *pectora pectoribus* rumpunt. (*Aen.* 11.614–15)

> *their horses collided, head on, so that breast*
> *Was broken and shattered on breast.*

Expecting the Roman context of a clash between two armies – Lucan himself employs the schema thus, at 7.573, *confractique ensibus enses* – the reader is asked to remember Lucan's introduction to the battle – *bellumque trahebat | auctorem ciuile suum* – and, beyond that, the proem's motif of the hand that turns on itself. The destruction has become internal, confined to Curio's army: the instigator of civil strife will die according to its laws.

---

[1] Note the progression, from *spissantur* 77 to *densaturque globus* 780, *constrinxit gyros acies* 781, *pressis* and *stipata* 782, and finally *compressum* 787.

[2] It would help to know the contexts of Enn. *Ann.* 572 V, and Bibac. fr. 10 M.

Lucan now completes his demolition of the recognized battle scene by telling us that the victors could not see the vanquished – unusual in itself – and that there were none of the customary streams of blood, or falling bodies, 784ff.:

> non tam laeta tulit uictor spectacula Maurus
> quam fortuna dabat; fluuios non ille cruoris
> membrorumque uidet lapsum et ferientia terram
> corpora: compressum turba stetit omne cadauer.　　(4.784–7)

*The victorious Moors did not enjoy to the full the spectacle that Fortune granted them: they did not see rivers of blood or bodies striking the ground; for each dead man was held bolt-upright by the dense array.*

Homer established the first motif and Apollonius and the Romans took it over; Lucan himself employs it elsewhere:

> sanguis ibi *fluxit* Achaeus,
> Ponticus, Assyrius; cunctos haerere cruores
> Romanus campisque uetat consistere *torrens*.　　(7.635–7)

*Here the blood of Achaea, Pontus and Assyria was poured out, and all that bloodshed the torrent of Roman gore forbids to linger and stagnate on the field.*

Ovid had made a great deal of it, for instance:

> cruor est *effusus* in auras　　(*Met.* 6.253)

*blood streamed into the air*

or again:

> plenoque e gutture *fluxit*
> inque toros inque ipsa niger carchesia sanguis　　(*Met.* 12.325–6)

*from the open wound in his neck the blood flowed over the couches and into the cups.*

Later, Valerius varies it with

> thorax egerit imbres
> sanguineos.　　(*Arg.* 6.186–7)

*a bloody rain was driven through their armour.*

Statius has his version too:

> eruptusque sinus uicit cruor.　　(*Theb.* 7.683)

*blood spurted out and stained his chest.*[1]

An unaccustomed direction is likewise given to the motif of the falling body. Virgil had taken it over from Homer with, for instance:

> at ille
> fronte *ferit terram* et crassum uomit ore cruorem.　　(*Aen.* 10.348–9)

> *so Dryops*
> *Struck the ground with his forehead and vomited up thick gore.*

[1] Cf. Hom. *Il.* 4.140, Ap. Rh. 3.1391–2, Ov. *Met.* 6.259–60; also Lucan 3.572–3, 589, 6.224, 7.625–6.

and again:

> sternitur infelix Acron et calcibus atram
> tundit humum. *(Aen.* 10.730–1)
>
> *and felled poor Acron, who dying drummed with his heels*
> *On the darkening ground.*

Later, in the probably Neronian Latin *Iliad* – a useful compendium of epic devices – we find for example:

> concidit et terram moribundo uertice *pulsat.* *(Il. Lat.* 376)
> *he fell and dying struck the earth with his forehead.*[1]

No streams of blood then, and no falling bodies: instead, a standing mass of corpses. There has been no battle in the usual sense of the word, not even an ordinary one-sided massacre: for Juba has been in the background, the Romans subjected in isolation to the relentless mechanics of internecine strife, a plight delineated through Lucan's alterations of the epic format. He wavers momentarily over Curio's death:

> non tulit adflictis animam producere rebus
> aut sperare fugam, ceciditque in strage suorum
> impiger ad letum. (4.796–8)
>
> *he would not stoop to survive defeat or hope for escape, but fell amid the corpses of*
> *his men, prompt to face death.*

As direct narrative takes over from the obliquities of the battle scene, one heroic deed is on the verge of rescue – but Lucan's negativity wins the day: *et fortis uirtute coacta* 'brave in forced courage' (4.798). In the cynical *coacta* we return from normal epic to the world of civil war.

In Book 5, during his account of Caesar's storm, Lucan's policy of negation recurs. Through the negation-antithesis, and a few slight changes in tradition, he enlivens the prodigies of the *poetica tempestas,*[2] converting them into images of nature's internal dissension – at the same time reversing the role of the hero. Nature no longer assails a helpless human victim: Caesar rides superior, as nature fears her own violence. The parallel with the war is clear: Caesar the superman, cause of civil strife, measures his stature against the fury of the storm, and laughs at a world at variance with itself.

Lucan's rehabilitation of disorder begins at line 597 with a *concursus uentorum.* If he had simply followed precedent, all four winds would have blown at once – and probably gone unnoticed. As it is, scientific theory is invoked to make us more aware of the breach in natural law.

---

[1] Cf. Virg. *Aen.* 9.708, 488–9, 12.926, *Il. Lat.* 370–1, 382; Miniconi (1951).

[2] For background, parallels, and bibliography, see Morford's extensive treatment (1967), chapters III and IV.

*non* Euri cessasse minas, *non* imbribus atrum
Aeolii iacuisse Notum sub carcere saxi
crediderim; *cunctos* solita de parte ruentes. . .          (5.608–10)

*I cannot believe that the threats of the East wind were still then, and that the South
wind black with storm was idle in the prison of Aeolus' cave: all the winds rushed
forth from their usual quarters.*

This time, cleverly, the negations help to reinstate the norm of previous epic:
but in Virgil and Homer physical laws were not the thing at issue. Reminding
us of science Lucan causes apprehension about a world we thought we knew.
All four winds now blow with a vengeance. What is more, the military imagery
previously used for the assault of nature on man is now redeployed to show
a world at odds with itself: the winds fight one another, the seas migrate, and
mountains are submerged. And the threat to nature continues, when the waters
that surround the earth begin to send in their waves:

*non* ullo litore surgunt
tam ualidi fluctus, alio*que* ex orbe uoluti
a magno uenere mari, mundumque coercens
monstriferos agit unda sinus.          (5.617–20)

*No shore gave birth to these mighty waves: they came rolling from another region
and from the outer sea, and the waters which encircle the world drove on these
teeming billows.*

Lines 620–4, with their comparison of the cataclysm, confirm our fear that
the boundaries of the world are on the verge of dissolution: and still no
battle of hero and the elements. Soon, a summary of the menace to the
universe; but first a variation on the traditional ideas of darkness and upward-
surging waves:

*non* caeli nox illa fuit: latet obsitus aer
infernae pallore domus nimbisque grauatus
deprimitur, fluctusque in nubibus accipit imbrem.          (5.627–9)

*The darkness was not a darkness of the sky: the heavens were hidden and veiled
with the dimness of the infernal regions, and weighed down by clouds; and in the midst
of the clouds the rain poured into the sea.*

In previous epic the waves reached the sky, but this is now impossible since
there is no sky – no intervening space between cloud and sea. Lucan replaces
the usual upward movement with a movement downwards, causing the upper
world to vanish from sight: hence the only darkness can be that of the lower.
Scientific observation – of the depression of cloud in a storm – helps once more
to resuscitate convention, and further our fears on nature's behalf. For another
department of the world has now disappeared.

Having disposed of the sky, Lucan discards lightning, again enlisting science:

> lux etiam metuenda *perit, nec* fulgura currunt
> clara, *sed* obscurum nimbosus dissilit aer.  (5.630–1)

*Light, albeit fearful, disappeared as well: no bright lightnings darted, but the stormy sky gave dim flashes.*

In a state of total cloud there cannot be collisions: hence lightning is replaced with a dark internal dissolution of the atmosphere.[1] Nature continues to suffer, and another element is lost – *lux* as well as *caelum*: for the prefatory negation ending in *perit* has larger designs than the simple *fulgura clara*.

Having infringed the literary order for the description of confusion, replacing the old conceits with scientifically based prodigies, Lucan now presents us with a picture of universal chaos:

> tum superum conuexa fremunt, atque arduus axis
> intonuit, motaque poli compage laborant.
> extimuit natura chaos; rupisse uidentur
> concordes elementa moras, rursusque redire
> nox manes mixtura deis: spes una salutis,
> quod tanta mundi nondum periere ruina.  (5.632–7)

*Next, the dome of the gods quaked, the lofty sky thundered, and the heavens, with all their structure jarred, were troubled. Nature dreaded chaos: it seemed that the elements had burst their harmonious bonds, and that Night was returning to blend the shades below with the gods above; the one hope of safety for the gods is this – that in the universal catastrophe they have not yet been destroyed.*

Thunder provides the starting point, but then the simple allied notion of the falling sky – Virgil's *caeli ruina* – receives eschatological development into the idea of *mundi ruina*: Lucan's vocabulary – *mota...compage, concordes... moras* – becomes reminiscent of those places in his epic where war involves the demise of earthly order, while *extimuit natura chaos* leaves no doubt that the victim of this storm is nature herself. In other storms it is the *compages* of the boat which is threatened, not the structure of the universe: and it is the hero, not the gods, who fears for his safety. Lucan's Caesar, who had exclaimed:

> caeli iste fretique
> non puppis nostrae labor est  (5.584–5)

*yonder trouble concerns the sky and sea, but not our barque,*

[1] See Morford (1967) 43.

proves right: he remains outside it, unscathed.[1] Nature's role and that of the hero have been interchanged: so much so, that the turmoil is no menace to Caesar, rather a measure of his demonic genius:

> credit iam digna pericula Caesar
> fatis esse suis     (5.653–4)

*he considers at last that the danger is on a scale to match his destiny.*

No deity began the storm. It was Caesar who wanted to sail, despite the protests of the humble Amyclas. And it is almost as if it has been he who has directed the storm, not the gods or nature, when the tenth wave, which normally brings destruction, places him and his boat on dry land:

> haec fatum decimus, dictu mirabile, fluctus
> inualida cum puppe leuat, *nec* rursus ab alto
> aggere deiecit pelagi *sed* protulit unda,
> scruposisque angusta uacant ubi litora saxis,
> imposuit terrae.     (5.672–6)

*As he spoke thus, a tenth wave – marvellous to tell – upbore him and his battered craft; nor did the billow hurl him back again from the high watery crest but bore him onwards till it laid him on the land, where a narrow strip of shore was clear of jagged rocks.*[2]

What Lucan forgets to tell us is that the mission was a failure: for Caesar, who thrives on disorder, has risen superior to a world he has ruined.

[1] Lucan defers to tradition at 639 and 652–3, where sailors experience fear: but these *nautae* are generalized. The *magister* of 645 whose *ars* is defeated by *metus* is probably Amyclas, Caesar's humble companion. But he is an ordinary mortal, not a superman. Lucan continues the notion of a storm which cannot harm the usually helpless hero at 646, with *discordia ponti | succurrit miseris*: the last word is out of place, but Lucan nods on occasion, even given his own terms of reference.

[2] For the tenth wave, see Ov. *Met.* 11.530, *Trist.* 1.2.49–50. Lucan is thinking of *Odyssey* 5, where the hero was finally washed ashore by a 'great wave': but he had first been wrecked by a μέγα κῦμα ...δεινὸν ἐπεσσύμενον (ll. 313–14): cf. *ingens ... pontus* at Virg. *Aen.* 1.114. Caesar has just reversed another convention of the *poetica tempestas*, in his contempt for the thought of death, 656–71 (especially 668–9 *mihi funere nullo | est opus, o superi*): other epic heroes had trembled at the idea of lacking a proper burial. See Morford (1967) 44.

# 5

# FLAVIAN EPIC

## I. INTRODUCTORY

Each of the three epic writers of the Flavian era – Valerius Flaccus, Papinius Statius, Silius Italicus – sought to be Virgil's successor: a laudable but daring aspiration. Method and result differed widely. What is common to the epics is less important than what is distinct. This divergence is plainly revealed in their choice of subjects. Valerius selected the Argonautic myth, transmuting elements taken from Apollonius Rhodius in a Virgilian crucible: an audacious process for even the most skilful alchemist. Statius chose the war of the Seven against Thebes, a horrific saga of fraternal discord and moral dissolution but congenial to a poet steeped in the gloomy portentousness of Senecan tragedy and the spiritual nihilism of Lucan's *Bellum civile*. Silius rejected mythology, assuming the patriotic mantle of Ennius and Virgil: his was a national theme, the war waged by Hannibal and perfidious Carthage against the manifest destiny of the Roman people. The idea of composing a *carmen togatum* no doubt had a special appeal to one who had himself been a consul, provincial governor and statesman.

Within the context of European literature, only one of the three gained enduring eminence: Statius, whose *Thebaid* and inchoate *Achilleid* were highly valued and widely studied in late antiquity, in the Middle Ages and after. Dante, Boccaccio, Chaucer, Tasso, Spenser, Milton and Pope all bear witness to his stature. Valerius and Silius, by contrast, fell rapidly into neglect and oblivion; the *Argonautica* and *Punica* were not rediscovered until the Italian Renaissance and subsequently they provided pabulum for the nourishment of philologists rather than imitators. It would be quixotic to negate the verdict of history. Statius' achievement surpassed that of both his contemporaries. Valerius has, in recent times, found admirers, who have discovered in his unfinished epic the seeds of genius and the harvest of artistry. Silus' *Punica* has been rarely read but commonly disparaged: somewhat unjustly, for, despite its many and obtrusive blemishes, there is in it much that is not despicable. It is, however, too optimistic to expect that many readers should feel impelled to sift the seventeen books of the *Punica* in quest of its better passages.

It was only at the Renaissance too that Statius' shorter poems, the *Silvae*, were brought again to light. Four books of *vers d'occasion*, and the semblance of a fifth, prove that his literary skills were not confined to the grandeur of epic but were equally adapted to lesser genres. The *Silvae* rapidly acquired a high reputation among neo-Latin and vernacular writers. Today there are those who set a greater price upon them than upon the *Thebaid*, which Statius, adhering to the hierarchical view of poetic kinds, regarded as his masterpiece and his guarantee of immortality. Death prevented him from writing more than a fraction of the *Achilleid*. It breaks off at line 167 of the second book and what was composed is best regarded rather as a provisional draft than as a definitive version. How Statius intended to fulfil his ambitious project of narrating Achilles' life from birth to death must remain a matter of vain speculation.

Valerius, Statius and Silius had to come to terms with an array of predecessors whose claims to homage were coercive and dominant. Virgil, Ovid, Seneca and Lucan had established canons which could be neither ignored nor spurned. It is true that there was in the late first century a movement – Quintilian is its chief theoretical exponent – that saw much to condemn in the stylistic innovations that Seneca and his nephew Lucan, in the wake of Ovid, had developed and fostered. Virgilian purity, however, could not be reproduced in the Flavian era. None of the three epics is a replica, in manner or ethos, of the *Aeneid*. It is permissible to speak of degrees of proximity to Virgil.

At the end of the *Thebaid*, Statius proclaims his acquiescence in the inevitable. His *chef d'œuvre* would for ever remain in a place second to the 'divine' *Aeneid* (12.816–17). In the *Silvae*, he mentions visits to the tomb of Virgil, his 'great teacher', in the hope of inspiration (4.4.53–5). This quasi-religious devotion was shared by Silius. Pliny, in his famous necrological notice, remarks that the author of the *Punica* was in the habit of celebrating Virgil's birthday with more pomp than his own and of reverencing his tomb like a temple (*Epist.* 3.7.8). Indeed, Martial informs us that Silius – already the proud possessor of a villa that had once housed Cicero – went so far as to purchase the site of, and to embellish, Virgil's *monimentum* (11.48, 49). In the *Punica*, an explicit tribute occurs at 7.592–4, where Silius, conventionally, asserts the equality of Homer and Virgil.

So much for claims. Despite his veneration, Statius stands farthest from Virgil, closest to Seneca and Lucan. *Silvae* 2.7 is a commemorative poem on Lucan: Statius' hyperbolic praises indicate a genuine admiration. Silius, saturated in the *Aeneid*, was too much of an eclectic to be fully or even predominantly Virgilian. He owed much to Ovid, much, by imitation or purposeful contrast, to Lucan – who had, after all, also based his epic on Roman history. Silius saw himself, too, as an heir of Ennius, providing him with a generous eulogy in the *Punica* (12.393–414). That Silius should revere Ennius at all is a portent, showing him to be a harbinger of second-century archaism. Statius, including Ennius in a catalogue of Roman poets, designated him 'unpolished' and 'harsh' (2.7.75). The precise contribution of Ennius' *Annales* to Silius' *Punica* is indeterminable: but even lip service testifies to an attitude of mind. Valerius Flaccus was nearest in spirit to Virgil, but the assessment of proximity depends on an observer's location. Ovid necessarily exercised a considerable effect on Valerius' formal techniques. It seems certain that in the *Argonautica* he aimed at a restraint in language and thought which he considered to be Virgilian. Quintilian, the apostle of classicism, noted with regret the passing of Valerius (*Inst.* 10.1.90) – doubtless recognizing in him a kindred spirit.

No less than the Augustans, the Flavians drank deep at the fountain of Greek poetry. Valerius' principal narrative source was Apollonius Rhodius, though there was little of the servile in the relationship. From Homer, the 'wellspring of all poesie', both Statius and Silius adapted much, introducing not only episodes already reshaped by Virgil but fresh ones as well. Both poets, for example, have incidents based on Achilles' fight with the River Scamander (*Iliad* 21.234ff.): Statius describes Hippomedon's battle with Ismenus (*Theb.* 9.404ff.), Silius Scipio's conflict with Trebia (*Pun.* 4.638ff.). The riches of Homer were inexhaustible, and Statius quarried freely. Silius saw no difficulty in welding Homeric motifs on to the framework of Roman history.[1] Homer's primacy in the genre and Virgilian precedent were, therefore, simultaneously recognized.

For Statius, it was natural to study the Greeks. He was of Hellenic descent, born in Naples, where, as he says in a poem addressed to his wife Claudia, *Graia licentia* and *Romanus honos* were happily conjoined (*Silv.* 3.5.94). His father was a poetaster and schoolmaster specializing in the explication of Greek texts (*Silv.* 5.3.146ff.). Statius' Hellenism is not, however, obtrusive. He utilized Euripidean tragedy – the *Phoenissae* and *Suppliant women* had obvious relevance to the *Thebaid* and the *Hypsipyle* may have added something to Books 4–6 – but never without radical transformation. From Callimachus he derived, among other things, some details for the myth of Linus and Coroebus (1.557–672). Apollonius Rhodius played a subsidiary role in the evolution of Hypsipyle's narrative in Book 5. Old theories that he drew material from the Cyclic *Thebaid* or from Antimachus of Colophon may be dismissed as unproven and improbable.[2]

For a long time the Flavian writers were regarded as little better than plagiarists. Recent investigations have revealed the inadequacy and injustice of this approach. This is especially true in Statius' case. His originality has been

---

[1] See the full investigations of Juhnke (1972).    [2] Cf. Vessey (1970) 118–43.

thoroughly vindicated. All ancient poets were bound by the principle of *imitatio*. This implied not merely respect for the past but a desire to reach new and individual standards of excellence. Statius was rarely, if ever, subservient to those whom he would have named with pride as his models. Valerius also took pains to create his own interpretation of the Argonautic myth, reassigning to Jason a heroic status which the cynical Apollonius had eroded. Even Silius, the most patently dependent of the three, did not hesitate to modify the events of the Punic War to illuminate a wider philosophical perspective.

## 2. STATIUS

### Family, friends and patrons; the Silvae

Statius may, then, be acquitted of plagiarism. He was a professional poet not a wealthy dilettante. He records, in a long epicedium (formal lament) for his father, that his family was financially straitened, stressing that his ancestors were freeborn and not without some distinction (*Silv.* 5.3.109–10, 115–17). The schoolmaster's son had, all the same, to make his way in the world by his own ingenuity. Prominent Neapolitans sent their sons to the elder Papinius for instruction in literature and other arts (*Silv.* 5.3.146ff., 176ff.). Such local connexions were, we may surmise, of assistance to Statius when he was establishing his reputation in Rome and seeking commissions for his work. He owed a profound debt to his father's guidance and precept in poetry (5.3.209ff.); the son was encouraged to follow in his father's footsteps by entering poetic contests, first in his home town, later in Rome.[1] Such laurels were valuable: they impressed potential patrons. Heredity and environment aided Statius in his chosen career. Inborn genius and artistic sensitivity crowned it.

The *Thebaid* was the offspring of twelve years of unremitting toil (12.811). It was published in its entirety in A.D. 90 or 91. Soon afterwards Statius began to issue the *Silvae*. Four books, each with an apologetic preface in prose, appeared between 91 and 95. The poems in them were obviously a selection from the large number of occasional pieces Statius must have written in previous years. The fifth book, so called, was put together, almost certainly, by an unknown literary executor – who may also have been responsible for the preservation of the *Achilleid*; it has no true preface, only a dedicatory epistle to the epicedium for Priscilla, wife of Flavius Abascantus.

The satirists' cynicism on the subject of patronage finds no confirmatory reflection in the *Silvae*. Statius does not present himself as a *cliens*. The recipients of his poems are not termed *patroni*. Friendship, deferential perhaps but sincere, is the bond that he claims. The *Silvae* are documents of great social

[1] *Silvae* 5.3.111–12, 141ff., 3.5.28ff.; 4.5.22ff. Statius failed to win the prize – to his chagrin – at the Capitoline contest, probably in 94: 3.5.31–3.

value; they reveal much about the outlook and pursuits of those who commissioned them. Taken as a group, they emerge as 'men of influence and wealth, either actively engaged in the imperial service or in a life of comfortable and affluent leisure. Cultured and critical dilettantes, many of them toyed with the art of poetry, dabbled in philosophy and spent their wealth in creating or acquiring objects of beauty.'[1] It was, in many ways, an unreal, exotic world. On these privileged denizens of Roman society Statius relied for support and encouragement. Nothing improper, vulgar or proletarian was permitted to intrude into the gilded and glittering *Silvae*.

Of the •Neapolitans, the most prominent was the millionaire Epicurean Pollius Felix, owner of extensive estates in Campania. To him the second book of *Silvae* was dedicated. 2.2 and 3.1 immortalize the architectural and visual splendours of his property at Surrentum. 4.8 is a congratulatory poem addressed to his son-in-law Julius Menecrates on the birth of a third child. Menecrates had been granted the *ius trium liberorum* by Domitian (4.8.20–2) and his brother had held a military tribunate in Africa (4.8.12). Even if Pollius Felix, for dogmatic reasons, abstained from political activity, his kin had no such scruples: Statius predicts a senatorial career for Menecrates' sons (4.8.59–62).

Some of Statius' patrons were men of power and standing in public life. The first book of *Silvae* was dedicated to L. Arruntius Stella. This moneyed patrician was progressing rapidly through the *cursus honorum* under Domitian; a suffect consulship awaited him in Trajan's principate. He was also an elegiac poet. He extended his patronage to Martial as well as to Statius. His marriage to the rich and beautiful Violentilla – of Neapolitan ancestry – is celebrated in 1.2. C. Rutilius Gallicus (1.4) had been *praefectus urbi* and twice consul. Vitorius Marcellus had political aspirations – as well as a fondness for literature. Statius dedicated Book 4 to him and he was the recipient of an epistle in it (4.4); the same Vitorius was dedicatee of Quintilian's *Institutio oratoria*. C. Vibius Maximus (4.7), already in Domitian's day a man of consequence, eventually attained the prefecture of Egypt. M. Maecius Celer (3.2) was to end a career successfully inaugurated under the last Flavian with a suffect consulship in 101. The youth Vettius Crispinus, panegyrized on the occasion of his appointment to a military tribunate (5.2), was son of the patrician Vettius Bolanus, consular, sometime propraetorial legate in Britain and proconsul of Asia. Though nothing further is know of Crispinus, his twin brother was consul in 111.

Other patrons eschewed the pursuit of power in favour of more tranquil occupations: philosophy, literature, connoisseurship. Statius offered Book 2 of his *Silvae* to the elegant and generous Atedius Melior. Within it, the death of Melior's slaveboy Glaucias is fittingly lamented (2.1). In more humorous vein, the passing of his parrot is bewailed (2.4). Also included is an aetiological

---

[1] Vessey (1973) 27.

fantasia on a curious plane-tree on Melior's estate (2.3). Flavius Ursus, urbane, rich and eloquent, received consolatory verses when he too was deprived by fate of a beloved *puer* (2.6). Septimius Severus, from Lepcis Magna and probably an ancestor of the homonymous emperor, followed an Epicurean style of life on his country properties. For him, Statius penned a Horatian ode, praising the virtues of carefree *otium* but not overlooking his patron's forensic skills (4.5). Lighthearted hendecasyllables were addressed to Plotius Grypus (4.9), another budding orator and minor *littérateur*, son of the consul of 88. Novius Vindex was a fanatical collector of art treasures – but not unappreciative of well-turned verses. Statius lovingly describes a statue of Hercules in Novius' possession, attributed to Lysippus himself (4.6).

There was, too, Claudius Etruscus: a freedman's son, it had to be admitted. But at the time of his death at an advanced age the elder Claudius could have looked back on a long period of power in the imperial household (3.3.59ff.). Furthermore, he had married into the nobility (111ff.). The fruit of that unequal union was a cultivated man, his intellectual gifts balancing his financial resources. His sumptuous bath-house is commemorated in 1.5. Flavius Earinus, Domitian's Ganymede from Pergamum, dispatched his shorn locks in a jewelled casket to the shrine of Asclepius in his birthplace: the Emperor commanded Statius to enshrine the auspicious event in verses (3.4). The resulting poem, if bizarre to modern ears, is nonetheless a valuable revelation of Domitian's claims to godhead. Also close to the earthly Jupiter was Flavius Abascantus, his private secretary: the consolation written by Statius on his wife's demise opens the fifth book, and the epistle dedicatory voices the poet's unshakeable loyalty to the divine house.

Domitian showed marks of favour to one who so deftly expressed official propaganda under a dazzling veil of verbal conceits. 1.1 records, in an ecphrasis, the consecration of a vast equestrian statue to honour the Emperor's Dacian victories in 89. Imperial largesse during a Saturnalian festival is wittily applauded in 1.6. 4.1 is a formal panegyric for Domitian's seventeenth consulship in 95, composed not long before the death of both *Princeps* and poet. 4.2 crystallizes the poet's gratitude for an invitation to dine with senators and knights within the palace itself: a visit to Olympus, a vision of deity never to be forgotten. The Via Domitiana, stretching from Sinuessa to Naples, was completed in 95. Statius summed up the thanks of travellers in hendecasyllables (4.3). It may not be accidental that three laudations of the Emperor and his acts appear in Book 4, which was published in 95 or 96. Domitian, nervously conscious of mounting hatred and barely latent opposition, would have welcomed vociferous plaudits at this time. Statius' prayer, put in the mouth of Janus, that his lord might be granted a long life (4.1.35ff.; cf. 46–7) did not deflect the course of destiny. Whether the poet survived to witness the extinction of the Flavian house in 96 is unknown. He had been its faithful spokesman and servant. Unlike Martial, he did not live long enough to revile his former master – even if he had wished to do so. For that reason, he has, ever since, been accused of degrading servility. But he had no opportunity for that recantation which, it seems, posterity demands of those who write under a despotism.

Artists respond to the society in which they live: by alienation or conformity. Statius conformed. The galaxy of patrons, in orbit around the imperial sun or following more idiosyncratic courses, could not have been easy to satisfy. Lesser poets than Statius, in the face of such creative asphyxiation, would have descended to the banal and the repetitious. His talent was such that he could metamorphose even the most intractable material into a new and memorable form. His patrons were educated men, not to be content with mere hackwork. To titillate their passion for *doctrina*, Statius made full use of allusion and recondite learning. In literature and in the visual arts, 'the taste of the Flavian period favoured brilliance and splendour above all';[1] Statius sought to make his verse jewelled, gleaming and ornate to reflect the spirit of the times. Simplicity was not a virtue that he esteemed, whether in language, imagery, structure or thought. Swift movement and startling colour characterize his work. Critics have remarked on his ability to evoke visual responses in a reader's mind. It is, in consequence, no simple task to appreciate his poetry. For those nurtured on Virgil and Horace, first acquaintance with the *Silvae* and *Thebaid* is aesthetically disorienting. It is a contrast between sobriety and inebriation. Justus Lipsius appositely remarked that Statius possessed a 'luxuria ingenii non indecora' and that he was 'sublimis et celsus poeta, non hercle tumidus'. Unfitting exuberance and grotesque tumidity were hazards that threatened him: but he, unlike many of his imitators, generally avoided the pitfalls.

Artistic surfeit had to be measured against formal austerities. Rhetoricians had by Statius' day established rules and patterns for the subdivisions of the epideictic genre. Prescriptions devised for prose orations had been transferred to poetry. Most of the *Silvae* can be allocated to recognizable *genera*.[2] There is one epithalamium (1.2). Epicedia account for a substantial group (2.1, 2.4, 2.6, 3.3, 5.1, 5.3, 5.5). Add two eulogies (4.1, 5.2), two *gratulationes* written to celebrate the birth of children (4.7, 4.8), two propemptica (3.2, 3.4). There are single instances of the soterion (1.4), the genethliacon (2.7) and the eucharisticon (4.2). A favourite form was the ecphrasis (*descriptio*), the detailed description of a building, an object of virtù or other static object. Eight of the *Silvae* may be assigned to this category and they include some of Statius' finest work (1.1, 1.3, 1.5, 2.2, 2.3, 3.1, 4.3, 4.6). It is not fanciful to trace a rapport between his taste for architecture and the visual arts and the vivid, picture-making

---

[1] Gossage (1972) 186.
[2] For the theory and characteristics of the rhetorical genres, see Cairns (1972).

quality of his verse. To the ancients, all the arts were in sympathy. In an ecphrasis, dumb stones were given the power of speech, the ability to explain themselves – just as sculptors and painters represented for the human eye incidents from poetry. Whether specific or secondary (as in formalized descriptions of gods, heroes, buildings, landscapes and the like in his epic), ecphrasis was for Statius a natural part of composition. Few poets have more successfully exploited the mode.

Panegyric was an element unavoidable in any epideictic kind. Statius was adept at telling his patrons what they wished to hear, cunningly interweaving *laudatio* with his central themes. In the hands of a skilled poet, generic patterns and the commonplaces (*topoi*) associated with them were a valuable asset. It was part of the decorum of eulogy not to stint one's praise. Not least in addressing the emperor: to expect moderation there, would be to have honey sour. Many of the themes in the *Silvae* had long been conventionalized. The problem for the conscientious artist was not to escape the dictates of tradition and maxim, but to remould inherited material in a fresh, but still recognizable, manner. If *ars* implied a knowledge of and respect for *regulae*, *ingenium* had to provide the original approach which tempered rigidity and triteness.

Genres could be used in an unusual way. The genethliacon for Lucan (2.7) has some of the characteristics of a funeral laudation: for Lucan was dead. 3.4 embodies elements from the propempticon: it is not a human being who is setting out on a voyage, but the locks of Earinus. 2.4, on the death of Melior's parrot, is a parody of the epicedium. Of the two *gratulationes*, one, for Vibius Maximus, is written in sapphic stanzas under the patronage of Pindar (4.7.5–9) and is therefore allowed to stray over diverse themes; the other, for Julius Menecrates, is more solemn and formal, in Statius' customary hexameters (4.8). A few of the *Silvae* cannot be assigned to fixed *genera*. 1.6, the *Kalendae Decembres*, is cast in lively hendecasyllables, as befits its purpose. The poem on Melior's tree (2.3), though a kind of ecphrasis, is, like the lament for his parrot, termed by Statius in the preface a light-hearted work, akin to epigram. 3.5 is a *suasoria* addressed by Statius to his wife, urging retirement from Rome to Naples. We find too an epistle for Vitorius Marcellus (4.4), some jesting verses for Plotius Grypus (4.9) and an alcaic ode for Septimius Severus (4.5). Standing on their own for brevity are 2.5, on Domitian's tame lion, and 5.4, an exquisite nineteen-line call to Sleep.

The principle of variety (*poikilia*) is observed generically and thematically in Books 1–4. It may be added that there is order in diversity. Just as Statius expended great effort on the inner structure of all his work, so the disposition of the poems in each book of *Silvae* is elaborately organized.

In Book 1, the first and last poems (1, 6) are both laudations of Domitian.

The epithalamium for Stella (to whom the book was dedicated) predictably stands in second place. It is balanced by 4, the soterion for Rutilius Gallicus: both are highly personal poems of felicitation, though widely different in occasion. 1, 3 and 5 are all ecphraseis. 2, 4 and 6 are united by the motif of rejoicing and festivity. We arrive, therefore, at the following simple schema:

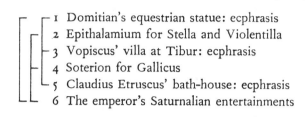

    1 Domitian's equestrian statue: ecphrasis
    2 Epithalamium for Stella and Violentilla
    3 Vopiscus' villa at Tibur: ecphrasis
    4 Soterion for Gallicus
    5 Claudius Etruscus' bath-house: ecphrasis
    6 The emperor's Saturnalian entertainments

In Book 2, the first poem, written for the dedicatee Atedius Melior, is an epicedium on the death of the slave-boy Glaucias: identical in kind and purpose is 6, for Flavius Ursus. 2 and 3, respectively for Pollius and Melior, are ecphraseis. 4 (on Melior's dead parrot) and 5 (Domitian's lion) are both devoted to remarkable animals. The genethliacon for Lucan (7), with its necrological aspects binding it to 2, 4 and 6, attains a climactic status as the last poem in the book. Again the plan is obvious:

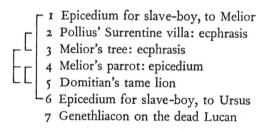

    1 Epicedium for slave-boy, to Melior
    2 Pollius' Surrentine villa: ecphrasis
    3 Melior's tree: ecphrasis
    4 Melior's parrot: epicedium
    5 Domitian's tame lion
    6 Epicedium for slave-boy, to Ursus
    7 Genethliacon on the dead Lucan

The arrangement here is slightly more complex than that of Book 1, for the group 3, 4 and 5 are notable for their facetious tone and form a central block within the whole. In Book 2, even more than in 1, we see, as an aspect of *variatio*, the mingling of tragic and comic in the bounds of a single collection.

The third book comprises only five poems. 1 is a *descriptio* of the temple of Hercules erected at Surrentum by the recipient of the dedication, Pollius Felix. 2 is a propempticon for Maecius Celer; 3 a long *consolatio* for Claudius Etruscus on his father's death; 4 the poem on Earinus' *capilli* and 5 the *suasoria* to the poet's wife. The solemn *consolatio* aptly occupies the central place.

Statius' enthusiastic *descriptio* of the Surrentine Herculeum, linked as it is with a laudation of Pollius and his wife, forms a natural complement to his eulogy of Naples in poem 5. Poems 2 and 4 are counterbalanced, for the *capilli*-poem is in part a propempticon, since it wishes the tresses a safe voyage over the sea to Pergamum, just as in 4 Maecius is the recipient of greetings for his journey to the orient. The book, therefore, is neatly disposed round the central pivot of the *consolatio*.[1]

The scheme requires no summary.

In the longest book (4), the first three poems are all concerned with honouring the Emperor. It has also a high proportion of non-hexameter poems: 3, 5, 7 and 9. 4 and 5, addressed to Vitorius Marcellus and Septimius Severus, make up a fitting pair, for the preface informs us that the two men were friends. 7 and 8 are joined by the fact that both were occasioned by the birth of a child. The schema may be presented in this way:

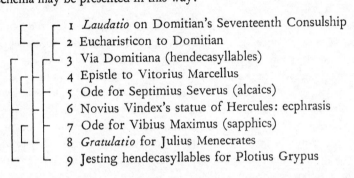

1 *Laudatio* on Domitian's Seventeenth Consulship
2 Eucharisticon to Domitian
3 Via Domitiana (hendecasyllables)
4 Epistle to Vitorius Marcellus
5 Ode for Septimius Severus (alcaics)
6 Novius Vindex's statue of Hercules: ecphrasis
7 Ode for Vibius Maximus (sapphics)
8 *Gratulatio* for Julius Menecrates
9 Jesting hendecasyllables for Plotius Grypus

This is the most complex structure of all. 1 and 2 occupy a special position as tributes to Domitian. Thereafter, hexameter poems alternate with those in other metres.

More might be said. These schemata are only outlines. The total structure of each book is enhanced by numerous and complex responsions within the poems: in theme and imagery, in mood, tone and tempo. Such analyses are evidence of the diligence with which Statius approached each detail of his literary work. But bad poems even well arranged would remain bad: what virtues stand out in the *Silvae* to commend them to us?

Statius has been arraigned for frigidity and obscurity, for an excessive use of mythology, for inventive aridity. Subjective criticisms cannot always be answered objectively. Romantic preconceptions about art in part account for Statius' fall from esteem. Insights must be sought from a different vantage point. An appreciation of craftsmanship may provide the foundation for a broader awareness of the beauty and subtlety of his best work.

There is no better proof of technical expertise than the epithalamium (1.2). The genre had been long established. A glance at Catullus' epithalamia (61, 62) is instructive. The neoteric poet, while making broad concessions to Roman rite and custom, in form and structure followed Hellenic precedents. Not so

---

[1] Vessey (1973) 29.

Statius. There are, as one would expect, parallels between his poem and the precepts laid down for hymenaeal orations by later Greek rhetors. In a wedding poem or speech, however, many features prescribed by theorists were but conventionalized commonsense: encomia of the bride and groom, a wish for marital harmony, a catalogue of the benefits of connubiality, a prayer for procreation. Even if Statius profited from contemporary rhetorical discussions of the genre, he permitted himself latitude for innovation. In his hands, the hymenaeal was personalized and reconstituted. Its smooth hexameters move sinuously between panegyric and aetiology, truth and fantasy, reality and myth, finding a resolution in a pithy final section which is a traditional epithalamium truncated (247–57).

Stella was bound to Statius by a common enthusiasm for the poetic art (247–8). The excellence of his amatory elegiacs is several times signalized (33, 96ff., 167ff., 197ff.). Tribute is paid to his constancy in love (32ff., 99ff.), his patrician ancestry (73–4), his physical charm (172), his military and civil achievements (174ff.). His bride, Violentilla, well-born (108) and wealthy (121), is a visible image of the Goddess of Love herself (236). It is a flawless diptych, displayed in a gilded frame. To demonstrate and to enhance the portrait, Statius, as commonly in the *Silvae*, turns to myth. He invents an aetiology, in the tradition of Callimachus, to explain the past and present love from which the blessed union has sprung.

His mythopoeia is grand and imaginative, epic in quality, lyrical in language. The wedding of Stella and Violentilla was forged in heaven to be a paradigm on earth. The tale of their love cannot be confined within the boundaries of mundane fact: the epithalamium is dominated by its mythic core. In 51–64, the scene is set on Olympus. Venus is in repose on her couch, circled by the Cupids, one of whom has inflamed Stella with an unequalled passion (83–4). He pleads with Venus to take pity on his victim, to grant fruition to his hopes (65–102). Venus accedes to his appeal in a speech which embodies a superb encomium of Violentilla's mental and physical attributes (106–40). The goddess descends to Violentilla's house in her chariot of swans; there she voices a persuasive plea for Stella. Violentilla should yield to love (162–93); old age will one day come and it is only through the power of love that the future can be created (184ff.). Her words are accepted by Violentilla, who recalls her suitor's 'gifts, prayers and tears' (195–6), his elegies written in her honour (197ff.). Two of the speeches introduced by Statius are *suasoriae*, one a *laudatio*. Rhetoric and fantasia are entwined to show that Stella's present bliss was divinely motivated.

There is no fixed calibration to determine frigidity in literature. To some, the aetiology invented by Statius will seem cold and artificial. The omnipresence of mythology in the *Silvae* requires explanation. It provided Statius, like other ancient poets, with a universal symbolic language, an instantly recognizable frame of reference. In the epithalamium, for example,

he utilises the myth to bring the marriage of Stella and Violentilla out of the particular moment of time into a reality that transcends time, into the world of the divine and the heroic, into a world where love, constancy, marriage, beauty are hypostatised. Through the mythic tale created by the poet, the marriage itself becomes as if a part of mythology, a universal *exemplum* rather than a specific event.[1]

In short, mythology was a valuable method of universalizing the particular, of giving a transcendental meaning to the transient events and situations that Statius was called upon to celebrate. It was a means, too, by which language could be dignified and the range of imagery expanded.

To demonstrate this, it is relevant to cite the passage in which Statius tells of Venus' descent to Rome and describes the house of Violentilla:

> sic fata leuauit      140
> sidereos artus thalamique egressa superbum
> limen Amyclaeos ad frena citauit olores.
> iungit Amor laetamque uehens per nubila matrem
> gemmato temone sedet. iam Thybridis arces
> Iliacae: pandit nitidos domus alta penates      145
> claraque gaudentes plauserunt limina cycni.
> digna deae sedes, nitidis nec sordet ab astris.
> hic Libycus Phrygiusque silex, hic dura Laconum
> saxa uirent, hic flexus onyx et concolor alto
> uena mari, rupesque nitent, quis purpura saepe      150
> Oebalis et Tyrii moderator liuet aeni.
> pendent innumeris fastigia nixa columnis,
> robora Dalmatico lucent satiata metallo.
> excludunt radios siluis demissa uetustis
> frigora, perspicui uiuunt in marmore fontes.      155
> nec seruat natura uices: hic Sirius alget,
> bruma tepet, uersumque domus sibi temperat annum.
> exsultat uisu tectisque potentis alumnae
> non secus alma Venus, quam si Paphon aequore ab alto
> Idaliasque domos Erycinaque templa subiret.      (140–60)

*So speaking, Venus rose, her limbs bright as the stars. She crossed the exalted threshold of her bower and summoned her Amyclaean swans to rein. Cupid yokes them and, seated on the gem-encrusted pole, he drives his joyful mother through the clouds. Soon they see the Trojan towers of Tiber. There stands a soaring palace, broad with gleaming halls. The swans in rapture beat their wings against its brilliant portals. It was a dwelling well worthy of divine visitation: even after the gleaming stars of heaven it was no shame for Venus to enter there. On this side, it was fashioned of*

---

[1] Vessey (1972) 183–4.

*Libyan and Phrygian marble; on that, of tough Laconian stone, green-glowing; there was serpentine agate and masonry veined blue as the ocean deeps; porphyry, too, bright sparkling – a source of envy to Oebalian purple and to the Tyrian dyemaker with his brazen vat. The ceilings float above, supported by columns beyond counting; the wooden beams glitter, glutted with Dalmatian gold. Cool shadows, streaming from ancient trees, offer protection from the sun's rays; and fountains play, living-clear, in conduits of marble. Nature does not preserve her natural courses: for here Sirius is cool and winter warm. The palace changes and governs the year as it wills. Beneficent Venus was overjoyed to see her mighty fosterchild's abode, no less than if she were drawing near to Paphos from the deep sea, or to her Idalian halls or to her fane at Eryx.*

Light and colour predominate in these lines: stars, jewels, marble of varying hues, gold, sunlight, running water, the sea. Vocabulary expressive of brightness is heaped up, clothing the whole passage in iridescent garb. As usual in Statius, words are used boldly (e.g. *pandit*, 145; *uirent, flexus*, 149; *pendent*, 152; *satiata*, 153; *uiuunt*, 155). Allusiveness and *doctrina* presuppose an informed receptiveness (*Amyclaeos...olores*, 142, *Thybridis arces | Iliacae*, 144–5; *Libycus Phrygiusque silex*, 148; *dura Laconum | saxa*, 148–9; *purpura | Oebalis*, 150–1; *Tyrii moderator...aeni*, 151; *Dalmatico...metallo*, 153; *Paphon...Idaliasque domos Erycinaque templa*, 159–60). On one occasion at least, the 'learning' reaches a point verging on grotesquerie (150–1). Hyperbole suffuses the description of Violentilla's palace, where even the columns are 'beyond counting' (152) and where, by a strained flight of rhetorical fantasy, neither summer nor winter can hold sway (156–7). Sound and metre reflect sense: *gaudentes plauserunt* (146) echoes the beating of the swans' wings at Violentilla's door; 155 evokes the movement of the fountains it mentions; the dactyls in 159–60 summon up the idea of speed in Venus' aerial flight over the ocean. Words are repeated to suggest significant comparisons: *superbum limen, clara limina*, 141–2, 146; *nitidos penates, nitidis astris*, 145, 147; *domus alta, alto mari, aequore alto*, 145, 149–50, 159. In 156–7, trope and paradox are combined to hammer home an exaggeration typical of Statius (*Sirius alget, bruma tepet*). The juxtaposition of contrasting images occurs several times: cloud and gems (143–4); stone and ocean (149–50); masonry, cloth and metal (150–1); masonry, wood and metal (152–3); heat and cold (154–5, 156–7); trees, water and marble (154–5); on a slightly different level, there is a pointed contrast between the toughness of the *saxa* in 148–9 and the verb implying growth in the same phrase (*uirent*, 149), as also between *pendent* and *nixa* in 152. All these features, however, are cohesively integrated: so swiftly do the verses move, so densely packed is the interplay of idea and image, so complex and agglutinative the poet's mode, that an intense and vivid picture is imprinted on the reader's mind. The developed Statian style is one of linguistic impressionism, demanding empathy and vicarious participation. This applies not only to the formal elements in the poems, but equally to subtler problems of symbolism, structure, imitation and philosophy.

In *Silvae* 1.2, Stella and Violentilla are subjected to a virtual deification, assuming static and timeless roles in a cosmos peopled by gods and heroes. Elsewhere Statius had to deal with a ruler who proclaimed himself a *deus praesens*. The poems on Domitian are hymns of praise to an incarnate deity; rich and curious incense is burnt before his altar. In the panegyric on the Emperor's seventeenth consulship (4.1), for example, it is Janus who, in almost hysterical vein, pours out the breathless paean (17–43). Janus has power over Time (*immensi reparator maximus aeui*, 11), and it is natural that he should sing of Domitian's relationship with Eternity and with a New Age which his consulship is to inaugurate (17–20). Domitian is the 'mighty father of the whole earth' (*magne parens mundi*, 17); miracles attended his assumption of the consular office (23–7). The whole history of Rome has reached its pinnacle in this blessed year; even Augustus has been excelled in glory:

> dic age, Roma potens, et mecum longa Vetustas,
> dinumera fastos nec parua exempla recense,
> sed quae sola meus dignetur uincere Caesar.                    30
> ter Latio deciesque tulit labentibus annis
> Augustus fasces, sed coepit sero mereri:
> tu iuuenis praegressus auos. et quanta recusas,
> quanta uetas! flectere tamen precibusque senatus
> promittes hunc saepe diem. manet insuper ordo            35
> longior, et totidem felix tibi Roma curules
> terque quaterque dabit.                                              (28–37)

*Come, give voice, almighty Rome, and with me reckon out, far-stretching Antiquity,
each detail of our annals. Cite no trivial instances, but those alone fit to be surpassed
by my Caesar. Thirteen times, as the years slipped by, did Augustus enjoy the consular
power in Latium: but true merit came late to him. You, while still young, have out-
done your forefathers. How often you have refused the honour! How often have you
debarred it! But you will yield. You will vow, in answer to the Senate's prayers,
time and again to repeat this day. A still longer course remains ahead. As often
again – no, three and four times as often, will Rome prove her good fortune by offering
you the curule chair.*

The prediction of sixty-eight further consulships to a *Princeps* in his mid-forties is, even when attributed to a celestial mouth, a daring feat of adulation. But gods are immortal: Domitian and Janus are establishing a new aeon in the universe (36), in which the Emperor will conquer all nations and extend his sway over the entire globe (39–43). Mystical and religious notions vie with a more traditional aspiration of Roman leaders: to succeed and to outstrip Alexander the Great, prototype of the divine world-ruler. Janus' prophecy is endorsed by heaven; Jupiter promises to Domitian, his earthly counterpart, unending youth and life eternal as his own (45–7).

As a guide to Domitian's attitude to the imperial cult, the lines contain much of value. What can be said of their poetic quality? To conceive and to execute such extremities of propaganda brought vices in its train. Distortion and absurdity, repellent to a modern ear; shallowness veiled by a specious profundity; an insincerity born of too great a yearning to seem sincere: these and other faults have been, and are, listed in the indictment. It is hard, however, not to feel some compassion for a poet of talent constrained, whether willingly or not, so to prostitute his art. It was no mean achievement in such circumstances to instil in his verses a certain grace and grandeur which in part compensate for the distasteful theme. Statius' private life was controlled by the demands of his *patroni* and by the imprisoning rigours of despotism: hence the *Silvae*. Only in the *Thebaid* could Statius find a degree of independence from the insistent pressures of society.

The construction of a twelve-book epic is a daunting task. Statius lavished infinite care on the *magnum opus* which would render his name famous in future ages. Parts of the *Thebaid* were made public by recitations: at which, so Statius tells us, senators were present on the benches (*Silv.* 5.2.161–3). The sarcastic Juvenal bears testimony to the popularity of these readings: but sneeringly implies that Statius pandered to his audience like a whore to her lovers (*Sat.* 7.82ff.). Statius was, admittedly, never indifferent to the judgement of others; to borrow Tacitus' remark on Seneca (*Ann.* 13.3), his *ingenium* was 'admirably suited to contemporary ears'.

Statius was the authentic voice of Domitian's Rome. He evolved a style as unique in Latin verse as that of Tacitus in prose: and as inimitable. The finest and most individual features traceable in the *Silvae* were perfected and finalized within the grand design of the Theban epic. In language, theme and thought, the Statian manner is that of deliberate extremism. The explorations of Ovid, Seneca and Lucan had mapped out the terrain. Statius fixed the boundaries beyond which, as his imitators proved, a writer journeyed at his peril.

*The Thebaid*

The *Aeneid* may have presented a challenge to Statius. He abstained from direct response to it. The *Thebaid* is not a Roman epic; it has no national or patriotic motive. The story of Oedipus and his sons was used to illustrate the broadest moral and philosophical dilemmas: appropriate enough in the Flavian age, no doubt, but divorced from too intimate a connexion with it.

The allegorical and spiritual facets of the *Aeneid* beggar definitive analysis:

no less many-sided are its artistic splendours: yet it is Augustan in the same sense as Spenser's *The Faerie Queene* is Elizabethan. The *Thebaid* is Flavian more in the fashion that *Paradise Lost* is linked to the England of Cromwell. Lucan, writing under Nero, could hardly have shared Virgilian values or have revivified the defunct ideals of the Restored Republic. His mind was at once more dogmatic and more superficial than Virgil's: doctrines and words were not so much his tools as his shackles. The suave urbanity of Ovid and the sententious brevity of Seneca had an instantaneous appeal for Lucan. His uncle reinforced style with Stoicism; the nexus was irresistible. Virgil's serene and flawless majesty must dim Lucan's pyrotechnics, however scintillating. Statius' verses glitter and coruscate – but they are still sharp and sudden like Lucan's, not constant and diffused like Virgil's.

The obsession with logodaedaly was initiated by Ovid. His successors in the first generation were Seneca and Lucan; the next heir was Statius. From Senecan tragedy and the *Bellum civile* he also borrowed a world-view for his epic. The *Thebaid* is a panorama in which cosmos and destiny, god and man, piety and sin, corruption and redemption are displayed within the compass of a single history. Seneca had written dramas – including an *Oedipus* and a *Phoenissae* – in which plots passed to him from the tragedians of Athens were reinterpreted to reveal – and to debate – the tenets of his own brand of Stoicism. Lucan narrated the war between Caesar and Pompey; the historical confrontation is universalized and defined in terms of philosophical absolutes. Though Statius eschewed the Stoic evangelism of the *Bellum civile*, he adopted its cosmic outlook and its psychological approach. Lucan's theme had led him into rash polemic: the Theban legend was safer, but no less amenable to setting forth the horrors of passion, ambition and tyranny.

The destruction, in successive generations, of an accursed house (*deuota domus*) was a favoured topic of Senecan tragedy. In the descendants of Tantalus and of Laius, madness – in Stoic view the ineluctable concomitant of passion (*ira*) – continually broke out afresh. Violence follows violence, crimes worsen and multiply. It is a bleak and anguished world, its savagery scarcely leavened by hope or goodness. The same dark miasma enwraps Lucan's epic. Caesar's tyrannical frenzy causes the dissolution of Roman liberty, of ordered society. Even Cato, the Stoic saint, is presented as a grim and forbidding figure. In the *Thebaid*, Statius recounts the horrendous chronicle of a doomed dynasty. Before him were Seneca's Theban dramas, his *Thyestes* and *Agamemnon*. Statius' Thebes is a diseased realm, ruled by a corrupt and insane tyrant. The prologue epitomizes the grimness of his theme:

> fraternas acies alternaque regna profanis
> decertata odiis sontesque euoluere Thebas
> Pierius menti calor incidit.                    (1.1–3)

*The Muses' fire pervades my mind, bidding it to expound war between brothers,*
*a kingdom apportioned to their alternate rule and fought for with sacrilegious hate,*
*Thebes the guilty.*

Family strife, war, hatred, depravity, guilt: the respondence with Seneca and Lucan is immediate and revealing. The opening words of the *Thebaid* echo *Bellum civile* 1.4 (*cognatasque acies*). Like the conflict between Caesar and Pompey, the war between Eteocles and Polynices is worse than civil (*bella... plus quam ciuilia, Bell. Civ.* 1.1). Fraternal discord had been exposed in all its horror in Seneca's *Thyestes* and *Phoenissae*. In the subsequent lines of his proem, Statius summarizes the long catalogue of madness and disaster that had afflicted the royal line of Thebes (5–16). He fixes the limits of his epic in the 'disturbed house of Oedipus' (*Oedipodae confusa domus*, 17): the last and worst act in a seemingly unending chain of doom and devastation.

Commentators have often written of Statius' pessimism. Its roots are palpable. Disillusion with the principate and the Stoic *Weltanschauung* had provided a double impetus to Seneca and Lucan in the days of Nero. Statius, admiring their style, took over profounder aspects of their work. No more tonally and symbolically fitting an introduction to the narrative could have been devised by Statius than 46ff. Oedipus, blind and vengeful, calls down a fearful curse upon his sons; his imprecation raises from hell the Fury Tisiphone who is afterwards a controlling force in the epic. Verbal echoes, as well as psychological similarities, link Statius' Oedipus with Seneca's. Tisiphone in the *Thebaid*, though related to Virgil's Allecto (*Aeneid* 7.323ff.), stands closer to the Fury who appears at the beginning of Seneca's *Thyestes*. Statius creates an infernal being who is a *figura* of hatred and madness. She owes her dominance in the rest of the epic principally to the irreversible effects of Oedipus' curse once it has been uttered – and confirmed by Jupiter, the executor of Fate (1.212ff.). Tisiphone is, in fact, nothing other than an objectified personification of the congenital evil that afflicts, and so destroys, the descendants of Laius: for it is Statius' custom to treat divine beings as allegories of abstract forces and ideas, in accordance with Stoic preconceptions. It follows that Tisiphone experiences no difficulty in inflaming Polynices and Eteocles with a legion of ruinous passions (1.125–30). They are members of a *deuota domus*, a *gens profana*, and so, by reason of their birth, predisposed to demonic possession. Seneca had examined the theme in depth; Statius made it a logical dynamic. And yet he tempered and moderated the harsh philosophy that he had assumed. Rays of light are allowed to illumine the gloom. Though the fatal results of *furor* occupy much of the *Thebaid* and though bestiality, insensate and uncontrolled, is almost omnipresent, piety and virtue are also given an exemplary role. Coroebus, Maeon, Amphiaraus, Menoeceus, Hypsipyle, Jocasta, Argia and Antigone all, in varying ways, figure forth a nobler vision of mankind.

The epic ends on a note of uplifting optimism. Theseus, king of Athens, a 'divine man' who embodies the highest ideals of justice and clemency, at last brings peace to Thebes and salvation to its people, cancelling the burden of punishment that had been imposed by Oedipus in Book 1. This purifying intervention is rightly kept until the final section of the *Thebaid* (12.464–813). Presentiments of it, foreshadowings of the Athenian king had indeed appeared earlier: only with the extinction of the whole House of Cadmus could equilibrium be fully restored and the plague be healed. By concluding his narrative with the dawning of a new age, Statius separated himself from the agonized, inflexible rigorism of Senecan tragedy. He pointed a contrast, too, with the ambiguous scene with which Virgil had closed the *Aeneid*. But the inner significance of this motif of renewal and redemption runs deeper. The Stoics believed in recurrence, that a new universe would arise after the destruction of the old. The advent of the saviour Theseus symbolizes this rebirth of the *mundus*. The Stoics argued that the cosmos would be overthrown by conflagration: Theseus' arrival is preceded by the cremation of Eteocles and Polynices (12.429ff.) and followed by the funeral rites of the Argive dead (12.797ff.). An *ecpyrosis* accompanies the refashioning of heaven and earth within the poetic universe of the *Thebaid*.

Predestination was a central dogma and problem in Stoicism. Free-will and the power of choice were excluded from a structured and interdependent *mundus*. What Fatum had fixed at the beginning of time was inescapable and had to be endured. The concept of *sympatheia* bound microcosm to macrocosm, man to nature. To modify any detail or particular in the working of destiny was not only impossible: it would bring about that primal chaos which ever hems in and threatens balance and order. Throughout the *Thebaid*, Statius adheres to the twin doctrines of inevitability and cosmic harmony. Events on earth are mirrored in heaven and in the physical world. The sins of men infect everything that exists, spreading the taint far and wide. The symptoms of this contagion may be ominous immensity. In Seneca's *Thyestes*, the blotting-out of the sun (a well-known part of the myth) attains a forceful dimension as a measure of the celestial and terrestrial disruption that has sprung from Atreus' ghastly vengeance (777ff., 789ff.). Thyestes himself invokes the universe, praying, in his torment of soul, that the darkness will be perpetual if condign punishment is not inflicted by the gods on his brother, guilty of 'boundless crimes' (1068–96). For Seneca, the *scelera* of one man are metamorphosed into an emblem of the inherent tension of the *mundus*, of the eternal conflict between moral polarities, threatening the stability of the whole system. It is a near-Manichaean standpoint: and one which Statius shares and to which he grants an informing validity in the *Thebaid*.

The reciprocal sympathy of animate and inanimate nature controls much of the imagery in Statius' epic – as well as some of its most impressive incidents. In Book 1, Polynices flees from Boeotia to Argos. He travels at night, through a storm of preternatural ferocity (1.336ff.). The elaboration of storm-scenes was a well-tried ingredient of epic: *Aeneid* 1 and Lucan, *Bellum civile* 5.504ff. provided Statius with a spur to emulation. Though both these predecessors may be justly said to have exploited the symbolic aspect of the storm-motif, Statius pressed still further in his integration of cosmos and psyche. The turmoil in the House of Cadmus, the madness of Polynices himself are mirrored in the troubled fury of the heavens. Nocturnal shadow is the setting for a journey which is to bring the corruption of Thebes to the still tranquil city of Argos. Indeed the ancient contrast between light and darkness, equated with life and death, good and evil, heaven and hell is to be cunningly developed throughout the *Thebaid*. In Book 2, Tydeus, after the failure of his embassy at Thebes, is ambushed at night by fifty Theban warriors sent by Eteocles to intercept him (2.496ff.). Though he defeats them single-handed, Tydeus is stimulated by this act of treachery to disseminate a gospel of war during the remainder of his journey and at Argos itself (3.1–164). It is just before dawn that King Adrastus of Argos, a man of peace enmeshed in the net of doom, finally agrees to launch a military expedition against Thebes in support of his son-in-law Polynices (3.684ff.). Shortly before the duel between the sons of Oedipus, Jupiter plunges the earth in gloom (11.130–3): for, at that moment, evil is triumphant. The fight, in which both brothers are killed, is watched by souls risen from the Underworld (11.422–3). The antithesis of light and darkness is a major facet in the symbolic pattern, repeated frequently but gaining, by its simplicity, an increasing vigour and imaginative strength. Other recurrent complexes may be viewed in similar terms: for example, the similes and metaphors identifying men with wild beasts, nautical imagery, allusions to storms and other violent natural phenomena, or – on a slightly different plane – the parallels drawn between Hercules, a popular subject for Stoic allegoresis, and the characters of the Theban story.

Dualism does not, however, underlie only the moral scheme of the *Thebaid*; it has also a structural importance. It explains, in part, the tendency which critics have traced for episodes to be doubled: such as the Council of the Gods in Books 1 and 7, or Tiresias' two magical operations in 4 and 10. The twin cities of Argos and Thebes, under their monarchs Adrastus and Eteocles, are themselves spiritual antitheses and the counterbalancing of them is thoroughly and pointedly specified. It may be seen expressed with especial clarity in the equivalent episodes in Books 3 and 4: whereas Adrastus seeks guidance from augury, bidding the pious priest Amphiaraus scan the supernal regions, Eteocles compels the blind prophet Tiresias to summon the ghost of Laius from the nether world by necromantic ritual. Thebes is truly a hell on earth. Its perverting mania spreads to Argos through Polynices' marriage to Argia; what was once a happy and blessed land becomes wretched and abased. Jupiter, in Book 1, decrees that both cities should suffer retribution for past misdeeds (224–7) and from that harsh mandate there can be no escape. It is notable that when Polynices and Tydeus – both agents of violence – arrive at Argos, the people have been celebrating a festival of Apollo, sun-god and lord of oracles; Book 1 ends with a sublime hymn to him by Adrastus. In direct contrast, Book 2 opens with the ascent of Laius from the Underworld at Jupiter's behest. He appears to Eteocles in a dream, redoubling the tyrant's loathing for his brother (94ff.). At the time of this grim visitation, the Thebans are in the midst of Bacchic *orgia* (83–8), rites redolent of blood and barbarism. In the end, it is only through the intervention of a third city, Athens, that peace is regained. At Athens stands the Altar of Mercy (12.481ff.): *clementia* is the only antidote to *ira*. Athens is the polar opposite to Thebes, but it is also Argos perfected. In the same way, its king, Theseus, is not only the diametric analogue of Eteocles (and his despotic successor Creon); he is also Adrastus shorn of weakness and failure.

The three cities have, therefore, the force of archetypes. In his characterization, Statius uses a figural technique. Its origin may again be traced to Seneca and Lucan, and to the Stoic psychology that they espoused. In Senecan drama, the principal characters are *figurae*, monochromatically represented. Caesar, Pompey, Cato are, for Lucan, largely exemplifications of specific types: tyrant, victim, sage. Though there are opportunities within this approach for a certain latitude, it can also be inhibiting. Statius defines in his proem the essential nature of several participants (1.33ff.). Eteocles and Polynices are *tyranni*. Tydeus is 'unrestrained in *ira*'. Amphiaraus is the pious minister of Apollo. Hippomedon is the turbulent warrior. Parthenopaeus is a pathetically gallant youth, Capaneus a blasphemer. These fundamental traits are sustained. They predicate the behaviour of *personae* in different situations. Sometimes this ploy is pressed too far. Neither Hippomedon nor Capaneus is sufficiently individualized: brute strength and sacrilege are their respective properties with almost nothing added. Eteocles is type-cast as a tyrant. Less prominent characters are similarly treated. In the House of Cadmus, we find Menoeceus, a sublime figuration of *uirtus* and *pietas*, Creon, indistinguishable from Eteocles in exhibiting the unlovely vices of absolutism. A degree of ambiguity may be detected in one or two portraits. Tydeus is a martial hero who, despite his better attributes, finally succumbs to the most bestial manifestation of *furor* at the moment of his death in Book 8; he is deprived of the apotheosis which Pallas wishes to grant him. Polynices is a potential but unfledged despot; though he cannot shed genetic predispositions, he is not completely devoid of moral sensibility. Adrastus is a wise and benevolent sovereign but he lacks fibre and foresight. More satisfying are Statius' womenfolk: the noble Hypsipyle, the majestically sorrowful Jocasta, the loyal Argia, the fearless Antigone, the modest Ismene. In general, however, Statius strictly observed the figural mode. Virgil's Aeneas is much more than a prototypical *exemplum* of piety. Statius' characters are statuesque rather than vital. The *Thebaid* was given an additional level of universality. It was also a surrender to dogma.

In his delineation of the gods, Statius likewise manifested a trend to full allegorization. Lucan denuded epic of divine machinery. Statius restored it – in consonance with his Stoic programme. Jupiter is omnipotent because he is responsible for effecting the designs of *Fatum*. The other deities have no power to thwart him, though they may modify attendant details. Often, as C. S. Lewis argued in *The allegory of love*, they are externalized depictions of internal processes in human minds.[1] Sometimes a little more: Bacchus is permitted to delay the Argive army at Nemea in Books 4 to 7, providing Thebes with a temporary respite. Apollo ensures that his protégé Amphiaraus descends, still living, from the battlefield to Elysian rewards (7.771ff.): in consequence of which Dis, enraged at an infringement of his prerogatives, ordains grim exits for the other Argive princes as well as Creon's folly in forbidding funeral rites to their corpses (8.65ff.). Diana aids Parthenopaeus in his boyish quest for glory in Book 9. In 10, Juno calls upon the assistance of Sleep, enabling the Argives to carry through a treacherous and brutal massacre of Thebans (49–346): she it is too who guides the Argive widows to Athens (12.134–6). Such celestial interpositions were sanctioned by Homer and Virgil, were part of the heritage of epic. Statius, however, does not allow the gods to disrupt his philosophical groundplan. *Fatum* is always paramount, *ira* always brings retribution. It is comprehensible that Statius presented, in company with familiar deities, other beings who are manifestly abstractions: no strangers to Roman religion but enhanced in stature. Virtus addresses Menoeceus before he resolves to sacrifice himself for Thebes in an uplifting act of patriotic *deuotio* (10.632ff.). Tisiphone is, as has been remarked, an overtly symbolic figure She is set in dramatic conflict with the personification Pietas shortly before the duel of Polynices and Eteocles (11.457ff.). Clementia, in Book 12 (481ff.), is a fructifying concept, suggestive of the highest impulses that can govern man and universe. At such points allegory and psychologization are united in the guise of *deorum ministeria*.

It has been commonly alleged that Statius was perverse in his inclusion of otiose material, that the *Thebaid* is incoherent. The falsity of such accusations can be demonstrated only by minute analysis. A story without a single hero has to rely on multiform cohesiveness. Statius clearly felt obliged to incorporate stock themes from received tradition: the mustering of armies (4.1–344, 7.243–373), nekyomanteia (4.419–645), funeral games (6.249–946), aristeia with

[1] Lewis (1936) 49–56.

lengthy battle scenes (Books 7 to 11). These need not impair unity provided that, as in the *Thebaid*, they are assimilated and made to serve broader themes. Statius created in 4 a military catalogue formally correspondent with prototypes in *Iliad* 2 and *Aeneid* 7. The other is cast as a teichoscopy loosely inspired by Euripides, *Phoenissae* 88ff. The *athla* in 6 are, in detail, a propædeutic anticipation of the impending war (Books 7 to 11). The *aristeiae* are distinctive and scrupulously balanced. Even more reprehensible, so it is said, are features such as the myth of Linus and Coroebus (1.557ff.), the long narrative of Hypsipyle (5.49ff.). Not so: these subsidiary elements are germinal and instructive. They encapsulate much that is crucial for understanding the *Thebaid*. The myth contains a summary of the leitmotifs of the whole epic; the experiences of Hypsipyle at Lemnos are a parabolic résumé of truths fully enunciated elsewhere. The devices of foreshadowing, parallelism, antithesis are widely utilized to bind episode to episode. The *Thebaid* is dynamic, associative and interwoven. It is, like Ovid's *Metamorphoses*, a *carmen perpetuum*, serpentine and polymorphic in its construction. Its parts are endowed with a self-sufficient but ultimately dependent cohesion. They form part of an integrated chain, each link discrete but devoid of significance outside its context. In the end, the *Thebaid* ought to be perceived as structurally related to the Stoic doctrine of the *series causarum*, that indissoluble pattern of cause and effect in which no particular can be divorced from the whole.[1]

Alert perceptiveness is required to appreciate the nuances of Statius' artistry. As in the *Silvae*, so in the *Thebaid* the finest passages impress themselves indelibly on a reader's mind. It is invidious to make a choice. Some incidents may, however, receive special mention for their imaginative vigour: Polynices' journey to Argos and his fight with Tydeus on arrival (1.312–481), Tydeus' monomachy (2.496–743), the two appearances of Laius' ghost, first in a dream (2.1–133), then through sorcery (4.419–645), the massacre at Lemnos as recounted by Hypsipyle (5.85–334), the chariot-race at Nemea (6.296–549), Hippomedon's fight with Ismenus (9.315–539), the tale of Hopleus and Dymas (10.347–448), Menoeceus' *deuotio* (10.628–782), the duel with its preliminaries and aftermath in Book 11, the meeting between Argia and Antigone outside Thebes in 12, which culminates in the divided flames on the funeral-pyre of Oedipus' sons: their hatred has passed beyond death itself (204–446). The colours are bold, the rhetoric taut and demanding; in such scenes, Statius validated his claim on eternity, as formulated in the epilogue (12.812–13).

[1] See further Vessey (1973) 317–28.

## The Achilleid

More debatable are the merits of the *Achilleid*. Judgements have shown pro-found disparity. Commenced at the end of the poet's life, it is a canvas on which only a few tentative brush-strokes have been laid. Its style is less ornate, less incisive than that of the *Thebaid*. It is probably best to see the fragment that remains as a cartoon, from which, by reworking and labour, a definitive version would at length have been evolved. In describing Achilles' youth, Statius is often poignant and deft: a lightness pervades the *Achilleid* that is found rarely in the Theban epic. And yet, his powers were waning, the fires were growing dim. Death brought the project to a premature end: but the *Achilleid*, despite its imperfections, has its own peculiar charm, arising from a directness of approach and a simplicity of tone lacking in Statius' other works.

### 3. VALERIUS

It is generally held that the grave claimed Valerius Flaccus before he had con-cluded the eighth book of the *Argonautica*. Of the man himself little can be said. Quintilian's brief notice (*Inst.* 10.1.90) is a solitary witness. A remark in Valerius' prologue may indicate that he was a *quindecemvir sacris faciundis* (1.5–7): if so, we may surmise that he was not without money and social standing. The epic was commenced before Statius' *Thebaid*, and it seems that work continued over a long period. An invocation of Vespasian, an allusion to Titus' destruction of Jerusalem, an obeisance towards the versifying of Domitian fix the proem to the early seventies (1.7–21). In Book 3, there is an apparent reference to the eruption of Vesuvius in 79 (207–8); elsewhere, it has been suggested, indirect mention is made of Domitian's campaigns against the Sarmatians in 89, even in 92 (6.162, 231ff.). Valerius, like Statius, presumably did not esteem rapidity of composition as a virtue. If he contemplated that the *Argonautica* should comprise twelve books, his progress during two decades was unusually slow. It may be that our chronological speculations are faulty; or, as C. W. Mendell has maintained, 'that the problem of how to finish the epic proved too much for the poet'.[1] The loss to the world, whatever the cause, may not be as great as Quintilian estimated.

Statius labelled the legend of the Argonauts among stale and hackneyed themes (*Silv.* 2.7.50–1). He also honoured the memory of Varro of Atax, who had, in the first century B.C., produced a version or adaptation of Apollonius (2.7.77). Varro had contributed something to the *Aeneid*; Quintilian damned his poem with faint praise (*Inst.* 10.1.87). Whether Valerius found guidance or inspiration in Varro is unknown. Apollonius was his prime source: in a

[1] Mendell (1967) 136.

sense to Valerius' detriment, for few would be prepared to dispute the innate superiority of the Greek poet. To have to contend for laurels not only with Virgil but also with Apollonius is Valerius' misfortune: add further the epic's incompletion and the total of disadvantages is formidable.

Apologists have nonetheless existed. One of Valerius' earliest champions, H. E. Butler, though admitting faults, held that he 'offends less than any of the silver Latin writers of epic', for 'he rants less and exaggerates less; above all he has much genuine poetic merit'. Butler saw that, in his choice of subject, Valerius faced difficulties: 'The Argonaut saga', he wrote, 'has its weaknesses as a theme for epic. It is too episodic, it lacks unity and proportion. Save for the struggle in Colchis and the loves of Jason and Medea, there is little deep human interest.' Compensation could, however, be found in 'variety and brilliance of colour', in 'romance' and 'picturesqueness'.[1] For some, the *Argonautica* has emerged primarily as a romantic epic, an adventure story, threading its way from incident to incident – a form predicated by its kinship with the *periplus*, the narrative of a coastal or circumnavigatory voyage. The first four lines perhaps bear out such an interpretation:

> Prima deum magnis canimus freta peruia nautis,
> fatidicamque ratem, Scythici quae Phasidis oras
> ausa sequi mediosque inter iuga concita cursus
> rumpere, flammifero tandem consedit Olympo.     (1.1–4)

*I sing of straits crossed first by the heroic offspring of gods, of the vessel with power to prophesy that dared the quest to the shores of Scythian Phasis and plunged headlong through the midst of the clashing rocks, at length finding its seat in the fiery heaven.*

At first sight, the words seem almost naively functional: but there may be hidden depths in them. The idea of a voyage through hazards to a celestial reward suggests both the metaphor of human life as a journey and of the earth as a ship with mankind as its crew: it is worth remembering that in antiquity the myth of the Argonauts was used in an 'Orphic', allegorical context. The crew of the *Argo* are denominated in 1 as heroes of divine ancestry; man and god are brought into juxtaposition. Valerius, compared to Apollonius, augmented the role of deities in his epic, stressing their influence over terrestrial events. The first word, *prima*, may well imply that the Voyage of the Argonauts is to be regarded as archetypal and revelatory. In such terms, the supposedly ornamental epithet *fatidica* applied to the *Argo* – although it alludes to a famous feature of the ship – gains an added significance. Scythian Phasis and the Cyanean Rocks are determinate synonyms for barbarism and violence, for obstacles in the path of life, only to be overcome by struggle and

[1] Butler (1909) 190–1.

85

audacity: they are contrasted with the bright, unchanging tranquillity of Olympus, which is the *telos* attained through endurance.

In general, Valerius followed the outlines of Apollonius' narrative. There are expansions and excisions, variations and changes. Among Valerian innovations, we may cite the suicide of Jason's parents Aeson and Alcimede (1.730–851) and the rescue of Hesione by Hercules and Telamon (2.451–578). The story of the Stymphalian birds, found in Apollonius' second book, is omitted by Valerius. Of what he had in common with his Greek exemplar, the Latin poet always made far-reaching realignments in tone, tempo and motivation: in the Lemnian episode (Book 2), in the tragedy of Cyzicus (Books 2–3), in the disappearance of Hylas (Books 3–4), in the encounter of Pollux and Amycus (Book 4), in the salvation of Phineus from the Harpies (Book 4). After negotiating the Clashing Rocks, the Argonauts reach Colchis: the details of Jason's dealings with King Aeetes and of his relationship with Medea (Books 5–7), though in many ways similar to the Apollonian version, are reshaped and altered. The unfinished eighth book tells of the theft of the Golden Fleece and of the departure of the Argonauts, with Medea, from Colchis.

Apollonius' epic is objective and urbane, exuding Hellenistic cynicism. It is brittle, often amoral, impersonal. In it, Homeric values are consciously, even maliciously, subverted. None of these traits was copied by Valerius. It was from the *Aeneid* that he sought his outlook and philosophy. The *Argonautica* bristles with Virgilian echoes, not only verbally but in incident and in characterization. Apollonius' Jason, as Gilbert Lawall has rightly said, is an anti-hero.[1] He lives in a harsh world where conventional virtue is irrelevant and inadequate; his success springs from a ruthless opportunism. Valerius recast Jason on the pattern of Aeneas. This reinstatement of Jason to full heroic stature is aptly signalized by Valerius' invocation of the Muse at 5.217–19:

> Incipe nunc cantus alios, dea, uisaque uobis
> Thessalici da bella ducis; non mens mihi, non haec
> ora satis.

*Now begin new songs, goddess; tell me of the wars waged by the Thessalian prince which you Muses saw; for my mind, my words cannot suffice.*

Jason has now reached Colchis. He is to be tested and tried as a warrior, just as Aeneas was after his arrival in Italy. These *bella* waged by Jason on Aeetes' behalf occupy Book 6. They have no counterpart in Apollonius. They serve to magnify Jason's heroism and also to unmask Aeetes' treachery. The Colchian king promises Jason the fleece if he defeats the Scythian army of his insurgent brother Perses: but reneges on his vow after Jason's triumph. Only when so perfidiously handled does Jason turn to Medea's goetic skills to achieve his

[1] Lawall (1966).

object. By such a metamorphosis of the plot, Valerius purifies Jason. It also gave him the opportunity of trying his hand at battle scenes in emulation of the *Aeneid*. His Aeetes is depicted in familiar form: a stock *tyrannus*, with a dash of Virgil's Mezentius. His son Absyrtus consequently becomes another Lausus.

·The cleansing and refining of characters, with concomitant denigration of others, at times leads Valerius into a sentimentality alien to Apollonius. Hypsipyle acquires a moral dignity, in part derived from Virgil's Dido but also indebted to Ovid, *Heroides* 6. The story of King Cyzicus is, as R. W. Garson has demonstrated, elaborated as a tragic drama.[1] A Virgilian motif is borrowed to provide a cause for its dénouement. Whereas Apollonius merely attributed the disaster to fate (1.1030), Valerius, in imitation of *Aeneid* 7.475 ff., establishes its origin in the fact that Cyzicus had angered the goddess Cybele by killing one of her sacred lions (3.19 ff.). This involuntary hybris brings about the peripateia, so that, in Book 3, Cyzicus is himself slain, in ignorance, by Jason. In his treatment of Hercules' loss of the boy Hylas in Book 3 (neatly complemented by the rescue of Hesione in 2), Valerius injects a wealth of amatory and pathetic colour lacking in Apollonius. He also invents a divine intrigue as the root of Hercules' misfortune. Theocritus 13 and Virgil were quarried. Apollonius depicts Hercules unflatteringly; Valerius consistently glorifies him. His Medea is perhaps more closely dependent on Apollonius. Torn between her filial duty (*pietas*) towards Aeetes and her passion for Jason, Medea, according to some, emerges not as a cunning and resolute sorceress but as a diffident and inexperienced girl. The view can be overstated. In Apollonius Medea is more robust and full-blooded. Valerius exhibits grace and charm, as well as sound psychological insight: but the resemblances to Apollonius are at all times substantial. Valerius rejects, however, the melodramatic Medea of Ovid, *Metamorphoses* 7 and Seneca's *Medea*.

When set beside Statius, Valerius is restrained and economical. Occasionally his terseness becomes jejune and effete. He sought Virgilian gravity as an antidote to the excesses of Seneca and Lucan; but, lacking his master's genius, he ran a perpetual risk of anaemia. The scenes of war in Book 6 are particularly tedious; they have none of the verve and panache of Books 7–11 of the *Thebaid*. His metre is often repetitive and unenterprising. An Ovidian smoothness prevails, but Valerius does not share Ovid's superb control over his medium – nor Lucan's fiery legerdemain which helped to offset his metrical sterility.

In Book 2, Hercules and Telamon, wandering on the coast of Phrygia, come upon Hesione, manacled to a rock. Hercules asks her identity, the reason for her predicament.

[1] Garson (1964) 269–70.

87

Hesione replies:

non ego digna malis, inquit; suprema parentum
dona uides, ostro scopulos auroque frequentes.
nos Ili felix quondam genus, inuida donec
Laomedonteos fugeret Fortuna penates.
principio morbi caeloque exacta sereno                    475
temperies, arsere rogis certantibus agri,
tum subitus fragor et fluctus Idaea mouentes
cum stabulis nemora. ecce repens consurgere ponto
belua, monstrum ingens; hanc tu nec montibus ullis
nec nostro metire mari. primaeua furenti                  480
huic manus amplexus inter planctusque parentum
deditur. hoc sortes, hoc corniger imperat Hammon,
uirgineam damnare animam sortitaque Lethen
corpora; crudelis scopulis me destinat urna.
uerum o iam redeunt Phrygibus si numina, tuque            485
ille ades auguriis promisse et sorte deorum,
iam cui candentes uotiuo in gramine pascit
cornipedes genitor, nostrae stata dona salutis,
adnue meque, precor, defectaque Pergama monstris
eripe, namque potes: neque enim tam lata uidebam          490
pectora Neptunus muros cum iungeret astris
nec tales umeros pharetramque gerebat Apollo.      (471–92)

*I am undeserving of such misfortunes, she said. You are looking at my parents' final gifts to me – rocks laden with purple and gold. We are scions of Ilus: once our race was blessed, till envious Fortune abandoned the halls of Laomedon. At first came plague; fair weather departed from the peaceful heaven. The fields were ablaze with a riot of funeral pyres. Then, suddenly, there was a thundering; waves shook the groves of Ida where beasts have their lairs. Straightway a vast and hideous monster emerged from the sea: you could not tell its size by comparison with any rocky pile, nor by our ocean. A youthful band was sacrificed to its frenzy, torn from the embraces, the lamentations of their parents. This was the command of the lot, this of horned Hammon: that a girl's life and body chosen by lot should be condemned to death. I it was that the savage urn doomed to the rocks. And yet, oh, if heaven's favour has returned to the Phrygians, if you have come as augury and divine lot foretold, if you are he for whom my father is at this moment pasturing white horses in the promised field, the fixed reward for my salvation, consent – save me, save Troy ravaged by monsters, for yours is the power to do so: for I have never beheld so broad a breast, not even while Neptune bound our walls to the stars – no, not even Apollo had such shoulders, such a quiver.*

For a maiden in dire distress, Hesione's speech is surprisingly bathetic. It is plain enough that Valerius has eschewed rhetorical exaggeration, favouring brevity and reticence. The yearning for classical purity has, however, led him to stale aridity. The generally short sentences are not clear and concise but feeble and attenuated: obscurity in Valerius usually arises from over-compression. When he ventures into hyperbole, as in 479–80 and 490–2, the effect is jarring and incongruous: indeed, Hesione's outburst on Hercules' massive physique verges on the absurd. Hardly less banal is the strained remark about her parents' *suprema dona* in 471–2. The adjective *Laomedonteos* in 474 is portentous without purpose. The conceit in *certantibus* (476) is inapt; the phrase *cum stabulis* (478) is pointless. The words *amplexus inter planctusque parentum* (481) are stilted and trivial. The repetition *sortes* (482), *sortita* (483), *sorte* (486), in conjunction with the elegant variation *urna* (484) produce drabness where excitement and tension are needed. *Monstrum ingens* in 479 is extracted from *Aeneid* 3.658, but the echo is frigid and unimpressive. Other objections might be made: all in all, Valerius presents himself as a Virgil without *ingenium*, an Ovid without *ars*.

It would be wrong to suggest that Valerius did not often rise to greater heights than this. He is at his weakest in speeches. There are times when his avoidance of 'rant' and 'bombast' – so often praised by his admirers – was stylistically beneficial. An instance of this is the absence of grotesquerie from the magical rites that precede the suicide of Aeson and Alcimede in Book 1 (730ff.). There Valerius, unlike Statius in Book 4 of the *Thebaid*, repudiated the extravagances of Seneca and Lucan (*Oedipus* 530ff., *Bell. Civ.* 6.419ff.). The resulting simplicity is refreshing and original. In the Lemnian episode Valerius shows imaginative power and technical ingenuity; the parting of Hypsipyle and Jason (2.400–24) gains in emotive strength from its succinctness. There are elegant and moving lines in his account of the abduction of Hylas. Often quoted for their musical poignancy are 3.596–7 – derived from Virgil, *Ecl.* 6.43–4:

> rursus Hylan et rursus Hylan per longa reclamat
> auia; responsant siluae et uaga certat imago.

*Again and again he cries 'Hylas, Hylas' through the endless wastes; the woods reply and straying echo vies with him.*

The verses find a responsive parallel at 724–5, when the Argonauts are sailing away from Phrygia without Hercules:

> omnis adhuc uocat Alciden fugiente carina,
> omnis Hylan, medio pereuntia nomina ponto.

*Still each of them calls 'Alcides' as the vessel flies away, each 'Hylas', but the names fade away in mid-sea.*

At the beginning of Book 4, Hercules, exhausted by searching, sees a vision of Hylas by the pool; the boy's words are harmonious and pathetic (25–37). The conclusion contrasts Hercules' triumphant destiny with the tender love that he felt for Hylas:

surge age et in duris haud unquam defice; caelo
mox aderis teque astra ferent; tu semper amoris
sis memor et cari comitis ne abscedat imago.          (35–7)

*Now rise: even in the midst of troubles do not succumb to weakness. Soon heaven will
be yours and your place will be with the stars. Never forget your love; never let
the vision of your beloved comrade slip from your mind.*

Godhead was approaching, but Hercules should not forget the passion that had
revealed his humanity.

The seventh book of the *Argonautica* is usually reckoned the best, despite
signs that it did not receive its author's final polishing. At 407ff. there occurs
a dialogue between Jason and Medea in the grove of Hecate. The hero makes it
plain that he is willing to die rather than return to Iolcos without the Golden
Fleece. This determination fills Medea with fear and hardens her in her resolve
to betray her father by using magical arts on Jason's behalf:

haec ait. illa tremens, ut supplicis aspicit ora
conticuisse uiri iamque et sua uerba reposci,
nec quibus incipiat demens uidet ordine nec quo
quoue tenus, prima cupiens effundere uoce
omnia, sed nec prima pudor dat uerba timenti.          435
haeret et attollens uix tandem lumina fatur.
'quid, precor, in nostras uenisti, Thessale, terras?
unde mei spes ulla tibi, tantosque petisti
cur non ipse tua fretus uirtute labores?
nempe ego si patriis timuissem excedere tectis          440
occideras, nempe hanc animam cras saeua manebant
funera. Iuno ubi nunc, ubi nunc Tritonia uirgo,
sola tibi quoniam tantis in casibus adsum
externae regina domus? miraris et ipse,
credo, nec agnoscunt haec nunc Aeetida silvae.          445
sed fatis sum uicta tuis; cape munera supplex
nunc mea; teque iterum Pelias si perdere quaeret
inque alios casus, alias si mittet ad urbes,
heu formae ne crede tuae.'          (7.431–49)

*Such were his words. She trembled, now that the suppliant hero's tongue was silenced
and she must make reply. In her frenzy she can devise for her words no beginning, no
logic, no conclusion: her desire is to tell everything at once: yet shame and fear restrain
her from utterance. She hesitates and then, at length, with a struggle, raises her eyes
towards him and says: 'Why, why, Thessalian stranger, have you come to our
country? Why have you any confidence in my help? The trials are great: but why do
you not face them relying on your own valour? If I had been afraid to leave my father's
halls, you would assuredly have fallen – and as assuredly grim destruction would have
awaited my soul on the morrow. Where now is Juno, where now is Pallas, since you have
no other supporter in such adversity but me, a princess of an alien dynasty? Even*

*you are astounded, I know it; not even these groves recognize me as Aeetes' daughter. But your destiny has conquered mine. Suppliant that you are, take now my gifts. And if Pelias again attempts to destroy you, if he sends you to meet other trials in other cities, do not, oh do not trust too much in your beauty.'*

Valerius' exposition has considerable refinement. Though Jason is the suppliant (431), it is Medea who is in the position of weakness, as she ironically divulges in 446–7. She is neither physically nor mentally in control of herself (*tremens*, 431, *demens*, 433). Her seething emotions cause temporary aphasia, a breakdown of reason (433–4); her response is too swift, too confused to permit orderly discourse (434–5). It is only by compelling herself to look at Jason that Medea overcomes her diffidence and replies to him (436). The psychological perceptiveness of the lines is intensified by the loose, oblique structure of 431–5, measured against the transparent clarity of 436. The speech is founded on an adroit *gradatio*. First, Medea enunciates a specious wish that Jason had never come to Colchis, while tacitly recognizing that his hope resides in her because the *labores* are too great even for his *uirtus* (438–9). She admits that she has betrayed her father; she sees now that her life and Jason's are interdependent (440–2). In the face of apparent divine indifference, Medea, although a princess and a foreigner, must assume a protective function; yet, by doing so, she alienates herself from her past, from her homeland and family (442–5). She acquiesces and submits, offering Jason all that she has (446–7). Then, at the end, she shows her awareness, almost wistfully, that it is physical love that has reduced her to her predicament (447–9). Medea is, therefore, at one and the same time saviour and victim. By giving Jason succour, she denudes herself of everything. Through his victory, she is conquered. Ignorant that she has been a plaything in a divine conspiracy (155ff.), she equates herself with the goddesses Juno and Pallas at a time when her human frailty is most clearly revealed.

Valerius deserves commendation for delicacy and insight in many parts of his epic. The problem, however, remains: what aim and purpose prompted him to compose the *Argonautica*? To hazard an answer is greatly complicated by its unfinished state. To view the work simply as a romance, as an exercise in storytelling, seems an over-simplification. Recent scholarship has shown that Apollonius' *Argonautica* uses myth to unveil and actualize a deep assessment of the human condition. The profundities of Virgilian metaphysics can never be fully or finally plumbed. It is hard to believe that Valerius had no more abstruse intent than to revamp the Argonautic saga according to his own aesthetic predilections.

As Apollonius realized, the *periplus* of the Argonauts is a useful framework for a commentary on moral and philosophical truths. That Valerius shared this view may, as has been suggested, be divined from his proem. The 'series of incidents' which make up the story is a golden opportunity to crystallize a whole range of contrasting situations and events. Some structural features are immediately detectable. In Book 2, the Argonauts disembark at Lemnos, a community that has suffered a devastating social trauma. Their visit, after some initial resistance (2.311ff.), brings about regeneration and renewal. Later, however, they reach the kingdom of Cyzicus. They are received with generous hospitality (2.634ff.); but their return, in a mental blindness imposed by Cybele's *ira*, spins the wheel of fortune; prosperity and happines are replaced by grief and ruin. The realms of Hypsipyle and Cyzicus are set out as a diptych. Jason's abandonment of the queen can be seen as a prefiguration of his killing of the king. Similarly, the rescue of Hesione by Hercules (in Book 2) corresponds with his loss of Hylas (in 3). The fight between Pollux and King Amycus (4.49ff.) has a symbolic equivalence with the scattering of the Harpies by Calais and Zetes (4.423ff.). Mopsus' homily on cathartic rites (3.377ff.) is dexterously connected with Orpheus' exposition of the myth of Io (4.351ff.); in both, sacral and religious concepts are set forth which illumine wider aspects of the Voyage. The prophecies of Cretheus (1.741ff.), Helle (2.587ff.) and Phineus (4.553ff.) form an ordered sequence. The passage of the Cyanean rocks (4.636ff.) signifies the completion of the first stage of the quest. After that, the scene shifts to Colchis and to Jason's attempts to gain possession of the Fleece. He tries negotiation (Book 5) and displays his martial valour (Book 6). It is finally through the power of love, leading to the use of thaumaturgy and theft (Book 7–8), that he achieves his end and departs from Colchis.

In Book 1, Jupiter provides a commentary on the Voyage in reply to complaints from Sol, Mars, Pallas and Juno. His speech is momentous within the fabric of the *Argonautica*. He begins by enunciating a stern doctrine of necessity, of the inflexible dominion that he has imposed on the universe:

> tum genitor: 'uetera haec nobis et condita pergunt
> ordine cuncta suo rerumque a principe cursu
> fixa manent; neque enim terris tum sanguis in ullis
> noster erat cum fata darem; iustique facultas
> hinc mihi cum uarios struerem per saecula reges.
> atque ego curarum repetam decreta mearum.'     (1.531–6)

*Then the Father replied: 'All these events were laid down by me long ago. They are proceeding in due order and remain unchangeable from the primal inauguration of the universe. When I ordained the course of Fate, no descendants of ours existed in any quarter of the earth. For that reason, I had the opportunity for strict impartiality in establishing divers sovereigns for ages still to come. Now I shall reveal to you what I have decreed in my providential care.'*

The words have a Stoic flavour, but the tenor of Jupiter's 'decrees' (*decreta*, 536) is unexpected. They disclose not a personal or a particular design but instead a historic *Weltbild*. The Argonautic voyage is to precede the transference of wealth and empire from Asia to Greece (543ff.). The art of navigation, now invented, will make international conflicts easier: hence the Trojan War, for which the Voyage is a preliminary (546ff.). Greece too will decline and fall. Her primacy will pass to another race. Jupiter does not specify the legatee, but it is Rome that is to have the *imperium sine fine*:

> arbiter ipse locos terraeque summa mouendo
> experiar, quaenam populis longissima cunctis
> regna uelim linquamque datas ubi certus habenas.     (558–60)

*By moving the centre of earthly governance I, as lord, shall prove what dominion I desire to be longest-enduring and universal, to whom I can, in safe assurance, entrust the reins of power.*

Finally Jupiter looks down at Hercules, at Castor and Pollux aboard the *Argo*, remarking:

> tendite in astra, uiri: me primum regia mundo
> Iapeti post bella trucis Phlegraeque labores
> imposuit: durum uobis iter et graue caeli
> institui. sic ecce meus, sic, orbe peracto
> Liber et expertus terras remeauit Apollo.     (563–7)

*Make your way to heaven, heroes! Only after war with savage Iapetus and struggles at Phlegra did I become ruler of the universe in my kingly palace. I have fixed for you a tough and onerous path to heaven. Only so did my own Liber, after traversing the globe, only so did my own Apollo, after dwelling on earth, return to Olympus.*

There is an obvious parallelism between the *cursus* of the universe (531), the path of history, the voyage of the Argonauts and the *iter* of the heroes to Olympus. Valerius had already stated that Jupiter's sway had abolished the peace (*otia*) of Saturn's reign (1.500). Henceforth it is to be through hardship and suffering that godhead will be won. The journey of the Argonauts initiated a new epoch (as Catullus had seen in his *Peleus and Thetis*), an epoch that gave birth, purposefully and inevitably, to the Roman empire. Power shifted from Asia to Greece: and then from Greece to Rome, where dwelt the scions of Asian Troy. The Argonauts became emblematic figures, not merely of the new men of a new *saeculum* but of the providential and cyclic movement of history, predetermined by divine will. If Hercules and the sons of Boreas are precursors of the Roman emperors, then Jason is ultimately representative of the qualities of outmoded Hellenism. The Golden Fleece is a token of Fate – a veiled symbol of that glittering, but perhaps illusory, ambition that man, whether as an individual or as a part of a larger community, seeks in the long pilgrimage of life, an *arcanum* which he cherishes but which can be only temporarily or fraudulently possessed.

93

Overt and covert glances towards the Roman *imperium* occur elsewhere in the epic. They are not simply antiquarian curiosities or meaningless Virgilian accretions. They are a crucial element in the interpretation Valerius imposed on the Argonautic myth. The full realization of his plan was foiled. The general trend may be divined. Statius was concerned with spiritual dilemmas, with the interconnexion of cosmos and psyche, of passion and virtue. Valerius wished to show humanity in a broad historical perspective. He envisaged the whole process of reality as divine, whether manifested in individual, in nation or in the *mundus*. In this sense, the philosophical structure of the *Argonautica* is Virgilian. The Voyage of the Argonauts seemed to Valerius a perfect instrument for such a comprehensive aim. Yet, in the end, the epic proves a failure. The scintilla of poetic greatness was not there. Even more important, by pitting himself so directly against Virgil, Valerius laid himself open to inhibiting constraints. He gave the fanatical assent of a convert to a credo; he attempted to live up to its demands. Dispassionate appraisal concludes that he had not grasped the implications of his faith or, at least, he was incapable of living up to it – an apprentice saint whose relics have produced no miracles.

## 4. SILIUS

If the *Argonautica* is thematically a prelude to the *Aeneid*, then the *Punica* is its fugue – but a fugue made monotonous by unsubtle variations. Jason's expedition was presented by Valerius as an anticipation of, or a rehearsal for, the settlement of the Trojans in Italy. The Punic Wars were for Silius a fated consequence of it. The author of the *Punica* enjoyed a long and remarkable career. His biography is pithily summarized by Pliny (*Epist.* 3.7). Sidelights are cast on it in Martial's epigrams: from them, we may deduce that Silius was a man of inordinate pretensions and vanity – a supposititious Cicero, a reborn Virgil, the founder of a consular dynasty (Martial 7.63, 8.66, 9.86). Pliny's obituary is more candid. Silius was alleged to have sullied his reputation under Nero by voluntarily acting as an informer. Appointed consul in the year of the tyrant's fall, he switched his allegiance to the party of Vitellius. Vespasian had rewarded his fluctuating loyalty with the proconsulship of Asia. Covered with glory, Silius retired to Campania and a life of *laudabile otium*. His days were divided between working on the *Punica* and conversing with friends and clients on topics of literary interest. His enormous wealth enabled him to acquire an abundance of villas, books, *objets d'art*. When he shortened a terminal illness by starvation in the reign of Trajan, he was still acknowledged as a *princeps ciuitatis*: but he had made no improper use of his prestige. As for his epic, despite Silius' habit of seeking criticism at public readings, it was written, so Pliny believed, *maiore cura quam ingenio*, with painstaking diligence rather than native aptitude.

Pliny's words have survived with the *Punica*, an equivocal motto but one that contains a studied appropriateness. In modern times, it has been twinned with H. E. Butler's aphorism that Silius is 'best known to us as the author of the longest and worst of surviving Roman epics.'[1] Readers have been more willing to forgive the inferiority than the prolixity. If the death of the man Silius prompted Pliny to reflect on human frailty (3.7.10–11), a perusal of his epic is likely to persuade a man to recall the value of such time as he may have. Life is brief, but Silius is not. In his poetry, he is a leviathan, wallowing in shallow waters that have been made turbid by his own frantic efforts to reach the open sea. Martial found it expedient to label Silius as Virgil's heir. The patrimony was ill-used.

The *Punica* is a hymn to the goddess Rome. It chronicles that heroic period of tribulation followed by triumph, when the Romans, abased by defeat, arose from it to dominion of the world. A stirring theme: Livy had recounted it in prose of memorable grandeur. Silius absorbed his *History*, and others, for the outlines of his national epic. His annalistic method harked back to the primitive but venerable Ennius. But it was Virgil who had fixed the boundaries of his *œuvre*. In the thirteenth line of the *Aeneid*, Carthage and Italy were set in eternal confrontation, spiritually more than historically. In *Aeneid* 4, Virgil had displayed the seeds of this long enmity. Dido herself had predicted the advent of an avenger, of wars that would be kindled from the tragic flames of her pyre (*Aen.* 4.625–9). There Silius picks up the tale. Hannibal is Dido's *ultor*. Typically, he also informs us, at length, of the adventures of Dido's sister Anna (*Pun.* 8.25–231).

Such a flashback into legend is but one feature of Silius' diligence (*cura*). The Punic War provided him with rich scope for discursiveness and for pedantic disquisition. His excessive zeal embellished historical narrative with all the conventional *topoi* of his chosen genre: the *nekyia* in Book 13 and the funeral-games in 16 suffice to show the grotesque inappropriateness of his syncretistic method. The combination of mythopoeic scenes with actual events soon becomes insufferable: patience and credulity are stretched to rupture. So too with the *deorum ministeria* which throng the *Punica*. Lucan's excision of such machinery was poetically wise as well as Stoically orthodox. Juno, Venus and the Sibyl find an acceptable habitation in the world of Aeneas. In the era of Hannibal and Scipio their presence is obtrusive. The disciple of Virgil was compelled to site the Punic War in heaven as well as on earth, to mingle gods and men in a bizarre setting. Such a *bêtise* was perhaps less offensive to Roman ears than to our own; it adds nothing to the *Punica* as a *laudatio rerum Romanarum*. It is hardly less than absurd to discover that Venus persuades Vulcan to evaporate the River Trebia as a boon to the defeated Romans

[1] Butler (1909) 236.

(4.467ff.) or to learn that Juno preserved Hannibal from death at Scipio's hands (17.523ff.), just as she had saved Turnus in *Aeneid* 10. No less tedious than such contrivances is Silius' penchant for obscure information, for catalogues and for encyclopaedic *doctrina*.

His chief errors, however, were inherent in the extent and nature of his theme. In the first book, Hannibal commences the war by his treacherous attack on Saguntum; in the seventeenth we reach Scipio's victorious return to Rome after Zama. Seventeen years of military campaigning would have taxed the acumen of a greater poet than Silius. Of the six great battles of the war, four – Ticinus, Trebia, Trasimene and Cannae – occurred in close chronological proximity. Silius has the first three in Books 4 and 5 – a surfeit of carnage. Cannae is delayed until Book 9; it is not until Book 12 that Hannibal reaches the walls of Rome. The battle of the Metaurus is described in 15, Zama in 17. Needless to say, all six engagements are set-pieces treated in accordance with Homeric and Virgilian norms. Between them, Silius had perforce to intersperse details of strategic manoeuvring with highly-elaborated digressions.

Typical of these is the story of Bacchus and Falernus (7.162–211). The pretext for introducing it is that the triumphant Hannibal, faced by Fabius' delaying tactics, was ravaging Campania and burning the vines growing in the Falernian region round Mount Massicus. Silius invents an aetiology to show the reason for the proverbial excellence of Falernian wine. The story is uncomplicated. In primeval times the aged Falernus farmed this area. One day, Bacchus – his divinity for a time hidden – came to Falernus' house and was entertained by him with a simple repast. Overjoyed by the hospitality he received, the god revealed himself, miraculously bestowing on his host the gift of wine and ordaining that for evermore the region should bear the name of Falernus and be renowned for its vineyards.

In inserting such a myth, Silius recalled the story of Hercules and Cacus in *Aeneid* 8.185–275. In form it is reminiscent of the tales to be found in Hesiodic poetry, in Callimachus' *Aetia*, in Propertius' fourth book and in Ovid's *Fasti*. It owed much, in word and idea, to the myth of Philemon and Baucis in Ovid's *Metamorphoses* (8.619ff.) and that of Hyrieus in the *Fasti* (5.495ff.). Under the influence of his Ovidian exemplars, Silius turns aside from the solemnity of epic to a lighter vein. His purpose in doing so, as he states it (161–2), is to pay pious honour to the god of wine.

The lightness of the episode contrasts vividly with the gloom that surrounds it. The tale of Falernus sets in relief the impenetrable darkness and impious horror of Hannibal's recent victories at Ticinus, at Trebia and at Lake Trasimene. Bacchus' beneficent action is in symbolic antithesis to the havoc wreaked by the Carthaginians. Falernus himself is an embodiment of Italian *pietas*, who fulfils ungrudgingly his obligations towards a stranger. For that reason, he is the recipient of a divine benison. Silius portrays him with warmth and humour: he bustles about in his eagerness to please his guest (176–8); the drunkenness which follows his introduction to wine is described with a mischievous realism (199–205).

This *aition* exhibits a deftness and dexterity of touch not generally attributed to Silius. For a moment he introduces into the sombre atmosphere of the *Punica* a shaft of Ovidian brightness. Nor is it totally without relevance to the wider content of the epic. Hannibal's devastation of Campania, the land blessed by Bacchus, presages his eventual defeat. In Book 11, Silius tells how the Carthaginian army and its leader are enervated and corrupted (through the scheming of Venus) by the luxury of Capua – not least by the gifts of Bacchus put to the service of vice and excess (11.285–6, 299–302, 307–8, 406–7, 414). This demoralization of Hannibal's forces was the turning-point in the Punic War. Furthermore, the younger Scipio, the 'divine man' and figure of *pietas*, who is ultimately to humble Carthaginian might at Zama, is depicted as a new Hercules, Bacchus and Quirinus. In Book 15, when Scipio, like Hercules at the crossroads, is confronted by a choice between Virtue and Pleasure (18–128), he is reminded by the personification Virtue of those celestial beings who had passed through the portal of heaven (77–8) and whom Scipio should emulate. Bacchus appears in his role as global *triumphator* at 79–81. Because Scipio chose the path of *uirtus* (spurning the blandishments of *uoluptas* to which Hannibal and his army had fallen victim at Capua), he too achieves apotheosis. The epic ends with his triumphant procession to the Capitol, where Silius compares him first to Bacchus and then to Hercules (17.646–50). Hannibal had paid the full price of his impiety. His destruction of the vineyards, miraculously established by Bacchus himself, did not go unpunished. In the myth told by Silius in Book 7, occurring at a time when Hannibal was at the height of his power, we can see a prefiguration of his final fall from glory into wretchedness, overcome by the superior might and virtue of Scipio, a Bacchus reborn to bring salvation to Rome.

Nor was it beyond Silius' reach to attain flashes of true poetic grace. In Book 13, the god Pan intervenes to preclude the burning of Capua. The poet gives the following account of his appearance and character:

> Pan Ioue missus erat, seruari tecta uolente
> Troia, pendenti similis Pan semper et imo
> uix ulla inscribens terrae uestigia cornu.
> dextera lasciuit caesa Tegeatide capra
> uerbera laeta mouens festo per compita coetu.　　　　330
> cingit acuta comas et opacat tempora pinus,
> ac parua erumpunt rubicunda cornua fronte;
> stant aures, imoque cadit barba hispida mento.
> pastorale deo baculum, pellisque sinistrum

uelat grata latus tenerae de corpore dammae.      335
nulla in praeruptum tam prona et inhospita cautes,
in qua non, librans corpus similisque uolanti,
cornipedem tulerit praecisa per auia plantam.
interdum inflexus medio nascentia tergo
respicit arridens hirtae ludibria caudae.      340
obtendensque manum solem inferuerscere fronti
arcet et umbrato perlustrat pascua uisu.
hic, postquam mandata dei perfecta malamque
sedauit rabiem et permulsit corda furentum,
Arcadiae uolucris saltus et amata reuisit      345
Maenala; ubi, argutis longe de uertice sacro
dulce sonans calamis, ducit stabula omnia cantu.    (326–47)

*Pan had been sent by Jupiter, who wished that the Trojan dwellings be preserved – Pan who seems to float in the air, who scarcely imprints a track upon the ground with his horned hoof. His right hand wantons with a thong of Tegean goatskin as he joyfully rains blows on the festal throng at the crossroads [at the Lupercalia]. Sharp pine wreathes his tresses and casts shadow on his temples and small horns break forth from his red-glowing forehead. Up-pointed are his ears and a bristly beard juts from the point of his chin. The god carries a shepherd's crook; the skin of a young roe pleasingly hides his left side. There is no rock so steep, precipitous and inhospitable where he cannot, balancing his body like a winged bird, pass over the headlong crags with horned stride. Sometimes he looks behind him to laugh at the merry antics of his hairy tail that sprouts from the middle of his back. He protects his forehead with his hand to ward off the scorching sun, and looks here and there over the pastures with shaded eyes. When he had fulfilled the commands of Jupiter, calming the malignant frenzy and soothing the hearts of the raging troops, he hastened back to the glens of Arcady and to his beloved Maenalus, on whose holy peak he makes enchanting music far and wide with harmonious reeds, drawing all the flocks after him with his melody.*

Silius' Pan owes a debt to Ovid (cf. *Metamorphoses* 1.699ff., 11.153ff.), but the passage has an overriding originality. The style is pictorial, but not narrowly descriptive. Silius reminds his readers of shared impressions of the sylvan god, so that they can build for themselves a composite image: it is not static, but lively and ebullient, consonant with the merriment, wild strangeness, half-human, half-animal nature of Pan. Verbal and metrical finesse is shown. The positioning of *parua* and *cornua* in 332 neatly suggests the sprouting horns. The heavy spondees of 336–7 are cunningly resolved in the swift-moving dactyls that follow, as we imagine fleet-footed Pan leaping down the precipitous crags. The echo of his pipes on Mount Maenalus is evoked by the framing words *argutis...calamis*. Alliteration is placed in effective service, especially at 329–30, 336–8 and 346–7: sound follows sense but, even more important, depths of sense are added by sound. The whole ecphrasis is a finely-wrought miniature. Silius' *cura* has for once produced a bounty, but to find such 'occasional gems, one must endure the dross'.[1]

One merit of Silius, even in his less inspired episodes, is linguistic perspicuity – a facet of his work that separates him from the tortuous complexities of Statius as well as from the sterile insipidity that afflicted parts of Valerius' *Argonautica*. This clarity of diction sprang, no doubt, both from Silius' reverence for Virgil and from his adoption of the annalistic tradition in epic. But even this merit has its limitations: it induces torpor. One spark of ardent animation – a quality that Lucan and Statius perhaps possessed in excess – would often have saved Silius from the chilling decorum, the fibreless and numbing dullness that pervades the *Punica*. In Pliny's terms, there was an absence of sustained *ingenium*.

It has sometimes been remarked that the *Punica* is an epic without a hero. It is in fact Hannibal, the consummate *exemplum* of Carthaginian perfidy, that dominates and controls the narrative. He is, like Turnus in the *Aeneid* (6.89), a rebirth of Achilles, the archetypal enemy of Troy–Rome; but he is also a Punic Aeneas, leading an invading force from North Africa to Italy in fulfilment of Dido's prophecy, but, because Punic, an impious Aeneas, foredoomed to defeat. In Book 2, the people of Spain present Hannibal with an engraved shield (395–496).[2] It is a heroic attribute, bringing him into relation with both Achilles and Aeneas. Hannibal's heroism is, however, superficial, for he lacks those virtues which enabled the progeny of Aeneas ultimately to overcome Carthage. Hannibal is a hero defeated by Fate, by the fact of his Punic origin as much as by his own innate depravity. It may not have been Silius' intention, but his portrait of Hannibal has a tragic nobility; the general with an inordinate lust for blood (cf. 1.40, 59–60, etc.) can nonetheless utter an exalted tribute to Aemilius Paullus when he comes upon his corpse after Cannae (10.572–8). The younger Scipio in the *Punica* is elevated to a semi-divine status, as we have seen. Yet, like Fabius Maximus Cunctator, Paullus and even Regulus, whose sufferings are described in retrospect in Book 6 (62ff.), Scipio, when measured against Hannibal, pales into the moral wanness of Stoic impeccability. The villain of the *Punica* is its fulcrum. For Silius the Stoic Hannibal may well have been the epitome of turpitude, just as was Scipio of rectitude. The war between Carthage and Rome may well have been an illustration for him of eternal verities in a similar fashion to Statius' treatment of the Argo-Theban conflict. But fact has, at the last, vanquished philosophy. Of all the characters that throng the *Punica*, Hannibal alone has a semblance of life, is more than a puppet. Silius' laudation of Roman majesty, of Roman *fides*, *pietas* and *uirtus* could not wholly expunge the glory of its mightiest foe, however *perfidus*,

[1] Vessey (1973) 2.
[2] On the significance of the shield, see Vessey (1975) 391–405.

99

*impius* and *saeuus*: or totally erase his greatness from record. Lucan had faced a similar problem with Caesar. In both the *Bellum civile* and the *Punica*, the axial polarization of good and evil, virtue and vice, painstakingly affirmed, has failed to persuade because the poets protested too much, too often and too stridently: perilous is the path of those who mythicize in verse the documents of history.

Statius, Valerius, Silius. Three poets with three distinct styles, purposes, attainments. Only the *Silvae* and, even more positively, the *Thebaid* can be accounted successful: within their limitations. Dante placed Statius in purgatory, where he freely acknowledges the supremacy of Virgil (*Purgatorio*, Canto 21); he names his cardinal sin on earth as prodigality (Canto 22). A not unfitting fancy: Statius was lavish in all his works of the *ars* and *ingenium* with which he was unquestionably dowered. Critically, the modern world has lodged him in a more straitened confinement than did Dante: with small hope of heaven. Silius is more justly damned. As Pliny saw, he had little else than *cura*: a literary Attis, who emasculated himself before the shrine of his gods. Valerius remains an enigma. Lacking the virtues of Statius and the vices of Silius, he reveals a mediocrity that, if not golden, has appeared to some at least well-burnished silver. A tribute from Quintilian: reward enough, perhaps, for the *Argonautica*.

# 6

# MARTIAL AND JUVENAL

On the usual dating,[1] the beginning of Juvenal's literary career coincided with Martial's later years: the composition of the first satire, which contains a reference to the trial of Marius Priscus in A.D. 100, was probably contemporaneous with the epigrammatist's retirement to Spain. Martial praised three emperors, and when it was safe to do so, condemned the memory of the first: but it is essentially the age of Domitian in which he moves. His work spans the last quarter century, a medley of adulation, obscenity, and off-hand observation on a tired, neurotic world. Perhaps gloating, he writes to Juvenal from Spain, comparing town and country: he is at ease, while Juvenal is harassed in the city (12.18). Juvenal, strangely impersonal despite his spleen and violence, has nothing in reply. For one obsessed with the world of the dead, friendship could have had few attractions. Tradition has it that he mellows with time: in fact he simply writes less well after the vitriolic ninth satire, and the paradigmatic, rhetorical tenth.[2] In Satire 15 the venom returns, but it is for his first two books, Satires 1–6, that he is chiefly celebrated. With time, his manner becomes less taut and less intense, more leisurely and reflective; the later Juvenal is a declaimer's poet, preoccupied with theses. In his earlier work he castigated vice and poured scorn on the insufficiencies of virtue, rejecting the ironic manner of Horace and the sermons of Persius, to adopt a deeply pessimistic, hysterically tragic stance.[3] Martial provided him with material and characters, but the mood is all his own. Nor must we overemphasize a direct connexion between the two writers, since epigram and satire deal in common currency. Both forms are traditionally unambitious, both take life as their province – presenting sometimes, occasionally transforming; the higher flights, of epic and tragedy, are

[1] For Juvenal, see Coffey (1976) 119–23; and for Martial, Friedländer (1886) pref.

[2] Highet (1954), with his insistence that Juvenal is growing old, illustrates the tendency to explain away the change of tone by simplistic appeal to the passing of time: for example 'Book IV is the work of an ageing man' (122); 'signs of age were visible in Juvenal's Third and Fourth Books. Book III was weaker. Book IV was mellower' (138). But this is perhaps not so tiresome as the theory that Juvenal could not have been the author of the later satires, as Ribbeck (1865) thought, even though his conclusions are supported by stylistic criteria. Writers modify their manner, and without biographical evidence, we cannot say why.

[3] See, e.g., Scott (1927), and Bramble (1974) 164–73.

by strict convention avoided. But nonetheless, when that is said, literary propriety could inhibit – and on that Juvenal is emphatic. A Roman Medea in his satire on women elicits the confession that the limits of form can no longer restrain him:

> fingimus haec altum satura sumente cothurnum
> scilicet, et finem egressi legemque priorum
> grande Sophocleo carmen bacchamur hiatu,
> montibus ignotum Rutulis caeloque Latino?
> nos utinam uani. sed clamat Pontia 'feci,
> confiteor, puerisque meis aconita paraui,
> quae deprensa patent; facinus tamen ipsa peregi.'     (6.634–40)

> *Am I making the whole thing up, careless of precedents, mouthing*
> *Long-winded bombast in the old Sophoclean manner*
> *That's quite out of place here under Italian skies?*
> *How I wish that it was all nonsense! But listen to Pontia's*
> *Too-willing confession: 'I did it, I admit I gave aconite*
> *To my children. Yes, they were poisoned, that's obvious.*
> *But I was the one who killed them.'* (Tr. Green)[1]

Earlier, in his fourth satire, an account of Domitian's council about 'a fish of wondrous size', he had recharged the resources of satire with devices taken from epic – and parody of Statius.[2] Likewise, in his second, the *Aeneid* had been used to vilify and condemn the profligacies of Otho.[3] Martial, on the other hand, will not disobey convention:

> a nostris procul est omnis uesica libellis,
> Musa nec insano syrmate nostra tumet.     (4.49.7–8)

> *Any form of turgidity is alien to my works,*
> *Nor does my Muse swell with unhealthy bombast.*

Life is his theme: epic and tragedy are unreal and divorced from the world that we know, offering nothing to the simple observer of *mores* and fashion. True, Martial will sometimes stray from his course, to attempt the *genus medium* in his non-satiric poems, but without a great deal of success. A fifty line set-piece like 3.58, with its expansive, well-wrought opening:

> Baiana nostri uilla, Basse, Faustini
> non otiosis ordinata myrtetis
> uiduaque platano tonsilique buxeto
> ingrata lati spatia detinet campi,
> sed rure uero barbaroque laetatur...

---

[1] Green's Penguin Translation of Juvenal (© P. Green 1970) is used throughout. Some of the translations of Martial are my own, some loose adaptations from Ker's version (1919).

[2] See Valla on 4.94, quoting four lines of Statius' *De bello Germanico* (*FPL* 134); also Highet (1954) 258–9, and Griffith (1969) 134–50.

[3] See, for instance, Lelièvre (1958) 22–5.

*Faustinus' villa at Baiae, Bassus, has no fruitless spaces of open land, laid out with idle myrtles, sterile planes or boxwood hedges, but is happy with real country and uncultivated land...*

inspires as little enthusiasm as Statius' occasional poems, with which it has obvious affinities.[1] Another example of such dalliance with the Muse, well-written but unconvincing, is the thirtieth epigram of Book 10:

> o temperatae dulce Formiae litus,
> uos, cum seueri fugit oppidum Martis
> et inquietas fessus exuit curas
> Apollinaris omnibus locis praefert.
> non ille sanctae dulce Tibur uxoris
> nec Tusculanos Algidosue secessus
> Praeneste nec sic Antiumque miratur;
> non blanda Circe Dardanisue Caieta
> desiderantur, nec Marica nec Liris
> nec in Lucrina lota Salmacis uena.

*O well-climed Formiae, pleasant shore, you, when he escapes austere Mars' town and weary sheds unquiet cares, Apollinaris prefers to every spot. Not so highly does he prize his chaste wife's dearest Tibur, the retreats of Tusculum or Algidus, Praeneste or Antium; not so deeply does he miss the charming headland of Circe and Trojan Caieta, or Marica or Liris, or Salmacis bathed in the Lucrine stream.*

Anyone could have written that: and twenty lines follow in the same tedious vein. But, for the most part, he adheres to epigram's prevalent ethos, of rhetorical point and cynical comment, couched in everyday speech.

Juvenal, as we have seen, is less obedient to the rules of his genre and sometimes even anarchic, his language a medley of high and low, his tone contemptuous, and, in any normal sense of the words, unconstructive, negative. Tragedy no longer capped life in its horrors: hence his self-granted permission to depart from the canons of Horace and Persius – his deliberate resort from the pedestrian muse to upper reaches trodden as yet only by schoolboys and bards. He tells us in the preface to his programmatic satire that so far he has only listened – to bombastic recitations, to the nonsense of the schools. Yet he too has the training: so why spare the paper any longer? And since life is now so ghastly, why not be immodest and depart from prior tradition?[2] Irony, too urbane and content a device, is replaced by malevolent verbal extravagance, and an arch and vengeful stance. His arena is that of Lucilius, depicted as a charioteer, then later as a warrior: the *inventor* of the genre would hardly have agreed to the pretensions of the portrait. And in tone as in style the sweeping

---

[1] For Statius' *Silvae*, see above, pp. 65–76.
[2] See in particular 1.1ff., 15ff., and the comments of Bramble (1974) 164–73, on the first satire's implications that the style should now be high.

gestures are evident. His audience is passive and lacking in opinion, seeking amusement from vice, and corrupted by the ease with which the schools disgorged their poets. So Juvenal is despotic, and refuses to be virtuous: he treacherously takes part with his reader, then bullies him to admit that his tastes are sick and weak, that the world he has seduced him with is more vile than he suspected. Like the Stoic or the Cynic, for whom nothing was obscene, nothing so forthright as never to be said, Juvenal mockingly entertains us with the vice we all demand, but takes it much too far, disturbing us with half-voiced questions about the basis of our values. His ancestor is the Thersites of the *Iliad*'s second book, unwilling to acquiesce in accepted beliefs, and the butt of our distaste when our sensibilities pretend offence.[1]

Martial, by way of contrast, never plays the fool, and never makes us think. He is succinct, at the expense of others, with never a moral reflection; he is always uninvolved, protected by his reader's tastes. He is poetic – on occasions – and the rules remain intact: even Quintilian, perhaps against his will, receives an epigram (2.90). With no doubts and no anxieties about his position in society, he acts the courtier, no doubt receiving rewards, and from beneath the cover of the unobjectionably trivial or else the safely obscene, he delivers the jokes that he leads us to expect. A tradition stands behind him – venerable writers whose page was lascivious[2] – and so he stays unruffled, no victim to emotion, and without claim to be a poet. His Muse is his reader – *dictauit auditor*, as he puts it in the preface to Book 12 – and life is his theme, his justification for asking no questions: *hominem pagina nostra sapit* (10.4.10). Juvenal the misanthrope will not comply. His reader is assaulted, assumptions set at nought. His verse makes jokes in earnest, but is full of tragic colour. An emperor is invoked but once, and that without flattery.[3] Perverts are greeted with obscenities in Satires 2 and 9, but without that element of complicity which we come to expect from Martial. And as for tradition, Lucilius is brought back to life, while the Horatian mode is forgotten:[4] Persius is closer to him, but he does not use his methods.[5] Above all, he knows the dangers, and the insult, of standing as listener: *semper ego auditor tantum?* No audience could

[1] For Thersites ('The Railer'), see Elliott (1960) 130ff., and in general, the excellent study of the figure of the fool by Welsford (1935), although she overlooks Thersites.

[2] See below, p. 116 n.1.

[3] At 7.1ff. See Townend (1973) 149ff., and Rudd (1976) 84ff.

[4] For Juvenal's portrait of Lucilius – a portrait which the founder of satire would not have recognized, painted as it is in military and epic colours – see Anderson (1961a) 12 n.25, and Bramble (1974) 169ff. For the essentially humble nature of satiric *sermo* see Fiske (1920): in fact Horace followed Lucilius in keeping his Muse pedestrian. It is Juvenal who enters new territory. Apart from 1.51 where the reference stands for satire in general, Juvenal only mentions Horace in the seventh satire, as an example of a text for the schools, and a poet who composed on a full belly: 7.62 *satur est cum dicit Horatius 'euhoe'*.

[5] Significantly, though only once, Persius is cynical at the expense of his professions, in the picture of Stoicism at 3.52ff.: an instance of amoral rhetorical obfuscation, of the kind we expect from Juvenal.

dictate to him: he sees the hypocrisy and collusion of the poet and his victim. Martial's reader is not for him: self-expression, pretended or real, replaces the urge to pander.[1] Like Persius, he knows that poetry cannot simply cater for hackneyed, senseless tastes.[2] Martial, an accepted poet, a figure from the ranks, would have recognized the content, but hardly the spirit, of Juvenal's dread questions; for patrician rage was out of date, or at least an unsatiric gesture, conservative though the form might be. Irony was the usual tool, but an unsuitable vehicle for Juvenal's *indignatio*. Epigram admittedly had never been the form for matters of much moment – Catullus, too, was trivial, though more sincere than Martial: enmity, love, the social *faux pas*, and sometimes poetry – those were his themes, but he entered them and lived them. His moods were uncommissioned, his technique more random and honest. But satire until Juvenal's day had answers as well as questions: steady, sane and sober, the form avoided the emotions in favour of normative morals. In Horace it was individuals, accepted individuals, and not society that sinned. For Persius, the norm was Stoic, and though the writing was brilliant, the answers were systematic. Neither faltered in their assumptions, and neither questioned virtue. It was not usual, even amongst the older Cynics, for negativity and anger to extend beyond human transgression to the basis of our morals: nature, or the golden age, were always there as a salve. Hence Juvenal's question – given that the world is wrong, our world, the world of Nero or Domitian, no matter with names and dates, can we play the Cato now, or are our values dying? – could not have fallen on sympathetic ears, at least amongst conservatives; could not have broken down reserves, except with some discomfiture.

Martial, indeed, would have found Juvenal too powerful. Yet even though he is a minor figure, he sets the precedent for later epigram: his cynicism, his invective, his obscenity – these were the qualities his imitators strove for. He never wearies of the credentials of tradition, and hence he never stumbles. He owes little to the Greeks, if we follow his own version. In the preface to the first book, he only mentions Romans: *sic scribit Catullus, sic Marsus, sic Pedo, sic Gaetulicus, sic quicumque perlegitur* 'So writes Catullus, Marsus, Pedo, Gaetulicus, anyone who is popular.' A popular form: these authors are read through and through. Pliny likewise omits the Greeks (5.3.5–6). Yet in the first century A.D., Argentarius, the second Nicarchus and Lucillius are composing epigrams in Greek in the pointed rhetorical vein. Meleager's *Garland*, collected around 80 B.C., and covering two centuries, does not offer parallels: except, perhaps, for Leonidas, who could be cynical and scabrous.[3] Nor does Latin display the mordant note until the time of Catullus: Ennius merely set

---

[1] The first satire is full of insistences that he must and will write satire: see Bramble (1974) 164f.

[2] In his first satire, Persius is at pains to show that few are left with discernment. Juvenal's audience was probably rather wider, but he maintains a similar stance.

[3] See Gow and Page (1965) I 107–39 and II 307–98.

the style for inscriptions, while Catulus, Aedituus, and Licinus were mannered poets of love, contemporaries of Meleager.[1] Catullus had no fixed metre; but elegiacs and hendecasyllables predominate. Nor, in this like Meleager, does he call his poems *epigrammata*; instead, they are *uersiculi, ineptiae*, or *nugae*. As much an iambist as an epigrammatist, Catullus looks forward at times to the abrasive side of Martial. In the ancient world 'iambic' is a tone of voice – biting, angry, aloof – and epigram has its iambic side. Archilochus and Hipponax, the impassioned iambists of Greece, were matched in Rome by figures as disparate as Lucilius, Catullus, Horace and Bibaculus: so runs the list of the grammarian Diomedes (*GLK* 1 485). Of Marsus, Pedo and Gaetulicus we cannot really speak. But in Greek the trend is clear: the second of the two great anthologies, the *Crown* of Philip, published under Caligula, is witty and pointed, whereas the *Garland* of Meleager was polished and sentimental; and the satiric epigram, the form we associate with Martial, has arrived on the scene with the work of Nicarchus and Lucillius. But, as we have noted, on Greek epigram Martial is silent, and Pliny is too: so rather than a direct debt, perhaps better to assume that developments in Rome had been the same – that the successors of Catullus had written like the Greeks, in the declamatory pointed fashion, abandoning the seductive tone of Alexandria to pursue the affiliation with iambic.

Martial is Juvenal's senior, and, as we have said, his work covers the twenty years which provided the satirist with the matter for much of his first two books – the twenty-year period during which the satirist still listened. Born somewhere between A.D. 38 and 41 at Bilbilis in Spain, Martial came to Rome in A.D. 64, to be received by Seneca and Lucan, the important writers of the day. Although he appears to have composed juvenilia (1.113), we have nothing to show for his first sixteen years; then, in A.D. 80, he produced the *Liber spectaculorum*, on the occasion of the opening of the Flavian Amphitheatre by Titus. Books 13 and 14 of our present collection – the *Xenia* and *Apophoreta*, brief, sometimes ingenious mottos for presents – followed in A.D. 84, or thereabouts, and then, in A.D. 86, appeared Books 1 and 2 of his epigrams, more substantial, but still very much to the popular taste. A new book was published roughly each year from A.D. 87 to 96; in A.D. 97, a shorter edition of Books 10 and 11 was produced for the Princeps (12.8), then, in A.D. 98, he returned to his homeland.[2] Finally, in the winter of A.D. 101, after a three-year gap, Book 12 was published from Spain. Martial's death is recorded by Pliny in a letter of A.D. 104 (*Epist.* 3.21.1). His first nine books appeared under Domitian, and contain the expected adulation. He changed his tune in the remaining three, now damning the tyrant,

---

[1] See *The Late Republic*, p. 1.
[2] 10.103.7ff. He had already spent some time abroad, in Cisalpine Gaul, whence he published the third book: see 3.1.

to laud the new masters, Nerva and Trajan. There are 1,561 epigrams in all: 1,235 written in elegiacs; 238 in hendecasyllables; 77 in scazons, and a few in hexameters and iambics. He knew, or at least addressed, the important figures of the Flavian literary establishment – Silius, Valerius, Pliny, Quintilian – and Juvenal as well.

Of Juvenal's career we know much less. Birth dates of A.D. 67, 60 and 55 have been suggested, but arguments are not conclusive.[1] Of his name, it has been argued that the gentile name Junius suggests possibly Spanish origin, while Juvenalis, his cognomen, is perhaps a sign of lowly birth.[2] Much has been made of an inscription from Aquinum – a place seemingly close to the satirist (3.318ff.); but it is unlikely that we shall ever know for certain if the Junius Juvenalis there mentioned, *duumvir quinquennalis*, *flamen* of Vespasian, and tribune of the soldiers, is the poet of the satires.[3] Juvenal claims autopsy of Egypt (15.45), but that need not have been as a soldier; nor is there strong reason for linking the reference to Ceres at the end of the third satire with the Ceres honoured in the inscription. We have several ancient lives, but they represent a single tradition.[4] According to the common source,[5] Juvenal, son of a wealthy freedman, declaimed into middle age – a story which may be based on extrapolation from the satires themselves (1.15ff.), and perhaps, to some extent, on conflation with Horace, *libertino patre natus* (*Sat.* 1.6.6). Then follows the tale of exile: Juvenal, now an old man, is sent to hold command on the furthest borders of Egypt, in disgrace for his comments about Paris the actor. The story is a part of Domitian's bad press, a concoction of later antiquity, intended to supply the wanted evidence for a writer about whom hardly anything was known – yet in recent times the tale has been revived: bitter and poor from his exile, Juvenal starts to write to voice the hatreds of his youth.[6] In fact, we know no more than that his output is a product of the first quarter of the second century. If he was active in the nineties, our only evidence would be Martial's seventh book, composed in A.D. 91–2, where the epithet *facunde*, addressed to Juvenal in the ninety-first epigram, perhaps suggests poetry: but declamation could explain it too, and Juvenal, it seems, had been a rhetorician. In A.D. 102, he might have been engaged on Book 1 of his satires – if that is what Martial has in mind when, in that year, he describes Juvenal as leading the life of a *cliens*. The clues are slight, but enough to make one think of the wretched existence portrayed in the early satires:

---

[1] As Coffey (1976) 120 points out, A.D. 55, the date offered by the *Vita*, is too early. Syme (1958) 774f. argues for A.D. 67, Highet (1954) 5 and 11–12, unconvincingly, for A.D. 60.

[2] See Coffey ibid.

[3] For details, see Highet (1954) 32ff.

[4] See Highet (1954) 21ff. and 238 with bibliography.

[5] Text in Clausen (1959) 179. For the other *Vitae* see Jahn (1851) 386–90.

[6] Highet's book in particular is vitiated by this biographical mode of approach, but most studies show traces of it.

dum tu forsitan inquietus erras
clamosa, Iuuenalis, in Subura
aut collem dominae teris Dianae;
dum per limina te potentiorum
sudatrix toga uentilat uagumque
maior Caelius et minor fatigat. . .                    (12.18)

*while no doubt you restlessly wander in the noisy Subura, Juvenal, or tread the hill
of lady Diana; or while you fan yourself by the movement of your sweaty toga, as
you visit the porches of the great, wearied by climbing the two Caelian hills. . .*

The comparison which follows with Martial's easy life in Spain would hardly
be charitable, unless Juvenal's life in Rome were a figment taken from his
poetry. Ancient writers were often characterized in terms of the contents of
their work,[1] so if Martial is following suit, Book 1 of the satires is already under
way. But perhaps after all there is an element of *Schadenfreude*: at least, in
Martial 7.24, animosity is denied, which perhaps makes one suspect that the
friendship was not a smooth or simple matter. Beyond this – and Martial is
the only contemporary who even mentions Juvenal – we glean a few dates
from the satires themselves, some of them perhaps indicating time of composition, though usually not yielding more than a *terminus post quem*, some of
them dramatic. Marius Priscus, tried in A.D. 100, is mentioned twice (1.47–50
and 8.120), perhaps because Pliny invested the case with some notoriety (*Epist.*
2.11.12 and 6.29.9). In the fourth satire there is an allusion to Domitian's
death in A.D. 96, although the *mise en scène* belongs to A.D. 82 (4.153–4).
Tacitus has been invoked to explain the second satire when it refers to Otho's
antics as worthy of annals or history: the dates in question would be A.D. 105,
when the *Histories* were under way, or A.D. 109, when published, or again,
A.D. 115 in the case of the *Annals*. But the passage has a general ring, and no
names are mentioned (2.102–3). We must wait till Satire 10 for Tacitean influence, in the portrait of Sejanus. Our other dates belong to the second and third
decades of the second century: Trajan's harbour at Ostia, finished in A.D. 113,
is mentioned at 12.75–81; a comet and earthquake of A.D. 115 occur at 6.407–
12; the address to Hadrian[2] at 7.1ff. probably antedates his departure from Rome
in A.D. 121; and finally, at 15.27, there is a reference to an event of A.D. 127.[3]

In the first, third, and fifth satires, it is Martial's Rome of which he writes;
and elsewhere in the first two books the scenery and the characters are unmis-
takably those of epigram.[4] But the scope is more extensive, the colours more
garish, the mood more fantastic. Juvenal's world is a mixture of memory,

---

[1] For instance, Gallus in the tenth *Eclogue*, and Tibullus in Hor. *Odes* 1.33 are depicted after the
manner of their elegies.

[2] Some argue that the emperor is Trajan, or even Domitian – without much likelihood: see Rudd
(1976) 85ff.

[3] For further details, see Highet (1954) 11ff.          [4] See Townend (1973) 148f.

imagination, and literary reminiscence, peopled by monsters and caricatures. Twenty years had passed, allowing the times of Domitian to become a paradise of crime, corruption, luxury and injustice. Juvenal's *cena*, the inequitable dinner of Satire 5, is based on Martial 3.60, a flatter, more objective account of the gap between client and patron:

> cum uocer ad cenam non iam uenalis ut ante,
>  cur mihi non eadem quae tibi cena datur?
> ostrea tu sumis stagno saturata Lucrino,
>  sugitur inciso mitulus ore mihi:
> sunt tibi boleti, fungos ego sumo suillos:
>  res tibi cum rhombo est, at mihi cum sparulo.
> aureus inmodicis turtur te clunibus implet,
>  ponitur in cauea mortua pica mihi.
> cur sine te ceno cum tecum, Pontice, cenem?
>  sportula quod non est prosit. edamus idem.

*When I am asked to dinner, not, as before, a dependant on the dole, why is the same food not served to me as you? You enjoy oysters fattened in the Lucrine lake, I suck a mussel, and cut my lips on the shell; you have mushrooms, I get some dubious fungus— you tackle turbot, I tackle brill; you take your fill of a golden turtle-dove, its rump all bloated with fat, while I am served a magpie that died in its cage. Why do I dine without you, Ponticus, although I dine with you? Let us make something of the abolition of the dole: let us eat the same.*

But here, apart from the black humour about the magpie dead in its cage, and the point of the penultimate line, there is little to remind us of Juvenal's scathing manner. Likewise, the third satire owes something to Martial 3.30:

> sportula nulla datur; gratis conuiua recumbis:
>  dic mihi quid Romae, Gargiliane, facis?
> unde tibi togula est et fuscae pensio cellae?
>  unde datur quadrans? unde uir es Chiones?
> cum ratione licet dicas te uiuere summa,
>  quod uiuis, nulla cum ratione facis.

*The dole exists no longer; your reward is now a free dinner. Tell me, Gargilianus, what can you do in Rome? Where do you get your threadbare toga, where the rent for your dark garret? How do you get the money for a bath, how do you afford Chione? You might say that you've rationalized your life to the last farthing, but your living at all is not a rational act.*

Chione, the garret, the penury – all reappear in Juvenal, and the third satire actually contains the words *quid Romae faciam?* (3.41). But Martial lacks bitterness and hyperbole, simply supplying the idea, 'a joker', as Townend calls him,[1] 'never shocked or distressed by the most horrific details that he

---

[1] Ibid.

relates from everyday life'. Likewise, the first satire recreates the world of Martial. To quote from Townend again:

when Juvenal opens his first sketch of Roman life in i.23, he leaves no doubt that this is Martial's scene, already several years, probably as much as twenty, in the past. Mevia, Crispinus, Matho are all Flavian figures from Martial, as Massa and Carus are informers from Domitian's last years, and the *magni delator amici* in line 33 can hardly be other than the great Regulus. Marius Priscus, the one apparent exception because his prosecution falls in the year 100 under Trajan, is nonetheless a creature of Domitian's reign, already in line for the proconsulate of Africa for 97/8, and perhaps actually appointed before Domitian was murdered in September 96. What Juvenal is doing in this section, and throughout the rest of the first satire, is to announce that his material belongs to a previous generation but is still first-rate scandal, to be reproduced with mock horror, and enjoyed with gusto.

True, as far as concerns Martial, and Juvenal's immersion in the past. But given Juvenal's fascination with bygone corruption, is he simply amoral, is his horror merely false?

There has been much debate. Critics have differed, some claiming Juvenal for a rhetorician, some for a social realist, others for a moralist – but not that many for a satirist.[1] Some appear worried that his characters are dead: but that hardly affects the issue. Given that his Rome is a recreation from the past, do his writings simply amuse, or imply that life might be different? Do we require a moral solution? Must his writings always be faithful? Ulrich Knoche, in his book on Roman satire, goes some way – further than most critics – towards answering these questions. Warning against the verisimilitude of Juvenal's Rome, he remarks on his subjectivity yet his apparent lack of philosophic commitment:

The individual case is usually raised to the level of the norm and for this reason the individual picture itself is in turn raised to the monumental. The picture is meant to be the direct expression of the poet's thought and opinion with all their emotion and fervour. In Juvenal there is, generally speaking, no overlapping of pictures and thought as is perhaps characteristic of Persius. But there is an intensification of thought through an extremely concentrated build-up of successive pictures in a step-by-step process. Judgment as a rule results automatically from this without further deliberation and then it almost seems as if Juvenal just records it.[2]

Which, I think, is to say that there is no direct moral intervention, no evangelistic design: the images are not informed by any obvious idea, the process of

---

[1] H. A. Mason in Sullivan (1963) 93–167, for instance, stresses the quality of rhetorical entertainment in Juvenal, denying him moral concern, while Wiesen (1963) attempts to exculpate him from the charge of moral anarchy by appeal to individual maxims; Green (1967), on the other hand, in the preface to his translation, emphasizes the social aspect. An important study of rhetoric in Juvenal is that by De Decker (1913).

[2] Knoche tr. Ramage (1975) 152.

selection is apparently random and objective, but at root intensely personal. Emotion is lavished on the object, not on its significance. Juvenal is possessive with his material, but will not arrange it into easy patterns or expected sermons; and so he abandons the precedent of Horace, with all his disguising irony, and the methods of Persius, for whom reality was a web of Stoic prohibitions and ideals. To quote from Knoche again:

He confronts monstrous depravity, which he identifies everywhere, bravely and boldly as an individual. He is not the man to take refuge in the realms of mythology as so many other poets of the time did. He identifies anger and indignation as the driving forces of his satiric poetry, and these are genuine and strong. It is not fair either to Juvenal's attitude or to his poetic achievement to brush him off as a declaimer, for as such he would not be part of his subject, and what he had to say would have only a virtuoso value. Juvenal's poetry aims at being a personal creed, and the poet is always directly concerned with his subject. Actually, he could be criticised for an excess of inner commitment rather than the opposite. The subject matter, as a matter of fact, takes him prisoner, and he hardly ever has the power to separate himself from it and to raise himself above it. This is the powerful source of his descriptive strength, but it is also probably the main reason that Horace's joy in understanding, especially understanding the weaknesses of his fellow man, is missing in him, as is the ironic laughter which finds its high point in the amiable self-irony of the earlier satirist.

From this outlook of his Juvenal gathers the power to praise and condemn without compromise, the right to make everything either black or white. Attempts have been made to deny him this right also, since it has been asserted that he lacked any ideal that had to be based on philosophical principles. Certainly, while the influence of popular moral philosophy, especially that with a Stoic direction, on Juvenal's satires may be indisputable, a philosopher the poet most certainly was not, and he himself rejected a commitment to philosophy. But a guiding principle is by no means missing from his judgments on this account.

His opinion is firmly and clearly determined by his wide practical experience and his respect for the old Roman traditions; he clings firmly to these. And since the life of his time ran directly contrary to these ideals, because he also recognised the impossibility of bringing the old values into play again generally, and because, moreover, all of this appeared to him to be natural necessity arising from the human plan, he had to pass unilateral judgment, and frequently with a sharpness and accentuation which from the modern point of view does not always completely suit the subject. This, however, is no *declamatio* (declamation), but in spite of all the strangeness in the individual instance, the indignation is always genuine and sincere. Here is where the essential point of this brittle poetic personality with its fundamental pessimism lies. Of course, personal disillusionment and bitterness may have had a part to play in shaping his conception of life, but this determines the degree of his censure, not its subject matter and direction.[1]

Knoche's position is possibly too simple: Juvenal can be more distanced and less positive than he suggests; nor does he take into account the less abrasive

---

[1] Ibid. 150–1.

output of the later books. But his analysis is intelligent and approaches more closely to Juvenal's general ethos than many more recent discussions: more closely, for instance, than H. A. Mason's assessment, which finds no moral centre, and unfairly condemns him through comparison with the confidence of Johnson's unquestioned moral standards; or D. Wiesen's apologia, which attempts vindication by appeal to moral apophthegms taken out of context.[1] Juvenal, it must be repeated, is a satirist, not a moralist. He does not record, or pass immediate, obvious judgement: he creates, and closes in on chimaeras, pretending uncertainty, to make us uncertain too. We are assaulted by the attractions of vice, attractions that he has fabricated, but then we are refused the prerogative of coming to a verdict. Seduced by the glamour of a world he forces on us, we find our morals failing when we try to interpose objections: for Juvenal will allow no absolutes, no self-satisfied ideals. Black honesty is his only retort to our feeble cries for justice, yet somehow it unnerves us more. Myths which nourished ancestors are exposed for what they are – easy and insubstantial, the progeny of false rhetoric and poetic nostalgia. Vice and corruption had shocked, or titillated before – but puritan answers were present, in the shape of golden age myths and pastoral idylls. Utopianism had been the keynote of much popular philosophy,[2] and the Romans with their sense of original sin and collective guilt – their feeling that Romulus and Laomedon had somehow mortgaged their innocence[3] – were inordinately disposed to excuse their unwillingness, or inability, to reform by self-righteous identification with caricatures of virtue, with honour now lost. Juvenal, by way of answer, is negative, or at least assumes a negative posture, in order to question the values that we vaunt, but sometimes more than that: for negativity on occasions can redeem outworn ideals. Pretending to worthlessness, through the *persona* of the perverted Naevolus, the querulous male prostitute of the ninth satire, or through the indignant but ineffectual client of the first book, Juvenal's way is to intimate that our golden age yearnings are literary, self-conscious and futile, that his are being poisoned too, by the insufferable communal worldliness, but that, because at least he has some insight, his own corruption is less. Not an innocent, and perhaps, except for intimations, never one, Juvenal takes hell as a given fact, as something banal; he is insistent but resigned, sometimes persecuted, and yet he never grovels: there is no overt self-pity, little pity for others except occasionally glimpsed – but then maybe that is because it is he himself that suffers, with his regretful laughter and censorious anger, far more than his unfeeling crowd. Yet although he will entertain no solutions, he is not the monumental despairer, he never dabbles in *ennui*, he is

---

[1] See above, p. 110 n. 1.
[2] See Ferguson (1975) and the important collection of texts in Lovejoy and Boas (1935).
[3] See Jal (1963) 406–11.

never seen directly commanding his creatures, is never so unkind as to rise superior to his figments – in this, so different from Petronius, the detestable ring-master, a figure that could have occurred in his satires, albeit dead and maybe harmless. His bitterness alone, undeprived of energy and sometimes illumination, acts as a salve in the world which Rome has ruined, a world where worthless vices have tantalized moralists and despoiled their credibility, because they could not laugh. No doubt in some of his readers the moral sense was too trite for discomfiture; but some, at least, must have squirmed, not so much because they recognized themselves amongst his monsters, but because they saw their values indicted, as archaic and inadequate.

Martial is no match for his successor in seriousness of tone, but he tells us of the times that Juvenal had lived through before he began to write, of the bygone society that provided him with material for satire. Juvenal openly admits that his characters are dead:

> experiar quid concedatur in illos
> quorum Flaminia tegitur cinis atque Latina.        (1.170–1)

> *For myself, I shall try my hand on the famous dead, whose ashes*
> *Rest beside the Latin and the Flaminian Ways.*

And the dangers he envisages as attending the writing of satire are just as artificial, survivals from the past:

> pone Tigellinum: taeda lucebis in illa
> qua stantes ardent qui fixo gutture fumant,
> et latum media sulcum deducis harena.        (1.115–17)

> *But name an Imperial favourite, and you will soon enough*
> *Blaze like these human torches, half-choked, half-grilled to death,*
> *Those calcined corpses they drag with hooks from the arena*
> *And leave a broad black trail behind them in the sand.*

Nero's favourite, Tigellinus, is selected to illustrate the risks of the satirist's profession: but Tigellinus is dead, chosen like the other figures to make us recall a stereotype, a past where colours are stronger, but a past that has infected the present, and a past which might recur. Horace had declined to attack any living person when told of the dangers of satire:

> sed hic stilus haud petet ultro
> quemquam animantem et me ueluti custodiet ensis
> uagina tectus.        (*Sat.* 2.1.39–41)

> *But this pen of mine will not gratuitously assail any living person but will protect me,*
> *like a sword laid up in its sheath.*

That seems to have influenced Juvenal when he professed to restrain his freedom of speech. But at a more general level all three extant satirists appear to have paid court to the rhetorical theory of humour: jests must be constructive, not aimed in any spirit of vindictiveness at accidental defects, directed instead at culpable faults. It would have been illiberal, according to theory, to deliver indiscriminate broadsides at individuals; hence epigram, iambic, and satire – although in the last case there was the related tradition about the legal and personal perils of mentioning names – made the equitable insistence that their verse contained no malice, no *animus* against persons. Instead, although sometimes with irony, and sometimes self-contradiction, they adopted the liberal posture, presuming to defend the individual and his right to anonymous contemplation of vice other than his own. Martial, like the other practitioners of the lower genres, claims to take the general and the typical as his province, disregarding individuals: hence no offence to reputation or privacy. He sums up the doctrine at 7.12.9: *parcere personis, dicere de uitiis* 'to spare the individual, and talk about the vice'. Persons will be spared, in favour of generalities. The policy is stated elsewhere: at the very start, in the preface to Book 1, where he expresses the intention to avoid personal attacks – contrary to the practice of the older authors, meaning Catullus, and probably Lucilius – also in random epigrams scattered throughout the collection, for instance 2.23, 7.12, and 9.95. So when at the end of his first satire, Juvenal talks of the dangers of mentioning names, and says that his intention is to satirize the dead, he not only has in mind the conventional fear of the law relating to libel, but is also sending up the equally conventional theory appertaining to charity in humour. In attacking the dead he pretends to avoid the opprobrium attached to invective against the living – to be devoid of malice, a gentleman acquainted with the polite theories of rhetoric. But his conflation of the dangers of libel with the theory of the liberal jest turns out to be negative and sardonic: by exchanging malice towards the living for malice towards the dead, he incurs the wrath of his reader. For through this deliberately tasteless gesture he implies that his audience is smug and respectable, far too content to view a generalized spectacle of vice from a position of comfort. We do not wish to be reminded of the way we might react to his criticism, of the way that our self-righteouness has necessitated flight from the present and refuge in safe stereotypes taken from the past. True, the exemplary status of names now dead and gone allows satire and epigram a general dimension: rhetorical education ensured a wide publicity for the anecdotes and associations surrounding the names of famous men. *Exempla* literature – typical stories with self-contained morals, like the tale of Cato's Stoic death, or Sulla's cruel proscriptions – provided a storehouse of symbols, a short-hand for satire. But Juvenal, the reader wishes, might have been more tactful in telling us what we want, in reminding us of the rhetorical techniques at his disposal: his fault is that of honesty, of being too explicit about the conventions of his genre – and, it must be said, of wishing to wound through pointed bad taste.[1]

Martial, too, has his share of bad taste, but in theory all is defined and correct. There is no wish to outrage the reader, merely the desire to produce an acceptable shock. As at the feast of the Saturnalia, so in epigram there is the opportunity for a reversal of the normal code of behaviour. But the reversal is institutionalized, as much a part of the Roman way of life as the stern morality of Cato which on occasions it replaces:

> triste supercilium durique seuera Catonis
>   frons et aratoris filia Fabricii
> et personati fastus et regula morum,
>   quidquid et in tenebris non sumus, ite foras.
> clamant ecce mei 'Io Saturnalia' uersus:
>   et licet et sub te praeside, Nerua, libet.
> lectores tetrici salebrosum ediscite Santram:
>   nil mihi uobiscum est: iste liber meus est.          (11.2)

*Begone sad frowns and rigid Cato's pursed brow, daughters of Fabricius from the plough, masks of disdain and moral rules – all the things we are not when private in darkened rooms. See, my verse proclaims the Saturnalia: with Nerva as my emperor there is no interdiction: reversal is my pleasure. Go learn by rote the arid pedant Santra,[2] all prudish readers: my business is not with you. This book is mine alone.*

Martial is the court jester, his role so well defined that nobody can take offence. Respectable men, orators and statesmen, had written epigrams before him: Pliny cites grave precedents and Martial does as well. Domitian, like Nerva, had been instructed in the topsy-turvy rationale of the form – epigram is not the place for traditional Roman morals:

> contigeris nostros, Caesar, si forte libellos,
>   terrarum dominum pone supercilium.
> consueuere iocos uestri quoque ferre triumphi:
>   materiam dictis nec pudet esse ducem.
> qua Thymelen spectas derisoremque Latinum,
>   illa fronte precor carmina nostra legas.
> innocuos censura potest permittere lusus:
>   lasciua est nobis pagina, uita proba.          (1.4)

*If by any chance, Caesar, you come across my books, do not wear the look that sternly rules the world. Your triumphs are accustomed to jests and frivolities, nor is there disrespect when wit sends up a general. I beg you to read my poems with the expression that you have when you watch disreputable mimes. Innocuous verse has no need of a censor: my page is lascivious, my life without rebuke.*

---

[1] On the theory of humour and disclaimer of malice, see further Bramble (1974) 190ff.
[2] A grammarian of Republican times.

Catullus, Ovid, and Pliny had made similar protestations: literature is one thing, life is quite another.[1] Martial has a lot to say about his chosen genre: there are prose prefaces to Books 1, 2, 8, 9 and 12, and in addition many poems which belong to the area of literary apologetics. Epigram is thin – *tenuis*, whereas tragedy and epic are fat – *pinguis*.[2] Martial's poems are *nugae*, or *ioci*, slight occasional pieces, with few literary pretensions. The parallel with mime is frequently adduced. In the preface to Book 1, he mentions the games of Flora:

> epigrammata illis scribuntur qui solent spectare Florales

> *epigram is written for those whose pleasure is in watching the plays at the Floralia.*

Similarly, at 9.28 he likens himself to the mimic actor Latinus, calling himself a member of the guild of *mimi*, careful nonetheless to justify his private ways and remain the servant of the emperor:

> sed nihil a nostro sumpsit mea uita theatro
> et sola tantum scaenicus arte feror:
> nec poteram gratus domino sine moribus esse:
> interius mentes inspicit ille deus.
> uos me laurigeri parasitum dicite Phoebi,
> Roma sui famulum dum sciat esse Iouis. (9.28.5–10)

> *But my own life has not been influenced in any way by the theatre I present, and it is only through my art that I have affinities with mime. Nor could I have pleased the emperor my master if my morals were deficient: that god on earth sees into the recesses of our minds. You may call me a mimic, an inferior member of laurelled Phoebus' guild, as long as Rome is certain that I am a servant of her lord.*

Cautious and respectful, Martial has no doubts about his position in society. His mode is *sal Romanus*, Roman wit, more crude and abusive than its Greek counterpart, *sal Atticus*: he has licence, *lasciuia*, *petulantia*, the freedom to say whatever he wants, in a forthright brutal way – this he calls *simplicitas*, the deliberate employment of words which elsewhere would have been shocking and abrupt. But unlike Juvenal the satirist he never intends offence. He will titillate, he will shock: but that is merely part of a game whose rules are known. He is so hedged around with defences, with excuses and apologies, that no exception can be taken.

Finally, before a survey of some elements in Juvenal's satires, a word on Martial's humour, and the structure of his poems. Kruuse[3] makes the distinction between emotional, metaphoric humour, and intellectual, logical humour –

---

[1] Catull. 16.5–6, Ov. *Trist.* 2.353–60, Plin. *Epist.* 7.9; cf. Apul. *Apol.* 11, Auson. *Idyll.* 360f., *Anth. Pal.* 12.258.

[2] Catullus, his predecessor, is variously called *tenuis*, *argutus*, *lepidus*, *tener*, and *doctus*. Epic is criticized at, for instance, 3.45.1–2; 4.29.8; 4.49.3–6; 5.53.1–2; 9.50; 10.35.5–7; 14.1.11. See above, p. 102, for the realism of epigram, as against epic and tragic bombast; and, e.g., 8.3.19–20 *at tu Romanos lepido sale tingue libellos:* | *adgnoscat mores uita legatque suos.*

[3] Kruuse (1941) 248f.

the first of which relies upon the single image as the comic vehicle, the second, upon a logical or paradoxical argument, comprehended in entirety. The humour of the single image is obviously self-contained, whilst that of the intellectual, argumentative poem is a function of all its parts. Martial's humour belongs in the main to this second kind, where what matters is the whole, together with the qualities of point and paradox that are dependent on the whole. The preparation for the point, or the paradox, is sometimes amusing in itself, but more often than not, the poem relies upon a witty, intellectual conclusion, without which it would be almost meaningless. Concision and brevity are the distinguishing feature of Martial's final apophthegms. Sometimes it is a single word that concludes the poem, more often, a pair of words, or else a shortish phrase: the tendency is to compress, and jolt the reader's expectations. In terms of organization, there are, according to Kruuse, two main types of structure, the bipartite and the tripartite. In the first, the reader's curiosity is aroused by some statement or proposition, then satisfied by a final commentary or question. In the second, to this basic pattern of proposition and commentary, or proposition and question, a third element is added, usually one of reply: hence we find schemes of proposition–question–reply; question–reply–commentary; and occasionally proposition followed by two questions. Not all of Kruuse's instances are equally convincing, but it is fair to say that the majority of the epigrams fall into the categories he describes; and it is, perhaps, here, in the intellectual organization of his pieces, that Martial's merits most truly reside. His wit is ordered, on occasions too much so, but there is little feeling for language: the words he uses are normally secondary to a governing conceit or an intellectualized scheme.

Juvenal too will build up to a climax, or paradox – but he has more feeling for words, for their epic, or vernacular qualities, and often the force of his wit derives from a single word or phrase, strategically placed at the beginning or end of a line. Sometimes it is the trivial which his rhetorical development sets in relief. Of the many horrors of city life the culmination is – bad poetry under a blazing sun:

> ego uel Prochytam praepono Suburae:
> nam quid tam miserum, tam solum uidimus, ut non
> deterius credas horrere incendia, lapsus
> tectorum adsiduos ac mille pericula saeuae
> urbis et Augusto recitantes mense poetas? (3.5–9)

> *Myself, I would value*
> *A barren offshore island more than Rome's urban heart:*
> *Squalor and isolation are minor evils compared*
> *To this endless nightmare of fires and collapsing houses,*
> *The cruel city's myriad perils – and poets reciting*
> *Their work in August!*

Likewise, in the eighth satire, the technique is to pinpoint the unimportant and the laughable in order to increase our sense of a need for real values. Nero's crimes are comparable to those of Orestes; but the Roman comes out as the worse – because he wrote an epic:

> par Agamemnonidae crimen, sed causa facit rem
> dissimilem: quippe ille deis auctoribus ultor
> patris erat caesi media inter pocula. sed nec
> Electrae iugulo se polluit aut Spartani
> sanguine coniugii, nullis aconita propinquis
> miscuit, in scaena numquam cantauit Orestes,
> Troica non scripsit. (8.215–21)

> *Orestes' crime was the same, but circumstances made it*
> *A very dissimilar case* – he *killed with divine sanction*
> *To avenge a father slain in his cups. Orestes never*
> *Had Electra's blood on his head, he never murdered*
> *His Spartan wife, or mixed up a dose of belladonna*
> *For any close relative. He never sang on the stage*
> *Or composed a Trojan epic.*

In both of these cases Juvenal reserves his paradox till the end of a progression, but the development is less highly organized than the type we find in epigram. There is nothing especially intellectual about either of these passages – and perhaps that is one reason why we sense a kind of nihilism. Nor is there an obvious structure in the way he arrives at his point. Instinctive and emotional – albeit with reserve – Juvenal lies in wait with his apparent moral anarchy to shock us into judgement. His procedure is accumulative and verbal, the opposite of Martial's.

Juvenal is preoccupied with realities – trivial, sordid, and irksome – yet there is little *simplicitas*, little of Martial's candid speaking. He values words too highly, and cannot resist hyperbole: his verse is loud, though brittle, its texture rich, concerned for much of the time with setting the past against the present, the noble against the real, or simply with the glorification of horrors and vices that go beyond all precedent. As Quintilian says: *tum est hyperbole uirtus, cum res ipsa, de qua loquendum est, naturalem modum excessit* 'hyperbole is permissible, when the subject matter to be discussed is something which has exceeded all natural limits' (*Inst.* 8.6.76). Hence, because of Juvenal's conception that vice is at its peak, the exaggerations, the grandiloquence – the struggle to create a grotesque yet epic pageant out of the Rome that inhabits his mind. At the outset of this study, we referred to Satire 6, and Juvenal's departure from the tradition of Persius and Horace: because the Medeas and Clytemnestras of myth are now once more alive, active and horrific in contemporary Rome, the *lex priorum* no longer holds, and stronger language is needed. He will rifle the resources of the tragedians and epicists, since life is larger than myth. We have seen from Satire 8 that Nero's crimes were worse than those of Agamemnon's son. And we find a similar lesson in his account of cannibalism in Egypt:

> nos miranda quidem, sed nuper consule Iunco
> gesta super calidae referemus moenia Copti,
> nos uolgi scelus et cunctis grauiora cothurnis,
> nam scelus, a Pyrrha quamquam omnia syrmata uoluas,
> nullus apud tragicos populus facit. accipe, nostro
> dira quod exemplum feritas produxerit aeuo.          (15.27–32)

> *The incident I shall relate,*
> *Though fantastic enough, took place within recent memory,*
> *Up-country from sunbathed Coptos, an act of mob violence*
> *Worse than anything in the tragedians. Search through the mythical*
> *Canon from Pyrrha onwards, you won't find an instance of a*
> *Collective crime. Now attend, and learn what kind of novel*
> *Atrocity our day and age has added to history.*

Juvenal, typically, has just written a review of Ulysses' after-dinner tales, casting doubt on their credibility. Reality, as he says, exceeds the proportions of myth: hence why should he submit to a set of stylistic laws which were evolved for the description of follies and minor offences? Horace's bland disquisitions and Persius' self-assured sermons are therefore replaced by parodistic flights of sublimity and a wryly anarchic *terribilità*.

Yet the effect is not always unconstructive. True, his mock heroics occasionally do little more than exaggerate vice to epic proportions – without a reminder that life could be noble. But sometimes through the parody we glimpse a nostalgia for lost ideals, and a more honest, worthwhile world: although even then there is often a pessimism that curbs simplistic faith in the past. When he calls his compatriots '*Troiugenae*', as he is fond of doing, he invokes grand associations: but if he writes about the past, he will often undercut that too.[1] Pathic Otho with his mirror occasions evocation of Turnus' spoils in war:

> ille tenet speculum, pathici gestamen Othonis,
> Actoris Aurunci spolium, quo se ille uidebat
> armatum, cum iam tolli uexilla iuberet.          (2.99–101)

> *Here's another clutching a mirror – just like that fag of an*
> *Emperor Otho, who peeked at himself to see how his armour looked*
> *Before riding into battle.*

This time the upshot is positive: the Virgilian quotation works, like the catalogue of heroes in the poem's finale, as a touchstone for judgement:

[1] For the place of allusions to the heroic past in Roman satire see Bramble (1974) 29ff., and Lelièvre (1958) 22–5.

Curius quid sentit et ambo
Scipiadae, quid Fabricius manesque Camilli,
quid Cremerae legio et Cannis consumpta iuuentus,
tot bellorum animae, quotiens hinc talis ad illos
umbra uenit? (2.153–7)

*how would our great dead captains*
*Greet such a new arrival? And what about the flower*
*Of our youth who died in battle, our slaughtered legionaries,*
*Those myriad shades of war?*

Here, the indignation is pure, unsullied by comedy – even though Juvenal
has only recently made a farce out of the infernal geography inhabited by the
great ghosts. Likewise, *pace* Mason, the *divina tomacula porci* at the end of the
tenth satire are merely a humorous, indignant finale to a solid and stoical
comment on life: yes, by all means pray, for something that matters, but
please avoid nonsensical ritual. But elsewhere epic allusion has no obvious
moral function – as, for example, in the reference to Meleager during the fifth
satire's lavish menu:

anseris ante ipsum magni iecur, anseribus par
altilis, et flaui dignus ferro Meleagri
spumat aper. post hunc tradentur tubera, si uer
tunc erit et facient optata tonitrua cenas
maiores. 'tibi habe frumentum,' Alledius inquit,
'O Libye, disiunge boues, dum tubera mittas.' (5.114–19)

*Himself is served with a force-fed goose's liver,*
*A capon as big as the goose itself, and a spit-roast*
*Boar, all piping hot, well worthy of fair-haired*
*Meleager's steel. Afterwards, if it's spring time,*
*And there's been sufficient thunder to bring them on,*
*Truffles appear. 'Ah Africa!' cries the gourmet,*
*'You can keep your grain supply, unyoke your oxen,*
*So long as you send us truffles!'*

In this passage, the mythological reference is cynical, serving to do little more
than amaze us with the host Virro's propensity for show: the moral sting is
reserved for Alledius' words, with their insistence on gourmandise to the detriment of nature, and ordinary people. As in the case of the black image of the
pike fed on sewage at line 105, the idea is one of a natural order perverted by
civilized whim – a notion found slightly earlier in this satire, at lines 92ff.,
where greed is described as having despoiled all the seas.

Epic and tragic allusions are rife, often positive, as reminders of bygone ideals,
sometimes negative, as reinforcements of Juvenal's caricatures of evil, but
sometimes merely neutral, yet another aspect of his fondness for epideixis.
A favourite device is the intrusion of vernacular elements: obscenities, diminu-

tives, Grecisms, words from the lower literary strata – these have the function of insisting on reality, and when they are placed next to grandiloquent language, what often greets us is a sense of dislocation, a feeling that there is a gap between life as it might be and life as it is.[1] Satire 4 is a case in point, where, with admirable control, Juvenal manipulates the associations of epic, and the silly business about the catching of the fish, in order to impress us with the notion that Rome is sick, unworthy of the pompous assumptions with which she hides her weakness. Epicisms here are at one and the same time cynical and positive: cynical because the trappings are vain, mere cloaks for deformity, but positive in that the language employed to describe them looks back to earlier days when Rome could take pride in an empire. Juvenal constantly belabours us with military and imperial allusion, contrasting it with diction which pinpoints cold realities. He begins with a preamble about Crispinus and a mullet: if an upstart Egyptian can spend so much on a fish, what should we expect when it comes to the tastes of the master of the world? The high style first appears when Crispinus buys his fish:

> mullum sex milibus emit,
> aequantem sane paribus sestertia libris,
> ut perhibent qui de magnis maiora loquuntur. (4.15–17)

> *He bought a red*
> *Mullet for sixty gold pieces – ten for each pound weight,*
> *To make it sound more impressive.*

Soon, Crispinus and the fish are put into perspective by the use of ordinary language:

> hoc tu,
> succinctus patria quondam, Crispine, papyro?
> hoc pretio squamas?

> *Did you pay so much for a fish, Crispinus, you who once*
> *Went around in a loin-cloth of your native papyrus?*

Through the delayed and unexpected gibe in *papyro*, and the bald realism of *squamas*, the pretence is undermined. But better is to come, in the passage of transition from Crispinus to Domitian, where low and high language meet, to remind us of what Rome should be, and thereby indict the sordid actualities that are hidden by mere names:

> qualis tunc epulas ipsum gluttisse putamus
> induperatorem, cum tot sestertia, partem
> exiguam et modicae sumptam de margine cenae,
> purpureus magni ructauit scurra Palati;
> iam princeps equitum, magna qui uoce solebat
> uendere municipes fracta de merce siluros? (4.28–33)

[1] For Juvenal's diction, see in particular Anderson (1961*b*) 51–87; also id. (1957) 33–90.

*what kind of menu was it*
*That the Emperor guzzled himself, I wonder, when all that gold –*
*Just a fraction of the whole, the merest modest side-dish –*
*Was belched up by this purple-clad Palace nark, this*
*Senior knight who once went bawling his wares*
*(Job-lots of catfish from some wholesaler's auction)*
*Through the Alexandrian back-streets?*

In the tension between the vernacular *gluttisse* and the epic archaism *induperatorem*, Juvenal summarizes his amusement and despair: Rome has sunk from her one-time magnificence into greed and self-abasement. His moral is the same in line 31, where *purpureus* and *magni* promise great things, only to be belied by the vulgarity of the two words which follow, *ructauit* and *scurra*. Finally, through the juxtaposition of the line about catfish and the official elevation of the title *princeps equitum*, the initial invective is completed; the old order is dead, replaced by a travesty. Now, after an ironic invocation of the muse, and an insistence that his story is true, Juvenal launches into the main part of his satire with full-blown epic parody:

> cum iam semianimum laceraret Flauius orbem
> ultimus et caluo seruiret Roma Neroni,
> incidit Hadriaci spatium admirabile rhombi;
> ante domum Veneris, quam Dorica sustinet Ancon,
> impleuitque sinus... (4.37–41)

*In the days when the last Flavian was flaying a half-dead world,*
*And Rome was in thrall to a bald Nero, there swam*
*Into a net in the Adriatic, hard by Ancona,*
*Where the shrine of Venus stands on her headland, a monstrous*
*Turbot, a regular whopper...*

Once more, the idea is that life is a hyperbole, hence warrants epic diction: foreign enemies and threats to the state have now given way to turbots. High-sounding words are used, but the whole thing is a mockery:

> iam letifero cedente pruinis
> autumno, iam quartanam sperantibus aegris,
> stridebat deformis hiems praedamque recentem
> seruabat; tamen hic properat, uelut urgueat auster.
> utque lacus suberant, ubi quamquam diruta seruat
> ignem Troianum et Vestam colit Alba minorem,
> obstitit intranti miratrix turba parumper.
> ut cessit, facili patuerunt cardine ualuae;
> exclusi spectant admissa obsonia patres.
> itur ad Atriden. (4.56–65)

*Now autumn*
*With its pestilential winds was yielding to winter's frosts;*
*Now patients were hopeful for milder, third-day fevers,*
*And icy blasts helped keep the turbot refrigerated.*
*On sped the fisherman, as though blown by a south wind,*
*Till below him lay the lakes where Alba, though in ruins,*
*Still guards the flame of Troy and the lesser Vestal shrine.*
*A wondering crowd thronged around him, blocking his way for a little*
*Till the doors on their smooth hinges swung inward, the crowd gave way,*
*And the Senators – still shut out – saw the fish admitted to*
*The Imperial Presence.*

Domitian is anyone but *Atrides*, a second Agamenmon. He is as unworthy of that title as the Senate are of theirs – and that idea is paralleled by the epic paraphernalia about the time of year: another context might deserve it, but certainly not the present, where nature does her utmost, in the highest of all diction, to keep the turbot fresh. Similarly, the palace doors swing open with too much drama. But Juvenal is not just mocking the apotheosis of the trivial: the Trojan fire and Vesta remind us of Rome's heritage, saving the epic parody from its potentially negative status. For we remember that such language has a more appropriate, noble use, and that memory once stirred gives direction to the satire.

Not that Juvenal's cynicism normally falls into abeyance when he has past ideals in mind. One of his favourite formulae is the contrast *olim. . .nunc* :[1] the present is quite ghastly, but the past is seldom entirely spared. Sometimes his anarchic instinct will not leave well alone, and then all values seem to crumble. But more often than not, there is a saving humour which leaves the principle intact, even though the myth might be inadequate in some ways. We catch him on the verge of dissolving our convictions – but usually he stops short of the seemingly inevitable iconoclasm, by converting his disillusionment into a joke, or importing the insinuation that salvation might be possible, if only we were more subtle, less dedicated to the search for facile panaceas, and more prone to acquiesce in a recognized second best. His third satire is full of this – a realistic spirit which refuses to regard a rustic moral archaism as a simple or obvious cure. Where Horace had no doubts about the ethical value of his farm – the medicinal properties of his stream, the simplicity of his diet, above all, the mental hygiene of a life in accordance with nature – Juvenal's moral pastoral, like the 'frugal' dinner of Satire 11, has no mildness or composure, no pretence to self-assurance. In his account of the country festival at lines 171ff., he comes nearest to commitment, but even here there is something which fails to convince us entirely – a brittleness of tone, and something ridiculous in the

---

[1] See Bramble (1974) 30 n. 1.

image of the *rusticus infans*. Likewise his recommendation of a house out in the provinces turns into a miniature satire of the values supposedly espoused:

> hortulus hic puteusque breuis nec reste mouendus
> in tenues plantas facili diffunditur haustu.
> uiue bidentis amans et culti uilicus horti.
> unde epulum possis centum dare Pythagoreis. (3.226–9)

> *A garden-plot is thrown in*
> *With the house itself, and a well with a shallow basin –*
> *No rope-and-bucket work when your seedlings need some water.*
> *Learn to enjoy hoeing, work and plant your allotment*
> *Till a hundred vegetarians could feast off its produce.*

Horace, too, had his joke about the vegetarian Pythagoreans. But Juvenal is more abrasive, and there is worse to come:

> est aliquid, quocumque loco, quocumque recessu
> unius sese dominum fecisse lacertae. (3.230–1)

> *It's quite an achievement, even out in the backwoods,*
> *To have made yourself master of, well, say one lizard, even.*

The joke about the lizard is rather weak, but the procedure is quite typical: a Parthian shot let loose, at the very end of a section, at a set of ideas which have hitherto been promoted. Towards the close of the satire we find the same technique, but employed with less bad taste:

> qua fornace graues, qua non incude catenae?
> maximus in uinclis ferri modus, ut timeas ne
> uomer deficiat, ne marrae et sarcula desint.
> felices proauorum atauos, felicia dicas
> saecula, quae quondam sub regibus atque tribunis
> uiderunt uno contentam carcere Romam. (3.309–14)

> *Our furnaces glow, our anvils*
> *Groan everywhere under their output of chains and fetters.*
> *That's where most of our iron goes nowadays; one wonders*
> *Whether ploughshares, hoes and mattocks may not soon be obsolete.*
> *How fortunate they were (you may well think), those early*
> *Forbears of ours, how happy the good old days*
> *Of kings and tribunes, when Rome made do with one prison only.*

Deliberate scurrility is absent from the passage: but even though the echoes of Virgil in the lines about the farm implements produce a moral insistence on the virtues of agriculture – albeit that in Virgil it was epic swords, not mean, ignoble fetters, that were forged from the innocent ploughshare[1] – there is treachery afoot in Juvenal's parting gesture, in the cynical suggestion that even Rome's heroic days harboured a few criminals.

---

[1] Virg. *Geo.* 1.506f. and *Aen.* 7.635f.

Likewise Juvenal has his fun at the expense of the golden age proper. At the opening of the sixth satire, the times traditionally extolled by idealizing poets are amusingly transformed into an uncomfortable prelude to corruption and decay. But amidst the sardonic humour there is the thought that at least in those backward days women looked like women:

> credo Pudicitiam Saturno rege moratam
> in terris uisamque diu, cum frigida paruas
> praeberet spelunca domos ignemque Laremque
> et pecus et dominos communi clauderet umbra,
> siluestrem montana torum cum sterneret uxor
> frondibus et culmo uicinarumque ferarum
> pellibus, haut similis tibi, Cynthia, nec tibi, cuius
> turbauit nitidos extinctus passer ocellos,
> sed potanda ferens infantibus ubera magnis
> et saepe horridior glandem ructante marito.          (6.1–10)

> *During Saturn's reign I believe that Chastity still*
> *Lingered on earth, and was seen for a while, when draughty*
> *Caves were the only homes men had, hearth fire and household*
> *Goods, family and cattle all shut in darkness together.*
> *Wives were different then – a far cry from Cynthia,*
> *Or the girl who wept, red-eyed, for that sparrow's death.*
> *Bred to the woods and mountains, they made their beds from*
> *Dry leaves and straw, from the pelts of savage beasts*
> *Caught prowling the neighbourhood. Their breasts gave suck*
> *To big strong babies; often, indeed, they were shaggier*
> *Than their acorn-belching husbands.*

Juvenal concedes a point with his comparison to the poetic mistresses, Cynthia and Lesbia – but then, typically, he half retracts it, in his unattractive portrait of the caveman's full-blown wife. But half the point remains: cavewomen were closer to nature than the corseted specimens of today. Irreverence is similarly the keynote of the golden age picture drawn in the thirteenth satire. Here Juvenal writes of the gods, and their forfeited innocence, perhaps developing a point from the preamble to Satire 6, where, a few lines later than the passage just quoted, Jupiter's age is an index of honesty:

> multa Pudicitiae ueteris uestigia forsan
> aut aliqua exstiterint et sub Ioue, sed Ioue nondum
> barbato, nondum Graecis iurare paratis
> per caput alterius...          (6.14–17)

> *Some few traces, perhaps, of Chastity's ancient presence*
> *Survived under Jove – but only while Jove remained*
> *A beardless stripling, long before Greeks had learnt*
> *To swear by the other man's head, or capital...*

But in Satire 13, the message is clearer, written up in a more leisurely manner. A broader humour, even signs of humanity, replace the accustomed malevolent posture – the old anger and indignation have gone:

> quondam hoc indigenae uiuebant more, priusquam
> sumeret agrestem posito diademate falcem
> Saturnus fugiens, tunc cum uirguncula Iuno
> et priuatus adhuc Idaeis Iuppiter antris;
> nulla super nubes conuiuia caelicolarum,
> nec puer Iliacus formosa nec Herculis uxor
> ad cyathos, et iam siccato nectare tergens
> bracchia Vulcanus Liparaea nigra taberna;
> prandebat sibi quisque deus, nec turba deorum
> talis ut est hodie, contentaque sidera paucis
> numinibus miserum urguebant Atlanta minori
> pondere; nondum imi sortitus triste profundi
> imperium Sicula toruos cum coniuge Pluton,
> nec rota nec Furiae nec saxum aut uolturis atri
> poena, sed infernis hilares sine regibus umbrae. (13.38–52)

> *That was how primitive man lived long ago, before*
> *King Saturn was ousted, before he exchanged his diadem*
> *For a country sickle, when Juno was only a schoolgirl,*
> *And Jupiter – then without title – still dwelt in Ida's caves.*
> *No banquets above the clouds yet for Heaven's inhabitants,*
> *With Hebe and Ganymede there to hand round drinks, and Vulcan,*
> *Still black from the smithy, scrubbing the soot off his arms*
> *With spirits of – nectar. Each God would breakfast in private;*
> *There wasn't our modern rabble of divinities, the stars*
> *Ran to far fewer deifications, the firmament rested lighter*
> *On poor old Atlas' back. The throne of the nether regions*
> *Stood vacant still – grim Pluto and his Sicilian consort,*
> *The Furies, Ixion's wheel, the boulder of Sisyphus,*
> *The black and murderous vulture, all these were yet to come:*
> *While they'd got no monarch, the shades could enjoy a high old time.*

Charm is hardly a quality one would usually associate with Juvenal – but here, at last, the wryness is fetching, not acid; the tone comic, not abrasive. Not that we really believe in the one-time innocence of the gods: but at least our satirist looks closer now to laughter than to bitterness or tears.[1] We admit his parody this time because it does not threaten us.

But, as we began by saying, it is for his earlier work that Juvenal is remembered: and there the world was out of joint, in almost all its aspects. Even our positives, our favourite opinions were subject to his scrutiny, and often his

---

[1] On the transition from the indignation of Satires 1–6 to the laughter of Satires 10–16 (arguing that the third book is transitional) see Anderson (1964) 174ff.

derision. Juvenal – the Juvenal, predominantly, of Satires 1 to 6 – allows us no moral respite, no refuge from his questions. Yet despite his treachery and deceptions – and one of them is pretending that the experience is literary, that all is words and rhetoric, a commodity made to please – despite his peevish aggression, towards the reader and his values, his uncharitable arrogance, something emerges which is tenuously hopeful, potentially constructive – the plain idea that honesty, though nasty, even vile, can direct us past appearances to see truths that live within. Contact may be sickening, when façades are stripped away: but interior truths once recognized, amendment can begin.

# 7

# MINOR POETRY

## I. PHAEDRUS

Phaedrus holds no exalted rank amongst Latin poets, but he claims serious attention by his choice of subject matter and his individualistic treatment of it. He was, as far as we know, the first poet, Greek or Roman, to put together a collection of fables and present them as literature in their own right, not merely as material on which others might draw. And on this collection he firmly imprinted his own personality, complacent, querulous, cantankerous. In prologues, epilogues, and occasionally elsewhere he reveals his grievances and aspirations. His fables contain elements of satire and 'social comment', not at all gentle: if he had chosen to write satire proper, he might have vied with Juvenal in trenchancy and bitterness.

Animal fables, usually purveying a simple moral, have a long prehistory in folklore. Thereafter they provided speakers and writers with a ready store of homely illustrations and precepts. The Greeks of the fourth century B.C. ascribed a mass of these fables to the wise and witty slave Aesop: how many of those which survive in fact go back to this shadowy figure we do not know, but we approach firmer ground with the collection of fables, attributed to Aesop or in the Aesopian tradition, compiled in prose by Demetrius of Phalerum (c. 300 B.C.). This book itself is lost (unless some parts have come to light on a papyrus)[1], but very probably it was Phaedrus' main source, perhaps his only source. We know of no other collections available to him. Certain recurrent features in Phaedrus may well derive from Demetrius, in particular *promythia*, initial statements of theme or moral, intended originally for the convenience of orators or others in search of illustrations. By couching his fables in verse Phaedrus gave them literary pretensions: they could no longer be regarded as rough material, to be shaped by others, for now the poet himself has done the polishing (1 *prol.* 1–2). Brevity is the virtue on which he most prides himself or which he feels conscious he must attain (2 *prol.* 12, 3 *epil.* 8, 4 *epil.* 7), but he is also aware of the need for variety (2 *prol.* 10) and strives to achieve it. He had virtually no precedents to guide him, since hitherto

[1] See Perry (1965) xiv–xv.

128

fables had appeared only incidentally in poetry, as in Horace amongst others, sometimes elaborated, sometimes brief. Horace's carefully developed story of the town and country mouse (*Sat.* 2.6.79–117) possesses a delicate humour worlds removed from the crude psychology which Phaedrus regularly offers. We have something nearer to Phaedrus' manner in the story of the fox and the corn-bin (*Epist.* 1.7.29–33). No doubt Horace had some influence on him, but it was not very deep. Phaedrus stands apart from the main stream of Augustan and post-Augustan poetry.

Demetrius' single book of fables could not supply Phaedrus with sufficient number or variety of themes. And so, particularly in Books 3–5, he adds much new material of his own (see 4 *prol.* 11–13), in part of contemporary interest, Roman rather than Greek. Hence such poems as 2.5 (the emperor Tiberius and the officious footman), 3.10 (the woman falsely suspected of adultery), and 5.7 (the inordinate conceit of the musician Princeps). In thus using the fable as a vehicle for very diverse themes Phaedrus is not uniformly successful, nor can he sustain overall the qualities of simplicity and artlessness which he affects. 3.10 and 5.7 are long-winded and tedious, as is 4.11 (the thief and the lamp), a fable more in the Aesopian vein, but apparently Phaedrus' own creation (see ll. 14–15). He is more interesting when he writes of his own poetry, as in 4.7, a derisive riposte to a detractor, reminiscent in some respects both of Persius and Martial. But even here, by clumsily appending an *epimythium* quite out of place in a personal poem, he reveals that he is ill at ease with his medium.

At the outset Phaedrus affirms that his purpose is to amuse and instruct, and he discharges this intention as best he can, baldly obtruding instruction in *promythia* or *epimythia*. He may, intermittently at least, have another, ulterior purpose, covertly to allude to circumstances and personalities of his day. We learn from 3 *prol.* 38ff. that he fell foul of Sejanus. What poems in Books 1–2 excited Sejanus' anger we cannot tell: they may, of course, be amongst those now lost. Phaedrus says (3 *prol.* 49–50) that he does not seek to brand individuals, but to display the manners of society generally. Whether that be true or not, it is not surprising that he caused offence, for the Romans of this period were alert to *double-entendre* and quick to sense an affront. And he does not always veil his thoughts: thus 1.1 is explicitly directed against those who 'use trumped-up charges to crush the innocent' and 1.15 is devised to illustrate that 'on a change in government the poor merely get a master with a different name'. For one of his humble status Phaedrus is singularly outspoken. And he is no *detrectator sui*: 3 *prol.* ought to have been a modest apologia, but it proves to be an impudent self-justification. Housman said that Phaedrus' 'spiritual home was the stable and the farmyard'. He might, one may feel, have been even more at home in the Subura: he would certainly not have denied that 'the proper study of mankind is man'.

Phaedrus' language is generally plain and commonplace, occasionally coarse. He admits colloquial and prosaic terms avoided by most of the poets. He does not try to create a distinct style for his fables: at the most we may discern a few mannerisms and favourite expressions. He chose to employ senarii like those of the early dramatists rather than the more restrictive trimeters used by Catullus and Horace amongst others: the looser verse-form was indeed better suited to his motley subject matter and unselective vocabulary. Linguistically he shows much similarity to satire and epigram, and a marked affinity to mime, as represented by the excerpted *sententiae* of Publilius Syrus.

Phaedrus has certain merits. Like Publilius, he can point a memorable phrase. His stories can be charmingly lucid and simple. But they would have been much improved by excision of *promythia*: here was a *damnosa hereditas* from Demetrius which, for all his independence, Phaedrus lacked the good sense to abandon. Again, his brevity is not always commendable: many of the fables seem flat and jejune, devoid of the detail and colour which their subjects invited. In antiquity Phaedrus won little recognition. He is ignored by all first-century writers, with the possible exception of Martial.[1] And when at a later day Phaedrus' poems were recast into prose, his name was removed from them. Avianus knew of his work, but scarcely used it, preferring to follow Babrius. Nowadays he seems wholly to have lost the appeal which he exercised in the seventeenth and eighteenth centuries. Yet animal stories are more popular now than ever before, although (or because) our society as a whole is remote from countryside and farmyard. Phaedrus' fall from favour may be explained variously. Only limited time is now available in schools for Latin reading and we tend to concentrate from the start on a few major authors. Again, moralizing has long been out of fashion, and Phaedrus' moralizing is trite and wearisome. Seneca has suffered a similar neglect for similar reasons, though we have recently seen a revival of interest in his works. Perhaps Phaedrus too will obtain some rehabilitation, but one may doubt it. His poems possess neither the substance nor the vigour nor the imagination necessary to secure them against the test of time.

## 2. CALPURNIUS SICULUS

That the seven eclogues of Calpurnius, the two Einsiedeln eclogues, and the panegyric on Piso all date from Nero's principate has long been accepted doctrine. They originate perhaps from a single literary coterie, centred upon the

[1] Mart. 3.20.5 *aemulatur improbi locos Phaedri* 'he imitates the passages [*sic*] of naughty Phaedrus', is doubly problematic. The paradosis *locos* is untenable and may reasonably be corrected to *iocos* 'jests' or *logos* 'fables'. The latter correction, if right, would strongly suggest that the fabulist is meant. But we cannot be sure that it is right. Again, it is debatable whether *improbus* fits the Phaedrus we know.

patron represented as Meliboeus in Calp. 1 and 4. Enthusiasm about a new golden age, evinced both by Calpurnius and the Einsiedeln poet, links these writers together and accords with other evidence for the optimism and sense of revival which seem to have marked Nero's accession to power. The period was prolific in literature, major and minor, and some modern critics attempt to determine the relationships which obtained between various writers or groups. Not enough evidence exists to support such reconstructions. And recently the conventional dating of Calpurnius' poems has itself been called in question.

Calpurnius is overshadowed by Theocritus and Virgil, who provided his main inspiration. But he kept bucolic poetry alive by somewhat extending its scope: though he acknowledges Virgil as a supreme model (4.64ff.), he does not entirely restrict himself to the paths which Virgil has trodden. Three of Calpurnius' eclogues (1, 4, 7) are more fully and obviously concerned with contemporary affairs than any of Virgil's, except (arguably) his fourth. In that poem (1–3) Virgil would fain excuse his unusual theme, but Calpurnius adopts such themes unhesitatingly, though he is careful to frame them still within a background of fantasy. Again, he draws readily upon other genres, particularly love elegy (3.45–91), didactic (5), and descriptive epigram (7.23–72). That is not wholly surprising, for bucolic had always been flexible: witness Theocritus' versatility, and Virg. *Ecl.* 6 and 10, which include material from 'miniature epic' and elegy. Certainly, by Calpurnius' time, variation on exclusively pastoral themes, limited in range, would have been uninteresting and arid. He had to offer something of a mixture: purism was not then in fashion in Latin poetry, if it ever had been.

Calpurnius' book of eclogues has an intentionally patterned structure: the first, central, and concluding poems (1, 4, 7) relate to the real world around him, while the others (2, 3, 5, 6) stand, ostensibly at least, apart from present circumstances. Again, the poems which have dialogue throughout (2, 4, 6) are interwoven with those which contain long monologues (1, 3, 5, 7). These patterns are plain enough, but what they signify, if anything of importance, is not easy to grasp. Further, while *Ecl.* 1 might well date from the beginning of Nero's rule (A.D. 54 or 55) and *Ecl.* 7 from some years later (not before A.D. 57), the order of the poems does not necessarily reflect sequence of composition. Some scholars argue that *Ecl.* 3, to their taste the crudest of the collection, is the earliest, and perhaps pre-Neronian. It may be so, but such arguments bring us on to perilously subjective ground.

Calpurnius' language is neither colourless nor wholly derivative. He had powers of observation and could deftly describe details or scenes. And he is generally quite lucid and unaffected. Though no ancient writer mentions

Calpurnius, he had a competent imitator in Nemesianus, who might have bypassed him and reverted directly to Virgil, and he is known to a few even later poets.

### 3. 'BUCOLICA EINSIDLENSIA'

These two incomplete and enigmatic eclogues may be dated to Nero's principate, but not to an exact time within it. 1.38ff. alludes to Nero's *Troica* as contemporary, but in what year that work first stunned the world is uncertain. The second poem is concerned with a new golden age, introduced by a ruler who assimilates himself to Apollo. This fits Nero, and best perhaps his early years. We cannot be sure that the poems are by the same author, but a few minor metrical differences do not preclude common authorship. It is notable, however, that *Buc.* 2, unlike *Buc.* 1, diverges from tradition in sometimes changing speakers within lines.

In the first eclogue two shepherds compete in singing the praises of the poet-emperor. The flattery which they effuse is exceptionally extravagant, and when, at 48–9, Mantua is represented as so conscious of Virgil's inferiority to Nero that it seeks to obliterate his works, we may well wonder whether the intention is not comic and derisive. The second eclogue is not a little perplexing. One of the speakers says that his joy is disturbed by care, and, pressed for explanation, that satiety is his trouble. Then he describes the blissful security which all may now enjoy. Perhaps he is playing with the old idea that peace is morally enervating, and, if so, offering a back-handed compliment to Nero's regime. There is thus a *prima facie* case for taking neither poem at face-value: sometimes, after all, impotent malice obtains refuge in riddles. The alternative is to dismiss both of them as vacuous and incoherent. The obscurity and clumsiness of their expression encourage the latter view, but the mutilation of the text enjoins hesitation.

### 4. 'LAUS PISONIS'

The 'Panegyric on Piso' is a distinctly odd composition and, if the poet expected Piso to approve of what he says, addressed to a distinctly odd person. He says first that Piso's personal qualities outshine his distinguished ancestry, then that he has won no military glory, but earned fame as a speaker in the courts and Senate (yet only a ceremonial speech is mentioned), and next, in 81–208 (about half of the poem), that he is affable, generous, and devoted to laudable recreations, cultural and physical, including a certain board game (190–208), at which he conspicuously excels. Having said this, he affirms (210) that Piso's merits defy adequate record, then importunes this up-to-date nobleman to become his patron, pointing out that the writers whom Maecenas favoured never feared an impoverished old age, and concludes by stating that he is not yet twenty. On first reading one might suppose the poem's aim to be other than it purports, even indeed that it is a burlesque. But its absurdities are not blatant enough to bear out this view. Much may be imputed to mere incompetence. Again, if the poem was indeed written under Nero, the writer had a delicate task: he could hardly extol military talents, proven or latent. It might have been better to abandon a hopeless enterprise: certainly the recurrent apologia seems very jarring in a eulogy. We may recall the inept *Elegies on Maecenas*. They, however, were posthumous and their subject retained general interest. Piso was no such subject, though perhaps he seemed to be to a circle of dependants. Altogether much in the *Laus Pisonis* remains unexplained.

The poem's style is commonplace and usually unexceptionable, sometimes bathetic or long-winded (e.g. 140ff.). In language and metre we find some affinities with Calpurnius and, to a lesser extent, with Lucan. Exact dating is unattainable.

## 5. 'AETNA'

Mt Etna, the most spectacular volcano known to antiquity, had challenged the descriptive skill of several poets, Pindar and Virgil amongst them. But no one, it seems, before the anonymous author of the didactic poem *Aetna* had in prose or verse attempted a separate and detailed treatment of volcanic activity. Those authorities, such as Posidonius, upon whom the *Aetna* depends treated volcanoes along with earthquakes, not separately. The conception of the poem is thus original, if its execution is not.

The *Aetna* is only 645 verses long, but it has a protracted introduction, in which the poet rejects mythological lore and poetic fancy, then emphasizes his own concern with truth. He proceeds to describe the earth's crust, which permits the activity of volcanoes. Then he begins to explain the cause of this activity, subterranean winds under high pressure, but breaks off into a lengthy digression on the value of natural science. Having at last dealt with the cause, he turns to discuss the fuel, lava-stone, on which volcanoes feed. Then, scientific discussion concluded, he adds an epilogue, first comparing natural spectacles with those of artistic or historical interest, and finally relating the story of the brothers of Catania. Various arguments converge to place the poem in the mid first century A.D. Clear debts to Ovid and Manilius show that it is post-Augustan. The brief, allusive references to mythological themes at 17ff. recall the impatience of Persius, amongst others, with such material. And very striking similarities in thought and expression to Seneca's *Natural questions* indicate a closer connexion with that work than merely a common source. The absence of any mention of Vesuvius gives A.D. 79 as a *terminus ante quem*.

A profound obligation to Lucretius (especially Book 6) is evident in thought and structure. The main scientific part of the poem is carefully divided into sections and subsections. Fallacious views are diligently refuted. And the poet repeatedly insists on a need for concrete evidence from the senses or appeals to graphic analogies. If his argumentation has one great fault, it is that he drives home his points too laboriously and unremittingly. In rejecting mythology (yet in the end using it), in asserting the virtues of his own approach, and in moralizing about worthwhile pursuits, he adopts attitudes conventional in didactic poetry and familiar elsewhere. Nevertheless, one detects in his writing a genuine enthusiasm for his task. Textual corruption makes it hard to assess the literary quality of the poem, but plainly its vocabulary is limited and its phraseology repetitious. Sometimes ideas and phrases flow easily, sometimes they seem halting and uneasy. The poet draws heavily on Lucretius, Virgil and Ovid, yet he is no slavish imitator. We find here nothing like the fumbling patchwork which disfigures the *Culex* and *Ciris*. We also find little distinctive or specially interesting, except a liking for personification and skilful use of various imagery, particularly that of warfare. The *Aetna* is not devoid of merit. One may applaud its firm structure, its earnest tone, its controlled and occasionally effective rhetoric. But it lacks freshness, warmth and imagination. Few Latin poems so completely fail to involve the reader.

### 6. EPIGRAMS ASCRIBED TO SENECA AND PETRONIUS

Amongst the Latin epigrams transmitted from antiquity are about a hundred, mainly in elegiacs, a few in other metres, which have, with varying degrees of plausibility, been ascribed to Seneca and Petronius. In nine cases out of ten the ascription is modern, and susceptible neither of proof nor disproof: the most we can usually do is to record the presence or absence of similarities in thought and expression between these poems and the authentic works of the two authors. Language and metre show scarcely any clear indications of composition later than the first century A.D., but, given the limited extent of the material and the conservatism of epigrammatic style, this negative consideration is not very weighty. Again, caution is enjoined both by the well known tendency for pieces originally anonymous to be fathered on a famous writer (witness the *Appendix Vergiliana*) and by the equally well known proneness of anonymous items in anthologies to be taken as belonging to the named authors of preceding items.

One or two of the poems ascribed to Seneca relate explicitly or very probably to his exile (*Anth. Lat.* 409, 236–7), while others treat of matters which interested him (though not him alone), such as mortality (*Anth. Lat.* 232), Cato (*Anth. Lat.* 397–9), and contempt for fortune (*Anth. Lat.* 444). One group of verses, on Claudius' British triumph (*Anth. Lat.* 419–26), seems to be fixed at Seneca's time by its subject matter, but other pieces look like variations on standard themes, such as Xerxes' expedition (*Anth. Lat.* 442, 461) and the fate of Pompey (*Anth. Lat.* 400–4), or school exercises (*Anth. Lat.* 462–3). Competence, and nothing higher, is the level attained. If a single writer is involved, he was one who did not always know when to stop. The treatment of the conquest of Britain is tediously repetitive and the indictment of the deceptions of hope (*Anth. Lat.* 415) labours under an excess of examples (contrast Tib. 2.6.19–28). These faults are perhaps not alien from Seneca. But where are his habitual merits? Pungency, for instance, is often lacking where it is most required, as at the conclusion of *Anth. Lat.* 412. Here, as elsewhere, one might have expected from a Seneca more novelty and ingenuity, as well as livelier expression.

Of the poems ascribed to Petronius several accord well with themes and attitudes to be found in the *Satyrica*, and may be fragments of that work, such as *Anth. Lat.* 466 (scepticism about the gods), *Anth. Lat.* 690 (oddities of nature), *Anth. Lat.* 469 (encouragement to a hero or mock-hero, who could be Encolpius), and *Anth. Lat.* 475 (an amusing parody of epic simile). The last two pieces, amongst others, are clearly taken from a narrative context, and not in fact epigrams at all. This favours attribution to the *Satyrica*, and incidentally makes the verses hard to judge in their own right. A few of the self-contained poems are of high quality, such as *Anth. Lat.* 706 (a pretty conceit about a snowball, but rather tender in tone for the Petronius we otherwise know) and *Anth. Lat.* 698 (a fine poem on a restless slave of love, after the manner of Tibullus and Ovid, but again hardly reminiscent of Petronius). We cannot, of course, tell how various were the moods which Petronius' fertile genius could compass. He might have written *Anth. Lat.* 698, 706 and several others which no internal evidence suggests that we should impute to him. To doubt it is not so much to question his versatility as simply to insist that attributions, if they are to be considered seriously, require some positive support.

### 7. 'PRIAPEA'

The book of epigrams concerned with Priapus (*Priapea*) is uninhibitedly obscene. Clearly the poet[1] revelled in the jokes which sexual activities so readily encourage, and would probably have been surprised to find that he had shocked, rather than diverted his readers. But the diversion which mere impropriety affords is ephemeral. Such stuff may catch a reader's attention, but will not long retain it unless presented with considerable artistic skill. Happily

---

[1] That these epigrams belong to one poet has been established beyond reasonable doubt by V. Buchheit (see Appendix).

the author of the *Priapea* possesses this skill in abundance. He is original, elegant, and witty, in command of different metres, adept at varying and conflating motifs, and subtle in the planning of his book as a whole. These qualities secure him a high rank amongst Latin epigrammatists.

Priapus figures somewhat tenuously in Greek poetry, and on occasion as an object of genuine cult. In Roman poetry he is almost exclusively associated with custodianship of gardens and with sexual matters, and easily lends himself to become an object of banter and ribaldry. He is treated light-heartedly or at best semi-seriously: so Hor. *Sat.* 1.8, Tib. 1.4, [Virg.] *Priap.* 1–3, *Copa* 23–5. From Martial he obtains a number of pieces (in particular 6.16, 49, 72, 73, 8.40), but they are very limited in thematic range and development. In contrast the book of *Priapea* offers a remarkable diversity of themes, which includes curses (e.g. 78), mockery (e.g. 12), riddles (e.g. 54), dedications to Priapus (e.g. 27), comparison of Priapus with other gods (e.g. 9), Priapus turning a blind eye (64), Priapus in despair (26), and Priapean interpretation of Homer (68). Amongst the characters the author sketches or derides we find prostitutes, pathics, the amorous but unamiable, poets, and respectable matrons. He can maintain suspense, even though we anticipate some obscene conclusion, he can deftly move into parody (e.g. 52. 11–12), and he can produce a neat pun (e.g. 55.6) or delightfully unexpected turn of phrase (e.g. 37. 13–14). And he enlivens hackneyed material, such as dedication of offerings, by ingenious novelty of treatment: conspicuously so in 37. The book is a *tour de force* and intended to be such: it shows the multiplicity of variations admitted by a subject at first sight extremely restricted.

Skilful though the author is in presenting Priapus from new aspects, items very similar in conception naturally occur in a corpus of eighty poems. Hence, to avoid tedium, he varies length, changes metre, and disperses, collocates, and interweaves his themes as they correspond or contrast. This is all so adroitly done that the overall planning appears only on close analysis. And it is not overdone: there is no obsession with patterns here. His artistry has enabled the poet to explore all the possibilities of his subject without wearying his reader. Perhaps his success deterred Martial from making much of Priapus, but, if that seems contrary to what we know of Martial, who might have been expected to take up the challenge, our author could well be the later.

# 8

## PROSE SATIRE

### 1. 'APOCOLOCYNTOSIS DIVI CLAUDII'

For sparkle and malicious wit few works of Latin literature can match the only complete Menippean satire which has survived,[1] a skit upon the life and death of Claudius Caesar ascribed in manuscripts which transmit it to Seneca. It is commonly identified with a piece about Claudius which Cassius Dio tells us Seneca wrote under the title *apocolocyntosis*. This word, though hardly translatable,[2] clearly involves allusion to a pumpkin, *colocynta*, perhaps as a symbol of stupidity, and may well involve, as Dio supposed, parody of the idea of deification. But how does it relate to the actual work, in which Claudius becomes neither a pumpkin nor a god? No one has yet explained. We have either to contend that the joke is limited to the title itself or, if we feel that a work and its title ought to have some discernible connexion, admit that a very real problem remains with us. As to authorship, Seneca could certainly have written the satire. There is nothing surprising in the contradiction here of all the earlier adulation of the *Ad Polybium* (even if that had been sincere, his protracted exile gave Seneca reason enough to detest Claudius) or in the satire's liveliness and scurrility (Seneca was versatile and not lacking in wit). Nero himself derided the dead Claudius and presumably allowed his courtiers to do the same. If Seneca wrote his skit shortly after Nero's accession he would have found an appreciative audience. But, though Seneca possessed the talent, motive, and opportunity to produce the work, so too did others, and famous names attract attributions. It is not absurd to retain some doubts.

After protestations of truthfulness (1–2), sure token of a tall story, the satirist narrates the death of Claudius (3–4), his ascent to Olympus and vain attempt to be enrolled as a god (5–11), and his descent via Rome, where he witnesses his own obsequies, to Hades and final damnation (12–15). The narrative varies in tempo, but is usually brisk and not overburdened with detail. Transition from prose to verse, a distinctive feature of the Menippean

---

[1] A passage of some size is lost in a lacuna at 7.5.

[2] There are two difficulties. Apparently close translation, such as 'pumpkinification', will not be English. And, more seriously, since many theories are current about the word's meaning, some plausible, none cogent, we cannot with assurance settle for any one.

genre, is aptly and amusingly contrived. In general frivolity prevails, but the praise of Nero (4.1) can be taken seriously and, of course, many of the charges against Claudius, made by Augustus (10) and elsewhere, are in themselves grave enough. One must hesitate, however, to impute any of the views expressed to the author. For instance, the sneer at Claudius' extension of the citizenship (3.3) tells us nothing about the real opinions of Seneca or any other individual. The satirist adopts a stance, that of the plain and forthright man in the street, much as Aristophanes had done long before. His satire is political in that it is concerned with a political figure, but not because he says anything of political moment.

The work's prosimetric form links it most obviously with Varro's *Menippeans*, and, though nothing closely comparable in theme appears amongst Varro's fragments, a considerable debt is likely. Something too may be owed directly to Menippus: similarities to Lucian, notably his *Icaromenippus* and *Deorum concilium*, could indicate Menippus as a common source. And one need hardly doubt that Lucilius' council of the gods hovered somewhere in our author's mind. In Lucilius the gods pass judgement on the deceased Cornelius Lentulus Lupus, as they do here on the deceased Claudius. To these literary influences, readily absorbed and exploited by a fertile imagination, we may add the effects of a long Roman tradition of political abuse and invective. The special circumstances of the time of composition allowed that tradition, having long run underground, to surface again. Modern critics may take exception to the treatment of Claudius' personal deformities as being in bad taste. It would not have seemed objectionable to Catullus or Cicero.

The greatest of the many delights which this minor masterpiece affords lies in the way hits are scored in every quarter. Historians, for instance, are mocked for their claims to impartiality (1.1) and avoidance of quotations (9.2). Augustus is made to talk like an animated inscription (10.2). The formalities of senatorial debate are playfully caricatured (9.5, 11.5). So too are poetic conventions and poetic language, not excluding that of Seneca's tragedies. Irony, bathos, and all sorts of comic incongruity abound. The Latin is light and racy when necessary, and witticisms flow with effortless ease. Proverbs and colloquialisms lend the work almost a plebeian air, and issue rather charmingly from the mouths of the gods. Olympus indeed seems as motley and clamorous as the streets of Rome. The satire is utterly disrespectful (save, of course, towards Nero), a fitting entertainment for the Saturnalia. Its unsparing derision of Claudius and uproarious laughter do not, as some suspect, betoken hysteria, but rather the healthy exuberance of a man at last pleased with himself and the world around him.

## 2. PETRONIUS

Petronius' *Satyrica*, commonly but incorrectly known as *Satyricon*,[1] raise abundant problems for literary historians and critics alike. Some of these problems, concerning scale, structure, and plot, are due solely to the mutilation of the text: if it were complete, they would vanish. Others, concerning genre, style, and intention, are more deeply rooted, and could only be resolved if several earlier works, now lost or fragmentary, were rediscovered. No Latin writer excites more lively interest. Unfortunately it is not always accompanied by due recognition of our ignorance.

The old dispute about date and authorship remains tenuously alive. As to date, the social and economic situation presupposed, the cultural interests revealed, and a few plausibly datable references[2] argue for composition during Nero's reign, and a dramatic setting somewhat earlier. And, if Petronius echoes Lucan, composition in the sixties, not the fifties, is indicated. Further, no valid evidence supports a later dating. As to authorship, the work's character accords well with what Tacitus records (*Ann.* 16. 18–19) about Nero's 'arbiter of elegance' Petronius Niger, connoisseur and voluptuary extraordinary. Again, the rare name *Arbiter*, attached to the author in certain manuscripts and elsewhere, may well have derived (exactly how is unclear) from the denomination *arbiter elegantiae*. Such arguments fall short of proving identity, and a strict historian may still suspend judgement.

The title *Satyrica*, 'satyr histories' or, more freely, 'tales of wantonness', recalling, for example, *Milesiaca*, 'Milesian tales', and *poemenica*, 'Shepherd stories', suggests affinity to the Greek romantic novel, a genre which was establishing itself and probably already popular by Petronius' time. But some scholars maintain that *satyrica* is ambivalent: it would also, they think, have recalled the superficially similar word *satura*, and thus suggested a satirical purpose. Petronius' contemporaries could perhaps have confused these basically different words, but they hardly needed to be told of a connexion with satire evident throughout his work. His debt to the satirists is seen in subject matter, for instance the dinner party (cf. Hor. *Sat.* 2.8), in characterization, particularly of minor figures, and in employment of parody and burlesque. And he may have taken the prosimetric form of his novel from Varro's *Saturae Menippeae*: the genre was still alive, as the nearly contemporary *Apocolocyntosis divi Claudii* shows. In spite of difference in scale, we might regard the *Satyrica* as a natural development of Varro's satire, but a prosimetric fragment, recently published, of what seems to be a Greek picaresque novel argues that he had closer antecedents.[3] And Varro wrote a number of separate pieces (one ad-

---

[1] See Appendix.  [2] Rose (1971) 20ff.
[3] Parsons (1971) 63–6.

mittedly of some length), Petronius a coherent, if often discursive, narrative. That difference is decisive: emulation of Varro cannot alone account for Petronius' enterprise.

Petronius presents the adventures of a hero, or anti-hero, Encolpius, a conventionally educated young man, without money or morals, and his catamite, Giton, handsome and unscrupulous. Other characters come and go and reappear, amongst them Quartilla, priestess of Priapus, and Eumolpus, poet, teacher, and reprobate. How importantly any of these subsidiary characters figured in the whole work it is impossible to tell. Encolpius, as narrator and observer, holds the story together. He is a ludicrous victim of fortune's whims, raised up and thrown down, living for the day; he is a voyeur plagued with impotence, a swashbuckling coward, querulous, aimless, and neurotic. In the Greek romances hero and heroine are wont to be buffeted by fortune; their perils and escapes are dire and astonishing; but in the end true love obtains its reward. Petronius burlesques this kind of plot. His homosexual lovers are faithless and unfortunate. Virtue tested and triumphant is replaced by vice rampant and frustrated. But no moral is intended: Petronius seeks only to subvert or mock or suggest comic resemblances. He finds ample material, in epic as in romance. Encolpius, an unheroic wanderer, is pursued by Priapus' wrath, as Odysseus was by Poseidon's and Aeneas by Juno's. Like Odysseus he meets a Circe (127ff.), like Aeneas he sallies forth to wreak vengeance (82. 1–2). Petronius writes for a highly literate audience, able to recognize widely scattered allusions. Thus, for example, Habinnas' entrance at Trimalchio's party (65.3ff.) is based on Alcibiades' in Plato's *Symposium*. His exploitation of many poets and prose-writers has encouraged the opinion that Petronius of set purpose blended diverse genres, romance, satire, epic, elegy, mime, diatribe, and declamation, to produce an amalgam both original and anti-classical. But a less revolutionary explanation will account for the evidence: for his theme, Petronius' obligation is principally to romance, sentimental or picaresque, and his own inventiveness, for the form adopted, partially perhaps to Varro, while all debts to other genres are incidental. These other genres inform his treatment of episodes or individuals, but not his whole work. Ovid's variation of treatment in his *Metamorphoses* is somewhat analogous.[1]

Two longer poems included in the *Satyrica* (89 and 119–24), *Troiae halosis*, 'The capture of Troy', consisting of 65 iambic verses, and *De bello civili*, 'On the civil war', consisting of 295 hexameters, pose teasing difficulties of interpretation, the latter particularly. What is Petronius here attempting: to show how epic should be written, to parody Lucan, or something more subtle? Parody may be discountenanced: Lucan's thoughts and expressions are not

[1] I owe this point to Professor Kenney.

arrestingly adapted, the gods, whom Lucan discarded, fulfil their accustomed role, and, for a parody, the poem is inordinately long. It could, one must admit, have been intended to be exemplary, though few have seen any merits in it. We had best seek guidance from its context. Eumolpus (who is presented elsewhere as a scoundrel, if not a charlatan) offers it as a specimen of the elevated treatment which the subject demands of a poet, as against the mundane treatment which should properly be left to historians. And Lucan, we remember, was commonly abused for writing like a historian, not a poet. Petronius, it may be, had as little regard for traditional epic, purveyed by Eumolpus and his like, as for current innovations. His shrewd contemporary, Persius, was certainly disillusioned about all such effusions. And, since the *De bello civili* contains enough phrases and rhythms similar to Lucan's to argue, though not to prove, that Petronius knew something of Lucan's work, he may wish to point the irony of a conservative like Eumolpus being infected by modern vices. If so, Lucan is indirectly criticized. Much the same implicit criticism may be found in the iambic piece. Though not a parody of Seneca, it illustrates how easily vapid iambics, not unlike Seneca's, can be strung together.

Both in incident and character Petronius' novel is highly realistic, indeed startlingly so, if compared with sentimental romances. Violence, vulgarity, and decadence disfigure the society which he depicts. His erotic scenes are sometimes titillating, sometimes callously comic, sometimes both: but sympathetic humour is almost as hard to find here as sentiment. However, in his description of Trimalchio's party (26.7–79.7) we are feasted with humour, of a hilariously rumbustious brand. Petronius' presentation of the freedman millionaire and his cronies is as adept as it is original. No one had hitherto so fully portrayed the thoughts, attitudes, and mode of speech of a specific social class, and at that a low one, though something at least comparable had been effected in comedy and mime. And Petronius is not content with caricature. Beneath a brash and ridiculous façade he discloses unrealizable aspirations and chronic insecurity. His Trimalchio is a complex character: he now wallows in luxury and self-deception, but was once resilient and faced a hard world on its own terms. For all his coarseness and ostentation he is not utterly unlikable.

After every allowance for the fragmentation of our text, the novel still seems very episodic, and the episodes seem to vary considerably in scale. Occasionally topics of general interest (education, for instance) are handled at length, and the narrative slows down. Such fluctuation of tempo and the generous treatment of many details may reinforce the manuscript evidence (sometimes questioned) for sixteen or more books. References to several episodes now lost add confirmation. And the scene must have changed more than once. The parts of the story we have are centred somewhere in Campania, after escapades at Massilia. Doubtless Encolpius moved on, as those who live on their wits (and on the fringes of the law) commonly do. We have then no organic, inevitably developed plot. It is uncertain even whether the theme of Priapus' hostility ran from beginning to end or merely through a portion of the novel.

Two distinct styles stand out in our fragments, that of the narrative and the 'educated' characters and that given to Trimalchio and the other freedmen. For unaffected ease and raciness many passages where the former style is used are quite unsurpassed. It is also an extremely flexible medium, admitting endless changes of nuance. And the opportunity Petronius enjoys to switch into verse, without syntactical break if necessary, is a useful resource: sometimes he can in verse better convey emotion or indicate amusing parallels. He is particularly skilful in reproducing the absurdities and pomposity of the superficially educated. Encolpius and Giton, when in extremity, discourse as if in a school of rhetoric (114.8–12); other characters rant, gush, or pontificate whenever they get the chance. There is no less verisimilitude in the freedmen's conversation, fruity, solecistic, and irrepressible. They are characterized by what they say (e.g. 61.6–62.14), as well as by the way they speak. Admittedly Petronius exaggerates somewhat. That so many homely saws, so much slang, and so much gutter wit were ever in real life accumulated in such short compass is hard to believe. Sam Weller at his best could not compete. But the language used is not far removed from reality, as independent evidence for colloquial Latin attests. Of course some questions arise, for instance over the appreciable number of Grecisms. Are they representative of colloquial speech in this milieu only, or generally? And one other question is especially tantalizing. Did Petronius in the books now lost attempt to copy the language of clearly identifiable social groups? He may have done so, for we must remember that Trimalchio's party is only an extended episode, and not to be accorded unique importance.

Evidence for substantial use of Petronius in later Latin literature is hard to find. Apuleius, in his novel's conception and style, pursued a different course, though similarities too may be detected. In modern times we encounter numerous works which bear a passing resemblance to Petronius', but few traces of direct imitation. Fragments are not perhaps very tempting to imitators. The Spanish picaresque novels seem to owe more to Apuleius. Again, though Petronius should have been congenial to some of our eighteenth-century novelists, Fielding, Smollett, and Sterne, reminiscences there are tenuous indeed. But a deep and subtle influence has been discerned in certain classics of the present century, including Joyce's *Ulysses* and Eliot's *Waste Land*. The latter acknowledges a connexion in his epigraph.

# 9

# HISTORY AND BIOGRAPHY

## I. VELLEIUS PATERCULUS

Several major historians, including Aufidius, Servilius, and Pliny, flourished in the century between Livy and Tacitus, but change of fashion or ill chance has robbed us of their works. Of the historical writing of this period only two representatives survive, Curtius (whose subject matter separates him from the main stream) and Velleius. Such is the dearth of other evidence that, if the criticisms directed against Velleius, for bias and incompetence, were trebly deserved, he could still not be neglected.

Velleius' history is neither epitome nor rudimentary summary, but a highly personal and selective outline, marked by special interests and very much overloaded. He vastly expands his scale of treatment as he approaches his own times, and some have supposed that everything which precedes Augustus and Tiberius is mere introduction: Velleius hurries on to talk about contemporary history, desiring to present in Tiberius the consummation of Roman virtues. If that were entirely true, his earlier exposition would have been derivative and perfunctory. In fact it is often studied and independent, albeit patchy. The same attitudes and techniques are indeed evident throughout: in particular he constantly seeks to evaluate the worth and achievements of individuals, rather than to describe the political circumstances of past ages. For him character and personality form history's very essence, and, though this recurrent obsession prompts some memorable sketches (e.g. 2.29, 2.35, 2.127), it also weakens and distorts the whole picture.

Modern discussion of Velleius centres on Tiberius' principate: Velleius is commonly condemned for flattery of Tiberius and Sejanus. Something may be said on the other side. Most importantly, much of his account of Tiberius is true. As Velleius, one of his officers, well knew, Tiberius was an extremely competent general; he cared about his men; he did not, like Augustus, lose his nerve in the crisis of A.D. 6–9; he inspired and rewarded loyalty. Velleius is a valuable source for Tiberius' campaigns in Illyricum and Germany, though he deceives or at least misleads his readers at 2.106.2. Further, he is fair to Gaius Caesar (2.101–2) and rightly critical of Varus (2.117–18). His evasion of delicate issues concerning Tiberius' 'exile' at Rhodes is venial enough, and his panegyric of the emperor at 2.126 was an unavoidable obligation for a contemporary, though he may genuinely have believed what he says. Again, his treatment of Sejanus at 2.127–8, ostensibly very favourable, does not prove him one of Sejanus' adherents. Velleius completed his work at a time of tension and uncertainty, as his impassioned concluding prayer (2.131) reveals. Though staunchly loyal to Tiberius and perhaps the more inclined to praise him as his general popularity waned, he still foresees grave dangers. In the political situation of A.D. 30 he could be no more explicit. Such is a case for the defence, not devoid of force. But bias, however plausibly accounted for, prevents Velleius from judging recent history objectively. And, while panegyric as such at 2.126 is understandable, the blessings which Tiberius allegedly effected pass all credence, the more so because much the same has been said about Augustus at 2.89.3–4. Augustus' last years were indeed troubled, but honesty, authority, and discipline had not vanished, only to be resuscitated instantaneously by Tiberius' accession. Revival of lost virtues was or was to become a commonplace: that is no excuse for a historian. Is Velleius then just a propagandist for Tiberius? In the strictest sense (if Tiberius' prior approval is implied), no. Like other retired officers, he probably had the itch to write and could guess what would be acceptable. Thus he provides good evidence for various concepts and conventions nowadays comprehended under the unduly formal rubric 'ideology of the Principate'.

Velleius is much indebted to Livy and Sallust, more to the former, though he sets great store by brevity (see, e.g., 1.16.1, 2.29.2, 2.124.1). But he achieves brevity by his handling of material rather than contracted expression or Sallustian abruptness. He elaborates certain topics, while omitting or summarily dismissing others, even matters of undeniable importance (e.g. 2.52.3). And, for all his anxiety about speed, he not only lingers but also digresses: at the end of Book 1 he actually conjoins two digressions, on colonies and literature. The latter digression (cf. 2.9), in a work so circumscribed, is rather remarkable. He says that he is irresistibly fascinated by the brief flowering of great talents, in Greece and Rome. No doubt he is, and, in finding space for such material, he displays a refreshingly catholic approach to the study of history. Indeed one may debate whether this is history at all as the ancients understood it.

Velleius' writing is predictably artificial. He likes verbal point; he employs many patterns of word and phrase; he partially anticipates Seneca's ingenious antitheses and Tacitus' unfailing novelty. But he is often pleonastic and sometimes constructs long periods, after Livy's manner. Emotional and high-flown passages (e.g. 2.66.3–5) stand near to sections of colourless and skimpy narration. Velleius' style is not homogeneous.

In writing outline history Velleius had respectable predecessors, such as

Atticus (Cic. *Brut.* 14–15) and Nepos (Cat. 1.5–7). We cannot tell whether he found in them precedent for reference to his family and personal experiences, or for giving his dedicatee, M. Vinicius, an unwarranted historical prominence. Plainly Velleius was self-centred and prejudiced, a wilful amateur: he neither enquired nor reflected enough. But, if he merits scant esteem, he still claims much attention. No one would hesitate to exchange him for Cremutius Cordus, let alone Aufidius or Pliny, but he somehow survived when his betters were lost. Hence he is indispensable for students of history. For students of literature he represents a transitional phase in Roman historiography, permitting some appraisal of gradual change and blending of style.[1]

## 2. Q. CURTIUS RUFUS

Curtius' *History of Alexander* is enthralling and exasperating. He enthrals if we want to read of drama and high adventure. He exasperates if we want essential facts and a consistent assessment of them. And he has greatly perplexed modern scholars. Some find in him a rhetorician pure and simple, concerned only to entertain and excite his readers, comparable with our historical novelists rather than our historians. Others claim that, however many blemishes may mar his work, he seriously endeavoured to write history and must be treated seriously.

Much may be said on both sides. Curtius' irresponsibility and nonchalance are demonstrated repeatedly by inaccuracies, contradictions, implausible fabrication of detail, in speeches and elsewhere, and above all freely confessed willingness to mislead. He admits (9.1.34) that he has copied down more than he believes to be true. In selecting material for elaboration Curtius prefers whatever is pathetic, romantic, extraordinary; his geography is deplorable, but he adeptly describes scenic beauty or curiosities of nature (e.g. 5.4.6–9); his reports of battles are often unclear, indeed unintelligible, but he very carefully depicts oriental pageantry (e.g. 3.3.8–28). He neither grasps the major historical issues which Alexander's career raises, nor does he present Alexander credibly and coherently. His final remarks about the king (10.5.26–36) are at variance with the picture of progressive corruption, derived from Peripatetic teaching, which largely colours the preceding narrative (see e.g. 6.2.1–4). In a word, he is unreliable and, if he had priorities, got them badly wrong. On the other side, it is clear that Curtius independently employed several sources, including one or two good sources not otherwise now accessible: he did not merely reproduce an inferior tradition, embodied in Clitarchus. Hence he preserves precious items of information, hidden

[1] I am greatly indebted to Dr A. J. Woodman, who has kindly shown me two of his papers before publication and taught me much about Velleius.

sometimes under the rhetoric of his speeches, and explains various matters (particularly Persian actions and motives) nowhere else explained. He can be as shrewd as he is impish[1] and perverse, and, though not in Arrian's class, remains indispensable. Again in a word, he intermittently troubled himself about content as well as form.

Curtius writes volubly, almost precipitately, as if embarrassed by a surplus of material, but he is never in real difficulties. Trite reflections and incisive comments are invariably at his command; he can expand, abbreviate, vary tone and mood, even discard his usual rhetoric, all with consummate ease; if he is at times clumsy and repetitious in expression and inept in thought, it is probably through negligence, not incompetence. Apart from his historical sources, certain literary influences may be detected, notably epic poetry and Livy, perhaps Herodotus, but no single writer known to us exercised a dominant effect on him. His style is not so derivative or distinctly marked as to give firm evidence of date, but his frequent *sententiae*, his sentence structure (he readily uses short, abrupt sentences), some features of his syntax (e.g. very free use of future participles), light poetic colouring, and absence of extravagant archaizing all point to the beginning or middle of the first century A.D., and this dating is confirmed by similarities in thought and expression to Seneca and Calpurnius Siculus.

Why this accomplished dilettante chose to write about Alexander we cannot know: perhaps he explained in his preface, if he condescended to write one. But Alexander was a standard theme in the schools of rhetoric and it was not difficult to see the rich opportunities which a full-scale treatment of his life and deeds offered. If our tentative dating is right, the more general revival of interest in Alexander prompted by Trajan is irrelevant. Curtius is typical of much historiography of the first century A.D.: it was stuff such as his, showy and untrustworthy, but not devoid of substance, which Tacitus used and superseded.

## 3. TACITUS

Tacitus never became a classic or school-book in antiquity, for he arrived too late to enter a limited repertoire.[2] As a traditionalist in an age of declining standards he was averse from outline history and scandalous biography, and his brevity defied the tribe of excerptors and abbreviators. If he courted popularity, he failed to win it. A few Christians know of him and in Ammian he has a distinguished follower. Thereafter followed long neglect, precarious and truncated survival, and late rediscovery. But, once rediscovered, Tacitus

---

[1] 'There are things in Curtius which look like pure impishness, designed to annoy serious readers', Tarn (1948) II 103.

[2] Though, admittedly, a few comparatively late poets, such as Lucan and Juvenal, became classics of a sort.

compelled the attention of many of the best scholars and thinkers of the fifteenth and sixteenth centuries. He interested them not only because of his style and theme, but also because his views (real or supposed) seemed applicable to contemporary politics and statecraft. This latter interest faded long ago, but a basic dilemma remains in studying Tacitus, a consummate stylist and rhetorician who is also a major historian. To what extent is his content separable from his style?

In the *Agricola*, his earliest work, Tacitus amalgamates biography and historical monograph. But the success of the combination is questionable. He gives roughly two thirds of the work to Agricola's governorship of Britain, and treats the climax of Agricola's campaigns at length, providing direct speeches for the two leaders, almost as if he were experimenting with full-scale history. Such extensive development of a part, albeit an important part, unbalances the whole. Again, most of what he tells us about Agricola's personality is conventional and unrevealing. Characterization in more depth was reasonably to be expected, though not, in an avowedly laudatory composition (3.3), any critical assessment. Some contend that Tacitus exaggerated Agricola's achievements and wilfully misconstrued his relations with Domitian. We cannot be sure, but certainly many matters in the *Agricola* are unclear or, like the insinuation of poisoning against Domitian (43.2), ill substantiated. There is, however, a case for the defence. Tacitus probably found little else worth relating about Agricola except the governorship, and hence made the most of it. In thus concentrating on military and administrative achievements, he followed a hallowed Republican tradition, attested in surviving epitaphs and eulogies (cf. Nep. *Epam.* 1.4). A Roman aristocrat should possess and display *uirtus*, above all in warfare: to this pattern Agricola conformed. Thus one old-fashioned attitude underlies a work somewhat novel in conception.

Concern with *uirtus*[1] was to reappear in the *Germania* and recur often in the major works. Agricola, a colourless individual, is instructive as a type: indeed he probably influenced Tacitus' judgement of more important historical figures. Even under a ruler hostile to the Senate *uirtus* may still, Tacitus thinks, be exercised to good purpose, though very liable to be frustrated by envy and spite. Thus Agricola prefigures Germanicus and Corbulo in the *Annals*. He also represents dignified moderation, a theme to which Tacitus reverts at *Ann.* 4.20.2–3, where he debates whether a viable middle course exists between contumacy and subservience. The problem affected prominent senators acutely. Hence this thread of thought runs through Tacitus' writings, just as the bitter sense of guilt and humiliation, disclosed at *Agricola* 45.1–2, infects

---

[1] *Virtus* has no precise English equivalent. Neither 'manhood' nor 'excellence' nor 'virtue' hits it exactly.

his view of the first century A.D. generally. To understand Tacitus we must pay special attention to the *Agricola*. Later he effectively conceals what he would not have us know. Here his protective mask is still uncemented.

For the speeches at 30–4 Tacitus is much beholden to Sallust and Livy, for his powerful and moving conclusion to Cicero. As yet he had not formed his historical style, controlled, incisive, only intentionally ambiguous. In the *Agricola* we find infelicities and obscurities, not all imputable to textual corruption, and some padding. One may contrast the *Dialogus*. Here an appropriate style was already available and Tacitus employed it with complete mastery. For the *Agricola* no such guidance offered itself, and in style, as in structure, this first essay is imperfect.

The *Germania* has been subjected to microscopic study, and, where content is concerned, survived the test tolerably well. Independent evidence tends to confirm the information which Tacitus provides. He probably obtained it from Book 104 of Livy, Pliny's lost *Bella Germaniae*, and (through them or directly) certain Greek authorities, but seems to use considerable judgement in selection. He may call on first-hand experience, his own or others', to supplement and control his sources.

In 1–27 Tacitus deals with country and people generally, in 28–46 with the individual tribes. The title *De origine et situ Germanorum*, 'On the origins and homeland of the Germans', is well attested and probably genuine, but he is just as interested in their character and way of life, *mores* and *instituta* (27.2). No model for his work survives, unless we consider Herodotus as such, but Livy's approach in Book 104 may have been similar, as may Seneca's in his lost writings on Egypt and India. Tacitus may also have been influenced by Sallust's excursus on the Black Sea in *Histories* 3, and by geographical digressions in other historians. This affiliation to history helps to explain why the *Germania* is not purely descriptive, but full of comment and evaluation. Tacitus wants to explain an alien people in terms which Romans can readily understand. He shows that the Germans retain virtues which Rome once possessed, but does not idealize them or hide their weaknesses. There is no sustained contrast here, no consistent sermonizing. But Tacitus saw, as Seneca had seen (*De ira* 1.11.4), that the Germans posed a real, perhaps imminent, threat to the empire, and plainly indicates as much (33.2 and 37.3–5). Insofar as it embodies this message, the *Germania* is a 'tract for the times', though not intended to prompt or justify a specific policy. It is best described as an ethnographical treatise written from a historical viewpoint.

Stylistically this is Tacitus' least happy work. A starkly scientific approach was for such a writer inconceivable, but simple subject matter deserved simple treatment. Instead we find an excess of crude rhetoric and verbal dexterity. By repeated self-obtrusion Tacitus gives the unpleasant impression of seeking to demonstrate his talents rather than to instruct his readers. Sometimes, one may admit, point and epigram arise quite naturally, as at 19.1 *nemo illic uitia ridet, nec corrumpere et corrumpi saeculum uocatur* 'no one there makes a joke of vice, nor is seducing and being seduced called the way of the world'. But, most irritatingly, he cannot even state plainly the plain fact that the Germans have no precious metals (5.2): *argentum et aurum propitiine an irati di negauerint dubito* 'I know not whether divine grace or anger has denied them silver and gold'. Such meretricious adornments, only too conventional, disfigure an ostensibly serious treatise. The style of the *Germania* has justly been likened to Seneca's: there is much balance and antithesis here, all rather cloying. Fortunately Tacitus never again pandered thus to a decadent fashion.

The *Dialogus*, a book rich in ideas if tantalizingly elusive in purport, is separated from everything else Tacitus wrote by its Ciceronianism. In his classic works on oratory Cicero found a highly apposite style for literary treatment of the subject. And Tacitus, using (as Cicero often used) a dialogue form, was *ipso facto* further committed to emulating Cicero: his own historical manner would have been utterly unsuitable. Since the *Dialogus'* style was so much conditioned by genre, this style scarcely helps us in dating the work relatively to Tacitus' other writings. Dating depends here principally on obligations to Quintilian's *Institutio* and similarities, in expression or thought, to Pliny's *Panegyricus*. This evidence points to the early years of the second century, and accords with the subjective impression that the *Dialogus* is a mature, not a juvenile work.

Tacitus' theme, the decline of oratory, was familiar. It had been tackled by Quintilian, touched upon by Petronius and 'Longinus'.[1] Indeed, from the late Republic onwards, Roman critics, not all conservatives, battled over the merits of old and new styles. Tacitus treats the subject alertly and many-sidedly, conscious of the complex factors involved, particularly educational theory, literary fashion, and political change. The *Dialogus* has three protagonists, Maternus (a poet), Aper (an advocate), and Messalla (a connoisseur of oratory). Its argument runs thus: Aper questions Maternus' preference for poetry, extolling the advantages and satisfaction which oratory affords, while Maternus asserts that poetry, more delightful in itself, brings enduring fame; discussion now shifts to the dispute between 'ancients' and 'moderns', and Aper argues that contemporary orators should concede nothing to their predecessors, pioneers in their day, but by present standards inadequate, while Messalla replies that Cicero and his contemporaries are unsurpassed, and attributes decline to bad training and limited education; then a lacuna in the

---

[1] The Περὶ ὕψους was probably written in the first century A.D., but the interesting similarities in thought between Tacitus and 'Longinus' are not such as to prove a direct connexion.

text engulfs the end of Messalla's speech;[1] when the text resumes Maternus is explaining that oratory is nurtured by suitable political conditions, that Republican dissensions encouraged it, but the blissful stability of the Principate renders it largely superfluous. This bald sketch naturally gives no impression of the dialogue's manifold subtleties.

Critics are much concerned with the work's structure and intention, asking whether it is an organic whole and whether Tacitus endorses any of the opinions expressed. But, let us remember, there are writers who do not invariably press their own views, and dialogue form, realistically employed, hardly permits unbroken development of a single argument. All the views conveyed in the *Dialogus* obtain eloquent and persuasive presentation, just as they would from Cicero: none of the speeches wholly cancels out or annuls another. Those who find Tacitus' verdict embodied in Maternus' final contribution must explain how Maternus can not only accept the Principate but regard it as far superior to what preceded. If he speaks for Tacitus, he speaks with heavy irony. More probably Tacitus' thoughts and personality find partial and unclear reflection in Aper's modernism no less than Messalla's nostalgia and Maternus' detachment. No simple conclusion emerges, but his theme itself shows that he admits a decline in standards. The *Dialogus* holds together intelligibly, if loosely, in three stages: oratory is examined in the contexts of literature, education, and politics. The discussion is broad and discursive, but not random or undisciplined.

In vocabulary, phrasal structure, figures of speech, and expansive geniality the *Dialogus* is markedly after Cicero's manner, though not purely Ciceronian. Tacitus' language here is livelier and more polished than Quintilian's and richer and more virile than Pliny's. Cicero never had a better imitator.

In A.D. 98 (*Agr.* 3.3) Tacitus planned to write 'a record of former servitude and acknowledgement of present blessings', but the scheme partly aborted. He deferred Nerva and Trajan (*Hist.* 1.1.4), a rich but delicate theme, limiting his *Histories* to A.D. 69–96. This task occupied him for several years, as Pliny attests. Perhaps, after the common fashion, the *Histories* became known initially by private circulation and recitation. When he completed this first part of his major work is uncertain. And we cannot tell whether he proceeded immediately to the second, the Julio-Claudian period, the subject of our *Annals*. One thing is clear, that Tacitus' interests were drawn back inexorably into the past: at *Ann.* 3.24.3 he states that, if he embarks on another theme, it will be Augustus' era, thus, it seems, finally abandoning contemporary history. The more he pondered upon the events he records, the more he looked for explanation in earlier developments.

---

[1] If the lacuna contained only Messalla's conclusion and the beginning of Maternus' speech, we may usefully discuss the whole plan of the work. If it contained another speech, structural analysis is insecure.

Tacitus begins his *Histories* in annalistic manner, with the consular year 69, but compensates somewhat for thus starting *in mediis rebus* by his memorable survey of the state of the empire (*Hist.* 1.4–11). He begins the *Annals*, originally titled or subtitled *ab excessu divi Augusti*, non-annalistically, but then, in *Ann.* 1–6 at least, adheres quite strictly to an annalistic layout. How, we may wonder, did he conclude the work? If with Nero's death, not the end of A.D. 68, then he nowhere recorded about six months of that year, a curious gap in an otherwise complete narration. Some scholars have criticized his decision to commence with Tiberius' accession. Other starting-points, they say, would have been better historically. Perhaps so, but none would have been perfect.

Several structural questions remain unanswerable: how, for instance, did Tacitus dispose his material in the missing portions of the *Histories* and *Annals*, and did he attach special importance to grouping in sections comprising six books? Again, having virtually no firm evidence for date, we cannot say much about stages of composition. We may detect some considerable linguistic differences between *Hist.* 1–5, *Ann.* 1–6, and *Ann.* 11–16, but they prove only that Tacitus was incessantly experimenting. Again, in these three sections, we observe changes in historiographical technique: in *Hist.* 1–5 the material is tightly packed, the narrative rapid, the centre of interest often shifting, in *Ann.* 1–6 Tacitus proceeds in more leisurely manner, diverging little from a simple framework, and centring attention on one dominant figure, while in *Ann.* 11–16 the structure is looser, the presentation of material varied and episodic. But these changes are largely imputable to the subject matter; the momentous events of A.D. 69 required a wide scale and sustained intensity of treatment, Tiberius, as an individual, was more interesting than his three successors, and under Claudius and Nero there were distinct phases, historical and dramatic, for which soberly annalistic narration, focused on Princeps and Senate, was not altogether ideal. But we still face the disquieting possibility that the *Annals* were never completed and that Books 13–16 are unrevised. The occasional laxity in structure, certain inconsistencies, some imprecision in nomenclature, and arguable lack of polish in expression may so suggest. Much of this can, however, be explained by carelessness over detail (such as we sometimes find elsewhere in his work) or mere exhaustion or increasing self-assurance.

Tacitus claims (*Hist.* 1.1.3 and *Ann.* 1.1.3) to write dispassionately, untouched by malice or partisanship. That conventional assertion appears in many writers, Greek and Roman. Historians were expected to tell the truth and the whole truth (cf. Cic. *De or.* 2.62), but, of course, not all of them did. In his prefaces and at *Hist.* 2.101.1 Tacitus scathingly castigates certain predecessors, some of whom he must have employed as sources: they falsified history through ignorance (not knowing what went on) or flattery (to please those in power) or spite (once free to abuse the dead). To judge from Velleius and what source-investigation can recover about such writers as Cluvius Rufus, this damning verdict is justified. Tacitus' own sincerity and good intentions need not be doubted, but we may ask whether he lived up to his ideals. Though he had no reasons for personal bias in much of what he wrote, he could still be affected by other, more insidious causes of misconception and inaccuracy. Again (a point rarely noted), he blandly assumes and implies that he at least is well informed and qualified to pass valid judgements. Perhaps so, but egotism and consular rank are no safeguards against credulity or error.

A historian's first task is to collect and evaluate evidence. Some nineteenth-century scholars believed that ancient writers of history shirked this labour, content to follow a single source, altering only the style. Their views have rightly been abandoned or tempered. The obligation to compare and assess earlier writings was commonly recognized (cf. Plin. *Epist.* 5.8.12), and Tacitus, amongst others, tried to discharge it. Thus at *Hist.* 3.28 he admits uncertainty, faced with equally possible opinions from Pliny and Messalla, at *Ann.* 4.57.1 questions a conventional theory, and at *Ann.* 13.20.2 notes Rusticus' prejudice in favour of Seneca. He seems to adumbrate his own approach at *Ann.* 4.10.1: he will report what the majority of reliable sources say, but may append divergent views or comments of his own. Tacitus drew his material from general and special histories (cf. *Ann.* 1.69.2), memoirs (cf. *Ann.* 4.53.2). personal enquiry (cf. Plin. *Epist.* 6.16.1), and the official report of senatorial proceedings, *acta senatus*.[1] It is debatable whether he made the fullest use of these diverse sources. Perhaps he might have used the *acta* as some partial control upon the historians, but in fact he seems to use them only intermittently, for variety or to preserve a semblance of traditional subject matter: thus minor senatorial business tends to appear at the end of each year's record. We cannot well judge how conscientiously Tacitus handled primary evidence, since he mainly depends on secondary sources. If we had the later books of the *Histories*, we might better appraise his quality: here, for much of the Flavian period, there were no secondary sources to reshape and supersede, and here, if anywhere, he was liable to personal bias.

Tacitus may often, as he says, follow the consensus of witnesses or the more trustworthy. But analysis of his work and comparison with Cassius Dio, Suetonius, and Plutarch, who partly depend on the same sources, sometimes suggest another picture: Tacitus may indeed utilize several predecessors, yet, at any particular place, he is, like Livy, prone to follow one mainly, inter-

---

[1] This is no complete list. Much miscellaneous material was available, such as published speeches, eulogistic biography, and collections of memorable deeds and sayings. And there was unpublished material, for instance in the imperial archives, to which he might have had access, though probably he never bothered.

weaving details or opinions from subsidiary authorities. Sometimes favourable and unfavourable views of the same individual are mixed or juxtaposed, as with Antonius Primus in the *Histories* and Annaeus Seneca in the *Annals*. Such discrepancies may well be due to imperfect assimilation of two or more traditions. While absolutely unswerving use of any single source may be discounted, the presence of dominant or, at least, specially influential sources may not. Thus the picture of Tiberius as a hypocritical and rancorous tyrant, shared with Dio and Suetonius, was probably sketched in essentials by a first-century historian. Again, we learn much by comparing *Hist.* 1–2 with Plutarch's lives of Galba and Otho, since Plutarch largely reproduces a writer whom Tacitus follows in substance, but with many variations. Here, via Plutarch, we may virtually test Tacitus against one of his major sources, and observe how he can come near to plagiarism (even epigrams are taken over), while diverging radically in approach. The source (probably the elder Pliny) was very full and detailed, readily intelligible, and apparently a little superficial. Tacitus omits much detail, highlighting only carefully chosen aspects or scenes, rearranges and trajects material, for greater effect or other reason, and ignores or subverts facile interpretation, preferring complexity and indecision. He was no bringer of order into chaos: when he found order he was indeed only too ready to disrupt it. The wilful selection and manipulation of detail, along with independence of attitude, which comparison with Plutarch attests, may further be established by comparison with those parts of Suetonius where the same common source again is evident. Plutarch and Suetonius copy: Tacitus chooses and blends, not always judiciously.

Like many predecessors, Tacitus conceives that history should be moralistic and instructive (*Ann.* 3.65.1). Therefore he looks for examples of good or bad conduct, regularly praises and censures, and quite seriously attempts to probe the psychology of historical characters and discover their motives. Unfortunately, the thoughts of persons long since dead are rarely recoverable, and Tacitus imputes motives for which no evidence can exist, often very discreditable ones. Though he professes instruction as his principal aim, he is no less anxious to captivate and entertain his readers. Hence he does not always give most space to matters most important historically, but frequently chooses to elaborate such material as readily invites colourful and exciting treatment. Hence too he ever pursues variety, in subject matter and presentation. He can be simple or complex, detached or committed, solemn or (witness *Ann.* 12.5.3) ironical. Such are the proper skills of a first-class rhetorician. Tacitus was more than that because he also attempted to explain and interpret the events he narrates, and did not invariably accept easy and plausible explanations.

Did Tacitus adhere to his professed ideals? Not altogether. In particular he took over and developed a presentation of Tiberius which is ill-founded and psychologically unconvincing. No doubt he was influenced in so doing by later events and his own experience of Domitian, but this is no adequate excuse. Struggling to reconcile his preconceived view of Tiberius with the facts available to him, he had to resort to many illegitimate and reprehensible devices to make those facts seem other than they were or to explain them away. Thus, to suggest that Tiberius' conduct is not to be explained straightforwardly, he constantly reiterates the ideas of hypocrisy, dissimulation, and hidden malice. And he presents the Tiberian treason-trials in an unjustifiably horrific and lurid way. But he does not suppress or pervert evidence, and indeed he supplies us with the means to refute his own contentions. *Ann.* 1–6 show a sad lack of judgement and historical perspective, but not dishonesty. And, we may fairly add, the world's literature would be much poorer without Tacitus' Tiberius, a haunting and tragic figure.

Tacitus' historical style is a masterful and strange creation, difficult to characterize. It appears abnormal, but was any general norm recognized at this period? If there was a standard prose, we may find it in Quintilian, and, for history, Curtius may be typical. But, in spite of the strong influence of tradition, fashion was very fluid and individuality acceptable. Tacitus tried, as others did, to be colourful, original, and arresting. He also cultivated a hauteur in expression and attitude unlike anything else in Latin literature. Some adjudge him tortuous and artificial, and certainly his writing is anything but facile. Close analysis reveals innumerable changes of preference: for a time Tacitus favours particular words and phrases, then suddenly drops and supersedes them. No constant development is evident, but he is ever striving to be different, reacting against his own earlier experiments as well as against other styles. He is also, however, acutely conscious of a need for overall consistency of texture.

Tacitus adopted many prominent features of Sallust's style: choice and unusual vocabulary, asyndeton, avoidance of balanced phrases and rounded periods, and, above all, brevity. But in almost every respect in which he imitates Sallust he also diverges, usually showing more taste and restraint than his model. Thus he does not accept all Sallust's vocabulary: some of it was too outlandish and archaic. Again he does not employ asyndeton as frequently or as extravagantly. And, though he surpasses Sallust in brevity, he does not affect the same abruptness. Rejecting the Ciceronian period, Sallust devised a broken, staccato sentence-structure. Tacitus can write like this occasionally, but elsewhere, to replace the period, he uses a lop-sided and overloaded form of sentence, in which important thoughts are appended one to another, often by the use of ablatives absolute, and where what is formally the main clause may in fact be of little weight. In one way only does he go further than Sallust, in his inordinate love of variation, a feature which pervades his historical writing. Tacitus' style is in general more smooth and homogeneous than Sallust's, for Sallust, though his conciseness deserved and won applause, can sometimes be hispid and verbose. Such insouciance was not for Tacitus, and, when he adapted the famous sketch of Catiline to Sejanus (*Ann.* 4.1), he pared away the unevenness and superfluities of the original.

The stylistic influences on Tacitus, apart from Sallust, are many and various, and some too deeply interlocked to be separated out. Cicero and Seneca are important here, not only because he rebelled against them. Livy's influence is underestimated: we may trace it in vocabulary and in treatment of minor scenes and, occasionally, larger episodes. Then there are the poets, above all Virgil, and here we encounter some misunderstanding. Tacitus, like any educated Roman of his day, was steeped in Virgil's poetry: it coloured his language and from time to time, perhaps, his thought. But it was no major formative influence. He does not often, as some suppose, use allusions to Virgil to enrich and enhance his narrative, nor does he find in Virgil inspiration for his handling of incident and character. Doubtless a few of his Virgilian echoes are intentional, but most of them lack special significance. Following a tradition of historical writing in which Sallust and Livy were conjoined,[1] Tacitus worked day by day with the historians of the first century A.D., his main sources: they cannot have failed to affect his style. We may form some impression, from Velleius and Curtius, of what the historiography of this period was like. It was probably marked by keen interest in personality, elaboration of parts of the story, abbreviation of others, a good deal of moralizing comment, and a great deal of pointed, epigrammatic expression. The characterization may have been crude or schematic, the moralizing trite, and the expression inadequate, but there lay an opportunity which Tacitus could seize. He consummated what several predecessors had attempted.

Tacitus was certainly an innovator: he coined words, strained usage, and once or twice, as in the 'impressionistic' writing of *Ann.* 1.40.4–41.2, almost abandoned syntax. But he was not such a radical as he seems at first glance. The loss of his sources, as of Sallust's *Histories* and much of Livy, enjoins cautious appraisal of apparent Tacitean novelties. Many words first attested in Tacitus must have existed earlier. Again, some of our first-century evidence, drawn from poets or other genres of prose, suggests strongly that Tacitus was wont to extend and vary established modes of expression, not to make wholly new departures. He shied away from affectation and preciosity, and we may well imagine the distaste he must have felt for the pedantic, archaizing fancies of Hadrian's era, if he survived to contemplate them.

[1] Perhaps separate traditions, Sallustian and Livian, continued through the first century. But the surviving texts scarcely confirm this opinion. Is Velleius, for instance, Sallustian or Livian? It looks as if the two streams converged quite early.

It is often useful to consider the sort of expressions which particular Latin writers seem to avoid. And in Tacitus this approach has been very rewarding, although some of his preferences and dislikes are inexplicable, except by whim and idiosyncrasy. In general he avoids flat, lifeless, and over-used words, and abstracts (especially when vivid and concrete synonyms are available), also technical terms and official parlance, such as we find on coins and public inscriptions. Conversely he likes words which, without being extraordinary, are yet fresh, graphic, and memorable. His discontent with much normal and seemingly innocuous vocabulary may be attributed partly to a conscious desire for dignity, partly to pathological aversion from the half-truths and clichés of his society. But there is also a more mundane explanation: Tacitus, who after all often perforce uses standard terms, sometimes replaces them simply to escape the tedium of repetition. Like most stylists, he is anxious not to bore his readers.

'Although the style of Tacitus cannot match that of Livy for variety, it nevertheless changes perceptibly according to the nature of the subject matter.'[1] Perhaps, out of a concern for stylistic unity, Tacitus deliberately restricted his room for manoeuvre. But he still found opportunity enough to be flexible and varied. Some scenes obtain rich coloration, for instance *Ann.* 1.65, where poeticisms cluster, and *Ann.* 4.46-51, where asyndeton is strikingly used. When emotionally involved, as at *Ann.* 14.64, he can be stridently rhetorical. When relating routine business, he can write quite simply. In speeches he diverges somewhat from his narrative style: we find here more balanced clauses, various devices of style infrequent elsewhere, and generally a comparatively flowing and expansive manner. Some suppose that, though tradition and propriety excluded reproduction of the exact words of authentic speeches (see *Ann.* 15.63.3), Tacitus attempted to recall or recreate styles appropriate to his characters. It is doubtful whether this interesting theory can be sustained, but he apparently paid some regard to what was actually said, when the information was accessible. The original of Claudius' speech at *Ann.* 11.24 partly survives on an inscription (*CIL* XIII 1.1668). Tacitus preserves something of its gist and a little of its phraseology, hardly enough, however, to resurrect Claudius' singular ineptitude. Again, the speech given to Seneca at *Ann.* 14.53-4, certainly a free composition by Tacitus, is perhaps intended to satirize the speaker, but, if so, it is the banality of thought which effects this object, not the expression, which is far from being Senecan. And again, while Tiberius' letters and speeches show a few distinct features, notably in vocabulary, we cannot prove that these features derive from Tiberius himself. We may assert that some of Tacitus' speeches have a more individual character than others, for instance *Hist.* 4. 42, which is remarkably Ciceronian. Beyond this we embark on speculation.

[1] Adams (1973) 124.

Verbal sharpness, concomitant with brevity, is of the essence of Tacitus' style. He extracts the maximum force from individual words and their collocations, sometimes unexpected and paradoxical. This continual seeking for effect is most obviously apparent in *sententiae*, the craze and curse of his generation as of several generations preceding.[1] By common consent Tacitus' *sententiae* rank as the best in Latin prose, probably because he troubled himself about content as well as form. Some convey ideas not found before. Others have a long history: Tacitus added the final polish. Here are some examples: *Agr.* 30.4 *ubi solitudinem faciunt, pacem appellant* 'where they make a desert, they call it peace', *Hist.* 2.77.3 *qui deliberant, desciuerunt* 'discussion of rebellion is rebellion', *Hist.* 3.25.3 *factum esse scelus loquuntur faciuntque* 'they tell of crime done and do the same', *Ann.* 3.27.3 *corruptissima re publica plurimae leges* 'the more corrupt a state, the more numerous its laws'. Tacitus, more successfully than most writers, blends point and epigram into his narrative, as a longer excerpt, Arminius' obituary (*Ann.* 2.88.2–3), will show:

.·.liberator haud dubie Germaniae et qui non primordia populi Romani, sicut alii reges ducesque, sed florentissimum imperium lacessierit, proeliis ambiguus, bello non uictus. septem et triginta annos uitae, duodecim potentiae expleuit, caniturque adhuc barbaras apud gentes, Graecorum annalibus ignotus, qui sua tantum mirantur, Romanis haud perinde celebris, dum uetera extollimus recentium incuriosi.

*. . .beyond doubt Germany's deliverer and one who, unlike other kings and generals, challenged not an infant Rome, but Rome's empire at its height, with various fortune in battles, unconquered in war. He lived thirty-seven years and had power for twelve, and he is sung of still by barbarian tribes, albeit unknown to Greek histories (the Greeks only admire their own achievements), nor properly noticed in ours, for we celebrate the remote past, uninterested in things recent.*

Volumes have been devoted to Tacitus' opinions, thought, and outlook on the world. But there is little to show for all this effort. A few ideas, attitudes, and special interests may securely be attributed to Tacitus. Beyond that uncertainty reigns, largely because we cannot often tell whether views which Tacitus reports, above all in speeches, are views which he himself shares. Again, views presented in one place are sometimes contradicted in another. To put it harshly, he can be confused and inconsistent, or, to put it mildly, complex and elusive. But fault, if fault there be, lies rather with those who want a historian also to be a philosopher.

Tacitus' attitudes are coloured by his class and rank. He has often to relate the degradation and servility of the Senate, but to do so pains and embarrasses him (*Ann.* 14.14.3), and he continues to regard the Senate as centrally important (see perhaps *Hist.* 1.84.4). For the urban *plebs* he displays much contempt

---

[1] A *sententia* is a thought briefly and pointedly expressed, self-contained and therefore, if originally linked to a context, separable from it.

(*Hist.* 1.32.1 and 3.85), though he is interested in their behaviour and psychology, as indeed he is in the behaviour of mobs generally (witness his elaborate treatment of the mutinies in *Ann.* 1.16–49). He recognized the existence of public opinion, but usually treats it as negligible and sometimes sets against it the judgement of informed observers, *prudentes*. He assumes an air of superiority which becomes quite absurd at *Ann.* 11.21.1, where he refuses to discuss Curtius' low birth, and *Ann.* 4.3.4, where he implies that Livia's crime would have been less heinous had her seducer been a nobleman. Whether Tacitus was himself a *novus homo* is uncertain, but it is very possible. He certainly shows interest in the influx of newcomers into the Senate, and considers that older and better standards were preserved in provincial Italy and beyond (*Ann.* 3.55.3 and 16.5.1). However this may be, he writes like a descendant of a dozen consuls, with an added censoriousness which the elder Cato would have relished.

When Tacitus touches on major moral or religious questions, he is either quite at a loss or sceptical of solutions offered. He gives no convincing appearance of belief in the gods. Indeed his occasional references to them, like his reports of prodigies, may merely be part of the tradition he inherited, a part he was loath to discard, since these references could be useful stylistically, by adding weight and colour to his narrative. Thus at *Hist.* 1.3.2 he very effectively concludes an outline of his theme by asserting that events demonstrated *non esse curae deis securitatem nostram, esse ultionem* 'that the gods are concerned to chastise, not protect us'. Here he may seem to admit divine intervention, and yet, at *Hist.* 1.10.3, as at *Ann.* 14.12.2, he is utterly cynical about any kind of providence. Again, at *Ann.* 6.22, discussing astrology, he confesses complete uncertainty whether the life of man is guided by destiny or just the plaything of chance, and neither here nor elsewhere does he adopt the tenets of any philosophical school. If he tends to any view, it is that *fortuna*[1] directs the black comedy of life (*Ann.* 3.18.4): *mihi, quanto plura recentium seu ueterum reuoluo, tanto magis ludibria rerum mortalium cunctis in negotiis obuersantur* 'the more I think upon recent or earlier history, the more the universal farcicality of human affairs is apparent to me'. Tacitus was a pessimist through and through: not for him easy consolation and popular anodynes.

Tacitus' outlook on politics and political history is generally realistic and detached, sometimes distorted by his own unhappy experiences or tinged with nostalgia. The struggles and achievements of Rome's past excite his enthusiasm (*Ann.* 4.32.1), and he believes that liberty once flourished, though destined to a lingering death under the Principate (*Ann.* 1.74.5). But the old regime was not wholly admirable, least of all in its last years (*Ann.* 3.28.1). Internal dis-

---

[1] What Tacitus means by *fortuna* in such places as *Ann.* 3.18.4 and 4.1.1 (an important passage) is hard to determine. It is probably something more than chance, though far short of providence.

sension and lust for power brought tribulation, to the provinces as well as Rome (*Ann.* 1.2.2). Then the Principate established peace, at a price and without much honour. Tacitus is disillusioned with ideals and outdated causes, though he pays indirect homage to the Republican heroes Brutus and Cassius (*Ann.* 3.76.2). But about a few matters he cares deeply, perhaps above all freedom of speech. We see how much he cares about this in the *Agricola*, the prefaces to his historical works, and his treatment of the trial of Cremutius Cordus at *Ann.* 4.34–5, where, after Cremutius' speech and condemnation, he directly expresses his own feelings. Here we need have no doubt of what he thinks. In many other cases, where there is no express endorsement, it is perilous to assume that arguments given to others obtain his approval. He is, after all, adept, as any rhetorician should be, at finding the words suitable to the occasion. Thus at *Hist.* 1.15–16 Galba is made eloquently and forcefully to commend adoptive succession to the Principate. That was appropriate in the circumstances (disastrous though this particular adoption proved), but it does not follow that Tacitus, enamoured of Trajan, supposed adoptive succession to be the panacea for all Rome's troubles. He probably thought them past cure.

It is wiser to take Tacitus as he is than, as so many critics have done, require that he should be what he is not. He has grave weaknesses as a historian, if he is judged, as he often has been, by the most exacting modern standards. But he never consciously betrayed his own standards, such as they were: he sought to discover the truth, probing, questioning, rejecting mere plausibility. And he is a supremely gifted writer. In his mature works he commanded with ease the rhetoric which enslaved most of his contemporaries: such difficulties as he had were self-imposed. Yet he laboured long and hard not to write for his own day alone. Hence the magic of his style survives.

### 4. PLINY THE YOUNGER

Among Latin letters those of Pliny stand second only to Cicero's in interest and importance, though they are very different in character. In recent times they have attracted much attention, particularly, one suspects, because they provide such an excellent starting-point for study of the social history of the early Empire. But the fascinations of Pliny's subject matter should not divert us altogether from the more specifically literary questions, of form, style, and intention, which the letters raise. In what follows we shall look mainly at Books 1–9, the private correspondence published by the author. The letters to Trajan in Book 10 are not without literary interest, either in style (they are framed more simply than those in 1–9) or in content (they tell us much of Pliny's merits and limitations), but, since apparently he did not himself collect and publish them, they cannot be judged in the same terms as the others.

The primary questions are easy to pose and hard to answer. What kind of letters have we here and how were they chosen for publication? More particularly, were they sent to the addressees, then published in their original form, are they revised versions of authentic originals, are they literary exercises which never passed through the post at all, or do some belong to one of these categories, some to another? In his prefatory epistle (1.1) Pliny says: 'you have often urged me to collect and publish such letters as I had written with some special care. I have collected them, disregarding sequence in time (I was not writing a history), but as each one came to hand.' He adds that, if he finds or writes any more, he will not suppress them. At first sight this all seems helpful: it seems less so on further examination. To begin with, writing a letter is not for Pliny necessarily dependent on a call to send one: he explicitly testifies in 7.9 that epistolography was a commendable literary pursuit, an aid to versatility in style. Again, a rough chronological sequence has been established between the nine books, and some sequence may be found even within books. Thus 'disregarding sequence in time' is hard to credit. And the choice of letters for each book cannot be so random as 'as each one came to hand' suggests, for Pliny has plainly effected a balanced variety of themes within each of Books 1–7 (in 8–9 he begins to run short of sufficiently diverse material) and, to some extent, from book to book. There is then a conflict between what Pliny professes and what he has in fact done.

With few exceptions, each letter treats of a single subject: this is usually proposed or sketched at the outset, then developed, discussed, and illustrated. That the letters are planned as organic wholes is further attested by recurrent structural patterns, such as statement followed by three examples. Pliny clearly recognizes certain rules of epistolography, and he senses a need for apology if he breaks them: unity and brevity are especially important. He rarely hurries, or rambles, or adds a postscript. This control and conscious planning divorce Pliny's letters from real life and set them in marked contrast to Cicero's. If we consider the relationship between many of the letters and their addressees, we get a similar impression of unreality. Often, to be sure, subject matter and addressee are related (e.g. family affairs and Fabatus, history or rhetoric and Tacitus), but numerous letters might, as far as we can tell, have been addressed to anyone whom Pliny chose to flatter by his notice. And not infrequently, when he initially links theme and addressee, he proceeds as if oblivious of the addressee's continued existence. Compliment and courtesy are evident here, but it is a far cry from the lively dialogue of genuine correspondence. One may wonder how many of Pliny's letters would have elicited replies. When he has, as so often, not merely proposed a topic but handled it at length, what was a correspondent to add? For instance, is not 4.30 more a courteous acknowledgement of Sura's interest in natural science than a serious request for information and decision? Again, the number of separate addressees is noteworthy: 105 for 247 letters. Thus, while some get a fair number of letters, most get very few. Why is there such a multiplicity of names? After all most letter-writers have intimate friends, to whom they write frankly and often. The exclusion of revealing and embarrassing letters from a correspondence published by the writer is readily intelligible, but it remains surprising that no really close friends emerge, if these are real letters or even edited versions of real letters. A sceptic might say that, for variety or some other reason, Pliny decided to introduce as many addressees as possible: if there were no appropriate letters in his files, he could soon create them. The frequency of standardized openings perhaps supports this scepticism. But mere name-dropping was not Pliny's purpose: many influential contemporaries are not addressed. We need not doubt that the addressees were personally known to him. Having the critical reader much in mind, Pliny was concerned with verisimilitude as well as diversity. He selected or composed the letters accordingly.

Most of the letters fall easily into regular types, according to subject matter: public affairs, personalities, anecdotes, literature, personal business, descriptions, advice, recommendation, and so on. Some of these types correspond with recognized topics for epistolography. Nevertheless the letters probably give a fairly accurate reflection of Pliny's range of interests, which are various but unremarkable. Some subjects, familiar in other writers of the period, scarcely appear at all: antiquarian lore, language and grammar, religion, and, most surprisingly, philosophy. Pliny was not a learned man nor a thinker: it is hard to discover any recondite information in his letters and vain to look for profound or original thoughts. Again, he generally eschews or has erased adverse comment upon contemporaries, except for his *bête noire* Regulus (1.5, 2.20, 4.2, 4.7). And he is singularly delicate about literary matters. Though he talks much of the practice of detailed reciprocal criticism, he presents nothing of the kind in the published correspondence: instead mere appreciations, often vague or flattering. Similarly, in some correspondence about matters of business (such as 3.6), various mundane details, which must have been in the 'real' letters, have been edited out. Pliny was, it seems, guided in his revision not only by discretion but also by a sense of literary propriety and a fear of tedium. He clearly thought that his readers had tender stomachs, and sometimes, by weakening or indeed emasculating his original letters, he has lost the immediacy and realism which elsewhere he successfully retains.

There are numerous echoes of other writers in Pliny's letters, both in thought and in expression. Predictably Cicero and Virgil head the list, followed by Horace, Martial, and Statius amongst others. The Roman poets bulked large in Pliny's reading, as Quintilian would have enjoined: he seems not so well versed in Greek literature. Many of Pliny's reminiscences are such as mark the occasional writing of any educated man, but some may best be explained by conscious imitation and, if so, support the view that certain letters are literary exercises. We have a good 'test-case' in his account of the harbour at Centum Cellae (6.31.15–17: cf. Virg. *Aen.* 1.159–65 and Luc. 2.616–21). The place probably was much as Pliny presents it and as Virgil presented his imaginary harbour, but does that sufficiently explain Pliny's extensive obligation to Virgil for the terms of his own description here? In cases like this it is difficult to distinguish between subconscious association of ideas and deliberate intention to imitate. Elsewhere Pliny obviously wants to show that, in his new genre of prose writing, he can rival writers in more established genres. Thus in 1.15, a 'prose epigram' whimsical and teasing in tone, neat and elegant in style, he vies directly with Martial (5.78), more remotely with Catullus and Horace (13 and *Epist.* 1.5 respectively). Again, in 6.16 and 20, where he relates the eruption of Vesuvius, Pliny does not merely fulfil his ostensible purpose, to supply Tacitus with material. Though he will not write history himself (5.8), he will prove his ability to handle it even in letters, and at 6.20.14–15 he comes very near to Tacitus' most pathetic vein (cf. *Ann.* 4.62.3). But Pliny does not always succeed in carrying off other styles: his attempt at lofty and impassioned indignation in 8.6 proves a diaster. The grand manner ill suits him in the *Panegyricus*, and in his letters it is absurd. Happily such errors of taste are in the correspondence extremely rare.

Pliny's writing is flexible, graceful, and polished. Like Tacitus, he achieves variety without abandoning self-consistency. He is meticulously careful in his vocabulary and phraseology, indeed rather unadventurous. All the internal evidence confirms what he reports about the painstaking composition and revision of his works. Pliny's most characteristic (and classical) quality is restraint. He likes antithesis, but does not, as Seneca does, overplay it; he enjoys sound-effects, but does not, as Nepos does, pursue them until they become an idiosyncrasy; he shares the current craze for epigrams, but does not, as Tacitus does in his *Histories*, obtrude them on every possible occasion. If there is a virtue in being without vices, Pliny in his letters may lay fair claim to it. But he has some mannerisms and predilections which he has not completely restrained, above all delight in two-fold and three-fold asyndeta and, matched against love of anaphora and emphatic repetition, strenuous avoidance of repetition generally (see e.g. 7.27). Cicero is Pliny's ultimate model and inspiration: smooth and limpid phrases, well balanced architecture of clause and sentence, and recurrent rhythmic patterns all attest that predominant influence. But it was the Cicero of the speeches and treatises, rather than the letters, who fired Pliny to emulation. And so, not unaccountably, Pliny's style is much akin to Quintilian's, albeit in comparison somewhat thin and affected. By blending Ciceronian and modern ingredients Pliny created an apt medium for urbane and inhibited epistolography. In his letters we have the last flowering of classicism, before individual whim or the extravagances of the archaizers fatally infected prose style.

Pliny's view of his times is tinged with complacency and humbug: only a few letters reveal that this is not the best of all possible worlds. He readily and unquestioningly adopts the attitudes and conventions of the affluent and leisured class which he adorned. Social and cultural trivialities occupy him inordinately, and indeed his worst anxiety is lest public duties should distract him from the pleasures of friendship and study. For Pliny and his contemporaries, unlike Cicero and Sallust, literary activity needs no excuse. He is, of course, duly modest about his own compositions, as he might well be, if he were judged by the execrable verses he cites at 7.4.6 and 7.9.11, but, like so many Romans, he aspires to immortality. It is fortunate for his readers that his purview is not limited by the walls of his salon: he is a sharp and attentive observer of the world at large and he shows an intermittent regard for the beauties and complexities of nature (see e.g. 8.8). Perhaps his uncle's influence was at work here, though Pliny is as much a romantic *manqué* as a dilettante scientist. His best quality is a genuine kindness towards the less privileged: the sentiments expressed in 8.16 and elsewhere are not mere lip-service to the humanitarian fashion of the age. But Pliny's advertisement of his public and private benefactions remains highly distasteful. And he is not always honest with himself. He would like to believe, and have us believe, that he challenged dangers under Domitian: in truth he was a time-server, like most senators, and he would earn more respect if he admitted the fact. Perhaps Pliny intended his self-revelation to serve a didactic purpose: by displaying the satisfaction which a virtuous and cultured life brings, he could commend such a life to others.[1]

We do not come to know Pliny, as we know Cicero, from his correspondence. That is one inevitable result of selection and revision. Pliny's letters exhibit charm and variety in abundance, but they lack sinews. Pliny never grapples with hard problems, emotional or intellectual. He has neither trenchancy nor passion, and consequently he cannot move his readers. Yet, though he falls short of greatness, his achievement is substantial: he widened the scope of prose writing by demonstrating that a collection of personal letters, designed or reshaped for publication, could offer almost every opportunity for description, narration, and comment which a stylist and observer of life might conceivably desire. Pliny had no worthy imitator in antiquity nor much influence. Fronto possessed neither the ability nor the will to imitate him. Again, the arid Symmachus and the tortuous Sidonius are not successors he would have cherished. He finds them at last in Mme de Sévigné and Horace Walpole.

[1] I owe this interesting idea to Professor Kenney.

The *Panegyricus* ('Panegyric')[1] is the only complete Latin oration which survives from the first two centuries of our era. For that reason, if no other, it possesses considerable literary interest. Again, it throws some light upon a period otherwise poorly documented (A.D. 96–100), as upon several wider areas of social and political history. Nevertheless it has fallen, not undeservedly, into almost universal contempt. Pliny would have been wiser if he had not expanded and developed the more simple version actually delivered in the Senate (*Epist.* 3.18.1).

There is no earlier speech with which the *Panegyricus* is closely comparable, but it owes a good deal, particularly in style, to Cicero's *Pro Marcello*. Pliny describes and extols Trajan's virtues, denigrates Domitian, and, like Seneca in his *De clementia*, sets forth certain ideals of princely conduct (cf. *Epist.* 3.18.3). He had a delicate task, and on some topics, military and dynastic, he has to be extremely circumspect. When he affects outspoken independence or blends banter with praise (e.g. 59.3–6), one recalls Tacitus' sour words *ea sola species adulandi supererat* 'that was the only brand of adulation as yet untried'. No doubt Trajan merited acclaim as the best of emperors, but Pliny spoils his case by enthusing interminably over trivialities and by his obsession with Domitian, with whom Trajan is repeatedly contrasted. It is after all an odd form of eulogy to reiterate that a man is not a profligate, not a sadist, not a megalomaniac, and indeed Pliny apologizes for these comparisons at 53.1–3, not altogether convincingly. At first sight the *Panegyricus* may seem exuberantly optimistic, but occasionally a thread of deep gloom shows through. Bad emperors may return (see e.g. 88.9), and what the Senate has suffered in the past it may suffer again. Pliny's outlook is not utterly different from Tacitus', whom he sometimes imitated or prompted to imitation. But a ceremonial occasion imposed restrictions over and above those which inhibited freedom of speech generally: the most interesting matters in the *Panegyricus* are to be read between the lines.

The speech is couched in the grand style, being elaborately expansive, patterned in phrase and clause, and full of florid conceits and rhetorical artifice of every kind. The lucidity which distinguishes the letters is here liable to eclipse. And, while the antitheses and epigrams which Pliny readily excogitated are often as wearisome as they are vacuous (see e.g. 61.4, 62.9, 67.3, 84.5), it is probably his woolly repetitiveness, rather than misplaced ingenuity, which in the end reduces most readers to despair. He himself wonders (*Epist.* 3.18.10) whether more sober treatment might have been preferable, but plainly he remained in love with his own vices.

---

[1] This title may not be original. At *Epist.* 3.13.1 and 18.1 Pliny talks of *gratiarum actio*, 'expression of thanks', but that is not necessarily his title either.

## 5. SUETONIUS

Suetonius published many works, scholarly rather than literary, though this distinction was no more clear-cut in his time than it is now. For some years at least he was a member of the emperor's secretariat. And, while closely acquainted with the schools of grammar and rhetoric, he was probably never a professional teacher. We have here a talented and versatile man of letters, comparable with Varro, though hardly his equal. Doubtless Suetonius' writings required much anxious parturition (cf. Plin. *Epist.* 5.10): the two which survive, *De vita Caesarum*, 'On the life of the Caesars' and (fragmentarily) *De viris illustribus*, 'On eminent men', are evidently based on diverse and extensive reading.

Following an approach to biography used by some of the Alexandrian scholars, Suetonius treats his subjects very schematically, according to divisions and categories such as antecedents, birth, career, achievements, morals, appearance, and death, but with some variations according to the particular subject matter. This form of biography was perhaps originally employed for literary figures, and thence transferred, not by Suetonius alone (cf. Nep. *Epam.* 1.4), to persons distinguished in public life. He could, however, have chosen another form, well represented in Greek by his near contemporary Plutarch, and going back at least to the early Peripatetic school. Plutarch views and assesses his subjects' lives coherently and chronologically: he prefers narration, with occasional moralizing, to analysis and tabulation. And plainly Plutarch's approach is, unlike Suetonius', closely akin to that of the historians. But there is more in Suetonius' method than misguided application of Alexandrian pedantry. Roman funeral speeches and epitaphs were traditionally centred on the deceased's honours, deeds, and prowess: they did not characterize him in the round. The *Res gestae* of Augustus helps to explain Suetonius' attitudes and choice of material. He, for instance, like Augustus, records offices held, donatives, and buildings. The Alexandrians gave him a framework: he easily brought within it matters of established Roman interest. He was perhaps the first to recognize that the Caesars should be treated as a special class. Supreme power and the way of life it engendered set them apart. Here lies his best claim to originality.[1]

Some critics assert that, for all his categorizing, Suetonius pays serious regard to chronology. That, to an extent, is true. In passages where he outlines parts of a man's career he naturally tends to follow temporal sequence. And, when his material is specially curious and inviting, he may set it out consecutively and with abundant detail, as in his account of the last days of Nero (*Nero* 40.4–49.4), perhaps the best thing he ever wrote. In general, however,

[1] I owe this view of Suetonius' originality to Professor Kenney.

he has his plan, and adheres to it. Though his schematism was inimical alike to wide historical survey and gradual delineation of character, it suited him well enough, for he has but a fumbling grasp of history and psychology. He perceives, for example, that Tiberius' principate somehow changed for the worse, but offers no convincing explanation of this change. Indeed his picture of Tiberius is glaringly self-contradictory, unless we can stomach metamorphosis of a moderate, old-fashioned aristocrat into a perverted and sadistic tyrant. Here, as elsewhere, Suetonius' characterization anticipates the story of Jekyll and Hyde. Witness the monumental crudity of his division of Caligula's actions (*Cal.* 22.1) into those attributable (*a*) to a prince, and (*b*) to a monster. But he is not always beside the mark. In his *Julius* he conveys something of Caesar's extraordinary magnetism, and in his *Augustus* illustrates the complexities of Augustus' personality. And he is adept at finding the revealing anecdotes which are so essential to biography. Yet rarely, if ever, does he complete his picture, and, by rigorous exclusion of material, however important, not immediately relevant to the individual with whom he is concerned, he usually leaves the background blank. Thus his approach was not properly adjusted to treatment of major historical characters, who must be set in a full context, though arguably adequate for minor celebrities, such as poets and orators. In what remains of the *De viris illustribus* we have some admirable miniatures, and here, on a tiny scale, he provides the necessary background, by sketching the development of grammar and rhetoric at Rome.

Suetonius drew on many sources for his *Vitae Caesarum*, and had little compunction about copying them word for word. That he is generally uncritical is the more to be regretted since, when he chooses to investigate a problem, he can be sharp and judicious, as in his discussion of Caligula's birthplace (*Cal.* 8). In the first three lives he uses and cites much primary evidence, notably letters of Augustus. He had carefully scrutinized many of the original documents (see *Aug.* 87-8), presumably housed in the imperial archives and accessible to him while he held high rank in the secretariat. But, from his *Tiberius* onwards, the number of citations of such material decreases markedly, and, furthermore, the later lives are generally less detailed and precise, in nomenclature and in reference to sources. The reason for this change is still debated. Probably, after his dismissal from public service in (perhaps) 122, he could no longer freely consult the records he had previously exploited. It is harder to explain why he began to take fewer pains himself in the use of evidence available to anyone.

Suetonius writes simply and straightforwardly. He is brief, but not pregnant or epigrammatic. He neither rounds his sentences into periods nor overloads them with appended clauses. Indeed, apart from some liking for variation, he seems largely indifferent to niceties of style. Yet his vocabulary is interesting, not so much because of its occasional idiosyncrasies as because it is generally indiscriminate. Suetonius recognizes no obligation to select and exclude, though he may consciously avoid high-flown expressions. He is largely content with current usage, and not averse even from mongrelized words and official terminology. Being unconcerned about unity of texture, he can dispense with the art of paraphrase and admit, without embarrassment, any quotations large or small, including Greek. He also takes over some oddities from his sources: at least a considerable minority·of the rare or unique words found in his writings may be attributed to pillage rather than innovation, and much resemble the riches of the magpie's nest. He might be contrasted with Gellius, who necessarily quoted often and at length, but who is much more fussy about his own style and altogether more self-conscious.

Except in the comparatively few places where he exercises his critical powers, Suetonius' value is that of his sources, and hence very mixed. He accommodates insubstantial rumour as generously as hard attested fact. He is inconsistent, as well as gullible. And he loves scandal, particularizing very meticulously on sexual vices, whether of emperors, poets, or grammarians (for example *Tib.* 43–5, *Nero* 28–9, *Gramm.* 23.5–6). Yet he tries, with some success, to give an impression of honest, impartial reporting, unemotional and not intentionally humorous, or, to borrow an apt term from a recent critic, dead-pan. Suetonius does not, like the historians, win effect by dramatizing his material. He leaves it to speak for itself, which it does well enough when it is intrinsically interesting and he troubles to present it fully. So, for example, some may prefer his description of Vitellius' ignominious death (*Vit.* 16–17) to Tacitus' selective and dramatized version (*Hist.* 3.84.4–85), precisely because he retails every sordid detail, without the pathos and comment which the theme invited. Though he never attempted to vie with writers of major history, he provides a wealth of information indispensable for any understanding of the first century A.D. But it requires careful sifting and redeployment.

We learn little about Suetonius from his writings. But it is clear enough that he possesses no original mind and that his attitudes, as far as he reveals them, are unsophisticated. Pliny attests (*Epist.* 1.18.1) that he was superstitious, and he certainly appears to take omens and prodigies very seriously. Some have found in the lives traces of hostility towards Hadrian. On inspection, they seem extremely tenuous. Others detect criticism of Tacitus, and perhaps Suetonius' discussion of Nero's poems (*Nero* 52) is directed against *Ann.* 14.16.1. But we have no unshakeable evidence that he was familiar with the *Annals.*

Suetonius has enjoyed lasting popularity. In the *Historia Augusta* (*Firm.* 1.1, *Prob.* 2.7), a mendacious compilation partly modelled on his *De vita Caesarum*, he is praised for honesty and candour. And of late his unpretentiousness has seemed an asset, now that airs and graces are at a discount. But, in the final assessment of his work, we must ask whether, to the best of his ability, he consistently tried to discover the truth and report it. The answer to that question cannot be favourable.

## 6. FLORUS

### The historian

Florus' outline of Roman history, ending with Augustus, was in late antiquity inaccurately described as an epitome of Livy. Doubtless Livy was his main source, directly or at second hand. But we may detect debts to Sallust and Caesar, amongst others, and poetic influence, particularly Virgil's and Lucan's. And Florus records events later than the conclusion of Livy's history. Again, his attitudes differ from Livy's: he seems, for instance, largely uninterested in religion. Some contend that he is attempting to create a new genre, a sort of historical panegyric, midway between prose and poetry. This view is rather fanciful, but Florus' panegyrical tone is unmistakable. He personifies the *populus Romanus* and makes it the hero of his whole narrative. So central indeed is the position he accords it that sometimes it is simply understood as the subject of sentences. Conversely the Senate's role is obscured, one of several ways in which he over-simplifies history. While he commonly regards Roman leaders as merely the people's agents, he still, like Velleius, shows intense interest in individuals. Perhaps he meant his work for school use: he arranges his material simply, provides occasional summaries, and is generally more of a story-teller than an enquirer. One may compare Dickens's *A child's history of England*: Dickens too preferred to omit recent history.

Florus has little to say which is new or remarkable. Thus he claims, reasonably but not originally, that both *uirtus* and *fortuna* contributed to Rome's greatness (*praef.* 2), and emphasizes, perhaps with Hadrian in mind, that it is harder to retain than acquire provinces (1.33.8 and 2.30.29). Tending to see the past in contemporary terms he falls into anachronism, for instance by misapplying the concept of *imperium Romanum* to comparatively early periods. He adopts, perhaps *via* one of the Senecas and ultimately from Varro,[1] an interesting but unsatisfactory comparison of the Roman people's history with four stages of human life, infancy, adolescence, maturity, and old age (*praef.* 4–8). This scheme is nowhere properly justified, and the last period (from Augustus to Florus' own times), which he does not handle, evidently caused him difficulty and embarrassment. The *populus* could no longer credibly figure

[1] Though we cannot be sure how Varro used his scheme of four ages.

as hero (see 2.14.4–6), though he has perforce to talk of its rejuvenation under Trajan. Otherwise he would be obliged to admit that the Empire's demise is imminent. And plainly he is an optimist: Rome always triumphs in the end, and fortune, though apt to waver momentarily, is never long unfaithful. There is a striking contrast here with Tacitus' profound gloom. Florus purveyed such intellectually undemanding diet as his contemporaries and later generations could easily digest: hence he was much used and occasionally much praised. Being principally concerned to present matter for admiration and eulogy, he makes few trenchant or perceptive observations. Most of his numerous comments are fatuous, or express child-like wonder and astonishment. It is hard to find another Latin writer so utterly empty-headed.

Florus' style, though often precious and florid, is virtually untouched by the archaisms familiar in Fronto and Gellius. And all the endeavours to discover in his work a distinct African Latinity have come to nothing. In fact he has very little individuality. His embellishments cannot conceal extreme poverty in vocabulary; his use of prose-rhythm is conventional; his imagery seems equally commonplace, and his epigrams, while sometimes effective, are usually forced. But he can write clearly and fluently and tell a good story. If he had heeded the maxim *rem tene, uerba sequentur* 'look after the facts and the words will look after themselves', he might have been no disgrace to Latin literature. Sadly such effort was beyond him.

### The rhetorician

We can only guess how Florus tackled the theme of his dialogue *Vergilius orator an poeta*, for we have merely part of its introduction, contrived, after Cicero's manner, to set the scene and introduce the participants. But the theme itself is of interest, recalling the first section of Tacitus' *Dialogus*, and comparable not only with a dispute mentioned by another near contemporary, Granius Licinianus (p. 33.9–10 Flemisch), whether Sallust is an orator rather than a historian, but also with arguments whether Lucan was a historian rather than a poet (see Serv. on *Aen.* 1.382). It looks as if such topics were frequently debated in schools of rhetoric: that did not preclude independent treatment. Perhaps Florus wanted to vie with Tacitus (a daunting enterprise), if, as is very possible, Tacitus' work was the earlier. His few surviving pages make lively and pleasant reading, though they are extremely self-centred. This is typical of the second century, when, as Fronto and Marcus Aurelius show, the anxieties and aspirations of individuals enjoy obsessive attention.

## The poet

No poem ascribed to Florus possesses any substantial merit, though *ego nolo Caesar esse*, 'I don't want to be a Caesar', is superlatively cheeky. The poem about roses (no. 2 Jal) might seem charming if later poetasters had not worried the idea to death. Some attribute to Florus that celebrated and lovable composition, the *Pervigilium Veneris*. Their opinion has no firm basis, and others believe that language and metre alike indicate the fourth century, if not the fifth.

# 10

# TECHNICAL WRITING

## I. POMPONIUS MELA

The earliest surviving Latin work on geography, Pomponius Mela's *De chorographia*, 'Of description of countries',[1] has not won the approval of geographers, though Pliny the Elder, hardly a discriminating critic, seems to have taken it seriously. The work is no systematic and professional treatise, but an outline for general readers, and it offers little new material, being largely based on written sources, including, though not necessarily at first hand, Nepos and Varro. Mela states (1.2) that he aims to describe the world's main divisions, then its coastal areas in more detail (cf. 1.24), and to add memorable particulars of individual regions and their inhabitants. His worst fault is that he supplies no measurements. And he was sadly misguided in basing his detailed survey on a sort of circumnavigation, after the manner of the Greek writings ascribed to Scylax and Scymnus, for as a result important inland areas, such as Bactria and Dacia, are wholly omitted. Again, in his choice of ethnographical matter he is quite uncritical. Judged even on its own terms, as a piece of popularization, the *De chorographia* cannot be applauded: the exposition might have been clearer and the expression more relaxed.

For all his errors (e.g. 2.57), obscurities, and omissions, Mela still possesses some interest. Occasionally (e.g. 3.31 on the Baltic and 3.38 on the Caspian) traces of unusually accurate information have somehow got through to him. And, while he will readily swallow fables or travellers' tales (e.g. 1.47 on the Blemyes and 3.81 on the Pygmies) or take over unacknowledged from Herodotus much of his account of the Scythians, he also preserves information not found elsewhere about places and beliefs (e.g. 3.19 on the Druids and 3.48 on the island of Sena). Again, some may detect merit in his elaborate descriptions, like that of the Corycian cave (1.72–6), even if they are rather out of proportion in a work of three short books.

The deprecation of Mela's preface is part of a conventional pose: having

---

[1] *Chorographia* differs from geography, which is more general, and topography, which is more restricted. But the differences cannot be pressed very far. In so far as they are valid, *chorographia* fits what Mela produces well enough.

asserted that his subject does not admit stylistic embellishment, he sets about providing it. Intricate word-order, anaphora, occasional asyndeta and ellipses, and variation in the shape of sentences, from expansive to starkly abrupt, are calculated to earn the reader's attention and regard. The influence of Sallust may be seen in words and phrases, but there is no sustained imitation. In some ways Mela resembles Florus: he shares, in particular, a fondness for expressing admiration and wonderment (e.g. 1.38, 2.57), and lacks any real intellectual curiosity. The passage on tides at 3.1–2 may well represent his work as a whole. It is most carefully written and intended to impress, but to instruct with evidence or convince by argument is not Mela's business.

### 2. COLUMELLA

Columella's *Res rustica*, 'Agriculture',[1] the fullest treatment of the subject in Latin literature, is a product of wide reading and long personal experience. Columella is appalled by the decline he sees in Italian agriculture (1 *praef.* 13ff.), and aims to show what knowledge and determination can do to put matters right. He sets a high value upon rural life, as opposed to urban, and indeed he shares most of the sentiments expressed by Virgil in his *Georgics*. But he is no starry-eyed idealist. If the perfection of farming, as of oratory, is remote and hard to attain (1 *praef.* 28ff.), that gives him no motive for despair: second-best is better than nothing. He demands discipline, efficiency, and profit, but does not therefore lack humanity, for he wants his farm to be happy and thriving as a whole. In his *Res rustica* we learn much of what life in the country was like in ancient Italy, hard indeed, but not invariably wretched.

Columella treats first of the site, layout, and staff of a farm (1), then cereals and vegetables (2), fruit-trees, in particular the vine and olive (3–5), larger mammals (6), smaller mammals (7), poultry and fish (8), bees (9), the garden (10), then (11) the duties of the *uilicus* 'overseer' and (12) the duties of the overseer's wife. Book 10 is in hexameter verse, so written, Columella tells us, at the behest of his dedicatee, Silvinus, and the encouragement of Virgil (*Georg.* 4.147–8), who left horticulture for posterity to handle.

Plainly Columella is much indebted to earlier agricultural writers, including his most recent predecessors Atticus, Celsus, and Graecinus. The length of his work is partly at least due to his desire to consider and, where necessary, controvert their views. Comparison with the older treatises of Cato and Varro would suggest that Columella filled out what they were content to sketch, adopting from them (and in particular Varro) many basic ideas and certain divisions in subject matter. He appears to have scrutinized established opinions very closely, but, when he disagrees, he is normally as courteous in his dis-

---

[1] For the *De arboribus*, 'On trees', which requires no separate discussion here, see Appendix.

sension as he is independent in his judgements. He is well read and not averse occasionally from general philosophical reflections (e.g. 3.10.9ff.).

Columella writes clearly, neatly, even elegantly. That he cares about style is evident from various comments made on his predecessors (e.g. 1.1.12, 2.1.2). Though he does not always avoid repetition, he has at his command a rich variety of vocabulary in dealing with matters, such as planting, which often recur. Contemporary fashions in literary prose leave him virtually untouched (one may contrast Pliny the Elder), for he does not seek to impress his readers by ingenuities of antithesis or epigrammatic point. He lacks also, and more regrettably, that pungency and bite which not infrequently enlivens the writing of Varro. And, in view of the size of his treatise, he makes comparatively little use of digressions and 'purple passages'. A few there are indeed (e.g. 7.12.1, 8.8.10), but they are not extravagantly developed. Columella is ever anxious to get on with his business, for which his unaffected and resourceful style is singularly well fitted.

One can hardly doubt that Columella was an infinitely painstaking and very successful farmer (see, e.g., 3.3.13–14). His enthusiasm for his theme is evident in many ways, not least when argument, which he enjoys, is happily interwoven with exposition: sometimes he seems to be conducting a dialogue with himself, as well as other authorities. And he takes a modest pride in appealing to the results of his own experiments. Today he might be a professor of agriculture. Or perhaps that is what he was, if, as has been conjectured, he and Silvinus ran some sort of agricultural school. Still, his treatise has flaws, in substance and in structure. Some are venial, such as the instances of super-stitious lore (e.g. 2.10.10ff.), of which more and worse may be found in other writers. But there are errors too (as in astronomical matters in Book 11) and some confusion or self-contradiction (e.g. 2.20.2, compared with 12.52.18). Again, Book 10 was a gallant, but ill-fated enterprise. If ever there was a case of versified prose, we have it here. Columella seems to have assembled the main material of Book 10 in his usual way, then forced it into hexameters and added some purely ornamental passages. Not that the poem is inept or faulty tech-nically: it is such as a well educated man of the period might be expected to contrive. But comparison with Virgil, which Columella invites, works heavily to his disadvantage. Again, the treatise was not planned as a whole in its present form. Columella composed and published in stages, taking account in what followed of opinions expressed on earlier books (see 4.1.1). This, added to his habit of leaving matters to be resumed later, makes for some complexity, if not muddle. And Books 11 and 12 are an addition to his original scheme, which might have been concluded with Book 10 (see 11.1.1–2). It is, however, instructive to see here, with unusual certainty, how a work of ancient literature changed and developed in the course of its composition.

The neglect of Columella in recent times is readily explicable. Much of what he has to say can interest only specialists, and his language, unlike Cato's and Varro's, can hardly claim exceptionally close attention. One may regret this neglect nevertheless, for in the *Res rustica* we encounter not only Columella's warm and engaging personality, but also a sane and business-like Latin style against which the achievements or aberrations of some more spectacular writers might not unprofitably be judged.

## 3. PLINY THE ELDER

Pliny is one of the prodigies of Latin literature, boundlessly energetic and catastrophically indiscriminate, wide-ranging and narrow-minded, a pedant who wanted to be a popularizer, a sceptic infected by traditional sentiment, and an aspirant to style who could hardly frame a coherent sentence. That is the impression given by his only surviving work, and no other evidence gainsays it. In a busy life, much of it in public service, Pliny found time for many intellectual activities, but not often for second thoughts.

The *Natural history*,[1] dedicated (A.D. 77 or 78) in an unwieldy and effusive preface to the heir apparent Titus, comprises list of contents (Book 1), cosmology (2), geography (3–6), anthropology (7), zoology (8–11), botany (12–19), botany (20–7) and zoology (28–32) in relation to medicine, and mineralogy (33–7). Digressions, historical references, and elaborate descriptions vary and enliven the work. Frequently Pliny is carried away into bombast by enthusiasm for his theme, indignation, or a maudlin brand of moralizing (e.g. 7.2–5 and 142–6). He drew no clear line between report and comment, and offered not a cold appraisal of fact but a panegyric upon the wonders of nature, in which man, her most marvellous creation, gets more than his due. Yet he genuinely sought to instruct, to set down information possibly useful to somebody sometime. Many passages look like conglutination of notes made during reading (Plin. *Epist.* 3.5.17): certainly disparate matters are unhappily conjoined. Pliny catered for diverse interests, but not for experts: the *Natural history* was written by a learned amateur for the benefit of unlearned amateurs. An abundant repertory of miscellaneous knowledge, it survived in entirety, though eagerly pillaged and excerpted. No Roman possessed the will and enterprise to supersede it.

Since Pliny lists the sources of each book (an unusual and noteworthy procedure), and often cites them for details, we escape one familiar difficulty. Numerous residual problems, about the authorities principally used in particular sections, are beyond our scope. One or two general points claim notice. Pliny

[1] *Naturalis historia* is the title now conventional, but Plin. *Epist.* 3.5.6 suggests that the work was originally called *naturae historiae*.

was both patriotic and gullible. His patriotism sometimes led him into exaggeration (e.g. 37.201–2) and encouraged him to take second hand from Roman sources what he could have had first hand from the Greeks. His gullibility led him into many absurdities (e.g. 7.64–5), but incidentally benefited us: along with marvels and anecdotes, apparently the staple diet of Roman readers (cf. Valerius Maximus), he records much abstruse wisdom and mumbo-jumbo, and thus illuminates obscure areas of folklore, quackery, and superstitition. Yet elsewhere he is aggressively rationalistic and a sour commentator on human ineptitude (e.g. 30.1–2). A more singular mixture is hard to imagine.

Norden[1] justly remarked that stylistically Pliny is amongst the worst of Latin writers, and not to be excused by his subject matter, since Columella and Celsus, faced with fairly comparable material, wrote well enough. In truth Pliny had neither literary skill nor sense of propriety, and he failed to discipline his thoughts. Instead of adopting the plain and sober style appropriate to his theme, he succumbs to lust for embellishment. The ornaments he parades differ somewhat from those employed by his contemporaries, mainly because they are more crude. But in his concern for instantaneous effect Pliny is wholly typical. He can be florid in the extreme, accumulating vacuous and picturesque phrases (e.g. 9.102–3), much as Apuleius was to do; he strings together tedious patterns of balanced clauses (e.g. 10.81–2); and he turns out epigrams of exceptional extravagance and insipidity. Predictably he eschewed Ciceronian periods, but, unlike Seneca and Tacitus, devised no original sentence-structure with which to replace them, unless casual parataxis, regular outside the 'purple passages', should be termed structure. He may be compared with Varro, who also wrote rapidly and voluminously, and had no gift for elegant expression. Equally he may be contrasted, since Varro probably cared little about expression anyway.[2]

In an assessment of Pliny the lost works cannot be disregarded. The 'Uncertainties of expression' had considerable influence on grammatical writings down to Priscian's time. 'The student',[3] which dealt in part at least with rhetorical artifices (see Gell. 9.16), accords with and confirms Pliny's evident addiction to transient scholastic fashion. 'The German wars' and 'Aufidius Bassus continued' amply justified Suetonius' inclusion of Pliny amongst notable historians. The latter work is probably the basic common source for the period from Claudius until and perhaps beyond A.D. 69 which we can recognize, but not for certain identify, behind Tacitus, Plutarch, Dio, and (sometimes) Suetonius.[4] Full and detailed, but simplistic in approach, this source presented ideal material for exploitation and recasting: Tacitus recast,

[1] Norden (1898) I 314.   [2] Laughton (1960) 1–3.
[3] Whether the title was *studiosus* or *studiosi*, and what exactly it meant, is debatable.
[4] Townend (1961 and 1964) *passim*.

others exploited. If it was Pliny, his stylistic weaknesses, as seen in the *Natural history*, would further have tempted his successors to do better themselves. The size and technicality of the *Natural history* condemn it to few readers. And, after all, the information provided is now mainly of antiquarian interest. Yet students of Latin language and style neglect Pliny at their peril. Here, better than in most other places, we may see the contortions and obscurities, the odd combinations of preciosity and baldness, and the pure vacuity to which rhetorical prose, handled by any but the most talented, could precipitously descend and would indeed often descend again.

## 4. FRONTINUS

Frontinus' two surviving works, *De aquis* and *Strategemata*, have somewhat limited pretensions to be literature. He calls them *commentarii*, a description comprising or overlapping with our 'notes', 'memoranda', 'records', and 'treatises'. A *commentarius* could be a polished composition in the plain style, or lack polish altogether: there was no firm tradition, as for the major genres of prose. The subject matter and the author's personality, rather than rules of genre, determined the character and quality of the writing.

The *De aquis* is exactly what it claims to be, a systematic account of the water-supply of Rome. This practical, business-like and perhaps original treatise (we know of no antecedents, though, of course, hydraulic engineering was not a new field) is mainly of historical interest, and otherwise concerns the linguist more than the literary critic. Its language seems in general unaffected, though one finds occasional embellishments and may fairly suppose that Frontinus wrote for a wider public than experts like himself. The *Strategemata* pose considerably more questions. Frontinus asserts that this work too is practical: the information he has arranged and classified will be of use to generals. Yet the book is strangely divorced from reality. Frontinus scarcely calls at all upon recent experience, such as his own, but purveys a mass of hackneyed material, Greek and Roman, compiled from literary sources, some of them, like Livy, painfully familiar. Restriction on freedom of speech under Domitian provides no complete explanation. Frontinus probably conformed with fashion. The Romans of the Empire had no little liking for the collection and retailing of snippets of information, historical, legendary, and anecdotal. One cannot fail to note the similarity, in type and mixed provenance of material (Roman and foreign), between Frontinus' work and the wider ranging *Facta et dicta memorabilia* of Valerius Maximus. The language of the *Strategemata*, while sometimes diverging from the commonplace (perhaps under the influence of history), is on the whole impoverished and repetitive. Of course a long series of brief items gave scant opportunity for elaboration, and Frontinus may well have sought a very plain style as befitting his theme and appropriate to a military man and administrator. But possibly he could produce nothing better. The numerous errors of fact in the *Strategemata*, when tested against other and better sources, enjoin a rather sceptical view of his abilities as a writer generally.

The authenticity of the fourth book of the *Strategemata* has been debated at length. Many, perhaps most, scholars today would accept it as genuine. The linguistic differences from Books 1–3 can be accounted for by an intervening lapse of time and a partial change of topic. And there are, as well as differences, some telling similarities. Apart from the main problem concerning Book 4, we have reason to suspect serious interpolation in various places and so some caution is needed in use of the work as any kind of authority.

# 11

# RHETORIC AND SCHOLARSHIP

## I. QUINTILIAN

Quintilian, the leading *rhetor*, 'teacher of rhetoric', of the Flavian period, fostered and, in his own writing, represented a reaction in literary taste against the innovations of Seneca, Lucan, and their contemporaries. There was no major revision of rhetorical theory: the difference lay rather in practice, in preference for older and, as Quintilian believed, better models, notably Cicero. This shift of attitude can be associated with a wider social change, recorded by Tacitus (*Ann.* 3.55), who says that the extravagances of Nero's times gave way on Vespasian's accession to more sober fashions, partly because new men, from Italy and the provinces, rose to prominence and reintroduced stricter codes of conduct. Quintilian, who had his origins in Spain, belongs amongst them. He was a man of wealth and influence, favoured by the ruling dynasty, and probably the first to obtain a state chair of Latin rhetoric (Suet. *Vesp.* 18). That he flatters Domitian (10.1.91–2) or talks of him in courtly terms (4 *praef.* 2–5) is neither blameworthy nor remarkable, but his bitter hostility towards contemporary philosophers (1 *praef.* 15, 12.3.12) raises interesting questions. Perhaps he honestly considers them depraved and pernicious (cf. Juvenal *passim*), but he may also be paying politic deference to the emperor's prejudices, as arguably he does in his conventionally scathing remark about the Jews (3.7.21). No doubt he saw himself as the latter-day champion of rhetoric in its ancient quarrel with philosophy. He concedes that the orator requires a knowledge of ethics, and therefore wants moral philosophy to be absorbed in (indeed subordinated to) the study of rhetoric (12.2.6ff.). He finds some support for this idea in the *De oratore*, but the intolerance which he here displays is utterly alien to Cicero.

The *Institutio oratoria* 'The training of an orator' is a happy amalgamation of an *ars rhetorica*, 'handbook of rhetoric', with a treatise on the functions and ideals of oratory, into which much discussion of education and literature is additionally blended. Quintilian is determined to put lots of flesh on dry bones (1 *praef.* 23–4). For a *rhetor* he ranges extraordinarily widely, concerning himself with the whole shaping of his ideal pupil, from early infancy to full maturity.

In the long technical sections of Books 3–9 Quintilian attempts mainly to evaluate existing theories rather than to propound new ones: he is flexible and undogmatic. More originality is seen when he deals with the education of young children (Book 1), the proper duties of a teacher (Book 2), and the merits or utility of individual writers (10.1). And several shorter sections possess both special interest and novelty, for instance 12.10.27–37, where he compares the potentialities of Greek and Latin for a stylist. While his technical disquisitions are largely (and avowedly) derivative, he draws on his own rich experience in discussing the actual business of teaching. And he is not averse from polemic, particularly against faulty method and debased standards. He consistently adopts a high moral tone, both in his conception of the orator as necessarily also a good man (1 *praef.* 9), elaborated in Book 12, and in the absolute rectitude which he enjoins upon the teacher (2.2.4ff.). It is therefore curious that he retains no little regard for Domitius Afer (Tac. *Ann.* 4.52.4, 66.1). He is also uncompromising in his demand that even the most eminent *rhetor* should undertake routine teaching (2.3.1ff.): only the best, in his opinion, is good enough. He tried to provide it, and also ventured on some modest reforms, not apparently with much success, since the whole system of rhetorical training was firmly entrenched and parents and pupils alike were intransigent in their desire to retain it unchanged. More than once he appears to be fighting for lost causes, mildly liberal.

Quintilian compels admiration, for his seriousness and dedication and for the sanity and perception of the judgements which he passes on methods of teaching and (sometimes) on literature. And we may warm to his genial humanity, even though it does not embrace philosophers. But he has grave deficiencies. One of them is astonishing: he seems to know little directly of the major Greek writers. Again, his vision is narrow. If it were not, he would have perceived that more was required to repair the inadequacies of current education than tinkering with details and occasional lip-service to wider culture. And he shows scant historical sense: how, we may ask, could the paragon who satisfied all Quintilian's requirements and emerged a perfect orator ever fully benefit from his training in (say) A.D. 90? Tacitus and 'Longinus' grasped the importance of that question.

Quintilian's style exemplifies many of the virtues which he commends. He diligently pursues perspicuity, and he avoids archaizing or modernistic affectations (cf. 8.3.24ff., 12.10.73). Cicero is his principal model, but he is no thoughtless imitator. He prefers discourse to harangue, and controls his rhetoric in places which others would have empurpled. For colour, relief, and variety he resorts above all to metaphor and simile: he was clearly endowed with sharp powers of observation. His epigrams are usually neat and unlaboured and arise naturally from their contexts. Altogether this is a mellow and easy style, neither wearisome like that of Seneca nor brittle like that of the younger Pliny. Occasionally, however, when he has a lot to say and wants to say it all at once, he involves himself in inextricable complexities of thought and sentence structure (e.g. 2.4.28ff.).

Quintilian exercised vast influence on critics and teachers of the fifteenth to seventeenth centuries: he seemed to offer precepts they could accept and ideals they could try to realize. Thus he contributed to the establishment of certain canons of taste and bounds of acceptability, chronological or moral, which have constricted the study of Latin literature over the last five hundred years. But the *Institutio* has been beneficent as well as stultifying: those who would understand the vocation of teaching may still learn the essentials here. And for students of Latin literature Quintilian remains one of the essential starting-points, however much we may question his opinions.

## 2. FRONTO

Amongst his contemporaries of the mid second century Fronto stood high, as Gellius, an admirer, attests. Acknowledged the leading Latin orator of the day, he was chosen as tutor to the princes Marcus and Lucius. For three centuries his fame survived: we find him placed not second to, but equal with Cicero. Thereafter he virtually disappeared from view, until in the early nineteenth century part of a collection of letters and miscellanea was rediscovered. The letters proved flaccid, trivial, and uninformative, the other pieces flimsy, and they provoked a chorus of derision. But exculpation, of a sort, is possible. First, these letters were probably never meant for publication or published by Fronto. Again, since they are mostly to or from members of the ruling dynasty, we cannot here expect the confidentiality and freedom of expression of friends who are also equals. This correspondence could not have resembled Cicero's with Atticus or Brutus: to lament the difference is absurd. Finally, Fronto was celebrated for eloquence and learning, not letter-writing. The letters scarcely justify surmise, let alone judgement, about his oratory.

Fronto's letters, and numerous letters to him (mainly from Marcus), contain little to interest anyone except the correspondents, and they were sometimes merely exchanging elaborate courtesies. Amongst the most recurrent topics we find protestation of affection (e.g. 1–5),[1] enquiry about or description of illness (e.g. 64), comment, complimentary or pedantic, upon compositions attempted (e.g. 90–2), and discussion, often superficial, of literary and rhetorical questions (e.g. 40–2). Fronto's intellectual range, compared with Pliny's, itself not wide, seems pathetically circumscribed. His repetitions and variations

---

[1] References are to pages of Van Den Hout.

on threadbare themes exude tedium: he would not have written thus for publication (cf. his criticism of Lucan, 151). Of business, in Senate, courts, and administration, we hear only rarely. Language, literature, and rhetoric absorbed Fronto's attention. If he had discussed affairs of state with his sovereign, he could hardly have contributed much. Again, important personal matters, which might have been tackled forthrightly, such as Marcus' preference for philosophy over rhetoric, though not unmentioned (e.g. 149), are often evaded. This weak and limited teacher had no enduring influence on his unstable, self-tormenting pupil: witness the perfunctory acknowledgement accorded Fronto at *Meditations* 1.11. The words which the emperor there addressed to himself jar against the cordiality of his letters. Marcus, though greatly changed, had kept up appearances. Fronto played the old tricks faithfully. This was not one of the unshakeable friendships of all time.

Fronto is a rhetorician through and through. That is confirmed by an introduction to his projected history of Lucius' Parthian campaigns (191–200): he apparently intended to work up Lucius' own notes. The specimen, flattery included, is dismally predictable: imitation of Sallust, generalizing reflections pointedly expressed, commonplace description of a general's proper behaviour when faced by hardship and demoralized troops. Fronto did not explore the truth. Given suitable material, he procured embellishment. Such is 'rhetorical' history, as regularly practised. Some scholars fancy that Fronto invented it.

The principal interest of the correspondence lies in language and style. Fronto, some say, sought to revive and reinforce Latin prose against the challenge of Greek, then vigorously renascent. Whether he clearly discerned any such rivalry is arguable, but he certainly tried to exploit anew the latent resources of Latin literature, by going back beyond the stylists of the early Empire, and beyond Cicero and his contemporaries, to extract from the archaic writers whatever he might effectively use. He greatly esteems Ennius (57) and Cato (192), and loathes Seneca (150). His appraisal of Cicero (57) is curiously anachronistic and biased: Cicero, he opines, never troubled to enrich his vocabulary with choice, unlooked-for words. Yet Fronto's own writing is not garishly coloured by archaisms, though occasional oddities leap to the eye. Concern for propriety tempers his pursuit of the unusual (92). We should not, however, consider him a purist and reactionary, or equate Latin archaizing with Greek Atticism. Fronto owes more than he readily admits to the new and mixed styles of the preceding hundred years; he is not averse from verbal artifice and epigrammatic point, and he is extremely partial to similes and extensively developed imagery; he wants to be both arresting and dignified. If we judge by the letters, his endeavour failed. His style is alternately lifeless and falsely inflated, unredeemed by imagination and flamboyance such as Apuleius', who continued more boldly with experiments which Fronto, amongst others, had begun.

The correspondence reflects, albeit incompletely, a society humane and refined, brittle and decadent. The Romans were forever looking back to their past, but in the second century A.D. this retrospection became obsessive. Fronto was accounted the prime ornament of his age because he embodied its ideal of culture and learning, and, Janus-like, sponsored both tradition and novelty. Since his speeches are lost, we had best refrain from further assessment.

### 3. AULUS GELLIUS

In his miscellany *Noctes Atticae*, 'Attic nights',[1] so called since it originated from his lucubrations in Attica (*praef.* 4), Gellius ranges haphazardly in many fields, including language, literature, history, law, and philosophy, looking out for topics of antiquarian interest and problems subtle and recondite in flavour. He explains in his preface that he has based his work on notes taken from reading and lectures, that the arrangement of this material is fortuitous, that he makes no pretence to laboured elegance, and that he aims to improve his readers' leisure rather than to instruct serious enquirers. We are not obliged to accept what he says, and may smile at his feigned modesty where style is concerned, but his prefatory statements are largely borne out by examination of his writing.

Miscellanies were much in favour in antiquity, amongst Greeks and Romans. They naturally differed considerably in size, range, and intention. Athenaeus' *Deipnosophistae* 'Connoisseurs at dinner' affords a fair analogy with the *Noctes Atticae*, and we may also recall Pliny's *Natural history*, though that is as much encyclopaedia as miscellany, and Valerius Maximus' collection of memorable deeds and sayings, though Valerius' scope is appreciably different. And perhaps Suetonius attempted a comparable mixture in his *Pratum*. There were also more remote Roman precedents, in works of Cato and Varro. Gellius is particularly notable because of his kaleidoscopic variety: the average space he accords to any single topic can hardly exceed two standard pages. Being both abundantly diverse and unpredictable, he well serves the needs of those who desire only an occasional dip into culture.

A 'perpetual student', not a professional teacher, Gellius venerated learning and retained an adolescent's awe for scholarly *tours de force*. In this we see the child of an age when few thought it strange that a rhetorician should become consul. He specially loved linguistic minutiae, and here too, perhaps, he reflects current fashion. But his modest deference to learned authorities

---

[1] Ancient anthologists and miscellanists commonly affected fanciful titles, as Gellius attests (*praef.* 5–10). He followed the fashion which he there elegantly deprecated.

has benefited us greatly, since he habitually names his sources, sometimes giving precise references. Hence we learn much about the activities of numerous scholars and critics. And we are above all indebted to Gellius for the preservation of many fragments of early Latin literature, not all of them meagre. Were it not for him (and Cicero), we could scarcely venture to appraise several important poets and prose-writers of the archaic period, for we should depend mainly on the scrappy and unrepresentative citations found in the grammarians. By citing at length, Gellius, like Cicero, enables us to judge for ourselves. His work is indeed 'a veritable monument of the second century's enthusiasm for all things archaic',[1] but he has no exclusive predilection for the antique, such as Hadrian allegedly showed. The fascinations of Ennius, Cato, and Gracchus never prevented him from enjoying Virgil and Cicero: his sober judgement and catholic taste deserve praise in warm terms such as he applies at 1.4.1 to Antonius Julianus. But another merit specially distinguishes him, his accuracy. Where we can test his reports against independent evidence, he seems nearly impeccable. He therefore claims a measure of trust elsewhere.

Some doubt whether Gellius ever read all the works he cited. To be sure many of his discussions involved study of extensive passages, not mere snippets, and he was eager to find old texts, long neglected (see 9.4.1–5). But perhaps, once he had taken pen in hand, he did not always go to the originals, if he could conveniently reproduce passages selected by others. He was certainly prepared to proceed thus with legal authorities (see e.g. 4.2.3 and 15.27.1). And on occasion he may have reported at second hand the opinions of older scholars, such as Varro, Hyginus, Verrius, and Probus. He has been suspected of playing down his debts to contemporaries. Perhaps he did sometimes, yet elsewhere he seems to attribute more credit to them than they deserve (see particularly 18.5.12). It is plain that his use of his sources admits of no simple explanation.

Gellius was not the kind of archaizer who would import artificial and obsolete terms wherever and whenever he could. Very occasionally they cluster, as at 2.29, where he may be paraphrasing Ennius, but for the main part he sprinkles his adornments lightly. And he generally prefers archaisms of a mild variety. Attentive reading discloses the immense pains he took to avoid repetitions and to find words both choice and apt. Lucid and uncomplicated in phraseology, Gellius writes Latin not vastly different from Quintilian's.

The *Noctes Atticae* was much used by later writers, not always with due acknowledgement. We may easily perceive why. Gellius retails numerous fascinating details of Greek and Roman life, language, and thought, suitably predigested. And he transmits some very good stories, amongst which

[1] Jocelyn (1964) 284.

'Androclus and the lion' (5.14) is justly celebrated. Again, his opinions are always worth hearing: witness his balanced discussion of Cato's speech 'In defence of the Rhodians' (6.3) and his comparisons of passages in Caecilius and Menander (2.23) and in Cato, Gracchus, and Cicero (10.3). He compels our attention, not only as a source of information, but in his own right. We should, for instance, before we presume to judge Latin literature, try to discover how the Romans themselves judged it. Here, as elsewhere, we have in Gellius a helpful and congenial guide.

# APPENDIX OF
# AUTHORS AND WORKS

## PERSIUS FLACCUS, AULES

### LIFE

b. 4 Dec. A.D. 34, a wealthy Etruscan knight. Knew Lucan and Thrasea Paetus, and was influenced by the Stoic Cornutus (addressee of *Sat.* 5). d. 24 Nov. A.D. 62. Sources: ancient *Vita*, based on material collected *c.* end of 1st c. A.D., printed by Clausen in his larger ed. (Oxford 1956) 35–9; tr. by J. C. Rolfe, *Suetonius* II (Loeb, 1914) 495–9.

### WORKS

Six Satires (650 hexameters), with a preface in scazons, pubd by Cornutus and Caesius Bassus after P.'s death.

### BIBLIOGRAPHY

TEXTS AND COMMENTARIES: TEXTS: W. V. Clausen (Oxford 1956); idem (OCT, 1966: with Juvenal); D. Bo (Paravia, 1969: with bibliography). COMMENTARIES: O. Jahn (Leipzig 1843; repr. 1967); J. Conington, 3rd ed. rev. H. Nettleship (Oxford 1893); F. Villeneuve (Paris 1918).

TRANSLATIONS: G. G. Ramsay (Loeb, 1918); N. Rudd (Penguin, 1979).

STUDIES: F. Villeneuve, *Essai sur Perse* (Paris 1918); T. Ciresola, *La formazione del linguaggio poetico di Persio* (Rovereto 1953); G. Faranda, 'Caratteristiche dello stile e del linguaggio poetico di Persio', *R.I.L.* 88 (1955) 512–38; D. Henss, 'Die Imitations-technik des Persius', *Philologus* 99 (1955) 277–94; R. G. M. Nisbet, 'Persius', in (ed.) J. P. Sullivan, *Satire* (London 1963); J. H. Waszink, 'Das Einleitungsgedicht des Persius', *W.S.* 76 (1963) 79–91; W. S. Anderson, 'Persius and the rejection of society', *Wiss. Zs. Univ. Rostock* 15 (1966) 409–16; O. Skutsch, *Studia Enniana* (London 1968) 25ff. and 126ff.; J. Bramble, *Persius and the programmatic satire* (Cambridge 1974); N. Rudd, 'Association of ideas in Persius', *Lines of enquiry* (Cambridge 1976) 54–83.

LEXICON: D. Bo (Hildesheim 1967).

# SENECA, LUCIUS ANNAEUS

## LIFE

Date of birth undetermined, but generally placed *c.* 4 B.C. (see M. Préchac, *R.E.L.* 11 (1934) 360–75; N. Scivoletto, *G.I.F.* 19 (1966) 21–31). b. Corduba, educ. Rome; already well known as writer and speaker by *c.* A.D. 39. Exiled to Corsica 41; recalled at the instance of Agrippina, made tutor to Nero, and designated praetor 49; joint chief adviser (with Burrus) in administration of empire from Nero's accession in 54 until 62; consul *suffectus* 55 or 56. Fell from favour 62, and virtually retired from public affairs. Shortly after discovery of Pisonian conspiracy (April 65) was charged with complicity, and committed suicide on Nero's orders. Ancient sources printed by W. Trillitzsch, *Seneca im literarischen Urteil der Antike. Darstellung und Sammlung der Zeugnisse* (Amsterdam 1971). Most important are Tac. *Ann.* 12–15; Dio Cassius 59–61; Suet. *Cal.*, *Claud.*, *Nero*; allusions in S.'s own works, esp. *Helv.* and *Ep.* See also *PIR*² 1 103–4 for a compendious statement of the sources for each of the main events in S.'s career.

## WORKS

Seneca's extant works descended through the middle ages in seven groups, each with its own more or less separate manuscript tradition; modern editors retain this grouping, as follows: (1) *Dialogorum libri XII*: collection of tracts datable to various periods from end to end of S.'s career. Apart from opening section of bk 9, there is no attempt at 'dialogue' in the Platonic or modern sense. 'Talks', or even 'chats' might be a more accurate rendering of the title. All treat of ethical or psychological topics, and, with the exception of the three books *De ira* (*Dial.* 3–5), are relatively short. Three are entitled Consolations: the *Consolationes ad Marciam* (*Dial.* 6, on the death of Marcia's son), *ad Polybium* (*Dial.* 11, ostensibly to console the famous freedman of Claudius on his brother's death, but evidently a plea for the remission of S.'s exile-sentence), and *ad Helviam* (*Dial.* 12, to his mother, consoling her for his absence in exile). Topics of remaining treatises sufficiently indicated by their transmitted titles.

(2) *De beneficiis* and *De clementia*. Neither title can be exactly rendered into English. The seven books of *De beneficiis* are concerned not so much with 'benefits' or 'favours' as with mutual kindness between man and man, and man and god – the very foundations of civilized and religious living. *De clementia*: originally in three books, only bk 1 and opening part of bk 2 survive. The only treatise in the corpus that is formally addressed to Nero, it is a statement of the right attitude of a monarch towards his responsibilities and his people. In this *clementia* plays an essential part; but it is a rational and humane quality, lacking the element of condescension implied in its English derivative.

(3) *Naturales quaestiones*: seems originally to have consisted of eight books, two of which (4A and 4B in modern edd.) are mutilated. Half the books are concerned nomi-

nally with meteorological phenomena; the remainder with terrestrial waters (bk 3), the river Nile (4A), earthquakes (6) and comets (7).

(4) *Epistulae morales ad Lucilium*: originally in at least twenty-two books, of which twenty (124 letters) have survived. For the specially complex history of this group's transmission, see L. D. Reynolds, *The medieval tradition of Seneca's letters* (Oxford 1965); strictly speaking it forms not one group, but two.

(5) Ten *tragoediae*, enumerated and discussed below.

(6) *Apocolocyntosis*: see pp. 205–6.

(7) *Epigrams*: see p. 204.

DATING: On dates of prose works see Münscher, under *Studies* (1) below, and K Abel, *Bauformen in Senecas Dialogen* (Heidelberg 1967: with bibliography). Following list shows those datings, or approximate datings, on which there is more or less general agreement. *Cons. ad Marciam*: within reign of Caligula (37–41). *De ira* 1–2: 41, between accession of Claudius and banishment of S. How much later bk 3 may be is still disputable. *Cons. ad Helviam*: early in S.'s exile-period; probably not later than summer 43. *Cons. ad Polybium*: in exile-period, before Polybius' death in 47; probably in summer 43. *De brevitate vitae* (*Dial.* 10): not later than 49; probably in exile-period. *De beneficiis*: between Nero's succession (September 54) and 64. *De clementia*: 56. *Naturales quaestiones*: between S.'s retirement from public affairs in 62, and his death in 65. Some reasons to put completion of work no later than 64. *Epistulae morales*: between S.'s retirement and death.

LOST WORKS: Titles and fragments last printed in full by Haase, under *Texts* below. Discussed by Münscher, under *Studies* (1) below. Four of them investigated by M. Lausberg, *Untersuchungen zu Senecas Fragmenten* (Berlin 1970). Representative selection follows: biography of Seneca the Elder, *De vita patris*; two geographical and ethnographical treatises, *De situ et sacris Aegyptiorum* and *De situ Indiae*; four physical treatises, *De motu terrarum volumen* (written by S. as a *iuuenis*, *Q. Nat.* 6.4.2), *De lapidum natura*, *De piscium natura*, and *De forma mundi*; published speeches (cf. Quint. 10.2.129 and Haase III 437–40); moral or philosophical works, *De amicitia*, *Exhortationes*, *De immatura morte liber*, *De matrimonio*, *Moralis philosophiae libri* (general systematization of his moral doctrines, in progress *c.* 62–5; cf. *Epist.* 106.2, 108.1, 109.17), *De officiis*, *De remediis fortuitorum*, *De superstitione dialogus*; treatise of unknown title which S. dictated on his deathbed, subsequently pubd (Tac. *Ann.* 15.63.7). For conjectures as to dates of lost works see Münscher, under *Studies* (1) below (results summarized 142–3).

DUBIOUS OR SPURIOUS: *Epistulae ad Novatum* (Haase fr. 109; cf. Münscher 44 n.2) and *ad Caesonium* (Haase fr. 109, Münscher 63), and a tract on shorthand symbols (Haase fr. 128). A number of spurious works circulating in the middle ages are extracts from, or rehashes of, extant Senecan treatises; such is the *De paupertate*

(Haase III 459–61). Most notorious of the certainly spurious compositions is the *Epistulae Senecae ad Paulum Apostolum et Pauli Apostoli ad Senecam* (ibid. 476–81); ed. C. W. Barlow (Rome 1938); see also K. M. Abbott, 'Seneca and St. Paul', in (ed.) D. C. Richel, *Wege der Wörter. Festschrift für Wolfgang Fleischhauer* (Cologne–Vienna 1978) 119–31, bibliography 119 n. 1.

TRAGEDIES: Transmitted as a group of almost bare texts: the MSS contain no arguments to the plays, no lists of dramatis personae, and no commentaries. The two recensions into which they divide do not agree on the order or number of the plays in the canon, or even on some of their titles. These two recensions are conventionally known as 'E' (after the recension's main representative, the *Codex Etruscus, c.* A.D. 1100) and 'A' (some 300 MSS; most dating from Italian renaissance; none earlier than 13th c. A.D.). Problems presented by the MSS discussed by Giardina,[1] Axelson,[2] and Philp.[3] Following table shows order and titles given by the two recensions:

| E: | A: |
|---|---|
| *Hercules* | *Hercules Furens* |
| *Troades* | *Thyestes* |
| *Phoenissae* | *Thebais* ( = E.'s *Phoenissae*) |
| *Medea* | *Hippolytus* ( = E.'s *Phaedra*) |
| *Phaedra* | *Oedipus* |
| *Oedipus* | *Troas* ( = E.'s *Troades*) |
| *Agamemnon* | *Medea* |
| *Thyestes* | *Agamemnon* |
| *Hercules* | *Octavia* |
| | *Hercules Oetaeus* |

Since E.'s existence was first made public by Gronovius,[4] most editors have adopted E.'s order and titles, except that they continue to distinguish the two Hercules plays, following A, as Furens and Oetaeus. Because the MSS further disagree as to the praenomen of the tragedian, and because neither Quintilian nor Seneca the Philosopher mentions expressly that the latter composed any tragedies, scholars long debated their authorship. Daniel Heinsius[5] distinguished no less than five dramatists in the Senecan corpus, and Milton was still among the doubters as to Senecan authoship (pref. to *Samson Agonistes*); general account of the controversy by Herrmann.[6] Question still not conclusively settled, but in recent times the general – and reasonable – consensus has been that the bulk of the corpus is by S. The present survey assumes that only two

[1] I. C. Giardina, *L. Annaei Senecae tragoediae*, 2 vols. (Bologna 1966: with bibliography).
[2] B. Axelson, *Korruptelenkult: Studien zur Textkritik der unechten Seneca-Tragödie Hercules Oetaeus* (Lund 1967).
[3] R. H. Philp, 'The manuscript tradition of Seneca's tragedies', *C.Q.* n.s.18 (1968) 150–79.
[4] J. F. Gronovius, *L. Annaei Senecae tragoediae* (Leiden 1661).
[5] D. Heinsius, 'De tragoediarum auctoribus dissertatio', in (ed.) P. Scriverius, *L. Annaeus Seneca Tragicus*, 2 vols. (Leiden 1621).
[6] L. Herrmann, *Le théâtre de Sénèque* (Paris 1924) 31–77, 85–99.

# APPENDIX OF AUTHORS AND WORKS

plays are spurious: the little *Octavia* (see Excursus on pp. 34–6), and the elephantine *Hercules Oetaeus*, apparently a semi-skilled imitation of the Senecan manner by a near contemporary; see Friedrich[1] and Axelson.[2] Dates of the eight plays here taken as genuine are uncertain. S. had probably written some of them, including *Hercules Furens*, by the end of 54 (evidence in Coffey[3]); possibly his dramatic activity was renewed in the years just before 62 (Tac. *Ann.* 14.52.3, *carmina crebrius factitare*, if here *carmina* means 'tragedies', as it does in *Ann.* 11.13.1). More precise datings based on supposed historical or political allusions (surveyed by Herrmann[4]) are not generally accepted.

## BIBLIOGRAPHY

TEXTS AND COMMENTARIES: TEXTS: (1) Prose works. Haase (Leipzig 1852: with fragments, *index rerum memorabilium*); J. W. Basore, T. H. Corcoran, R. M. Gummere (Loeb, 1917–72). *Dialogi*: L. D. Reynolds (OCT, 1977). *De beneficiis* and *De clementia*: C. Hosius, 2nd ed. (BT, 1914). *Naturales quaestiones*: P. Oltramare (Budé, 1929). (2) Tragedies. I. C. Giardina (Bologna 1966). COMMENTARIES. *Medea*: C. D. N. Costa (Oxford 1973); *Agamemnon*: R. J. Tarrant (Cambridge 1976).

TRANSLATIONS: F. J. Miller (Loeb, 1917); E. F. Watling, *Seneca: four tragedies and Octavia* (Penguin, 1966).

STUDIES: (1) S.'s BIOGRAPHY AND GENERAL STUDIES: K. Münscher, *Senecas Werke: Untersuchungen zur Abfassungszeit und Echtheit, Philologus* suppl. 16, Heft 1 (1922); Schanz–Hosius II 456–75; V. d'Agostino, 'Seneca Filosofo e Tragico negli anni 1953–1965: Saggio Bibliografico', *R.S.C.* 14 (1966) 61–81; W. Trillitzsch, *Seneca im literarischen Urteil der Antike. Darstellung und Sammlung der Zeugnisse*, 2 vols. (Amsterdam 1971); A. L. Motto, *Seneca sourcebook: guide to the thought of Lucius Annaeus Seneca* (Amsterdam 1970); G. Cupaiuolo, 'Gli studi su Seneca nel triennio 1967–1971', *Boll. di Studi Latini* 2 (1972) 278–317; A. L. Motto, *Seneca* (New York 1973); M. Griffin, *Seneca: a philosopher in politics* (Oxford 1976); M. Rozelaar, *Seneca: eine Gesamtdarstellung* (Amsterdam 1976). (2) PROSE WORKS AND FRAGMENTS: Bibliographies by A. L. Motto, *C.W.* 54 (1960–1) 13–18, 37–48, 70–1, 111–12 (for 1940–58); idem, *C.W.* 64 (1970–1) 141–58, 177–86, 191 (for 1958–68). Also A. Bourgery, *Sénèque prosateur* (Paris 1922); M. Lausberg, *Untersuchungen zu Senecas Fragmenten* (Berlin 1970). (3) TRAGEDIES AND OCTAVIA: Bibliographies by M. Coffey, *Lustrum* 2 (1957) 113–86 (for 1922–55), and in E. Lefèvre, *Senecas Tragödien* (Darmstadt 1972) 583–92 (for 1956–c. 1971). Also F. Leo, *L. Annaei Senecae tragoediae* I (Berlin 1878); M. Coffey, *FYAT* 316–23. (4) CONCORDANCE: R. Busa and A. Zampolli (Hildesheim 1975).

1 W. H. Friedrich, 'Sprache und Stil des Hercules Oetaeus', *Hermes* 82 (1954) 51–84.
2 Axelson, op. cit.
3 M. Coffey, *Lustrum* 2 (1957) 150.
4 Herrmann, op. cit.

# LUCANUS, MARCUS ANNAEUS

## LIFE

b. A.D. 39 at Cordoba, grandson of elder Seneca, nephew of younger (Vacca, *Vita Luc.*). Met Persius, and admired his poetry, at lectures of Stoic Cornutus (Probus, *Vita Pers.*). Involved in Pisonian conspiracy, forced to commit suicide A.D. 65, aged 26 (Tac. *Ann.* 15.56 and 70). Epigrams on his birthday to his widow Polla at Mart. 7.21–3 (cf. 10.64), also Stat. *Genethliacon Lucani, Silv.* 2.7; possible ref. to the young L. at Sen. *Helv.* 43.4.5; boast of excelling Virgil, Suet. *Vita Luc.*; stories of rivalry with Nero in both *Vitae.*

## WORKS

(1) EXTANT: *De bello civili* (so the MSS; Housman (under *Texts* below, 296), explains *Pharsalia nostra* at 9.985 as a ref. to the battle fought by Caesar, and described by L.): unfinished epic, breaking off at 10.546; several passages might have been excised on revision. In the *Vita Codicis Vossiani*, Seneca is wrongly accredited with first four lines of bk 1, probably as a result of a misinterpretation of *Annaeus* at Fronto 2.105ff., above p. 37 n. 2. Jerome mentions a commentary at *Apol. c. Rufin.* 1.16: cf. Lyd. *De mag.* 3.46. Two ancient commentaries survive, the *Commenta Bernensia,* ed. H. Usener (BT, 1869), and the *Adnotationes super Lucanum,* ed. J. Endt (BT, 1909). (2) LOST: A long list of works in Vacca, five of which are attested by Stat. *Silv.* 2.7.54–63, who also mentions an *Adlocutio ad Pollam.* We have fragments of the *Catachthonion, Iliacon, Orpheus* and *Epigrammata,* but the *Laudes Neronis, Silvae, Saturnalia, Medea, Salticae fabulae, De incendio urbis, Epistulae ex Campania* and *Prosa oratio in Octavium Sagittam* are only titles.

## BIBLIOGRAPHY

(for 1925–42, see R. Helm, *Lustrum* 1 (1956) 163–228; for 1943–63, W. Rutz, ibid. 9 (1964) 243ff.; also Morford (1967, under *Studies* below) 89–90, and Ahl (1976) 355–64)

TEXTS AND COMMENTARIES: TEXTS: C. Hosius, 3rd ed. (BT, 1919); A. Bourgery and M. Ponchont (Budé, 1926–9); J. D. Duff (Loeb, 1928); A. E. Housman, 2nd ed. (Oxford 1950), with review of 1st ed. by E. Fraenkel, *Gnomon* 2 (1926) 497. COMMENTARIES: C. E. Haskins, with intr. by W. E. Heitland (London 1887). Bk 1: P. Lejay (Paris 1894); R. J. Getty (Cambridge 1955); P. Wuilleumier and H. le Bonniec (Paris 1962). Bk 7: J. P. Postgate, rev. O. A. W. Dilke (Cambridge 1960). Bk 8: J. P. Postgate (Cambridge 1917).

STUDIES: C. Hosius, 'Lucan und seine Quellen', *Rh.M.* 48 (1893) 380ff.; R. Pichon, *Les sources de Lucain* (Paris 1912); W. Kroll, 'Das historische Epos', *Sokrates* 4 (1916) 2ff.; E. Fraenkel, 'Lucan als Mittler des Antiken Pathos', *Vorträge der Bibliothek Warburg* (1924) 229ff.; E. M. Sandford, 'Lucan and his Roman critics',

*C.Ph.* 26 (1931) 233–57; L. Eckhardt, *Exkurse und Ekphraseis bei Lucan* (Heidelberg 1936); E. Malcovati, *Lucano* (Milan 1940); B. Marti, 'The meaning of the Pharsalia', *A.J.Ph.* 66 (1945) 352–76; idem, 'La structure de la Pharsale', in *Entretiens* (1968 below) 1–50; J. André, *Étude sur les termes de couleur dans la langue latine* (Paris 1949); P. J. Miniconi, *Étude des thèmes guerriers de la poésie gréco-romaine, Publ. Fac. Lettr. Alger.* 2.19 (Paris 1951); idem, 'La joie dans l'Éneide', *Latomus* 21 (1962) 503–11; A. Guillemin, 'L'inspiration Virgilienne dans la Pharsale', *R.E.L.* 29 (1951) 214–27; I. Cazzaniga, *Problemi intorno alla Farsaglia* (Milan 1955); E. Longi, 'Tre episodi del poema di Lucano', *Stud. in on. di G. Funaioli* (Rome 1955) 181–8; H. Nowak, *Lukanstudien* (diss. Vienna 1955); G. K. Gresseth, 'The quarrel between Lucan and Nero', *C.Ph.* 52 (1957) 24–7; I. Opelt, 'Die Seeschlacht vor Massilia bei Lucan', *Hermes* 85 (1957) 435–45; H. P. Syndikus, *Lucans Gedicht vom Bürgerkrieg* (Munich 1958); L. Thompson and R. T. Bruère, 'Lucan's use of Virgilian reminiscence', *C.Ph.* 63 (1968) 1–21; P. Grimal, 'L'éloge de Néron au début de la Pharsale', *R.E.L.* 38 (1960) 296–305; idem, 'L'épisode d'Antée dans la Pharsale', *Latomus* 8 (1949) 55–61; L. A. Mackay, 'The vocabulary of fear in Latin epic poetry', *T.A.Ph.A.* 92 (1961) 308–16; O. S. Due, 'An essay on Lucan', *C.&M.* 22 (1962) 68–132; P. Jal, *La guerre civile à Rome* (Paris 1963); J. Brisset, *Les idées politiques de Lucain* (Paris 1964); P. Pecchiura, *La figura di Catone Uticense nella letteratura latina* (Turin 1965); K. Seitz, 'Der pathetische Erzählstil Lucans', *Hermes* 93 (1965) 204ff.; M. P. O. Morford, *The poet Lucan* (Oxford 1967); A. Ollfors, *Studien zum Aufbau des Hexameters Lucans* (Gothenburg 1967); *Entretiens XV: Lucain* (Fondation Hardt, Geneva 1968); O. C. Philips, 'Lucan's grove', *C.Ph.* 63 (1968) 296–300; A. W. Lintott, 'Lucan and the history of the civil war', *C.Q.* 21 (1971) 488–505; F. M. Ahl, *Lucan, an introduction* (New York 1976).

CONCORDANCE: R. J. Deferrari et al. (Washington 1940).

# FLAVIAN EPIC

## GENERAL WORKS

Bardon, H., 'Le goût à l'époque des Flaviens', *Latomus* 21 (1962) 732–48.

Bolaffi, E., 'L'epica del I secolo dell' impero', *G.I.F.* 12 (1959) 218–30.

Butler, H. E., *Post-Augustan poetry from Seneca to Juvenal* (Oxford 1909).

Gossage, A. J., 'Virgil and the Flavian epic', in (ed.) D. R. Dudley, *Virgil* (London 1969) 67–93.

Hadas, M., 'Later Latin epic and Lucan', *C.W.* 29 (1936) 153–7.

Mendell, C. W., *Latin poetry: the age of rhetoric and satire* (Hamden 1967).

Schönberger, O. 'Zum Weltbild der drei Epiker nach Lukan', *Helikon* 5 (1965) 123–45.

Steele, R. B., 'The interrelation of the Latin poets under Domitian', *C.Ph.* 25 (1930) 328–42.

Summers, W. C., *The silver age of Latin literature* (London 1920).
Williams, G., *Change and decline: Roman literature in the early Empire*, Sather Classical Lectures 45 (Berkeley–London 1978).

# STATIUS, PUBLIUS PAPINIUS

## LIFE

b. at Naples *c*. A.D. 45; his father a poet and schoolmaster. At Rome established himself as a poet (recitals, Juv. 7.82–7; see V. Tandoi, *Maia* 21 (1969) 103–22), and was favoured by Domitian (cf. *Silv.* 3.1.61ff.). d. at Naples *c*. 96. For a dubious allusion to S. by Martial, see H. Heuvel, *Mnemosyne* 3.4 (1937) 299–330; see also F. Delarue, 'Stace et ses contemporains', *Latomus* 33 (1974) 536–48. For his father, see *Silv.* 5.3, with G. Curcio, *Studio su P. Papinio Stazio* (Catania 1893) 3–18; A. Traglia, *R.C.C.M.* 7 (1965) 1128–34; D. Vessey, *Statius and the Thebaid* (Cambridge 1973) 49–54; K. Clinton, 'Publius Papinius ST[---] at Eleusis'; *T.A.Ph.A.* 103 (1972) 79–82.

## WORKS

*Silvae*: five books of poems, mostly in hexameters, pubd in stages from 92. *Thebaid*: epic in twelve books, pubd *c*. 91. *Achilleid*: epic, unfinished in bk 2 at S.'s death. Also (lost), *De bello Germanico* (schol. *ad* Juv. 4.94) and a pantomime, *Agave* (Juv. 7.87).

## BIBLIOGRAPHY

(for 1925–42, see R. Helm, *Lustrum* 1 (1956) 272–99)

TEXTS AND COMMENTARIES: TEXTS: Complete works: A. Traglia and G. Aricò (Turin 1980: with bibliography 55–72 and tr.). *Silvae*: A. Baehrens (BT, 1876); A. Klotz, 2nd ed. (BT, 1911); J. S. Phillimore, 2nd ed. (OCT, 1918; repr. 1962); H. Frère and H. J. Isaac (Budé, 1944); J. H. Mozley, rev. ed. (Loeb, 1955). *Thebaid*: H. W. Garrod (OCT, 1906; repr. 1965; with *Achilleid*); J. H. Mozley, rev. ed. (Loeb, 1955); A. Klotz, rev. T. C. Klinnert (BT, 1973). *Achilleid*: A. Klotz (BT, 1902); J. H. Mozley, rev. ed. (Loeb, 1955); J. Méheust (Budé, 1971); A. Marastoni (BT, 1974). COMMENTARIES: *Silvae*: F. Vollmer (Leipzig 1898; repr. 1968). *Thebaid*: Bk 1: H. Heuvel (diss. Groningen, Zutphen 1932); F. Caviglia (Rome 1973). Bk 2: H. M. Mulder (diss. Groningen 1954). Bk 3: H. Snijder (Amsterdam 1968), cf. P. Venini, in *Studi Staziani* (Pavia 1971) 110–24 = *Athenaeum* 58 (1970) 132–8. Bk 6.1–295: H. W. Fortgens (diss. Utrecht, Zutphen 1934). Bk 10: R. D. Williams, *Mnemosyne* suppl. 22 (Leiden 1972). Bk 11: P. Venini (Florence 1970). *Achilleid*: S. Jannoccone (Florence 1950); O. A. W. Dilke (Cambridge 1954). See also P. M. Clogan, *The medieval Achilleid of Statius* (Leiden 1968).

TRANSLATIONS: *Silvae*: D. A. Slater (Oxford 1908: with notes). *Thebaid*: J. B. Poynton, 3 vols. (Oxford 1971–5).

# APPENDIX OF AUTHORS AND WORKS

STUDIES: (1) GENERAL INTRODUCTION: R. Helm, *RE* XVIII.3 (1949) 984–1000; A. J. Gossage, in (ed.) D. R. Dudley, *Neronians and Flavians: Silver Latin* I (London 1972) 184–235.

(2) STATIUS AND DOMITIAN: K. Scott, *A.J.Ph.* 54 (1933) 247–59; idem, *The imperial cult under the Flavians* (Stuttgart–Berlin 1936); F. Sauter, *Der römischer Kaiserkult bei Martial und Statius* (Stuttgart 1934); D. Vessey, *Statius and the Thebaid* (Cambridge 1973) 28–36.

(3) PATRONS: R. Syme, 'Vibius Maximus, Prefect of Egypt', *Historia* 6 (1957) 480–7; G. Aricò, 'Stazio e Arrunzio Stella', *Aevum* 39 (1965) 345–7; P. R. C. Weaver, 'The father of Claudius Etruscus, Statius, Silvae III.3', *C.Q.* n.s.15 (1965) 145–54; D. Vessey, *Statius and the Thebaid* (Cambridge 1973) 15–28; P. White, 'Notes on two Statian ΠΡΟΣΩΠΑ', *C.Ph.* 68 (1973) 279–84 (Marcellus, Crispinus); idem, 'Vibius Maximus, the friend of Statius', *Historia* 22 (1973) 295–301; idem, 'The presentation and dedication of the Silvae and Epigrams', *J.R.S.* 64 (1974) 40–61; idem, 'The friends of Martial, Statius and Pliny and the dispersal of patronage', *H.S.C.Ph.* 79 (1975) 265–300 (Arruntius Stella, Atedius Melior, Claudius Etruscus, Argentaria Polla, Novius Vindex, Earinus).

(4) 'SILVAE': J. Danglard, *De Stace et surtout sur les Silves* (Lyon 1864); G. Luehr, *De P. Papinio Statio in Silvis priorum poetarum imitatore* (diss. Königsberg 1880); A. Herzog, *Statii Epithalamium, Silvae I.ii* (diss. Leipzig 1882: text and comm.); O. Lottisch, *Trostgedicht an den Claudius Etruscus (Silv. III.3) mit sachlichen und kritischen Erklärungen* (prog. Hamburg 1893: text and comm.); H. Lohrisch, *De Papinii Statii Silvarum poetae studiis rhetoricis* (diss. Halle 1905); J. F. Lockwood, in *Ut pictura poesis: studia Latina P. J. Enk septuagenario oblata* (Leiden 1955) 107–11 (*Silv.* 4.4); A. Marastoni, 'Per una nuova interpretazione di Stazio poeta delle Selve', *Aevum* 31 (1957) 393–414 and 32 (1958) 1–37; V. Buchheit, *Hermes* 88 (1960) 231–49 (*Silv.* 2.7); R. Argenio, *R.S.C.* 34 (1962) 128–32 (*Silv.* 5.3); idem, *R.S.C.* 37 (1965) 160–73 (*Silv.* 4.3); idem, *R.S.C.* 20 (1973) 221–62 (*Silv.* 2.1, 5.5); A. Traglia, 'De P. Papinio Statio Silvarum poeta', *Latinitas* 12 (1964) 7–12; H. Cancik, *Untersuchungen zur lyrischen Kunst des P. Papinius Statius* (diss. Tübingen 1965) = *Spudasmata* 13 (Hildesheim 1965); idem, *A.U.* 11 (1968) 62–75 (*Silv.* 2.2); Z. Pavlovskis, 'Statius and the late Latin epithalamia', *C.Ph.* 60 (1965) 164–77; idem; 'From Statius to Ennodius: a brief history of prose prefaces to poems', *R.I.L.* 101 (1967) 535–67; J. H. Bishop, in (ed.) M. Kelly, *For service to classical studies: essays in honour of Francis Letters* (Melbourne 1966) 15–30; H. Szelest, 'Die Originalität der sog. beschreibenden Silvae des Statius', *Eos* 56 (1966) 186–97; idem, *Meander* 22 (1967) 261–8 (*Silv.* 4.7 and 8); idem, *Meander* 23 (1968) 298–305 (*Silv.* 1.4); idem, 'Mythologie und ihre Rolle in den Silvae des Statius', *Eos* 60 (1972) 309–17; E. Mensching, *Hermes* 97 (1969) 252–5 (*Silv.* 2.7); D. Vessey, *A.C.* 39 (1970) 507–18 (*Silv.* 4.5); idem, 'Varia Statiana', *C.B.* 46 (1970) 49–64; idem, *Mnemosyne* 4.25 (1972) 172–87 (*Silv.* 1.2); idem, *A.C.* 43 (1974) 257–66 (Silv. 4.8); idem, *C.J.* 72 (1976–7) 134–40 (*Silv.* 3.5); G. Aricò, 'Sulle trace di una poetica staziana', *Ricerche Staziane* (Palermo 1972) 37–71 = *B.S.L.* I

(1971) 217–39; E. B. Holtsmark, *C.J.* (1972–3) 216–20 (*Silv.* 1.5); R. Häussler, *Živa Antika* 25 (1975) 106–13 (*Silv.* 5.4); S. T. Newmyer, *The Silvae of Statius: structure and theme*, Mnemosyne suppl. 53 (Leiden 1979).

(5) 'THEBAID' AND 'ACHILLEID': see the works cited by D. Vessey, *Statius and the Thebaid* (Cambridge 1973) 329–41, and the following: G. Aricò, 'Adrasto e la guerra Tebana (Mondo spirituale staziano e caratterizazione psicologia)', *Ricerche Staziane* (Palermo 1972) 109–31 = *Annali del liceo classico 'G. Garibaldi' di Palermo 7–8* (1970–1) 208–23; M. Goetting, *Hypsipyle in der Thebais des Statius* (diss. Tübingen 1966, Wiesbaden 1969); P. Venini, 'Ancora su Stazio e Lucano', *Studi Staziani* (Pavia 1971) 81–3; S. von Moisy, *Untersuchungen zur Erzählweise in Statius' Thebais*, Habelts Dissertationsdrucke, Reihe Klass. Phil. 11 (Bonn 1971); J. F. Burgess, 'Pietas in Virgil and Statius', *P.V.S.* 11 (1971–2) 48–61; idem, 'Statius' altar of mercy', *C.Q.* n.s.22 (1972) 339–49; E. Burck, 'Die Thebais des Statius, Die Achilleis des Statius', in (ed.) E. Burck, *Das römische Epos, Grundriss der Literaturgeschichte nach Gattungen* (Darmstadt 1979) 300–58.

(6) TEXT: L. Håkanson, *Statius' Silvae: critical and exegetical remarks with some notes on the Thebaid* (Lund 1969: select bibliography 7–11), reviewed by D. Vessey, *C.Ph.* 66 (1971) 273–6, and G. Aricò, *Maia* 25 (1973) 180–2; J. A. Willis, 'The Silvae of Statius and their editors', *Phoenix* 20 (1966) 305–24; L. Håkanson, *Statius' Thebaid: critical and exegetical remarks* (Lund 1973: select bibliography 89–91); G. Lotito, 'In margine alla nuova edizione teubneriana della Silvae di Stazio', *A.&R.* 19 (1974) 26–48.

CONCORDANCE: R. J. Deferrari and M. C. Eagan (Brookland 1943).

# VALERIUS FLACCUS, GAIUS

## LIFE

Unknown, except that he was *XVvir sacris faciundis* (1.5, 8.239–41). Only contemporary ref. is Quint. 10.1.90.

## WORKS

*Argonautica*: epic, unfinished in bk 8 at V.'s death A.D. 92/93.

## BIBLIOGRAPHY

(See L. Ieep, Bursian 23 (1896) 72–93; for 1925–42, R. Helm, *Lustrum* 1 (1956) 236–55; for 1940–71, W.-W. Ehlers, *Lustrum* 16 (1971–2) 105–42)

TEXTS AND COMMENTARY: TEXTS: A. Baehrens (BT, 1875); P. Langen, *Berl. Stud. f. class. Phil. u. Archäol.*, n.s.1.1–2 (Berlin 1896; repr. Hildesheim 1964);

# APPENDIX OF AUTHORS AND WORKS

O. Kramer (BT, 1913; repr. Stuttgart 1967); J. H. Mozley (Loeb, 1934; rev. ed. 1936, 1958, 1963); E. Courtney (BT, 1970). COMMENTARY: Bk I: H. G. Blomfield (Oxford 1916: with tr.).

STUDIES: H. Gebbing, *De C. Valerii Flacci tropis et figuris* (diss. Marburg 1878); J. Peters, *De C. Valerii Flacci vita et carmine* (Königsberg 1980); A. Grueneberg, *De Valerio Flacco imitatore* (diss. Berlin 1893); W. C. Summers, *A study of the Argonautica of Valerius Flaccus* (Cambridge 1894); R. Harmand, *De Valerio Flacco Apollonii Rhodii imitatore* (Nancy 1898); R. Stroh, *Studien zu Valerius Flaccus, besonders über dessen Verhältnis zu Vergil* (diss. Munich 1902 (1905)); R. Syme, 'The Argonautica of Valerius Flaccus', *C.Q.* 23 (1929) 129–37; K. Scott, 'The date of the composition of the Argonautica of Valerius Flaccus', resumé of diss., *T.A.Ph.A.* 64 (1933) lxvi; idem, 'La data di composizione della Argonautica di Valerio Flacco', *R.F.* 62 (1934) 474–81; F. Mehmel, *Valerius Flaccus* (diss. Hamburg 1934); J. Stroux, 'Valerius Flaccus and Horaz', *Philologus* 90 (1935) 305–50; R. J. Getty, 'The date of the composition of the Argonautica of Valerius Flaccus', *C.Ph.* 31 (1936) 53–61; idem, 'The introduction of the Argonautica of Valerius Flaccus', *C.Ph.* 35 (1940) 259–73; J. M. K. Martin, 'Valerius Flaccus, poet of romance', *G.&R.* 7 (1937–8) 137–48; W. Morel, 'Zu den Argonautica des Valerius Flaccus', *Rh.M.* 87 (1938) 60–74; A. Kurfess, *RE* VIII.I (1955) 9–15; V. Ussani, *Studio su Valerio Flacco, Studi e Saggi* 6 (Rome 1955); E. Merone, *Sulla lingua di Valerio Flacco, Bibl. del Giorn. It. Fil.* 8 (Naples 1957); H. MacL. Currie, 'Virgil and Valerius Flaccus', *V.S.L.S.* 48 (1959); W. Schetter, 'Die Buchzahl der Argonautica des Valerius Flaccus', *Philologus* 103 (1959) 297–308; R. W. Garson, 'The Hylas episode in Valerius Flaccus' Argonautica', *C.Q.* n.s.13 (1963) 260–7; idem, 'Some critical observations on Valerius Flaccus' Argonautica', *C.Q.* n.s.14 (1964) 267–79 and 15 (1965) 104–20; idem, 'Metrical statistics of Valerius Flaccus' Argonautica', *C.Q.* n.s.18 (1968) 376–9; idem, 'Homeric echoes in Valerius Flaccus' Argonautica', *C.Q.* n.s.19 (1969) 362–6; idem, 'Valerius Flaccus the poet', *C.Q.* n.s.20 (1970) 181–7; H. O. Kröner, 'Zu den künstlerischen Absichten des Valerius Flaccus', *Hermes* 96 (1968) 733–54; G. Cambier, 'Recherches chronologiques sur l'oeuvre et la vie de Valerius Flaccus', *Hommages à M. Renard, Coll. Latomus* 101–3 (Brussels 1969) I 191–228; R. Nordera, 'I virgilianismi in Valerio Flacco', *Contributi a tre poeti latini* (Bologna 1969) 1–92; J. Adamietz, 'Jason und Hercules in den Epen des Apollonios Rhodios und Valerius Flaccus', *A.&A.* 16 (1970) 29–38; idem, *Zur Komposition der Argonautica des Valerius Flaccus* (Munich 1976); E. Burck, 'Kampf und Tod des Cyzicus bei Valerius Flaccus', *R.E.L.* 47.2 (1970) 173–98; idem, 'Die Argonautica des Valerius Flaccus', in (ed.) E. Burck, *Das römische Epos, Grundriss der Literaturgeschichte nach Gattungen* (Darmstadt 1979) 208–53; W.-W. Ehlers, *Untersuchungen zur handschriftlichen Überlieferung der Argonautica des C. Valerius Flaccus, Zetemata* 52 (Munich 1970: bibliography 126–33); E. Lefèvre, 'Das Prooemium der Argonautica des Valerius Flaccus: Ein Beitrag zur Typik epischer Prooemien der römischen Kaiserzeit', *Abh. Akad. Mainz* 1971, 6; P. Venini,

APPENDIX OF AUTHORS AND WORKS

'Valerio Flacco e l'erudizione Apolloniana: note stilistiche', *R.I.L* 105 (1971) 582–96; idem, 'Sulla struttura della Argonautiche di Valerio Flacco', ibid. 597–620; idem, 'Su alcuni motivi della Argonautiche di Valerio Flacco', *B. Stud. Lat.* 2 (1972) 10–19; J. Strand, *Notes on Valerius Flaccus' Argonautica, Stud. Graec. et Lat. Gothoburg* 31 (Göteborg 1972); S. Contino, *Lingua e stile in Valerio Flacco* (Bologna 1973); J. P. Perkins, 'An aspect of style of Valerius Flaccus' Argonauticon', *Phoenix* 28 (1974) 290–313; J. G. Fitch, 'Aspects of Valerius Flaccus' use of similes', *T.A.Ph.A.* 106 (1976) 113–24.

CONCORDANCE: W. H. Schulte (Scottdale 1934; repr. Hildesheim 1965).

# SILIUS ITALICUS,
# TIBERIUS CATIUS ASCONIUS

## LIFE

Dates *c.* A.D. 26–101. Advocate in Rome, consul 68, supporter of Vitellius, governor of Asia *c.* 77. Starved himself to death after contracting an incurable disease. Sources: Pliny, *Epist.* 3.7 (obituary); Mart. 7.63, 8.66, 9.86, 11.48, 49 (all addressed to S.); Tac. *Hist.* 3.65 (S. and Vitellius). For inscription relating to his governorship of Asia, see W. M. Calder, *C.R.* 49 (1935) 216–17. Cf. also D. Vessey, 'Pliny, Martial and Silius Italicus', *Hermes* 102 (1974) 109–16; W. C. McDermott and A. E. Orentzel, 'Silius Italicus and Domitian', *A.J.Ph.* 98 (1977) 24–34.

## WORKS

*Punica*: epic in seventeen books on second Punic war, written from 88 onwards.

## BIBLIOGRAPHY

(for 1929–42, see R. Helm, *Lustrum* 1 (1956) 255–72)

TEXTS: L. Bauer (BT, 1890–2); J. D. Duff (Loeb, 1934); A. Petrucci (Milan 1947: with tr.).

STUDIES: L. Legras, 'Les "Puniques" et la "Thébaïde"', *R.E.A.* 7 (1905) 131–46, 357–71; L. B. Woodruff, *Reminiscences of Ennius in Silius Italicus, Univ. of Michigan Studies* 4 (New York 1910) 355–424; R. Rebischke, *De Silii Italici orationibus* (diss. Königsberg–Danzig 1913); R. B. Steele, 'The method of Silius Italicus', *C.Ph.* 17 (1922) 319–33; C. W. Mendell, 'Silius the reactionary', *Ph.Q.* 3 (1924) 92–106; A. Klotz, *RE* IIIA.1 (1927) 79–91; D. J. Campbell, 'The birthplace of Silius Italicus', *C.R.* 50 (1936) 56–8; J. Nicol, *The historical and geographical sources used by Silius Italicus*

(Oxford 1936); S. Blomgren, *Siliana: De Silii Italici Punicis quaestiones criticae et interpretariae*, *Årsskrift Upps. Univ.* 1938.7 (Uppsala–Leipzig 1938); M. Sechi, 'Silio Italico e Livio', *Maia* 4 (1951) 280–97; L. Ramaglia, 'La figura di Giunone nelle Puniche di Silio Italico', *R.S.C.* 1 (1952–3) 35–43; R. T. Bruère, 'Silius Italicus, Punica 3.62–162 and 4.763–822', *C.Ph.* 47 (1952) 219–27; idem, 'Color Ovidianus in Silius' Punica I–VII', in (ed.) N. I. Herescu, *Ovidiana* (Paris 1958) 475–99; idem, 'Color Ovidianus in Silius' Punica VIII–XVII', *C.Ph.* 54 (1959) 228–45; idem, 'Some recollections of Virgil's Drances in later epic', *C.Ph.* 66 (1971) 30–4; E. Wistrand, *Die Chronologie der Punica des Silius Italicus: Beiträge zur Interpretation der flavischen Literatur, Göteborgs Univ. Årsskrift* 62 = *Studia Graeca et Latina Gothoburgensia* 4 (Göteborg 1956); E. L. Bassett, 'Silius Italicus in England', *C.Ph.* 48 (1953) 155–68; idem, 'Regulus and the serpent in the Punica', *C.Ph.* 50 (1955) 1–20; idem, 'Silius, Punica 6.1–53', *C.Ph.* 54 (1959) 10–34; idem, 'Scipio and the ghost of Appius', *C.Ph.* 58 (1963) 73–92; idem, 'Hercules and the hero of the Punica', in (ed.) L. Wallach, *The classical tradition: literary and historical studies in honor of Harry Caplan* (New York 1966) 258–73; M. V. T. Wallace, 'The architecture of the Punica: a hypothesis', *C.Ph.* 53 (1958) 99–103; idem, 'Some aspects of time in the Punica of Silius Italicus', *C.W.* 62 (1968) 83–93; M. von Albrecht, 'Gleichnis und Innenwelt in Silius' Punica', *Hermes* 91 (1963) 352–74; idem, *Silius Italicus, Freiheit und Gebundenheit römischer Epik* (Amsterdam 1964: bibliography 215–37); idem, 'Silius Italicus: Ein vergessenes Kapitel Literaturgeschichte', in *Argentea Aetas: In Memoriam E. V. Marmorale, Univ. di Genova Ist. di Fil. Class. e Mediev. Pubbl.* 37 (Genoa 1973) 181–8; J. Delz, 'Die erste Junoszene in den Punica des Silius Italicus', *M.H.* 26 (1969) 88–100; P. Venini, 'Silio Italico e il mito Tebano', *R.I.L.* 103 (1969) 778–83; idem, 'Cronologia e composizione nei Punica di Silio Italico', *R.I.L.* 106 (1972) 518–31; idem, 'Tecnica allusiva di Silio Italico', ibid. 532–42; H. Juhnke, *Homerisches in römischer Epik flavischer Zeit: Untersuchungen zu Szenennachbildungen und Structurentsprechungen in Statius' Thebais und Achilleis und in Silius' Punica, Zetemata* 53 (Munich 1972); D. Vessey, 'Silius Italicus on the fall of Saguntum', *C.Ph.* 69 (1974) 28–36; idem, 'The myth of Falernus in Silius Italicus, Punica 7', *C. J.* 68 (1972–3) 240–6; idem, 'Silius Italicus: the shield of Hannibal', *A.J.Ph.* 96 (1975) 391–405; K. H. Niemann, *Die Darstellung der römischen Niederlagen in den Punica des Silius Italicus* (diss. Bonn 1975); E. Burck, 'Die Punica des Silius Italicus', in (ed.) E. Burck, *Das römische Epos, Grundriss der Literaturgeschichte nach Gattungen* (Darmstadt 1979) 254–99.

CONCORDANCE: N. D. Young, *Iowa Stud. in Class. Phil.* 8 (Iowa City 1939).

# MARTIAL AND JUVENAL

## GENERAL WORKS

(1) Juvenal in conjunction with Martial, literary life of the times.

Bardon, H., *Les empereurs et les lettres latines* (Paris 1940).

Colton, R. E., *Juvenal and Martial* (diss. Columbia 1951).

idem, 'Juvenal and Martial on literary and professional men', *C.B.* 39 (1963) 49–52.

idem, 'Juvenal's second satire and Martial', *C.J.* 61 (1965–6) 68–71.

idem, 'Juvenal on recitations', *C.B.* 42 (1966) 81–5.

Guillemin, A.-M., *Pline et la vie littéraire de son temps* (Paris 1929).

Marache, R., 'La poésie romaine et le problème social à la fin du Ier siècle chez Martial et Juvénal', *L'Information Littéraire* 13 (1961) 12–19.

Scivoletto, N., 'Plinio il Giovane e Giovenale', *G.I.F.* 10 (1957) 133–46.

Steele, R. B., 'Interrelation of the Latin poets under Domitian', *C.Ph.* 25 (1930) 328–42.

Townend, G., 'The literary substrata to Juvenal's satires', *J.R.S.* 63 (1973) 148–60.

White, P., 'The friends of Martial, Statius, and Pliny, and the dispersal of patronage', *H.S.C.Ph.* 79 (1975) 265–300.

(2) Roman satire

Coffey, M., *Roman satire* (London–New York 1976).

Duff, J. W., *Roman satire* (Cambridge 1937).

Knoche, U., *Die römische Satire*, 3rd ed. (Göttingen 1971).

Terzaghi, N., *Per la storia della satira*, 2nd ed. (Turin 1944).

Weinreich, O., *Römische Satiren*, 2nd ed. (Zurich–Stuttgart 1962).

# MARTIALIS, MARCUS VALERIUS

## LIFE

b. *c.* A.D. 38–41 at Bilbilis in Spain. At Rome knew Silius, Valerius, Pliny, Quintilian and Juvenal. Pliny subsidized his return to Spain, where he died *c.* 104 (Pliny, *Epist.* 3.21.1). See above, p. 602, and U. Scamuzzi, *R.S.C.* 14 (1966) 149–207.

## WORKS

Twelve books of epigrams, pubd 86–101; *Liber spectaculorum*, 80; *Xenia* and *Apophoreta* (now bks 13–14), *c.* 84. See above, pp. 602–3; H. F. Stobbe, *Philologus* 26 (1867) 44–80; E. T. Sage, *T.A.Ph.A.* 50 (1919) 168–76.

## BIBLIOGRAPHY

(for 1915–25, see M. Schuster, *J.A.W.* 211 (1927) 144–67; for 1925–42, R. Helm, *Lustrum* 1 (1956) 299–318, and 2 (1957) 187–206; for 1901–70, G. W. M. Harrison, *Lustrum* 18 (1975) 301–37)

TEXTS AND COMMENTARIES: TEXTS: W. M. Lindsay (OCT, 1903); W. C. A. Ker (Loeb, 1919); H. J. Izaac (Budé, 1930); W. Heraeus, rev. J. Borovskij (BT, 1976). COMMENTARIES: L. Friedländer (Leipzig 1886). Bk 1: M. Citroni (Florence 1975); P. Howell (London 1980).

STUDIES: A. Zingerle, *Martial's Ovid-Studien* (Innsbruck 1877); W. M. Lindsay, *The ancient editions of Martial* (Oxford 1903); K. Preston, 'Martial and formal literary criticism', *C.Ph.* 15 (1920) 340–52; K. F. Smith, *Martial the epigrammatist and other essays* (Baltimore 1920); C. W. Mendell, 'Martial and the satiric epigram', *C.Ph.* 17 (1922) 1–20; O. Weinreich, *Studien zu Martial* (Stuttgart 1928); J. W. Spaeth, 'Martial and Virgil', *T.A.Ph.A.* 61 (1930) 19–28; K. Barwick, 'Zur Kompositionstechnik und Erklärung Martials', *Philologus* 87 (1932) 63–79; F. Sauter, *Der römische Kaiserkult bei Martial und Statius* (Stuttgart–Berlin 1934); J. Kruuse, 'L'originalité artistique de Martial', *C.&M.* 4 (1941) 248–300; A. Nordh, 'Historical exempla in Martial', *Eranos* 52 (1954) 224–38; R. Helm, in *RE* VIIIA.1 (1955) 55–85; K. Barwick, *Martial und die zeitgenössische Rhetorik* (Berlin 1959); H. Szelest, 'Martials satirische Epigramme und Horaz', *Altertum* 9 (1963) 27–37; J. Ferguson, 'Catullus and Martial', *P.A.C.A.* 6 (1963) 3–15; P. Laurens, 'Martial et l'épigramme grecque du Ier siècle après J-C', *R.E.L.* 43 (1965) 315–41; E. Siedschlag, *Zur Form von Martials Epigrammen* (Berlin 1977).

CONCORDANCE: E. Siedschlag (Hildesheim–New York 1979).

# IUVENALIS, DECIMUS IUNIUS

## LIFE

b. A.D. 67 (?), d. sometime after 127 (last datable refs. *Sat.* 13.17, 15.27). Not mentioned by any contemporary except Martial (Mart. 7.24 and 91, 12.18). Did not achieve popularity until 4th c. A.D.; see Highet (1956, under *Studies* below), and Coffey (under *General works* (2) above) 144–6 with notes. See above, pp. 107–8, for the problems, and authors and evidence cited there in notes; also G. Highet, *T.A.Ph.A.* 68 (1937) 480–506; W. S. Anderson, *C.Ph.* 50 (1955) 255–7; G. Brugnoli, *Studi Urbinati* 37 (1963) 5–14; Coffey (1963, under *Bibliography* below) 165–70.

## WORKS

Fifteen complete satires, and a fragment of a sixteenth, divided into five books. *Sat.* 1 composed after 100, *Sat.* 15 after 127. Additional thirty-six lines, generally agreed to be genuine and belonging to *Sat.* 6, were discovered in 1899; see Housman (under *Texts* below) xxix–xxx and xxxix–xl; Coffey (1963, under *Bibliography* below) 179–84; J. G. Griffith, *Hermes* 91 (1963) 104–14; G. Luck, *H.S.Ph.* 76 (1972) 217–32. The contention of O. Ribbeck, *Der echte und der unechte Juvenal* (Berlin 1865) that the later satires are not authentic is now discounted. For author-variants, see J. G. Griffith, *Festschrift B. Snell* (Munich 1956) 101–11; for interpolations, E. Courtney, *B.I.C.S.* 22 (1975) 147–62.

## BIBLIOGRAPHY

(for 1918–40, see E. Lommatzsch, *J.A.W.* 204 (1925) 221ff., 235 (1932) 149–51, 260 (1938) 102–5; for 1941–61, R. Helm, *J.A.W.* 282 (1943) 15–37, and M. Coffey, *Lustrum* 8 (1963) 161–217); for 1937–68, W. S. Anderson, *C.W.* 50 (1956) 38ff., 57 (1964) 346–8, 63 (1970) 217–22. See also bibliographies in Adamietz (1972) and Gérard (1976), under *Studies* below)

TEXTS AND COMMENTARIES: TEXTS: A. E. Housman, 2nd ed. (Cambridge 1931); U. Knoche (Munich 1950); W. V. Clausen (OCT, 1959). COMMENTARIES: G. A. Ruperti (Glasgow 1825); L. Friedländer (Leipzig 1895), intr. tr. J. R. C. Martyn, *Friedländer's essays on Juvenal* (Amsterdam 1969); J. E. B. Mayor (London 1901); J. D. Duff and M. Coffey (Cambridge 1970); E. Courtney (London 1980). SCHOLIA: D. Wessner (BT, 1931). See G. B. Townend, *C.Q.* 22 (1972) 376–87. MANUSCRIPTS: U. Knoche, *Die Überlieferung Juvenals* (Berlin 1926); idem, *Handschriftliche Grundlagen des Juvenal-Textes*, *Philologus* suppl. 33 (1940); Coffey (1963, under *Studies* below) 170ff.; J. G. Griffith, *M.H.* 15 (1968) 101–38.

STUDIES: J. de Decker, *Juvenalis declamans* (Ghent 1913); I. G. Scott, *The grand style in the satires of Juvenal* (Northampton, Mass. 1927); P. de Labriolle, *Les satires de Juvénal: étude et analyse* (Paris 1932); F. Gauger, *Zeitschilderung und Topik bei Juvenal* (diss. Greifswald 1937); E. Smemo, 'Zur Technik der Personenzeichnung bei Juvenal', *S.O.* 16 (1937) 77–102; G. Highet, 'The philosophy of Juvenal', *T.A.Ph.A.* 80 (1949) 254–70; idem, 'Juvenal's bookcase', *A.J.Ph.* 72 (1951) 369–94; idem, *Juvenal the satirist* (Oxford 1954); W. C. Helmbold, 'Juvenal's twelfth satire', *C.Ph.* 51 (1956) 14–23; W. S. Anderson, 'Studies in book 1 of Juvenal', *Y.Cl.S.* 15 (1957) 31–90; idem, 'Juvenal and Quintilian', *Y.Cl.S.* 17 (1961) 3–93; idem, 'The programs of Juvenal's later books', *C.Ph.* 57 (1962) 145–60; idem, 'Anger in Juvenal and Seneca', *Univ. Calif. Publ. Class. Phil.* 19.3 (1964); A. Serafini, *Studio sulle satire di Giovenale* (Florence 1957); E. Thomas, 'Ovidian echoes in Juvenal', in (ed.) N. Herescu, *Ovidiana* (Paris 1958) 505–25; G. Lawall, 'Exempla and theme in Juvenal's tenth satire', *T.A.Ph.A.* 89 (1958) 25–31; E. J. Kenney, 'The first satire of Juvenal', *P.C.Ph.S* 8 (1962) 29–40; J. G. Griffith, 'Juvenal and the stage-struck patricians', *Mnemosyne* 4.15 (1962) 256–61; idem, 'The ending of Juvenal's first satire and Lucilius xxx', *Hermes* 98 (1970) 56–72; E. J. Kenney, 'Juvenal, satirist or rhetorician?', *Latomus* 22 (1963) 704–20; H. A. Mason, 'Is Juvenal a classic?', in (ed.) J. P. Sullivan, *Satire* (London 1963) 93–167; N. Scivoletto, 'Presenze di Persio in Giovenale', *G.I.F.* 16 (1963) 60–72; J. J. Bodoh, *An analysis of the ideas of Juvenal* (diss. Wisconsin 1966); idem, 'Artistic control in the satires of Juvenal', *Aevum* 44 (1970) 475–82; A. S. McDevitt, 'The structure of Juvenal's eleventh satire', *G.&R.* 15 (1968) 173–9; J. P.

Stein, 'The unity and scope of Juvenal's fourteenth satire', *C.Ph.* 65 (1970) 34–6; S. C. Fredericks, 'Rhetoric and morality in Juvenal's 8th satire', *T.A.Ph.A.* 102 (1971) 111–32; L. Edmunds, 'Juvenal's thirteenth satire', *Rh.M.* 115 (1972) 59–73; J. Adamietz, *Untersuchungen zu Juvenal, Hermes Einzelschriften* 26 (1972: on satires 3, 5 and 11); J. Gérard, *Juvénal et la réalité contemporaine* (Paris 1976).

INDEXES: L. Kelling and A. Suskin (Chapel Hill 1951); M. Dubrocard (New York 1976).

# PHAEDRUS (Augusti libertus)

## LIFE

Dates *c.* 18 B.C.–A.D. 50 (not universally accepted). Thracian slave, manumitted by Augustus. Offended Sejanus through allusions in his fables and received some unknown punishment. Sources: Phaedr. 3 *prol.*, 3 *epil.*, 4 *prol.*; Mart. 3.20.5; Avian. *Epist. ad Theod.* See A. de Lorenzi, *Fedro* (Florence 1955: speculative).

## WORKS

Remnants of five books of Aesopian fables in iambic senarii, pubd at intervals between *c.* A.D. 20–50. Order of books seems to correspond with sequence of composition, and bk 3 is definitely later than A.D. 31. The codex Pithoeanus transmits ninety-four fables and some seven other pieces, and some thirty other items are added by the *appendix Perottina* (a 15th-c. transcription by N. Perotti from a MS apparently less truncated than P). But the collection is still far from complete: paraphrases of prose translations give substance of fables not extant in metrical form. P. probably wrote at least 150 fables.

## BIBLIOGRAPHY

TEXTS: L. Müller (BT, 1877); L. Havet (Paris 1895); J. P. Postgate (OCT 1919); B. E. Perry, *Babrius and Phaedrus* (Loeb, 1965). See also L. Hervieux, *Les fabulistes latins depuis le siècle d'Auguste jusqu'à la fin du moyen âge*, vols. I–II, 2nd ed. (Paris 1893–4); B. E. Perry, *Aesopica* I (Urbana 1952).

STUDIES: A. Hausrath, in *RE* XIX (1938) 1475–1505; B. E. Perry, 'The origin of the epimythium', *T.A.Ph.A.* 71 (1940) 391–419; idem, 'Demetrius of Phalerum and the Aesopic fables', *T.A.Ph.A.* 93 (1962) 287–346, and in intr. to his edition, lxxiii–xcvi.

INDEX: A. Cinquini (Milan 1905).

# CALPURNIUS SICULUS, TITUS

## LIFE

Dates of birth and death unknown, but almost certainly wrote his poems under Nero (see particularly 1.44–5, 77–83, 7.23–4). Contra: E. Champlin, *J.R.S.* 68 (1978) 95–110. If his name is rightly transmitted, *Calpurnius* might indicate some unknown connexion with the Calpurnii Pisones, *Siculus* place of origin or association with Theocritean bucolic. Claims to be of humble rank.

## WORKS

Seven eclogues after the manner of Virgil: long conjoined with four others, shown by Haupt (1854, under *Studies* below) to belong to Nemesianus, *pace* A. E. Radke, *Hermes* 100 (1972) 615–23.

## BIBLIOGRAPHY

TEXTS AND COMMENTARIES: Calpurnius. TEXTS: *PLM*, vol III; H. Schenkl, in (ed.) J. P. Postgate, *Corpus poetarum Latinorum*, vol. II (London 1905); C. Giarratano (Turin 1924); J. W. and A. M. Duff, in *Minor Latin poets* (Loeb, 1934). COMMENTARIES: C. H. Keene (London 1887); R. Verdière (Brussels–Berchem 1954); D. Korzeniewski (Darmstadt 1971).

*Bucolica Einsidlensia.* TEXTS: *Anth. Lat.* 725–6; *PLM*, Giarratano, Duff (above). COMMENTARIES: Verdière and Korzeniewski (above).

*Laus Pisonis.* TEXTS: *PLM*, vol. I; Duff (above). COMMENTARIES: Verdière (above); A. Seel (Erlangen 1969).

STUDIES: M. Haupt, *De carminibus bucolicis Calpurnii et Nemesiani* (Berlin 1854) = *Opuscula* I (Leipzig 1875) 358–406; F. Chytil, *Der Eklogendichter T. Calpurnius Siculus und seine Vorbilder* (Znaim 1894); E. Groag, in *RE* III (1899) 1378–9; F. Skutsch, ibid. 1401–6, and V (1905) 2115–16; S. Lösch, *Die Einsiedler Gedichte* (diss. Tübingen 1909); B. L. Ullmann, 'The text tradition and authorship of the Laus Pisonis', *C.Ph.* 24 (1929) 109–32; J. Hubaux, *Les thèmes bucoliques dans la poésie latine* (Brussels 1930); A. Momigliano, 'Literary chronology of the Neronian age', *C.Q.* 38 (1944) 96–100 = *Secondo contributo* (Rome 1960) 454–61; W. Schmid, 'Panegyrik und Bukolik in der neronischen Epoche', *B.J.* 153 (1953) 63–96; idem, 'Nochmals über das zweite Einsiedler Gedicht', *Hermes* 83 (1955) 124–8; M. L. Paladini, 'Osservazioni a Calpurnio Siculo', *Latomus* 15 (1956) 330–46, 521–31; W. Theiler, 'Zu den Einsiedlern Hirtengedichten', *S.I.F.C.* 27–8 (1956) 565–77 = *Untersuchungen zur antiken Literatur* (Berlin 1970) 430–41; H. Fuchs, 'Der Friede als Gefahr: zum zweiten Einsiedler Hirtengedichte', *H.S.C.Ph.* 63 (1958) 363–85; D. Korzeniewski, 'Die "panegyrische Tendenz" in den Carmina Einsidlensia', *Hermes*

94 (1966) 344–60; G. Scheda, *Studien zur bukolischen Dichtung der neronischen Epoche* (diss. Bonn 1969); D. Korzeniewski, 'Die Eklogen des Calpurnius Siculus als Gedichtbuch', *M.H.* 29 (1972) 214–16; R. W. Garson, 'The Eclogues of Calpurnius. A partial apology', *Latomus* 33 (1974) 668–72; G. B. Townend, 'Calpurnius Siculus and the *Munus Neronis*', *J.R.S.* 70 (1980) 166–74; R. G. Mayer, 'Calpurnius Siculus: technique and date', ibid. 175–6.

## BUCOLICA EINSIDLENSIA

Two eclogues, discovered in a manuscript at Einsiedeln and first published by W. Hagen (*Philologus* 28 (1869) 338–41); text seriously mutilated. Generally dated, on internal evidence, to time of Nero. Authorship utterly uncertain, but differences in thought and attitude suggest that they were not written by Calpurnius Siculus, to whose work they are nevertheless somewhat akin. For bibliography, see under Calpurnius Siculus.

## LAUS PISONIS

A panegyric (261 hexameters) on a certain Calpurnius Piso, perhaps the conspirator (Tac. *Ann.* 15.48) or the consul of A.D. 57. Its language and metre may indicate, and certainly do not preclude, a Neronian date. Much speculation about the author: Calpurnius Siculus remains a possibility, but no more. For bibliography, see under Calpurnius Siculus.

## AETNA

Didactic poem on volcanic nature of Etna. Authorship unknown.

### BIBLIOGRAPHY

TEXTS AND COMMENTARIES: TEXTS: *PLM*, vol. I, rev. F. Vollmer; J. Vessereau (Budé, 1923); W. Richter (Berlin 1963); F. R. D. Goodyear, in *Appendix Vergiliana* (OCT, 1966). COMMENTARIES: H. A. J. Munro (Cambridge 1867); R. Ellis (Oxford 1901); F. R. D. Goodyear (Cambridge 1965: with index).

STUDIES: E. Bickel, 'Apollon und Dodona. Ein Beitrag zur Technik und Datierung des Lehrgedichts Aetna', *Rh.M.* 79 (1930) 279–302; P. de Lacy, 'The philosophy of the Aetna', *T.A.Ph.A.* 74 (1943) 169–78; W. Richter, 'Lucilius, Seneca, und das Aetnagedicht', *Philologus* 96 (1944) 234–49; K. Büchner, in *RE* VIIIA (1955) 1136–55; F. Weissengruber, 'Zur Datierung der Aetna', *W.S.* 78 (1965) 128–38; J.-H. Waszink, *Gnomon* 41 (1969) 353–62 (review of edd. by Richter and Goodyear).

# EPIGRAMS ASCRIBED TO
# SENECA AND PETRONIUS

Apart from various discountable items (*Anth. Lat.* 464–5, 667, 799, 804), three poems are transmitted under the name of Seneca (*Anth. Lat.* 232, 236–7) and sixty-seven ascribed to him by Scaliger and others (*Anth. Lat.* 396–463). There is nowadays much uncertainty, indeed scepticism, about the attribution of most of these pieces. So with Petronius. Five poems are transmitted under his name or cited as his by Fulgentius (*Anth. Lat.* 466, 476, 650–1, 690), fourteen are ascribed to him by Scaliger (*Anth. Lat.* 464–5, 467–75, 477–9), ten by Binet (*Anth. Lat.* 218, 691–9), who claims to take the ascription from a manuscript, and eight by Baehrens (*Anth. Lat.* 700–7). Great doubt attaches to the last two groups, but there are indications that some at least of the other pieces may be Petronian.

## BIBLIOGRAPHY

TEXTS AND COMMENTARY: TEXTS: *PLM*, vol. IV; *Anth. Lat.* COMMENTARY: C. Prato, *Gli epigrammi attribuiti a L. Anneo Seneca* (Rome 1964).

STUDIES: O. Rossbach, *Disquisitionum de Senecae filii scriptis criticarum capita duo* (Breslau 1882); C. W. Krohn, *Quaestiones ad anthologiam latinam spectantes* (Halle 1887); A. Collignon, *Étude sur Pétrone* (Paris 1892) 362–76; E. Herfurth, *De Senecae epigrammatis quae feruntur* (Jena 1910); K. P. Harrington, 'Seneca's epigrams', *T.A.Ph.A.* 46 (1915) 207–15; H. Bardon, 'Les épigrammes de l'anthologie attribuées à Sénèque le philosophe', *R.E.L.* 17 (1939) 63–90; V. Tandoi, 'Il trionfo di Claudio sulla Britannia e il suo cantore', *S.I.F.C.* 34 (1962–3) 83–129, 137–68; idem, 'Sugli epigrammi dell' Antologia Latina attribuiti a Seneca', *S.I.F.C.* 36 (1964) 169–89.

# PRIAPEA

Book of about eighty short poems, in hendecasyllables, elegiacs, and choliambs, addressed to or concerned with Priapus: has sustained some minor damage, but may otherwise be virtually complete. Commonly regarded as a collection of pieces by divers authors, assembled in or soon after Augustus' times, it is rather the work of a single poet, very possibly later than Martial.

## BIBLIOGRAPHY

TEXTS: *PLM*, vol. III; F. Buecheler, *Petronii saturae et liber Priapeorum* (Berlin 1912); *PLM*, vol. II rev. F. Vollmer; I. Cazzaniga, in *Carmina ludicra Romanorum* (Turin 1959).

STUDIES: F. Buecheler, 'Vindiciae libri Priapeorum', *Rh.M.* 18 (1863) 381–415 = *Kleine Schriften* (Leipzig 1915) 328–62; H. Herter, *De Priapo, Rel. Vers. u. Vorarb.* 23 (Giessen 1932); R. Helm, in *RE* XXII (1954) 1908–13; V. Buchheit, *Studien zum Corpus Priapeorum*, Zetemata 28 (Munich 1962).

## APOCOLOCYNTOSIS DIVI CLAUDII

Satire on the emperor Claudius, in a mixture of prose and verse. Of our three principal MSS two give the title *Ludus de morte Claudii* ('A sport on Claudius' death') and one *Divi Claudii apotheosis per satiram* ('The blessed Claudius' apotheosis, in satire'). The former may be an original title or sub-title, though this use of *ludus* is not attested in classical Latin, and in the latter *apotheosis* may be an explanatory gloss which has ousted an original title *apocolocyntosis*, preserved not by the direct tradition, but by Cassius Dio (60.35), who says, 'Seneca composed a piece which he called *apocolocyntosis*, a sort of deification as it were'. Most scholars accept that the work we have is that to which Dio refers as composed by Seneca. A minority hold that it is not the same and not necessarily Senecan, on the grounds (i) that neither *apocolocyntosis* itself nor Dio's explanation of the term fits the existing work, and (ii) that there are some indications that its attribution to Seneca in our medieval MSS has no great antiquity (see R. Roncali, *Belfagor* 29 (1974) 571–3). Whether Seneca's or another's the satire was probably written late A.D. 54, shortly after Claudius' death. Arguments for composition much later in Nero's principate have not carried conviction: see A. Momigliano, *C.Q.* 38 (1944) 96–100 = *Secondo contributo* (Rome 1960) 454–61.

### BIBLIOGRAPHY

(for 1922–58, see M. Coffey, *Lustrum* 6 (1961) 239–71)

TEXTS AND COMMENTARIES: TEXTS: F. Buecheler and W. Heraeus, in *Petronii saturae* etc., 6th ed. (Berlin 1922); O. Rossbach (Bonn 1926). COMMENTARIES: O. Weinreich (Berlin 1923); C. F. Russo, 4th ed. (Florence 1964).

STUDIES: R. Helm, *Lucian und Menipp* (Leipzig 1906); R. Heinze, 'Zu Senecas Apocolocyntosis', *Hermes* 61 (1926) 49–78; A. Momigliano, *Claudius: the emperor and his achievement* (Oxford 1934); H. MacL. Currie, 'The purpose of the Apocolocyntosis', *A.C.* 31 (1962) 91–7; K. Kraft, 'Der politische Hintergrund von Senecas Apocolocyntosis', *Historia* 15 (1966) 96–122; H. Haffter, *Römische Politik und römische Politiker* (Heidelberg 1967) 121–40; K. Bringmann, 'Senecas Apocolocyntosis und die politische Satire in Rom', *A.&A.* 17 (1970) 56–69; G. Binder, 'Hercules und Claudius', *Rh.M.* 117 (1974) 288–317; M. Coffey, *Roman satire* (London – New York 1976) 165–77; M. T. Griffin, *Seneca: a philosopher in politics* (Oxford 1976) 129–33.

CONCORDANCE: in R. Busa and A. Zampolli, *Concordantiae Senecanae* (Hildesheim 1975).

# PETRONIUS ARBITER

## LIFE

Not certainly documented, but the author is plausibly identified with T. Petronius Niger, consul *c.* A.D. 62, d. 66. Sources: Tac. *Ann.* 16.17–19 (character sketch and account of his suicide); Pliny, *N.H.* 37.20; Plut. *Mor.* 60e; Macr. *Somn.* 1.2.8. See R. Browning, 'The date of Petronius', *C.R.* 63 (1949) 12–14; H. C. Schnur, 'The economic background of the *Satyricon*', *Latomus* 18 (1959) 790–9; Sullivan (1968, under *Studies* below) 21–33; Walsh (1970, under *Studies* below) 67–70, 244–7; K. F. C. Rose, *The date and author of the Satyricon, Mnemosyne* suppl. 16 (1971).

## WORKS

*Satyrica* or *Satyricon libri*, not *Satyricon*, in at least sixteen books. We have fragments of bk 14, a long passage, the *cena Trimalchionis*, perhaps coextensive with bk 15, and fragments of bk 16 and probably later books too. Apparently written in second half of Nero's reign. Various pieces of verse, which may well be extracted from the *Satyrica*, are attributed to P. in the Latin Anthology and elsewhere.

## BIBLIOGRAPHY

(see G. L. Schmeling and J. H. Stuckey (Leiden 1977))

TEXTS AND COMMENTARIES: TEXTS: F. Buecheler, 6th ed. (Berlin 1922); A. Ernout, 4th ed. (Budé, 1958); K. Müller (Munich 1961); K. Müller and W. Ehlers (Munich 1965). COMMENTARIES: *Cena Trimalchionis*: L. Friedländer (Leipzig 1891); W. D. Lowe (London 1905); W. B. Sedgwick (Oxford 1925); P. Perrochat (Paris 1939); M. S. Smith (Oxford 1975). *De bello civili*: F. T. Baldwin (New York 1911); G. Guido (Bologna 1976).

STUDIES: E. Klebs, 'Zur Komposition von Petronius' Satirae', *Philologus* 47 (1889) 623–55; A. Collignon, *Étude sur Pétrone* (Paris 1892); R. Heinze, 'Petron und der griechische Roman', *Hermes* 34 (1899) 494–519; W. Heraeus, *Die Sprache des Petronius und die Glossen* (Leipzig 1899), revised in *Kleine Schriften* (Heidelberg 1937) 52–150; R. Cahen, *Le Satiricon et ses origines* (Paris 1925); W. Süss, *De eo quem dicunt inesse Trimalchionis cenae sermone uulgari* (Dorpat 1926); H. Stubbe, *Die Verseinlagen im Petron, Philologus* suppl. 25 (1933); J. W. Duff, *Roman satire* (California 1936) 84–105; W. Kroll, in *RE* XIX (1937) 1202–14; E. Courtney, 'Parody and literary allusion in Menippean satire', *Philologus* 106 (1962) 86–100; A. Stefenelli, *Die Volks-*

sprache im Werk des Petron im Hinblick auf die romanischen Sprachen (Vienna 1962);
P. Veyne, 'Le "je" dans le Satiricon', *R.E.L.* 42 (1964) 301–24; B. E. Perry, *The ancient romances* (California 1967); J. P. Sullivan, *The Satyricon of Petronius* (London 1968); A. M. Cameron, 'Petronius and Plato', *C.Q.* n.s.19 (1969) 367–70; A. Scobie, *Aspects of the ancient romance and its heritage, Beiträge zur klassichen Philologie* 30 (Meisenheim am Glan 1969); A. M. Cameron, 'Myth and meaning in Petronius: some modern comparisons', *Latomus* 29 (1970) 397–425; H. D. Rankin, 'Some comments on Petronius' portrayal of character', *Eranos* 68 (1970) 123–47; P. G. Walsh, *The Roman novel* (Cambridge 1970); P. Parsons, 'A Greek Satyricon?', *B.I.C.S.* 18 (1971) 53–68; F. I. Zeitlin, 'Petronius as paradox: anarchy and artistic integrity', *T.A.Ph.A.* 102 (1971) 631–84; G. Luck, 'On Petronius' bellum civile' *A.J.Ph.* 93 (1972) 133–41; P. A. George, 'Petronius and Lucan de bello civili', *C.Q.* n.s.24 (1974) 119–33; M. Coffey, *Roman satire* (London 1976) 178–203.

INDEX: I. Segebade and E. Lommatzsch (Leipzig 1898).

# VELLEIUS PATERCULUS

## LIFE

b. *c.* 20 B.C. Military tribune in Thrace and Macedonia; accompanied Gaius Caesar to the east A.D. 1; served under Tiberius in Germany and Pannonia for eight years. Quaestor A.D. 7, praetor A.D. 15. d. later than A.D. 30. Praenomen uncertain. Refs. to ancestors and career: Vell. 2.16.2, 69.5, 76.1, 101.2–3, 104.3, 107.1, 111.3–4, 113.3, 115.1, 121.3, 124.4. See Sumner (1970, under *Studies* below) 257–79.

## WORKS

Outline history in two books, pubd A.D. 30. Bk 1 (mythological times to 146 B.C.) is largely lost: we lack the preface, but have the narration from near the beginning to the foundation of Rome; vast lacuna follows to 167 B.C. Bk 2 (146 B.C.–A.D. 29) is virtually complete. No other works known. V. says several times that he intends to write a major history, but apparently never did so.

## BIBLIOGRAPHY

TEXTS AND COMMENTARIES: TEXTS: C. Halm (BT, 1876); F. Haase (BT, 1884); R. Ellis (Oxford 1898); F. W. Shipley (Loeb, 1924); C. Stegmann de Pritzwald (BT, 1933). COMMENTARIES: D. Ruhnken (Leiden 1779); F. Kritz (Leipzig 1840). 2.94–131: A. J. Woodman (Cambridge 1977).

STUDIES: H. Dodwell, *Annales Velleiani* (Oxford 1698); F. Milkau, *De Velleii Paterculi genere dicendi quaestiones selectae* (Regensburg 1888); C. Jodry, 'L'utilisation des documents militaires chez Velleius Paterculus', *R.E.L.* 29 (1951) 265–84; I. Lana, *Velleio Patercolo o della propaganda* (Turin 1952); H. J. Steffen, *Die Regierung des Tiberius in der Darstellung des Velleius Paterculus* (Kiel 1954): A. Dihle, in *RE* VIIIA (1955) 638–59; J. Hellegouarc'h, 'Les buts de l'oeuvre historique de Velleius Paterculus', *Latomus* 23 (1964) 669–84; A. J. Woodman, 'Sallustian influence on Velleius Paterculus', in *Hommages à Marcel Renard* I (Brussels 1968) 785–99; G. V. Sumner, 'The truth about Velleius Paterculus: prolegomena', *H.S.C.Ph.* 74 (1970) 257–97 A. J. Woodman, 'Velleius Paterculus', in (ed.) T. A. Dorey, *Silver Latin* II (London 1975) 1–25; idem, 'Questions of date, genre and style in Velleius', *C.Q.* n.s.25 (1975) 272–306.

# CURTIUS RUFUS, QUINTUS

## LIFE

Unknown, except that he lived under the principate and that not long before he wrote his history the empire went through a period of trouble and anxiety (10.9.1–6). His work, which has been placed as early as Augustus and as late as Alexander Severus, was most probably written under Claudius or Vespasian. He has been identified (without foundation) with a rhetorician mentioned by Suetonius (*De gramm. et rhet.* p. 2 Brugnoli), with a governor of Africa (Tac. *Ann.* 11.20.3–21.3), and with a son of the latter.

## WORKS

*Historiae Alexandri Magni* in ten books: first two lost and substantial gaps in 5, 6, and 10. Text transmitted in numerous MSS, but not in a very good state. No other writings known.

## BIBLIOGRAPHY

TEXTS: E. Hedicke (BT, 1908); J. C. Rolfe (Loeb, 1946); H. Bardon (Budé, 1947); K. Müller (Munich 1954).

STUDIES: S. Dosson, *Étude sur Quinte-Curce, sa vie et son oeuvre* (Paris 1887); E. Schwartz, 'Curtius', in *RE* IV (1901) 1871–91; W. Kroll, *Studien zum Verständnis der römischen Literatur* (Stuttgart 1924) 331–51; F. Wilhelm, *Curtius und die jüngere Seneca* (Paderborn 1928); J. Stroux, 'Die Zeit des Curtius', *Philologus* 84 (1929) 233–51; H. Lindgren, *Studia Curtiana* (Uppsala 1935); W. W. Tarn, *Alexander the Great* II (Cambridge 1948) 91–122; W. Rutz, 'Zur Erzählungskunst des Q. Curtius Rufus. Die Belagerung von Tyrus', *Hermes* 93 (1965) 370–82; J. Blaensdorf, 'Herodot bei Curtius Rufus', *Hermes* 99 (1971) 11–24.

INDEXES: O. Eichert (Hanover 1893); J. Therasse (Hildesheim 1976).

# TACITUS, PUBLIUS (or GAIUS) CORNELIUS

## LIFE

b. c. 55 A.D., family origins uncertain. Entered public life under Vespasian. Betrothed to Agricola's daughter 77. Praetor and *XVvir* 88; abroad 90–3, but back in Rome during Domitian's last years. Consul *suffectus* 97; delivered funeral oration over Verginius Rufus. Prosecuted Marius Priscus, ex-governor of Africa, on extortion charge 100. Proconsul of Asia c. 112/13, d. not earlier than A.D. 116. Sources: Tac. *Agr.* 2–3, 45 (refs. to Domitian), 9.6 (marriage), *Dial.* 1.1–2, 2.1 (study of oratory), *Hist.* 1.1.3–4 (general statement of career), *Ann.* 11.11.1 (praetor, *XVvir*); Pliny, *Epist.* 2.1 (funeral oration), 2.11 (prosecution of Priscus), 1.6, 1.20, 4.13, 4.15, 6.9, 6.16, 6.20, 7.20, 7.33, 8.7, 9.10, 9.14, 9.23; *CIL* VI 10229 (= *ILS* 8379a: possibly paired with Pliny in a will); *OGIS* 487 (proconsul); Pliny, *N.H.*7.76 (his father (?) a procurator in Gallia Belgica); *Hist. Aug. Tac.* 10.3 (his works ordered to be placed in libraries). See M. L. Gordon, 'The patria of Tacitus', *J.R.S.* 26 (1936) 145–51; R. Syme, *Tacitus* (Oxford 1958) 611–24; R. Hanslik, 'Die Ämterlaufbahn des Tacitus im Lichte der Ämterlaufbahn seiner Zeitgenossen', *A.A.W.W.* 102 (1965) 47–60; E. Koestermann, 'Tacitus und die Transpadana', *Athenaeum* 43 (1965) 167–208; S. Borzsák, in *RE* suppl. XI (1968) 375–99; R. P. Oliver, 'The praenomen of Tacitus', *A.J.Ph.* 98 (1977) 64–70.

## WORKS

Five works survive, in whole or part: *De vita Iulii Agricolae*, dating from A.D. 98, *De origine et situ Germanorum*, from the same year, *Dialogus de oratoribus*, probably later than 100, *Historiae* (12–14 bks), composed between c. 100–110, and *Ab excessu divi Augusti* or *Annales* (16–18 bks), later than *Hist.* and probably still being written in 116. Titles *Historiae* and *Annales* have little or no ancient authority, and, though these works are likely to have been first pubd separately, they also, from a date unknown, circulated in a joint edition of thirty books (see Goodyear on *Ann.* 1.1.1). Only *Agricola* and *Germania* (thus commonly known) remain intact. *Dialogus* is impaired by a lacuna of some size. Of *Historiae* we possess only 1–4, part of 5, and a few fragments. Of *Annales* we have 1–4, a small piece of 5, 6, part of 11, 12–15, and part of 16. Much controversy about number of books T. devoted to *Hist.* and *Ann.*: some favour distribution of twelve and eighteen, others of fourteen and sixteen. The only firm evidence (numeration of second Medicean MS) supports the latter view. The matter is further complicated by possibility that he did not live to complete the *Annales*. No other writings recorded.

## BIBLIOGRAPHY

(see Borzsák (1968, under *Studies* (1) below); F. R. D. Goodyear, *G.&R.*, *New surveys in the classics* 4 (Oxford 1970); H. W. Benario, *C.W.* 71 (1977) 1–32)

# APPENDIX OF AUTHORS AND WORKS

TEXTS AND COMMENTARIES: TEXTS: Minor works: E. Koestermann (BT, 1970); R. M. Ogilvie and M. Winterbottom (OCT, 1975). *Hist.*: C. D. Fisher (OCT, 1910); H. Heubner (BT, 1978). *Ann.*: C. D. Fisher (OCT, 1906); H. Fuchs (Frauenfeld 1946–9); E. Koestermann (BT, 1971); P. Wuilleumier (Budé, 1974–8). COMMENTARIES: *Agr.*: R. Till (Berlin 1961); R. M. Ogilvie and I. A. Richmond (Oxford 1967). *Germ.*: J. G. C. Anderson (Oxford 1938); R. Much, 3rd ed. rev. H. Jankuhn and W. Lange (Heidelberg 1967). *Dial.*: W. Peterson (Oxford 1893); A. Gudeman, 2nd ed. (Leipzig–Berlin 1914). *Hist.*: E. Wolff, vol. I, 2nd ed. (Berlin 1914), vol. II, 2nd ed. rev. G. Andresen (Berlin 1926); C. Heraeus, rev. W. Heraeus, vol. I, 6th ed. (Leipzig 1929), vol. II, 4th ed. (Leipzig 1927). Bks 1–2: A. L. Irvine (London 1952). Bks 1–4: H, Heubner (Heidelberg 1963– ). Bk 3: K. Wellesley (Sydney 1972). *Ann.*: H. Furneaux, vol. I, 2nd ed. (Oxford 1896), vol. II, 2nd ed. rev. H. F. Pelham and C. D. Fisher (Oxford 1907); K. Nipperdey, rev. G. Andresen, vol. I, 11th ed. (Berlin 1915), vol. II, 6th ed. (Berlin 1908); E. Koestermann (Heidelberg 1963–8). Bk 1: N. P. Miller (London 1959). Bk 1.1–54: F. R. D. Goodyear (Cambridge 1972). Bk 1.55–81 and Bk 2: F. R. D. Goodyear (Cambridge 1981). Bk 14: E. C. Woodcock (London 1939). Bk 15: N. P. Miller (London 1973).

STUDIES: (1) GENERAL: F. Leo, *Tacitus* (Göttingen 1896) = *Ausg. kl. Schr.* II (Rome 1960) 263–76; G. Boissier, *Tacitus and other Roman studies* (London 1906); R. von Pöhlmann, 'Die Weltanschauung des Tacitus', *S.B.A.W.* 1910, 1; E. Fraenkel, 'Tacitus', *N.J.W.* 8 (1932) 218–33 = *Kleine Beiträge* II (Rome 1964) 309–32; F. Klingner, 'Tacitus', *Ant.* 8 (1932) 151–69 = *Römische Geisteswelt*, 4th ed. (Munich 1961) 490–513; M. L. W. Laistner, *The greater Roman historians* (Berkeley 1947) 103–40; C. W. Mendell, *Tacitus: the man and his work* (New Haven 1957); R. Syme, *Tacitus* (Oxford 1958); E. Paratore, *Tacito*, 2nd ed. (Rome 1962); V. Pöschl, 'Der Historiker Tacitus', *W.G.* 22 (1962) 1–10; R. Häussler, *Tacitus und das historische Bewusstsein* (Heidelberg 1965); A. Michel, *Tacite et le destin de l'empire* (Paris 1966); S. Borzsák, 'P. Cornelius Tacitus', *RE* suppl. XI (1968) 373–512; D. R. Dudley, *The world of Tacitus* (London 1968); R. T. Scott, *Religion and philosophy in the Histories of Tacitus, Papers and monographs of the American academy in Rome* 22 (Rome 1968); R. Syme, *Ten studies in Tacitus* (Oxford 1970); R. H. Martin, *Tacitus* (London 1981).

(2) MINOR WORKS: F. Leo, review of Gudeman's ed. of *Dial.*, *G.G.A.* 1898, 169–88 = *Ausg. kl. Schr.* II 277–98; R. Reitzenstein, 'Bemerkungen zu den kleinen Schriften des Tacitus', *N.G.G.* 1915, 173–276 = *Aufsätze zu Tacitus* (Darmstadt 1967) 17–120; E. Norden, *Die germanische Urgeschichte in Tacitus' Germania*, 3rd ed. (Berlin 1923); E. Wolff, 'Das geschichtliche Verstehen in Tacitus' Germania', *Hermes* 69 (1934) 121–64; R. Heinze, '*Urgentibus imperii fatis*', in *Vom Geist des Römertums* (Leipzig–Berlin 1938) 255–77; R. Güngerich, 'Der Dialogus des Tacitus und Quintilians Institutio Oratoria', *C.Ph.* 46 (1951) 159–64; K. Barwick, 'Der Dialogus de oratoribus des Tacitus, Motive und Zeit seiner Entstehung', *Ber. Sächs. Akad. Wiss.* 1954, 4; A. Michel, *Le 'Dialogus des Orateurs' de Tacite et la philosophie de Cicéron* (Paris 1962);

# APPENDIX OF AUTHORS AND WORKS

E. A. Thompson, *The early Germans* (Oxford 1965); H. Gugel, *Untersuchungen zu Stil und Aufbau des Rednerdialogs des Tacitus*, Commentationes Aenipontanae 20 (Innsbruck 1969); R. Häussler, 'Zum Umfang und Aufbau des Dialogus de oratoribus', *Philologus* 113 (1969) 24–67; A. Köhnken, 'Das Problem der Ironie bei Tacitus', *M.H.* 30 (1973) 32–50.

(3) PREDECESSORS AND SOURCES: T. Mommsen, 'Cornelius Tacitus und Cluvius Rufus', *Hermes* 4 (1870) 295–325 = *Gesamm. Schr.* VII (Berlin 1909) 224–52; P. Fabia, *Les sources de Tacite* (Paris 1893); E. Schwartz, 'Cassius Dio', *RE* III (1899) 1684–1722, esp. 1714ff.; H. Heubner, *Studien zur Darstellungskunst des Tacitus* (Würzburg 1935); F. Klingner, 'Die Geschichte Kaiser Othos bei Tacitus', *Ber. Sächs. Akad. Wiss.* 1940, 1 = *Studien* (Zurich 1964) 605–24; A. Briessman, *Tacitus und das flavische Geschichtsbild*, Hermes Einzelschriften 10 (1955); F. Klingner, 'Tacitus und die Geschichtsschreiber des ersten Jahrhunderts nach Christus', *M.H.* 15 (1958) 194–206; C. Questa, *Studi sulle fonti degli 'Annales' di Tacito*, 2nd ed. (Rome 1963); G. B. Townend, 'Cluvius Rufus in the Histories of Tacitus', *A.J.Ph.* 85 (1964) 337–77; R. H. Martin, 'Tacitus and his predecessors', in (ed.) T. A. Dorey, *Tacitus* (London 1969) 117–47; D. Flach, 'Tacitus und seine Quellen in den Annalenbüchern I–VI', *Athenaeum* 51 (1973) 92–108.

(4) HISTORIOGRAPHY: F. Leo, 'Die staatsrechtlichen Excurse in Tacitus' Annalen', *N.G.G.* 1896, 191–208 = *Ausg. kl. Schr.* II 299–317; P. S. Everts, *De Tacitea historiae conscribendae ratione* (Kerkrade 1926); F. Krohn, *Personendarstellungen bei Tacitus* (Leipzig 1934); C. W. Mendell, 'Dramatic construction in Tacitus' Annals', *Y.Cl.S.* 5 (1935) 3–53; J. Vogt, 'Tacitus und die Unparteilichkeit des Historikers', *Würzburger Studien* 9 (1936) 1–20; I. S. Ryberg, 'Tacitus' art of innuendo', *T.A.Ph.A.* 73 (1942) 383–404; D. M. Pippidi, *Autour de Tibère* (Bucharest 1944); J. Cousin, 'Rhétorique et psychologie chez Tacite, un aspect de la deinosis', *R.E.L.* 29 (1951) 228–47; B. Walker, *The Annals of Tacitus* (Manchester 1952); F. Klingner, 'Tacitus über Augustus und Tiberius', *S.B.A.W.*, Heft 7, 1953 = *Studien* 624–58; E. Koestermann, 'Die Majestätsprozesse unter Tiberius', *Historia* 4 (1955) 72–106; idem, 'Die Feldzüge des Germanicus 14–16 n. Chr.', *Historia* 6 (1956) 429–79; idem, 'Die Mission des Germanicus im Orient', *Historia* 7 (1957) 331–75; S. G. Daitz, 'Tacitus' technique of character portrayal', *A.J.Ph.* 81 (1960) 30–52; M. Fuhrmann, 'Das Vierkaiserjahr bei Tacitus', *Philologus* 104 (1960) 250–78; E. Koestermann, 'Der Eingang der Annalen des Tacitus', *Historia* 10 (1961) 330–55; J. Tresch, *Die Nerobücher in den Annalen des Tacitus* (Heidelberg 1965); D. C. A. Shotter, 'Tacitus, Tiberius and Germanicus', *Historia* 17 (1968) 194–214; D. Timpe, *Der Triumph des Germanicus* (Bonn 1968); K. Wellesley, 'Tacitus as a military historian', in (ed.) T. A. Dorey, *Tacitus* (London 1969) 63–97; S. Borzsák, 'Zum Verständis der Darstellungskunst des Tacitus', *A. Ant. Hung.* 18 (1970) 279–92; D. Flach, *Tacitus in der Tradition der Antiken Geschichtsschreibung* (Göttingen 1973); K. Gilmartin, 'Corbulo's campaigns in the East', *Historia* 22 (1973) 583–626; D. O. Ross, 'The Tacitean Germanicus', *Y.Cl.S.* 23 (1973) 209–27.

(5) LANGUAGE AND STYLE: E. Wölfflin, 'Jahresberichte über Tacitus 1–3', *Philologus*

25 (1867) 92–134, 26 (1867) 92–166, 27 (1868) 113–49, excerpted in *Ausg. Schr.* (Leipzig 1933) 22–102; A. A. Draeger, *Über Syntax und Stil des Tacitus*, 3rd ed. (Leipzig 1882); F. G. Moore, 'Studies in Tacitean ellipsis: descriptive passages', *T.A.Ph.A.* 34 (1903) 5–26; E. Courbaud, *Les procédés d'art de Tacite dans les Histoires* (Paris 1918); R. Ullmann, *La technique des discours dans Salluste, Tite-Live et Tacite* (Oslo 1927); E. Löfstedt, *Syntactica* II (Lund 1933) 276–90; N. Eriksson, *Studien zu den Annalen des Tacitus* (Lund 1934); G. Sörbom, *Variatio sermonis Tacitei* (Uppsala 1935); H. Hommel, 'Die Bildkunst des Tacitus', *Würzburger Studien* 9 (1936) 116–48; E. Löfstedt, 'On the style of Tacitus', *J.R.S.* 38 (1948) 1–8; C. O. Brink, 'Justus Lipsius and the text of Tacitus', *J.R.S.* 42 (1952) 32–51; R. H. Martin, 'Variatio and the development of Tacitus' style', *Eranos* 51 (1953) 89–96; F. Klingner, 'Beobachtungen über Sprache und Stil des Tacitus am Anfang des 13 Annalenbuches', *Hermes* 83 (1955) 187–200; K. Seitz, *Studien zur Stilentwicklung und zur Satzstruktur innerhalb der Annalen des Tacitus* (Marburg 1958); A. Kohl, *Der Satznachtrag bei Tacitus* (Würzburg 1960); R. Enghofer, *Der Ablativus absolutus bei Tacitus* (Würzburg 1961); F. Kuntz, *Die Sprache des Tacitus und die Tradition der lateinischen Historikersprache* (Heidelberg 1962); B.-R. Voss, *Der pointierte Stil des Tacitus* (Münster 1963); N. P. Miller, 'Dramatic speech in Tacitus', *A.J.Ph.* 85 (1964) 279–96; R. H. Martin, 'The speech of Curtius Montanus: Tacitus, Histories iv, 42', *J.R.S.* 57 (1967) 109–14; F. R. D. Goodyear, 'Development of language and style in the Annals of Tacitus', *J.R.S.* 58 (1968) 22–31; N. P. Miller, 'Tiberius speaks', *A.J.Ph.* 89 (1968) 1–19; J. N. Adams, 'The language of the later books of Tacitus' Annals', *C.Q.* n.s.22 (1972) 350–73; idem, 'The vocabulary of the speeches in Tacitus' historical works', *B.I.C.S.* 20 (1973) 124–44; idem, 'Were the later books of Tacitus' Annals revised?', *Rh.M.* 117 (1974) 323–33.

LEXICA: W. Boetticher (Berlin 1830); P. Fabia, *Onomasticon Taciteum* (Paris–Lyons 1900); A. Gerber, A. Greef, C. John (Leipzig 1903).

# PLINIUS CAECILIUS SECUNDUS, GAIUS

## LIFE

b. A.D. 61/62 at Comum. On his father's death was brought up by the elder Pliny, his maternal uncle, and took his name when formally adopted by him in his will. At Rome studied rhetoric under Nicetes Sacerdos and Quintilian; began a long career in the lawcourts. Held all the regular magistracies (consul *suffectus* 100), and other administrative posts: *praefectus aerari militaris, praefectus aerari Saturni, curator alvei Tiberis.* Governor of Bithynia *c.* 111, d. *c.* 112. Sources: Pliny, *Epist. passim*; *CIL* v 5262. See T. Mommsen, *Hermes* 3 (1869) 31–140 = *Gesamm. Schr.* 4 (Berlin 1906) 366ff; W. Otto, *S.B.A.W.* 1919, 10; M. Schuster, in *RE* xxi (1951) 439–45; R. Syme, *Tacitus* (Oxford 1958) 75–85; A. N. Sherwin-White, *The letters of Pliny* (Oxford 1966) 69–82.

## WORKS

Two works survive: (1) the *Panegyricus*, P.'s expanded version of his speech of thanks to Trajan on becoming consul in A.D. 100, transmitted along with eleven much later speeches in the same vein (the so-called *Panegyrici Latini*), and (2) a collection of letters in nine books, dating apparently from about A.D. 97 to 108, and pubd in parts by Pliny A.D. 103–9 (in what parts exactly is still disputed). In addition there is a number of private and official letters to and from Trajan, written mainly *c.* 111 when P. was governor of Bithynia, pubd presumably after his death and added as a tenth book to P.'s collection. We hear from P. himself of several speeches which he revised and circulated (see, e.g., 1.8.2, 4.9.23, 5.20.2, 7.30.4, 9.13.1), of a laudatory biography (*Epist.* 3.10), and of verses in various metres. Of these nothing remains, except perhaps for the poem in *Anth. Lat.* 710. Specimens of P.'s versification in *Epist.* 7.4 and 7.9.

## BIBLIOGRAPHY

TEXTS AND COMMENTARIES: TEXTS: Complete works: H. Keil (Leipzig 1870); M. Schuster, rev. R. Hanslik (BT, 1958); B. Radice (Loeb, 1969). *Epistulae*: 1–10, E. T. Merrill (Leipzig 1922); 1–9, A.-M. Guillemin (Budé 1927–8); 10, M. Durry (Budé, 1959); 1–10, R. A. B. Mynors (OCT, 1963). *Panegyricus*: E. Baehrens (BT, 1874); W. Baehrens (BT, 1911); M. Durry (Budé, 1959); R. A. B. Mynors (OCT, 1964). COMMENTARIES: *Epistulae* 1–10: A. N. Sherwin-White (Oxford 1966). Bk 6: J. D. Duff (Cambridge 1906). Bk 10: E. G. Hardy (London 1889). SELECTIONS: E. T. Merrill (London 1903); A. N. Sherwin-White (Oxford 1967). *Panegyricus*: M. Durry (Paris 1938).

STUDIES: H. Peter, *Der Brief in der römischen Literatur* (Leipzig 1901); A.-M. Guillemin, *Pline et la vie littéraire de son temps* (Paris 1929); M. Schuster, in *RE* XXI (1951) 439–56; R. T. Bruère, 'Tacitus and Pliny's Panegyricus', *C.Ph.* 49 (1954) 161–79; S. E. Stout, *Scribe and critic at work in Pliny's letters* (Bloomington 1954); J. Niemirska-Pliszczyńska, *De elocutione Pliniana* (Lublin 1955); H. W. Traub, 'Pliny's treatment of history in epistolary form', *T.A.Ph.A.* 86 (1955) 213–32; B. Radice, 'A fresh approach to Pliny's letters', *G.&R.* 9 (1962) 160–8; A. N. Sherwin-White, 'Trajan's replies to Pliny', *J.R.S.* 52 (1962) 114–25; A. D. E. Cameron, 'The fate of Pliny's letters in the late empire', *C.Q.* n.s.15 (1965) 289–98; F. Millar, 'Emperors at work', *J.R.S.* 57 (1967) 9–19; B. Radice, 'Pliny and the Panegyricus', *G.&R.* 15 (1968) 166–72; A. N. Sherwin-White, 'Pliny, the man and his letters', *G.&R.* 16 (1969) 76–90; H.-P. Bütler, *Die geistige Welt des jüngeren Plinius* (Heidelberg 1970); S. MacCormack, 'Latin prose panegyrics', in (ed.) T. A. Dorey, *Silver Latin* II (London 1975) 143–205.

INDEX: X. Jacques and J. van Ooteghem (Namur 1968).

# SUETONIUS TRANQUILLUS, GAIUS

## LIFE

b. *c.* A.D. 70. Birthplace uncertain. After practising as a lawyer devoted himself to writing. Declined a military tribunate; obtained (though childless) the *ius trium liberorum* from Trajan through Pliny. Appointed secretary under Trajan and Hadrian, but dismissed 121/122 along with Septicius Clarus (dedicatee of *De vita Caes.*). d. later, perhaps much later, than A.D. 122. Sources: Suet. *Cal.* 19.3, *Nero* 57.2, *Otho* 10.1, *Dom.* 12.2, *De gramm. et rhet.* 4.9 (background); Pliny, *Epist.* 1.18 (lawyer), 1.24 possibly a schoolmaster), 3.8 (tribunate), 5.10 (slow to publish), 9.34 (P. asks about public recital of his verses), 10.94–5 (*ius t.l.*); *Hist. Aug. Hadr.* 11.3 (secretary, dismissal); Ioh. Lyd. *De mag.* 2.6 (dedication to Clarus). See E. Marec and H. G. Pflaum, 'Nouvelle inscription sur la carrière de Suétone, l'historien', *Comptes rendus de l'acad. des inscr.* 1952, 76–85, *A.É.* 1953, no. 73; J. A. Crook, 'Suetonius 'ab epistulis', *P.C.Ph.S.* n.s.4 (1956–7) 18–22; R. Syme, *Tacitus* (Oxford 1958) 778ff.; G. B. Townend, 'The Hippo inscription and the career of Suetonius', *Historia* 10 (1961) 99–109.

## WORKS

(1) *De vita Caesarum*: twelve biographies, from Julius Caesar to Domitian, in eight books, complete except for opening chs. of first life. Bk. 1, and possibly others, perhaps pubd 119–22. (2) *De viris illustribus*: numerous short biographies of persons eminent in literature and education, arranged in classes, perhaps (i) poets, (ii) orators, (iii) historians, (iv) philosophers, and (v) grammarians and rhetoricians. We have part of the section *De grammaticis et rhetoribus*, independently transmitted. Some lives from the *De poetis* are transmitted along with the poets themselves. Those of Terence, Horace and Lucan seem clearly Suetonian, and Donatus' life of Virgil contains at least some Suetonian material. Part of the life of the orator Passienus Crispus survives in the scholia on Juv. 4.81, part of the elder Pliny's accompanies his *Natural History*, and Jerome in his chronicle frequently draws on S. (3) Numerous treatises, some in Greek, on a wide range of subjects, such as critical signs, the Roman year, Roman customs, famous courtesans, and terms of abuse. Only occasional fragments remain. For further details see Schanz–Hosius III 58–64.

## BIBLIOGRAPHY

TEXTS AND COMMENTARIES: TEXTS: C. L. Roth (BT, 1858). *De vita Caes.*: M. Ihm (BT, ed. mai. 1907, ed. min. 1908). *De gramm. et rhet.*: A. Reifferscheid (Leipzig 1860: also the fragments); A. Brugnoli (BT, 1960). COMMENTARIES: D. C. G. Baumgarten-Crusius (Leipzig 1816–18). *Julius*: H. E. Butler and M. Cary (New York–Oxford 1927). *Augustus*: E. S. Shuckburgh (Cambridge 1896); M. A. Levi

(Florence 1951). *Galba–Domitian*: G. W. Mooney (London 1930). *Vespasian*: A. W. Braithwaite (Oxford 1927). *De gramm. et rhet.*: R. P. Robinson (Paris 1925). *De poetis*: A. Rostagni (Turin 1944).

STUDIES: A. Macé, *Essai sur Suétone* (Paris 1900); F. Leo, *Die griechisch-römische Biographie nach ihrer litterarischen Form* (Leipzig 1901); D. R. Stuart, *Epochs of Greek and Roman biography* (Berkeley 1928); G. Funaioli, in *RE* IVA (1931) 593–641; G. d'Anna, *Le idee letterarie di Suetonio* (Florence 1954); F. della Corte, *Suetonio eques Romanus* (Milan–Varese 1958); G. B. Townend, 'The date of composition of Suetonius' Caesares', *C.Q.* n.s.9 (1959) 285–93; idem, 'The sources of the Greek in Suetonius', *Hermes* 88 (1960) 98–120; C. Questa, *Studi sulle fonti degli 'Annales' di Tacito*, 2nd ed. (Rome 1963) 95–123; W. Steidle, *Sueton und die antike Biographie*, 2nd ed. (Munich 1963); T. F. Carney, 'How Suetonius' lives reflect on Hadrian', *P.A.C.A.* 11 (1968) 7–24; B. Mouchova, *Studie zu Kaiserbiographien Suetons*, Acta universitatis Carolinae phil. et hist. 22 (Prague 1968); J. Gugel, 'Caesars Tod', *Gymnasium* 77 (1970) 5–22; K. Bringmann, 'Zur Tiberiusbiographie Suetons', *Rh.M.* 114 (1971) 268–85; S. Döpp, 'Zum Aufbau des Tiberius-Vita Suetons', *Hermes* 100 (1972) 444–60.

INDEX: A. A. Howard and C. N. Jackson (Cambridge, Mass. 1922).

# FLORUS, JULIUS or L. ANNAEUS

## LIFE

Unknown, unless the same as P. Annius Florus (next entry). The Bambergensis calls him Julius Florus, other MSS L. Annaeus Florus: both names suspect. Internal evidence (*praef.* 8 and 1.5.5–8) suggests *c.* A.D. 140 as earliest time for his writing, and admits a considerably later date. Occasional praise of Spain (e.g. 1.22.38) may indicate connexions with that province.

## WORKS

*Epitoma de Tito Livio bellorum omnium annorum DCC* (so the MSS): this title, ancient but probably not F.'s, ill represents the contents; perhaps *tabella* (*praef.* 3) figured in F.'s title. B, marginally more authoritative than other MSS, divides the work into two books, the rest into four. The two books seem rather long, but this division makes some sense and may be tolerated.

## BIBLIOGRAPHY

TEXTS: O. Jahn (BT, 1852); O. Rossbach (BT, 1896); E. S. Forster (Loeb, 1929); E. Malcovati, 2nd ed. (Rome 1972); P. Jal (Budé, 1967).

STUDIES: P. Monceaux, *Les Africains. Étude sur la littérature latine d'Afrique. Les païens* (Paris 1894) 193–209; F. Schmidinger, 'Untersuchungen über Florus', *N.J.Ph.* suppl. 20 (1894) 781–816; O. Hirschfeld, 'Anlage und Abfassungszeit der Epitome des Florus', *Sitzb. Berl.* 29 (1899) 543–54; O. Rossbach, in *RE* VI (1909) 2761–70; E. Norden, *Die Antike Kunstprosa*, 4th ed. II (Leipzig–Berlin 1923) 598–600; S. Lilliedahl, *Florusstudien, Acta Universitatis Lundensis* 24.7 (Lund–Leipzig 1928); R. Zimmermann, 'Zum Geschichtswerk des Florus', *Rh.M.* 79 (1930) 93–101; R. Sieger, 'Der Stil des Historikers Florus', *W.S.* 51 (1934) 94–108; E. Malcovati, 'Studi su Floro', *Athenaeum* 15 (1937) 69–94, 289–307, and 16 (1938) 46–64; A. Nordh, 'Virtus and Fortuna in Florus', *Eranos* 50 (1952) 111–28; A. Garzetti, 'Floro e l'età adrianea', *Athenaeum* 42 (1964) 136–56; R. Häussler, 'Vom Ursprung und Wandel des Lebensaltervergleichs', *Hermes* 92 (1964) 313–41; I. Hahn, 'Prooemium und Disposition der Epitome des Florus', *Eirene* 4 (1965) 21–38; P. Jal, 'Nature et signification politique de l'ouvrage de Florus', *R.E.L.* 43 (1965) 358–83; W. den Boer, *Some minor Roman historians* (Leiden 1972) 1–18.

LEXICON: M. L. Fele (Hildesheim 1975).

# FLORUS, P. ANNIUS

## LIFE

Poet and rhetorician from Africa who competed in Domitian's *ludi Capitolini* (A.D. 86 or 90 or 94). After some years became a schoolmaster in Spain. Here he places a dialogue in which he is himself a protagonist. Its dramatic date cannot be much before A.D. 100, its composition may be appreciably later. Many identify him with the preceding entry, explaining away discrepancies in nomenclature. He may also be identifiable with the next entry.

## WORKS

Dialogue entitled *Vergilius orator an poeta*. Only the first few pages survive.

## BIBLIOGRAPHY

Partly as for preceding entry. Add R. Hirzel, *Der Dialog* II (Leipzig 1895) 64–70.

# FLORUS, (?) ANNIUS

## LIFE

A poet known to Hadrian, as poems interchanged by them (*Hist. Aug. Hadr.* 16.3–4) attest, and probably the Annius Florus whose letters to Hadrian Charisius cites

(66.10 and 157.21 Barwick), and the author of several poems under the name Florus in the *Anthologia Latina*. Charisius' mention of the name Annius supports identification with the writer of the dialogue. The further identification with the writer of the epitome is at best uncertain. To coalesce epitomator, rhetorician, and poet into one provides a tempting solution to many problems, but not a solution readily acceptable, when the nomenclature offered by our MSS is so various. Two men of similar name could have been writing at much the same time.

## WORKS

Short poems on various themes, and letters.

## BIBLIOGRAPHY

Partly as for last entry but one. Add *Anth. Lat.* 1.1.119–21 and 200–2; J. W. and A. M. Duff, *Minor Latin poets* (Loeb, 1935) 423–35.

# MELA, POMPONIUS

## LIFE

Dates of birth and death unknown, but was writing during early part of Claudius' principate. From Tingentera in Spain (2.96).

## WORKS

Geography, *De chorographia*, in three books. Completed late A.D. 43 or early 44 (3.49 conquest of Britain accomplished but Claudius' triumph still to come): see G. Wissowa, *Hermes* 51 (1916) 89–96. Apparently (1.2, though the passage has been interpreted otherwise), M. planned to write more fully on the same subject, but whether he did so is unknown: see P. Parroni, *R.F.I.C.* 96 (1968) 184–97.

## BIBLIOGRAPHY

TEXTS AND COMMENTARY: TEXTS: G. Parthey (Berlin 1867); C. Frick (BT, 1880); G. Ranstrand (Göteborg 1971: with index). COMMENTARY: C. H. Tzschucke (Leipzig 1806–7).

STUDIES: E. H. Bunbury, *A history of ancient geography* II (London 1879) 352–70; H. Oertel, *Über den Sprachgebrauch des Pomponius Mela* (Erlangen 1898); A. Klotz, *Quaestiones Plinianae geographicae* (Berlin 1906); D. Detlefsen, *Die Geographie Afrikas bei Plinius und Mela und ihre Quellen* (Berlin 1908); F. Gisinger, in *RE* XXI (1952) 2360–411.

# COLUMELLA, LUCIUS IUNIUS MODERATUS

## LIFE

Dates of birth and death unknown, but was writing under Nero and before A.D. 65 (3.3.3, Pliny, *N.H.* 14.49–51); b. in Gades (Cadiz). Moved to Italy at some stage and owned estates in various regions. His work is used by the elder Pliny in his Natural History. He was probably advanced in years when he completed it, but this view rests partly upon a doubtful reading at 12.59.5. See further 1.7.3, 2.10.18, 3.9.2, 8.16.9, 10.185; *CIL* IX 235 (C. a military tribune); W. Becher, *De L. Iuni Moderati Columellae vita et scriptis* (Leipzig 1897).

## WORKS

Two works survive: *Res rustica*, in twelve books (bk 10 in verse), and one book *De arboribus*. The *De arboribus* seems to be the second book (see its opening sentence) of a shorter and earlier treatise on agriculture in two or more books, and deals with the same material as books 3–5 of the larger work. Cassiodorus (*Inst.* 1.28.6) mentions sixteen books on agriculture by C. If the number is correctly transmitted, it may well relate to the longer and shorter treatises taken together. But the position is complicated by a reference in our MSS (*Res Rust.* 11, *ad fin.*) to a single book *De cultura vinearum et arborum* addressed to Eprius Marcellus. Interpretation and credibility of this notice are debatable. Perhaps it refers to the *De arboribus* and perhaps the whole shorter treatise was dedicated to Marcellus, as the larger is to Silvinus. C. tells us (11.1.31) of a work he wrote *Adversus astrologos* and (2.21.5–6) of his intention to write on lustrations and other sacrifices.

## BIBLIOGRAPHY

TEXTS AND COMMENTARIES: TEXTS: V. Lundström, Å. Josephson, S. Hedberg (Uppsala–Göteborg 1897–1968); H. B. Ash, E. S. Forster, E. H. Heffner (Loeb, 1941–55). Bk 10: J. Häussner (Karlsruhe 1889); J. P. Postgate, in *Corpus poetarum Latinorum* II (London 1905). COMMENTARIES: J. M. Gesner, in *Scriptores rei rusticae veteres Latini* I (Leipzig 1735); J. G. Schneider, in *Scriptores rei rusticae veteres Latini* II (Leipzig 1794).

STUDIES: R. Reitzenstein, *De scriptorum rei rusticae libris deperditis* (Berlin 1884); H. Stadler, *Die Quellen des Plinius im 19. Buche der n.h.* (Munich 1891); E. Weiss, *De Columella et Varrone rerum rusticarum scriptoribus* (Breslau 1911); A. Kappelmacher, in *RE* X (1919) 1054–68; B. Baldwin, 'Columella's sources and how he used them', *Latomus* 22 (1963) 785–91; T. Janson, *Latin prose prefaces, Studia Latina Stockholmiensia* 13 (Stockholm 1964) 83ff.; K. D. White, *Roman farming* (London 1970) *passim*.

INDEX: G. G. Betts and W. D. Ashworth (Uppsala 1971).

# PLINIUS SECUNDUS, GAIUS

## LIFE

b. at Comum A.D. 23/24; of equestrian rank. Served in Germany under Pomponius Secundus at periods from c. 46; commanded cavalry squadron. On return to Italy 57/58 pursued rhetorical and grammatical studies, and active as lawyer at some stage. Procurator in Spain c. 73. d. during eruption of Vesuvius A.D. 79. Sources: Pliny, *N.H. passim*; Pliny, *Epist.* 3.5 (works, lifestyle), 6.16 and 20 (death); Suet. *De vir. ill.* p. 92 Reifferscheid; *CIG* III 4536. See K. Ziegler, in *RE* XXI (1951) 271–85; R. Syme, 'Pliny the procurator', *H.S.Ph.* 73 (1969) 201–36.

## WORKS

Listed by the younger Pliny (*Epist.* 3.5.3–6), apparently in chronological order and sometimes with indication of date: *De iaculatione equestri*, *De vita Pomponi Secundi* (2 bks), *Bella Germaniae* (20 bks), *Studiosus* (training manual for orators; 3 bks), *Dubius sermo* (grammatical work 'on uncertainties of expression'; 8 bks), *A fine Aufidi Bassi* (continuation of Bassus' history; 31 bks), and *Naturae historiae* or *Naturalis historia* (37 bks). Only the last survives, apart from fragments, but the historical works were much used by later writers, including Tacitus.

## BIBLIOGRAPHY

(see H. le Bonniec, *Bibliographie de l'Histoire naturelle de Pline l'Ancien* (Paris 1946))

TEXTS AND COMMENTARIES: TEXTS: J. Sillig (Hamburg–Gotha 1851–5); L. Jan (BT, 1854–65); D. Detlefsen (Berlin 1866–82); C. Mayhoff (BT, 1892–1909); H. Rackham, W. H. S. Jones, D. E. Eichholz (Loeb, 1938–63). *Dubii sermonis reliquiae*: J. W. Beck (BT, 1894). COMMENTARIES: A. Ernout and others (Paris 1947–). Bk 2: D. J. Campbell (Aberdeen 1936). See also K. Jex-Blake and E. Sellers, *The elder Pliny's chapters on the history of art* (London 1896); K. C. Bailey, *The elder Pliny's chapters on chemical subjects* (London 1929–32).

STUDIES: J. Müller, *Der Stil des aelteren Plinius* (Innsbruck 1883); C. F. W. Müller, *Kritische Bemerkungen zu Plinius' Naturalis Historia* (Breslau 1888); F. Münzer, *Beiträge zur Quellenkritik der Naturgeschichte des Plinius* (Berlin 1897); D. Detlefsen, *Untersuchungen über die Zusammensetzung der Naturgeschichte des Plinius* (Berlin 1899); E. Norden, *Die antike Kunstprosa*, 4th ed. (Leipzig–Berlin 1923) I 314–18; W. Kroll, *Die Kosmologie des älteren Plinius* (Breslau 1930); W. Kroll, K. Ziegler, H. Gundel, W. Aly, R. Hanslik, in *RE* XXI (1951) 271–439; J. André, 'Pline l'Ancien botaniste', *R.E.L.* 33 (1955) 297–318; A. Önnerfors, *Pliniana* (Uppsala 1956); A. della Casa, *Il Dubius Sermo di Plinio* (Genova 1969); K. G. Sallmann, *Die Geographie des älteren*

*Plinius in ihrem Verhältnis zu Varro* (Berlin 1971); T. Köves-Zulauf, 'Die Vorrede der plinianischen Naturgeschichte', *W.S.* 86 (1973) 134–84.

# FRONTINUS, SEXTUS IULIUS

## LIFE

b. *c.* A.D. 35. Praetor 70, consul *suffectus c.* 74. Legate of Britain *c.* 76–8; subdued Silures. Appointed *curator aquarum* by Nerva *c.* 96–7. Consul again in 98 and 100. d. 103 or 104. Sources: Frontin. *De aquis* 1 (*curator*), *Strat.* 4.3.14; Pliny, *Epist.* 4.8.3 (P. succeeds F. as augur; see Sherwin-White, *ad loc.*), 5.15, 9.19, *Pan.* 61–2 (thrice consul); Tac. *Agr.* 17.2 (in Britain), *Hist.* 4.39 (praetor); Mart. 10.58; Ael. Tact. *praef.*; Veget. *De re mil.* 2.3; *PIR*² 1 322. See A. Kappelmacher, *RE* X (1919) 591–5.

## WORKS

(1) EXTANT: *Strategemata* (4 bks), written between A.D. 83 and 96, and *De aquis* (1 or 2 bks), *c.* A.D. 98. (2) LOST: Works on surveying (fragments, or adaptations, in C. Thulin, *Corpus agrimensorum Romanorum* 1 1 (BT, 1913)), and on the art of war (*Strat. praef.* and Veget. 1.8).

## BIBLIOGRAPHY

TEXTS: *Strat.*: G. Gundermann (BT, 1888); G. Bendz, 2nd ed. (Berlin 1978). *De aquis*: F. Buecheler (BT, 1858); F. Krohn (BT, 1922); C. Kunderewicz (BT, 1973). Both works: C. E. Bennett (Loeb, 1925).

STUDIES: G. Bendz, *Die Echtheitsfrage des vierten Buches der Frontinischen Strategemata* (Lund 1938); N. Wood, 'Frontinus as a possible source for Machiavelli's method', *J.H.I.* 28 (1967) 243–8.

INDEX: G. Bendz (Lund 1938).

# QUINTILIANUS, MARCUS FABIUS

## LIFE

b. *c.* A.D. 35 at Calagurris in Spain. Taught at Rome by the orator Domitius Afer. At some time returned to Spain, and recalled by Galba 68. Active as teacher and advocate for twenty years; first rhetorician to receive public salary. Received *ornamenta consularia* for educating Domitian's two great-nephews. d. probably not before A.D. 95, perhaps years later. Sources: Quint. *Inst.* 1 *praef.* 1 (duration of teaching), 2.12.12 (retirement), 4 *praef.* 2 (tutor to Domitian's heirs), 5.7.7 (Afer; see Pliny, *Epist.*

# APPENDIX OF AUTHORS AND WORKS

2.14.9), 6 *praef.* (death of his wife and sons), 6.1.14 (possibly in Rome 57), and *passim*; Mart. 2.90 (tribute); Juv. 7.186–90 (Q.'s wealth); Auson. *Grat. act.* 7.31 (*ornamenta consularia*), *Prof. Burd.* 1.7. (birthplace); Jerome, *Chron. sub* A.D 68 (Galba) and 88 (salary). See Colson (under *Commentaries* below) ix–xx; M. L. Clarke, *G. & R.* n.s. 14 (1967) 24–37.

## WORKS

*Institutio oratoria* (12 bks) alone survives: some details of composition in Q.'s prefatory epistle to his publisher Trypho. Pubd before Domitian's death, and probably not long before, but exact dating impossible. Q. had earlier pubd a treatise *de causis corruptae eloquentiae* (see *Inst.* 6 *praef.* 3 and 8.6.76), and one of his speeches, while versions of others were circulated without his consent (*Inst.* 7.2.24). Two extant collections of declamations are attributed to him. Some of them or some parts of them may be genuine, but there are very good reasons for doubt, particularly about the longer pieces (*declamationes maiores*).

## BIBLIOGRAPHY

TEXTS AND COMMENTARIES: TEXTS: G. L. Spalding (Leipzig 1798–1816); C. Halm (BT, 1868–9); L. Radermacher (BT, 1907, 1935, rev. V. Buchheit 1959); M. Winterbottom (OCT, 1970); J. Cousin (Budé, 1975–). COMMENTARIES: Bk 1: F. H. Colson (Cambridge 1924). Bk 3: J. Adamietz (Munich 1966). Bk 10: W. Peterson (Oxford 1891). Bk 12: R. G. Austin (Oxford 1948).

STUDIES: K. Barwick, *Remmius Palaemon und die römische Ars grammatica*, *Philologus* suppl. 15.2 (1922); J. F. d'Alton, *Roman literary theory and criticism* (London 1931); J. Cousin, *Études sur Quintilien* (Paris 1936); W. Kroll, 'Rhetorik', in *RE* suppl. VII (1940) 1039–1138; S. F. Bonner, *Roman declamation* (Liverpool 1949); M. L. Clarke, *Rhetoric at Rome* (London 1953); H. I. Marrou, *A history of education in antiquity* (London 1956); G. Kennedy, 'An estimate of Quintilian', *A.J.Ph.* 83 (1962) 130–46; F. Kuehnert, 'Quintilians Erörterung über den Witz', *Philologus* 106 (1962) 29–59, 305–14; M. Winterbottom, 'Quintilian and the vir bonus', *J.R.S.* 54 (1964) 90–7; G. Kennedy, *Quintilian* (New York 1969); T. Gelzer, 'Quintilians Urteil über Seneca', *M.H.* 27 (1970) 212–23; M. Winterbottom, *Problems in Quintilian*, *B.I.C.S.* suppl. 25 (1970); M. L. Clarke, 'Quintilian on education', in (ed.) T. A. Dorey, *Silver Latin* II (London 1975) 98–118; M. Winterbottom, 'Quintilian and rhetoric', ibid. 79–97.

LEXICON: E. Bonnell (Leipzig 1834).

APPENDIX (declamations ascribed to Q.): TEXTS: *Declamationes maiores*: G. Lehnert (BT, 1905). *Declamationes minores*: C. Ritter (BT, 1884).

# FRONTO, MARCUS CORNELIUS

## LIFE

b. at Cirta, Numidia, probably *c.* A.D. 100, perhaps earlier. Leading orator in Rome and teacher of Marcus Aurelius and Lucius Verus. Consul *suffectus* 143. d. *c.* 167, perhaps considerably later. Sources: Fronto, *Epist. passim*; Marc. Aur. 1.11; Gell. 2.26, 13.29, 19.8, 10, 13; *Pan. Lat.* 8.14.2; Macr. *Sat.* 5.1.7; *PIR²* C 1364 (Stein). See Haines (Loeb ed.) xxiii–xliii; G. W. Bowersock, *Greek sophists in the Roman empire* (Oxford 1969) 124–6; E. Champlin, 'The chronology of Fronto', *J.R.S.* 64 (1974) 136–57.

## WORKS

A collection of letters and essays, partially preserved in a 5th-c. palimpsest (nearly half lost and portions illegible). We have the remains of: letters to and from Marcus Aurelius (9 bks), Lucius Verus (2 bks), and Antoninus Pius (1 bk); letters to friends (2 bks); miscellaneous pieces. Securely datable items range from *c.* A.D. 139 to 166. Details of publication unknown: no indication that F. pubd the material himself; it is disordered and the merest ephemera are included. Of his speeches only fragments and titles survive.

## BIBLIOGRAPHY

TEXTS: S. A. Naber (Leipzig 1867); C. R. Haines (Loeb, 1919–20); M. P. J. van den Hout (Leiden 1954). See also L. Pepe, *Marco Aurelio Latino* (Naples 1957).

STUDIES: T. Mommsen, 'Die Chronologie der Briefe Frontos', *Hermes* 8 (1874) 199–216 = *Gesamm. Schr.* IV (Berlin 1906) 469–86; H. Peter, *Der Brief in der römischen Literatur* (Leipzig 1901) 124–35; E. Norden, *Die antike Kunstprosa*, 4th ed. I (Leipzig–Berlin 1923) 362–7; M. D. Brock, *Studies in Fronto and his age* (Cambridge 1911); R. Hanslik, 'Die Anordnung der Briefsammlung Frontos', *C.V.* 1 (1935) 21–47; R. Marache, *La critique littéraire de langue latine et le développement du goût archaïsant au IIe siècle de notre ère* (Rennes 1952); idem, *Mots nouveaux et mots archaïques chez Fronton et Aulu-Gelle* (Paris 1957); S. Jannaccone, 'Appunti per una storia della storiografia retorica nel II secolo', *G.I.F.* 14 (1961) 289–307.

# GELLIUS, AULUS

## LIFE

b. *c.* A.D. 129, date of death unknown. Only source his own work: *praef.* (in Attica), 7.6.12 (youth in Rome), 12.11.1 (Athens), 12.13.1, 14.2.1 (*iudex* at Rome), 13.13.1 (ref. to beginning of his career), 13.18.2–3 (his tutor Sulpicius Apollinaris), 19.12.1

# APPENDIX OF AUTHORS AND WORKS

(hears Herodes Atticus in Athens), and *passim*. On date of birth, see P. K. Marshall, *C.Ph.* 58 (1963) 143–9.

## WORKS

*Noctes Atticae*: learned miscellany in twenty books; beginning of Preface and all bk 8 (except ch. headings) lost. More projected (*praef.* 23–4) but apparently never written. Pubd not before A.D. 165 (*praef.* 1: children ref. to as adults) and perhaps appreciably later; see E. Castorina, *G.I.F.* 3 (1950) 137–45. No other works known.

## BIBLIOGRAPHY

TEXTS AND COMMENTARY: TEXTS: M. Hertz (Berlin 1883–5); C. Hosius (BT, 1903); P. K. Marshall (OCT, 1968). Bks 1–10: R. Marache (Budé, 1967–78). COMMENTARY: Bk 1: H. M. Hornsby (Dublin–London 1936).

STUDIES: H. Nettleship, 'The Noctes Atticae of Aulus Gellius', *A.J.Ph.* 4 (1883) 391–415 = *Lectures and essays* (Oxford 1885) 248–76; M. Hertz, *Opuscula Gelliana* (Berlin 1886); C. Knapp, 'Archaism in Aulus Gellius', *Classical studies in honour of H. Drisler* (New York 1894) 126–71; C. Hosius, pref. to his ed., 16–59; idem, in *RE* VII (1912) 992–8; P. Faider, 'A. Gellii Noctium Atticarum praefatio', *M.B.* 31 (1927) 189–216; R. Marache, *La critique littéraire de langue latine et le développement du goût archaïsant au IIe siècle de notre ère* (Rennes 1952); idem, *Mots nouveaux et mots archaïques chez Fronton et Aulu-Gelle* (Paris 1957); S. Jannaccone, 'Cicerone in Gellio', *Ciceroniana* 3–6 (1961–4) 193–8; L. Gamberale, *La traduzione in Gellio* (Rome 1969).

# METRICAL APPENDIX

## (1) BASIC PRINCIPLES

### (A) STRESSED AND QUANTITATIVE VERSE

In metres familiar to speakers of English, rhythm is measured by the predictable alternation of one or more stressed syllables with one or more unstressed syllables (distinguished by the notation – and ∪, or ′ and ˣ). Consequently, it is word-accent that determines whether or not a word or sequence of words may stand in a certain part of the verse. Thus the word *classical* may occupy the metrical unit represented by the notation –∪∪ by virtue of the stress imparted to its first syllable in everyday pronunciation. In contrast, the rhythms of classical Latin metres are measured by the predictable alternation of one or more 'heavy' syllables with one or more 'light' syllables (defined below, and distinguished by the notation – and ∪), so that in the construction of Latin verse the factor of primary importance is not word-accent but syllabic 'weight'. Thus the word *facerent*, although accented in normal speech on the first syllable, consists for metrical purposes of two light syllables followed by one heavy syllable, and for this reason can only occupy the metrical unit ∪∪–. Verse constructed upon this principle is conventionally designated *quantitative*: it should be emphasized that this term refers to the quantity (or 'weight') of syllables, and that throughout this account such quantity is described by the terms 'heavy' and 'light' to distinguish it from the intrinsic length of vowels; unfortunately, both syllabic weight and vowel-length are still generally denoted by the same symbols, – and ∪.

### (B) SYLLABIFICATION

A syllable containing a long vowel or diphthong is heavy (e.g. the first syllables of *pacem* and *laudo*).

A syllable containing a short vowel is light if it ends with that vowel (e.g. the first syllable of *pecus*), but heavy if it ends with a consonant (e.g. the first syllable of *pectus*).

To decide whether or not a short-vowelled syllable ends with a consonant (and thus to establish its quantity), the following rules should be observed:[1] (i) word-division

---

[1] The resulting division is practical only; for the difficulties involved in an absolute definition of the syllabic unit see Allen (1973) under (4) below, esp. 27–40.

should be disregarded; (ii) a single consonant between two vowels or diphthongs belongs to the succeeding syllable (thus *pecus →pe–cus*; *genus omne →ge–nu–som–ne*); (iii) of two or more successive consonants, at least one belongs to the preceding syllable (thus *pectus →pec–tus*; also *nulla spes →nul–las–pes*, though short final vowels are normally avoided in this position), except as allowed for below.

*Note*: for this purpose *h* is disregarded; *x* and *ʒ* count as double consonants, 'semi-consonantal' *i* and *u* as consonants (except in the combination *qu*, regarded as a single consonant).

To (iii) there is an important exception. In the case of the combination of a plosive and liquid consonant (*p, t, c, b, d, g* followed by *r* or *l*), the syllabic division may be made either between the consonants (e.g. *pat–ris*) or before them (e.g. *pa–tris*), resulting in *either* a heavy *or* a light preceding syllable. However, when two such consonants belong to different parts of a compound or to two different words, the division is always made between them, giving a heavy preceding syllable (e.g. *ablego →* *ab–lego*, not *a–blego*; *at rabidae →at–rabidae*, not *a–trabidae*). Lastly, when, after a short final vowel, these consonants begin the next word, the division is nearly always made before them, giving a light preceding syllable (e.g. *plumbea glans →plum–be–a–glans*).

## (C) ACCENT

The nature of the Latin word-accent (whether one of pitch or stress) and its importance in the construction of verse are both matters of controversy: for a clear discussion of the basic problems see Wilkinson under (4) below, 89–96, 221–36. By way of practical guidance in reading Latin verse, all that may be said is that for the present-day English speaker, accustomed to a naturalistic manner of reading poetry, it will sound as strange (and monotonous) to emphasize the heavy syllables of a metrical structure ('Quális Théseá iacuít cedénte carína') as it does to read Shakespearian verse with attention only to its iambic structure ('Now ís the wínter óf our discontént'); furthermore that, even in giving stress to the word-accent in Latin verse, heavy syllables will generally coincide with accented syllables with sufficient frequency to ensure that the metre is not forgotten – particularly at the beginning and end of many metres, as in the hexameter quoted above. It should be remembered, however, that what sounds natural is not thereby authentic, and that poetic delivery is highly susceptible to whims of fashion, idiosyncrasy and affectation. Even now it is not uncommon criticism of a Shakespearian actor that he 'mutilates' the shape of the verse by reading it as prose, while recordings of Tennyson and Eliot reading their poetry already sound bizarre (in different ways) to the modern ear.

# (2) TECHNICAL TERMS

*Anceps* ('unfixed'): term used to describe a metrical element which may be represented by either a heavy or a light syllable. The final element of many Latin metres is regularly of this nature, but not in certain lyric metres in which there is metrical continuity (*synaphea*) between as well as within lines.

*Brevis brevians*, or *the law of iambic shortening*: in comedy and other early Latin verse a heavy syllable may be lightened if it directly follows a light syllable and is adjacent to an accented syllable.

*Caesura* ('cutting') and *diaeresis*: division between words within a verse is termed *caesura* when occurring inside a metrical foot, or *diaeresis* when occurring at the end of a foot. The varied distribution of these plays an important part in avoiding monotony in the structure of verse; in particular, the caesura prevents a succession of words co-extensive with the feet of a metre (as found in Ennius' hexameter, 'sparsis hastis longis campus splendet et horret').

*Elision* and *hiatus*: a vowel (or vowel $+m$) ending a word is generally suppressed or *elided* when immediately preceding another vowel or *h*. When it is not elided in these circumstances (a phenomenon most frequently found in comedy), it is said to be in *hiatus*; by the rare process of *correption* a long vowel or diphthong in hiatus may be scanned short to make a light syllable. *Prodelision* (or *aphaeresis*) signifies the suppression of *e* in *est* after a final vowel or *m*, *hypermetric elision* the suppression of a vowel between lines (nearly always that of *–que*).

*Resolution*: the substitution of two light syllables for a heavy one.

# (3) COMMON METRES

For the sake of simplicity only the most basic characteristics of each metre are given here. For the numerous divergencies regarding anceps, resolution, position of caesura etc., see Raven under (4) below.

(a) Stichic verse (constructed by repetition of the same metrical line)
Iambic senarius (or trimeter):

$$\underline{\smile}-\smile-\,|\,\underline{\smile}-\smile-\,|\,\underline{\smile}-\smile\underline{\smile}$$

(commonest dialogue metre in early Roman drama; also used in Seneca's tragedies, Phaedrus' *Fables*, and, in alternation with an iambic dimeter ($=\underline{\smile}-\smile-\,|\,\underline{\smile}-\smile-$), Horace's *Epodes* 1–10)
Iambic septenarius (or tetrameter catalectic):

$$\underline{\smile}-\smile-\,|\,\underline{\smile}-\smile-\,|\,\underline{\smile}-\smile-\,|\,\smile-\underline{\smile}$$

(common dialogue metre of comedy)

Trochaic septenarius (or tetrameter catalectic):

$$-\cup-\underset{\smile}{} \mid -\cup-\underset{\smile}{} \mid -\cup-\underset{\smile}{} \mid -\cup\cup$$

(very common dialogue metre in early Roman drama)

Hexameter:

$$-\underset{\smile\smile}{} \mid -\underset{\smile\smile}{} \mid -\underset{\smile\smile}{} \mid -\underset{\smile\smile}{} \mid -\cup\cup \mid -\underset{\smile}{}$$

(regular metre for epic, satiric, pastoral and didactic poetry)

Pentameter:

$$-\underset{\smile\smile}{}-\underset{\smile\smile}{}- \mid -\cup\cup-\cup\cup\underset{\smile}{}$$

(following the hexameter this forms the elegiac couplet, which is regarded as an entity and hence as stichic; regular metre for love-poetry and epigram)

Phalaecean hendecasyllables:

$$\underset{\smile}{\frown} \mid -\cup\cup- \mid \cup-\cup-\underset{\smile}{}$$

(i.e. first foot may be a spondee, iamb or trochee; used by Catullus, Martial and Statius)

(b) Non-stichic verse (constructed by combination of different metrical lines)

| | | |
|---|---|---|
| Alcaic stanza: | $--\cup-- \mid -\cup\cup- \mid \cup\underset{\smile}{}$ | (twice) |
| | $--\cup---\cup-\underset{\smile}{}$ | |
| | $-\cup\cup-\cup\cup- \mid \cup-\underset{\smile}{}$ | |
| Sapphic stanza: | $-\cup-- \mid -\cup\cup- \mid \cup-\underset{\smile}{}$ | (three times) |
| | $-\cup\cup- \mid \underset{\smile}{}$ | (adonean) |
| Third asclepiad: | $-- \mid -\cup\cup- \mid \cup\underset{\smile}{}$ | (glyconic) |
| | $-- \mid -\cup\cup--\cup\cup- \mid \cup\underset{\smile}{}$ | (lesser asclepiad) |
| Fourth asclepiad: | $-- \mid -\cup\cup--\cup\cup- \mid \cup\underset{\smile}{}$ | (lesser asclepiad, three times) |
| | $-- \mid -\cup\cup- \mid \cup\underset{\smile}{}$ | (glyconic) |
| Fifth asclepiad | $-- \mid -\cup\cup--\cup\cup- \mid \cup\underset{\smile}{}$ | (lesser asclepiad, twice) |
| | $-- \mid -\cup\cup- \mid \underset{\smile}{}$ | (pherecratean) |
| | $-- \mid -\cup\cup- \mid \cup\underset{\smile}{}$ | (glyconic) |

(the First and Second asclepiad consist, respectively, of the lesser and greater asclepiad only; the latter $= -- \mid -\cup\cup--\cup\cup--\cup\cup- \mid \cup\underset{\smile}{}$)

All the above found in Horace's *Odes*; some in Catullus and Statius.

# (4) BIBLIOGRAPHY

Allen, W. S., *Vox Latina*, 2nd ed. (Cambridge 1978).

idem, *Accent and rhythm* (Cambridge 1973).

Raven, D. S., *Latin metre* (London 1965).

Wilkinson, L. P., *Golden Latin artistry* (Cambridge 1963) 89–134 and *passim*

# ABBREVIATIONS

| | |
|---|---|
| *Anth. Lat.* | A. Riese–F. Bücheler–E. Lommatzsch, *Anthologia Latina Latina* (Leipzig, 1894–1926). (Cf. *CLE*) |
| *ANRW* | H. Temporini, *Aufstieg und Niedergang der römischen Welt* (Berlin, 1972– ) |
| Bardon | H. Bardon, *La littérature latine inconnue* (Paris 1951–6) |
| BT | Bibliotheca Scriptorum Graecorum et Romanorum Teubneriana (Leipzig & Stuttgart) |
| Budé | Collection des Universités de France, publiée sous le patronage de l'Association Guillaume Budé (Paris) |
| Bursian | Bursian's *Jahresbericht über die Fortschritte der klassischen Altertumswissenschaft* (Berlin, 1873–1945) |
| *CAF* | T. Kock, *Comicorum Atticorum Fragmenta* (Leipzig, 1880–8) |
| *CAH* | *The Cambridge Ancient History* (Cambridge, 1923–39) |
| *CAH*² | 2nd ed. (Cambridge, 1961– ) |
| *CC* | *Corpus Christianorum.* Series Latina (Turnholt, 1953– ) |
| *CGF* | G. Kaibel, *Comicorum Graecorum Fragmenta* (Berlin, 1899) |
| *CGFPap.* | C. F. L. Austin, *Comicorum Graecorum Fragmenta in papyris reperta* (Berlin, 1973) |
| *CIL* | *Corpus Inscriptionum Latinarum* (Berlin, 1863– ) |
| *CLE* | F. Bücheler–E. Lommatzsch, *Carmina Latina Epigraphica* (Leipzig, 1897–1930). ( = *Anth. Lat.* Pars II) |
| *CRF* | O. Ribbeck, *Comicorum Romanorum Fragmenta*, 3rd. ed. (Leipzig, 1897) |
| *CSEL* | *Corpus Scriptorum Ecclesiasticorum Latinorum* (Vienna, 1866– ) |
| *CVA* | *Corpus Vasorum Antiquorum* (Paris & elsewhere, 1925– ) |
| Christ–Schmid–Stählin | W. von Christ, *Geschichte der griechischen Literatur*, rev. W. Schmid and O. Stählin (Munich, 1920–1924) 6th ed. (Cf. Schmid–Stählin) |
| *DTC* | A. W. Pickard-Cambridge, *Dithyramb, tragedy and comedy.* 2nd ed., rev. T. B. L. Webster (Oxford, 1962) |
| *DFA* | A. W. Pickard-Cambridge, *The dramatic festivals of Athens.* 2nd ed., rev. J. Gould–D. M. Lewis (Oxford, 1968) |

| | |
|---|---|
| DK | H. Diels–W. Kranz, *Die Fragmente der Vorsokratiker.* 6th ed. (Berlin, 1951) |
| EGF | G. Kinkel, *Epicorum Graecorum Fragmenta* (Leipzig, 1877) |
| FGrH | F. Jacoby, *Fragmente der griechischen Historiker* (Berlin, 1923– ) |
| FHG | C. Müller, *Fragmenta Historicorum Graecorum* (Berlin, 1841–70) |
| FPL | W. Morel, *Fragmenta Poetarum Latinorum* (Leipzig, 1927) |
| FPR | E. Baehrens, *Fragmenta Poetarum Romanorum* (Leipzig, 1886) |
| FYAT | (ed.) M. Platnauer, *Fifty years (and twelve) of classical scholarship* (Oxford, 1968) |
| GLK | H. Keil, *Grammatici Latini* (Leipzig, 1855–1923) |
| GLP | D. L. Page, *Greek Literary Papyri* (Cambridge, Mass. & London, 1942– ) |
| Gow–Page, *Hell. Ep.* | A. S. F. Gow–D. L. Page, *The Greek Anthology: Hellenistic Epigrams* (Cambridge, 1965) |
| Gow–Page, *Garland* | A. S. F. Gow–D. L. Page, *The Greek Anthology: The Garland of Philip* (Cambridge, 1968) |
| Guthrie | W. K. C. Guthrie, *A History of Greek Philosophy* (Cambridge, 1965–81) |
| HRR | H. Peter, *Historicorum Romanorum reliquiae* (Leipzig, 1906–14) |
| HS | J. B. Hofmann, *Lateinische Syntax und Stilistik*, rev. A. Szantyr (Munich, 1965) |
| IEG | M. L. West, *Iambi et Elegi Graeci* (Oxford, 1971–2) |
| IG | *Inscriptiones Graecae* (Berlin, 1873– ) |
| ILS | H. Dessau, *Inscriptiones Latinae Selectae* (Berlin, 1892–1916) |
| KG | R. Kühner–B. Gerth, *Ausführliche Grammatik der griechischen Sprache: Satzlehre.* 4th ed. (Hannover, 1955) |
| KS | R. Kühner–C. Stegmann, *Ausführliche Grammatik der lateinischen sprache: Satzlehre.* 3rd ed., rev. A. Thierfelder (Hannover, 1955) |
| Leo, *Gesch.* | F. Leo, *Geschichte der romischen Literatur.* I *Die archaische Literatur* (all pubd) (Berlin, 1913; repr. Darmstadt, 1967, w. *Die römische Poesie in der sullanischen Zeit*) |
| Lesky | A. Lesky, *A History of Greek Literature*, tr. J. Willis–C. de Heer (London, 1966) |
| Lesky, *TDH* | A. Lesky, *Die tragische Dichtung der Hellenen*, 3rd ed. (Göttingen, 1972) |
| LSJ | Liddell–Scott–Jones, *Greek–English Lexicon*, 9th ed. (Oxford, 1925–40) |
| Loeb | Loeb Classical Library (Cambridge, Mass. & London) |
| MGH | *Monumenta Germaniae Historica* (Berlin, 1877–91) |
| OCD² | *Oxford Classical Dictionary*, 2nd ed. (Oxford, 1970) |

| | |
|---|---|
| OCT | Scriptorum Classicorum Bibliotheca Oxoniensis (Oxford) |
| Paravia | Corpus Scriptorum Latinorum Paravianum (Turin) |
| PIR | E. Klebs–H. Dessau, *Prosopographia Imperii Romani Saeculi I, II, III* (Berlin, 1897–8), 2nd ed. E. Groag–A. Stein (Berlin & Leipzig, 1933– ) |
| PL | J.-P. Migne, *Patrologiae cursus completus* Series Latina (Paris, 1844– ) |
| PLF | E. Lobel–D. Page, *Poetarum Lesbiorum Fragmenta* (Oxford, 1963) |
| PLM | E. Baehrens, *Poetae Latini Minores* (Leipzig, 1879–83), rev. F. Vollmer (incomplete) (1911–35) |
| PLRE | A. H. M. Jones–J. R. Martindale–J. Morris, *The prosopography of the later Roman Empire* (Cambridge, 1971– ) |
| PMG | D. L. Page, *Poetae Melici Graeci* (Oxford, 1962) |
| PPF | H. Diels, *Poetarum Philosophorum Graecorum Fragmenta* (Berlin, 1901) |
| Pfeiffer | R. Pfeiffer, *A history of classical scholarship* (Oxford, 1968) |
| Powell | J. U. Powell, *Collectanea Alexandrina* (Oxford, 1925) |
| Powell–Barber | J. U. Powell–E. A. Barber, *New chapters in the history of Greek Literature* (Oxford, 1921), 2nd ser. (1929), 3rd ser. (Powell alone) (1933) |
| Preller–Robert | L. Preller, *Griechische Mythologie*, 4th ed., rev. C. Robert (Berlin, 1894) |
| RAC | *Reallexicon für Antike und Christentum* (Stuttgart, 1941– ) |
| RE | A. Pauly–G. Wissowa–W. Kroll, *Real-Encyclopädie der klassischen Altertumswissenschaft* (Stuttgart, 1893– ) |
| ROL | E. H. Warmington, *Remains of old Latin* (Cambridge, Mass. & London, 1935–40) |
| Roscher | W. H. Roscher, *Ausführliches Lexicon der griechischen und römischen Mythologie* (Leipzig, 1884– ) |
| SEG | *Supplementum Epigraphicum Graecum* (Leyden, 1923–71; Alphen aan den Rijn, 1979– ) |
| SVF | H. von Arnim, *Stoicorum Veterum Fragmenta* (Leipzig, 1903– ) |
| Snell | B. Snell, *Tragicorum Graecorum Fragmenta* (Göttingen, 1971– ) |
| Schanz–Hosius | M. Schanz–C. Hosius, *Geschichte der römischen Literatur* (Munich, 1914–1935) |
| Schmid–Stählin | W. Schmid–O. Stählin, *Geschichte der griechischen Literatur* (Munich, 1929–1948) |
| Spengel | L. Spengel, *Rhetores Graeci* (1853–6); I ii rev. C. Hammer (Leipzig, 1894) |
| Teuffel | W. S. Teuffel, *Geschichte der römischen Literatur* (Leipzig & Berlin, 1913–1920) |

# ABBREVIATIONS

| | |
|---|---|
| *TGF* | A. Nauck, *Tragicorum Graecorum Fragmenta*, 2nd ed. (Leipzig, 1889) |
| *TLL* | *Thesaurus Linguae Latinae* (Leipzig, 1900– ) |
| *TRF* | O. Ribbeck, *Tragicorum Romanorum Fragmenta*, 3rd ed. (Leipzig, 1897) |
| Walz | C. Walz, *Rhetores Graeci* (Stuttgart, 1832–6) |
| Williams, *TORP* | G. Williams, *Tradition and originality in Roman Poetry* (Oxford, 1968) |

# WORKS CITED IN THE TEXT

Abel, K. (1967). *Bauformen in Senecas Dialogen.* Heidelberg.

Adams, J. N. (1973). 'The vocabulary of the speeches in Tacitus' historical works', *B.I.C.S.* 20: 124–44.

Ahl, F. M. (1976). *Lucan, an introduction.* New York.

Allen, W. S. (1973). *Accent and rhythm: prosodic features of Latin and Greek.* Cambridge.

Anderson, W. S. (1957). 'Studies in Book I of Juvenal', *Y.Cl.S.* 15: 31–90.

(1961*a*). 'Venusina Lucerna. The Horatian model for Juvenal', *T.A.Ph.A.* 92: 1–12.

(1961*b*). 'Juvenal and Quintilian', *Y.Cl.S.* 17: 1–93.

(1964). *Anger in Juvenal and Seneca.* Berkeley.

André, J. (1949). *Étude sur les termes de couleur dans la langue latine.* Paris.

Anliker, K. (1960). *Prologe und Akteinteilung in Senecas Tragödien.* Bern & Stuttgart.

Auerbach, E. (1953). *Mimesis,* tr. W. R. Trask. Princeton.

Axelson, B. (1945). *Unpoetische Wörter.* Lund.

(1967). *Korruptelenkult: Studien zur Textkritik der unechten Seneca-Tragödie Hercules Oetaeus.* Lund.

Bardon, H. (1956). *La littérature latine inconnue.* II. *L'époque impériale.* Paris.

Barlow, C. W. (1938). (ed.). *Epistolae Senecae ad Paulum et Pauli ad Senecam quae vocantur.* Papers and Monographs of the American Academy X. Rome.

Bourgery, A. (1922). *Sénèque prosateur.* Paris.

Bramble, J. C. (1974). *Persius and the programmatic satire: a study in form and imagery.* Cambridge.

Brisset, J. (1964). *Les idées politiques de Lucain.* Paris.

Brower, R. A. (1959). *Alexander Pope: the poetry of allusion.* Oxford.

Butler, H. E. (1909). *Post-Augustan poetry from Seneca to Juvenal.* Oxford.

Cairns, F. J. (1972). *Generic composition in Greek and Roman poetry.* Edinburgh.

Canter, H. V. (1925). *Rhetorical elements in the tragedies of Seneca.* University of Illinois Studies in Language and Literature X.1. Urbana.

Caplan, H. (1954). (ed.). *Rhetorica ad Herennium.* Loeb. London & Cambridge, Mass.

Cizek, E. (1972). *L'époque de Néron et ses controverses idéologiques.* Roma Aeterna IV. Leiden.

# WORKS CITED IN THE TEXT

Clausen, W. V. (1959). *A. Persi Flacci et D. Iunii Iuvenalis Saturae*. Oxford.

Coffey, M. (1957). 'Seneca tragedies, 1922–1955', *Lustrum* 2: 113–86.

(1976). *Roman satire*. London & New York.

Conington, J. (1881). *P. Vergilii Maronis Opera* 1. London.

D'Alton, J. F. (1931). *Roman literary theory and criticism*. London.

De Decker, J. (1913). *Juvenalis declamans*. Ghent.

Dilke, O. A. W. (1960). (ed.). *Lucan book VII*. Revision of Postgate's edition (Cambridge 1913). Cambridge.

Due, O. S. (1962). 'An essay on Lucan', *Class. et Med.* 22: 68–132.

Duff, J. D. (1928). (ed.). *Lucan*. Loeb. London & Cambridge, Mass.

Eckhardt, L. (1936). *Exkurse und Ekphraseis bei Lucan*. Heidelberg.

Eliot, T. S. (1927). Introduction to *Seneca his tenne tragedies translated into English*, edited by Thomas Newton, anno 1581. London & New York.

Elliott, R. C. (1960). *The power of satire, magic, ritual, art*. Princeton.

Ellis, R. (1981). *Noctes Manilianae*. Oxford.

Ferguson, J. (1975). *Utopias of the classical world*. London.

Fiske, G. C. (1920). *Lucilius and Horace*. Madison.

Fraenkel, E. (1937). Review of Pasquali (1936), in *J.R.S.* 27: 262ff.

(1964). *Kleine Beiträge zur klassischen Philologie*. 2 vols. Rome.

Friedländer, L. (1886). (ed.). *M. Valeri Martialis Epigrammaton Libri*. 2 vols. Leipzig.

Friedrich, W. H. (1933). *Untersuchungen zu Senecas dramatischer Technik*. Leipzig.

(1954). 'Sprache und Stil des Hercules Oetaeus', *Hermes* 82: 51–84. Repr. in Lefèvre (1972) 500–44.

Garson, R. W. (1964). 'Some critical observations on Valerius Flaccus' *Argonautica*, 1', *C.Q.* n.s. 14: 267–79.

Giardina, I. C. (1966). *L. Annaei Senecae tragoediae*. 2 vols. Bologna.

Gigon, O. (1938). 'Bemerkungen zu Senecas Thyestes', *Philologus* 93: 176–83.

Goodyear, F. R. D. (1971). 'The *Dirae*', *P.C.Ph.S.* n.s. 17: 30–43.

Gossage, A. J. (1972). 'Statius', in *Neronians and Flavians: Silver Latin* 1. Greek and Latin Studies, ed. D. R. Dudley. London.

Gow, A. S. F. and Page, D. L. (1965). (eds.). *Hellenistic epigrams*. 2 vols. Cambridge.

(1968). (eds.). *The Greek Anthology. The Garland of Philip*. 2 vols. Cambridge.

Green, P. (1970). *Juvenal, the sixteen satires*. (Trans.) Harmondsworth.

Gresseth, G. K. (1957). 'The quarrel between Lucan and Nero', *C.Ph.* 52: 24–7.

Griffith, J. G. (1969). 'Juvenal, Statius, and the Flavian establishment', *G. & R.* n.s. 16: 134–50.

Grimal, P. (1949). 'L'episode d'Antée dans la Pharsale', *Latomus* 8: 55–61.

(1960). 'L'éloge de Néron au début de la *Pharsale*', *R.E.L.* 38: 296–305.

Gronovius, J. F. (1661). (ed.). *L. Annaei Senecae Tragoediae*. Leiden.

(1682). (ed.). *L. Annaei Senecae Tragoediae*. 2nd edn. rev. J. Gronovius. Amsterdam.

Guillemin, A.-M. (1951). 'L'inspiration virgilienne dans la *Pharsale*', *R.E.L.* 29: 214–27.

# WORKS CITED IN THE TEXT

Haase, F. (1852). (ed.). *L. Annaei Senecae Opera quae supersunt*. 3 vols. Leipzig.

Haines, C. R. (1919). (ed.). *The correspondence of Marcus Cornelius Fronto*. Loeb. London & Cambridge, Mass.

Helm, R. (1934). 'Die *Praetexta Octavia*', *Sitz.-Ber. Berlin* 283–347.

(1954). 'Praetexta', *RE* XLIV 1569–75.

Herington, C. J. (1961). 'Octavia praetexta: a survey', *C.Q.* n.s. 11: 18–30. Repr. in Lefèvre (1972) 376–401.

(1966). 'Senecan tragedy', *Arion* 5: 422–71.

Herrmann, L. (1924). *Le théâtre de Sénèque*. Paris.

Heseltine, M. (1913). (ed.). *Petronius*. Loeb. London & Cambridge, Mass.

Highet, G. (1954). *Juvenal the satirist*. Oxford.

Hosius, C. (1893). 'Lucan und seine Quellen', *Rh. Mus.* 48: 380–97.

(1922). (ed.). *Octavia Praetexta cum elementis commentarii*. Bonn.

Hughes, T. (1969). 'The Oedipus of Seneca' (poetic translation), *Arion* 7: 324–71.

Jahn, O. (1851). (ed.). *Junii Juvenalis Saturarum libri V*. Berlin.

Jal, P. (1963). *La guerre civile à Rome*. Paris.

Jocelyn, H. D. (1964). 'Ancient scholarship and Virgil's use of republican Latin poetry. 1', *C.Q.* n.s. 14: 280–95.

Juhnke, H. (1972). *Homerisches in römischer Epik flavischer Zeit: Untersuchungen zu Szenennachbildungen und Strukturentsprechungen in Statius' Thebais und Achilleis und in Silius' Punica*. Zetemata LIII. Munich.

Keseling, P. (1941). 'Horaz in den Tragödien des Seneca', *Philologische Wochenschrift* 61: 190–2.

Knoche, U. (1975). *Roman satire*, tr. E. S. Ramage. Bloomington.

Kruuse, J. (1941). 'L'originalité artistique de Martial', *Class. et Med.* 4: 248–300.

Laughton, E. (1960). 'Observations on the style of Varro', *C.Q.* n.s. 10: 1–28.

Lawall, G. (1966). 'Apollonius' *Argonautica*: Jason as anti-hero', *Y.Cl.S.* 19: 116–69.

Leeman, A. D. (1963). *Orationis ratio*. Amsterdam.

Lefèvre, E. (1972). (ed.). *Senecas Tragödien*. Darmstadt.

Lelièvre, F. J. (1958). 'Parody in Juvenal and T. S. Eliot', *C.Ph.* 53: 22–5.

Leo, F. (1878). (ed.). *L. Annaei Senecae Tragoediae*, I (*Observationes criticae*), II (critical text). Berlin.

(1897). 'Die Composition der Chorlieder Senecas', *Rh. Mus.* 52: 509–18.

Levin, H. (1952). *Christopher Marlowe: the Overreacher*. Cambridge, Mass.

Lewis, C. S. (1936). *The allegory of love: a study in medieval tradition*. Oxford.

(1942). *A preface to Paradise Lost*. London, New York & Toronto.

Longi, E. (1955). 'Tre episodi del poema di Lucano', in *Studi in onore di G. Funaioli* 181–8. Rome.

Lovejoy, A. O. and Boas, G. (1935). *Primitivism and related ideas in antiquity*. Baltimore.

MacKay, L. A. (1961). 'The vocabulary of fear in Latin epic poetry', *T.A.Ph.A.* 92: 308–16.

Marti, B. (1945). 'The meaning of the *Pharsalia*', *A.J.Ph.* 66: 352–576.

(1968). 'La structure de la *Pharsale*', in *Lucain*, Entretiens Hardt xv 1–50. Geneva.

Mason, H. A. (1959). *Humanism and poetry in the early Tudor period*. London.

(1963). 'Is Juvenal a classic?', in Sullivan (1963) 93–167.

Mendell, C. W. (1967). *Latin poetry: the age of rhetoric and satire*. Hamden.

Miniconi, P. J. (1951). *Étude des thèmes guerriers de la poésie greco-romaine.* Publ. Fac. Lettr. Algér. II sér. 19. Paris.

(1962). 'La joie dans l'Éneide', *Latomus* 21: 503–11.

Morford, M. P. O. (1967). *The poet Lucan*. Oxford.

Motto, A. L. (1970). *Seneca sourcebook: guide to the thought of Lucius Annaeus Seneca.* Amsterdam.

(1973). *Seneca*. New York.

Müller, G. (1953). 'Senecas Oedipus als Drama', *Hermes* 81: 447–64. Repr. in Lefèvre (1972) 376–401.

Münscher, K. (1922). *Senecas Werke: Untersuchungen zur Abfassungszeit und Echtheit. Philologus* Suppl.-Band XVI, Heft 1.

Nettleship, H. (1890). 'Literary criticism in Latin antiquity', *Journal of Philology* 18: 225–70.

Nisbet, R. G. M. (1963). 'Persius', in Sullivan (1963) 39–71.

Norden, E. (1898; repr. Stuttgart 1973). *Die antike Kunstprosa.* 2 vols. Leipzig.

Nowak, H. (1955). *Lukanstudien*. Diss. Vienna.

Ollfors, A. (1967). *Studien zum Aufbau des Hexameters Lucans.* Gothenburg.

Opelt, I. (1957). 'Die Seeschlacht vor Massilia bei Lucan', *Hermes* 85: 435–45.

(1969). 'Zu Senecas Phoenissen', in Lefèvre (1972) 272–85.

Otis, B. (1963). *Virgil: a study in civilized poetry*. Oxford.

Parks, E. E. (1945). *The Roman rhetorical schools as a preparation for the courts under the early Empire.* Diss. Baltimore.

Parsons, P. (1971). 'A Greek Satyricon?', *B.I.C.S.* 18: 53–68.

Pasquali, G. (1936). *Preistoria della poesia romana.* Florence.

Pecchiura, P. (1965). *La figura di Catone Uticense nella letteratura latina.* Turin.

Peiper, R. and Richter, G. (1902). (eds.). *L. Annaei Senecae Tragoediae.* Leipzig.

Perry, B. E. (1965). *Babrius and Phaedrus.* Loeb. London & Cambridge, Mass.

Phillips, O. C. (1968). 'Lucan's Grove', *C.Ph.* 62: 296–300.

Philp, R. H. (1968). 'The manuscript tradition of Seneca's tragedies', *C.Q.* n.s. 18: 150–79.

Pichon, R. (1912). *Les sources de Lucain.* Paris.

Pighi, G. B. (1963). 'Seneca metrico', *Rivista di Filologia e di Istruzione Classica* 91: 170–81.

Pound, E. (1918). In *The little review*, ed. M. Anderson. Chicago.

Préchac, M. (1934). 'La date de la naissance de Sénèque', *R.E.L.* 11: 360–75.

Regenbogen, O. (1927/8). 'Schmerz und Tod in den Tragödien Senecas', *Vorträge der Bibliothek Warburg* VII 167–218. (Repr. as monograph with same title, Darmstadt 1963).

Reynolds, L. D. (1965). *The medieval tradition of Seneca's letters*. Oxford.

Rieu, E. V. (1950). *Homer, the Iliad*. (Trans.) Harmondsworth.

Rist, J. M. (1969). *Stoic philosophy*. Cambridge.

Rose, K. F. C. (1971). *The date and author of the Satyricon*. Leiden.

Rudd, N. (1976). *Lines of enquiry: studies in Latin poetry*. Cambridge.

Rutz, W. (1965). 'Lucan 1943–1963', *Lustrum* 9: 243–340.

Sanford, E. M. (1931). 'Lucan and his Roman critics', *C.Ph.* 26: 233–57.

Scivoletto, N. (1966). ' Quando nacque Seneca?', *G.I.F.* 19: 21–31.

Scott, I. G. (1927). *The grand style in the satires of Juvenal*. Northampton, Mass.

Scriverius, P. (1621). (ed.). *L. Annaeus Seneca Tragicus*. 2 vols. Leiden.

Seitz, K. (1965). 'Der pathetische Erzählstil Lucans', *Hermes* 93: 204ff.

Skutsch, O. (1968). *Studia Enniana*. London.

Sluiter, Th. H. (1949). (ed.). *Octavia fabula praetexta*. Leiden.

Steyns, D. (1906). *Étude sur les métaphores et les comparaisons dans les oeuvres en prose. de Sénèque le philosophe*. Gand.

Sullivan, J. P. (1963). (ed.). *Critical essays on Roman literature. Satire*. London.

Summers, W. C. (1910). *Select letters of Seneca*. London.

Syme, R. (1958). *Tacitus*. 2 vols. Oxford.

Tandoi, V. (1969). 'Il ricordo di Stazio "dolce poeta" nella sat. 7 di Giovenale', *Maia* 21: 102–22.

Tarn, W. W. (1948). *Alexander the Great*. I *Narrative*; II *Sources and Studies*. Cambridge.

Thompson, L. and Bruère, R. T. (1968). 'Lucan's use of Virgilian reminiscence', *C.Ph.* 63: 1–21.

Tillyard, E. M. (1943). *The Elizabethan world picture*. London.

Townend, G. B. (1961). 'Traces in Dio Cassius of Cluvius, Aufidius, and Pliny', *Hermes* 89: 227–48.

(1964). 'Cluvius Rufus in the *Histories* of Tacitus', *A.J.Ph.* 85: 337–77.

(1973). 'The literary substrata to Juvenal's satires'. *J.R.S.* 63: 148–60.

Trillitzsch, W. (1971). *Seneca im literarischen Urteil der Antike. Darstellung und Sammlung der Zeugnisse*. 2 vols. Amsterdam.

Vessey, D. W. T. C. (1970). 'Statius and Antimachus: a review of the evidence', *Philologus* 114: 118–43.

(1972). 'Aspects of Statius' epithalamion: *Silvae* 1.2', *Mnemosyne* 4.25: 172–87.

(1972–3). 'The myth of Falernus in Silius, *Punica* 7', *C.J.* 68: 240–6.

(1973). *Statius and the Thebaid*. Cambridge.

(1975). 'Silius Italicus: the shield of Hannibal', *A.J.Ph.* 96: 391–405.

Welsford, E. (1935). *The Fool, his social and literary history*. London.

Wiesen, D. (1963). 'Juvenal's moral character, an introduction', *Latomus* 22: 440–71.

Williamson, G. (1951). *The Senecan amble: prose form from Bacon to Collier*. Chicago.

Zwierlein, O. (1966). *Die Rezitationsdramen Senecas*. Meisenheim am Glan.

# INDEX

*Main references are distinguished by figures in bold type. References to the Appendix (which should normally be consulted for basic details of authors' lives and works, and for bibliographies) are given in italic figures.*

# INDEX

14516